OF FIRE AND WATER

Sifu Tak Wah Eng with his original cover art.

SYMBOLOGY OF THE COVER ART

The artwork on the cover was painted by Sifu Tak Wah Eng[1] of New York's Chinatown. It reflects the dynamic interaction between Yin and Yang, Dragon and Tiger, Sun and Moon, Fire and Water, and the Five Elements in the circle of life. It therefore suggests the alchemical transformation in the *I-Ching*, "Book of Changes." It portrays a dialectic: opposites are drawn into the cauldron, the dualism is dissolved, and a new, higher state of spirit or consciousness is achieved. It is the apotheosis in the esoteric practice of alchemy. The transformative process begins with the first two hexagrams of the *I-Ching*, Heaven/Tian (Hexagram 1) and Earth/Kun (Hexagram 2). As they "mate" they give birth to Water/Kan (Hexagram 29) and Fire/Li (Hexagram 30). Eventually there is a Reversal (Hexagram 63 and *Tao Te Ching* 40). That is the bare outline in the quest for perfection, but it is more intricate. In the actual praxis, as the different meridian pathways and different *dan tian* (elixir field) locations (lower, middle, upper) come into play, the body becomes the stove and different ingredients from within and without are drawn into the "field" to be transformed. An Immortal Fetus, actual or symbolic of a new consciousness, is born in the Great Work. Transformation happens in everyday life although we are not aware of it. Through the different arts like music, poetry, painting, martial art, qigong, alchemy, acupuncture, herbology, meditation, fengshui, we are transformed. The enso is indescribably profound, a single spontaneous sumi-e stroke of the brush creates a circle that in zen depicts the self or the world in search of completion and perfection, the twin goals of ancient alchemy. More could be said but let the painting speak for itself.

OF FIRE AND WATER

ALCHEMY AND TRANSFORMATION

Rene J. Navarro

www.TambuliMedia.com
Spring House, PA USA

First printed on December 8, 2023 by Tambuli Media

ISBN: 978-1-943155-40-8

LCCN: 2022942385

Cover Painting by Eng Tak Wah
Back Cover Photo by Christoph Halbe
Interior layout by Summer Bonne
Essays compiled by Manny Maramara
Edited by Mark V. Wiley

Tambuli Media
1121 N. Bethlehem Pike #60-179
Spring House, PA 19446
www.TambuliMedia.com

www.ReneNavarro.Org

Dedicated to my father Ricardo Yuson Navarro
(January 15, 1916-December 31, 2001)
who introduced me to the novels
"Candide" by Voltaire, and "Crime and Punishment" by Dostoevsky,
"Rubaiyat" by Omar Khayyam," boxing and the virtue of kindness.

Foreword

There is so much to say about Grandmaster Rene J. Navarro, that a biography should be written to document his adventures, study, contributions to Philippine culture, healing traditions, and martial arts. Until then, we have this truly inspiring and insightful memoir hidden within the essays of his encounters with extraordinary teachers the world over.

What is immediately self-evident in reading is Rene's passion and drive toward self-empowerment through cultivation of his mind, his body, and his spirit. And I don't list these terms as watered-down self-branded gurus and healers that get tossed about as mere jargon. In Rene's case, he is indeed a scholar, well read, a writer and poet (mind); he is a half-century long practitioner of kung-fu, arnis, tai chi, massage, and qigong (body); and he is an advanced meditator, energy healer, reciter of mantra and sutra, and a loving man (spirit). His life-long pursuit of these excellences has taken him around the world many times to meet great masters under whom to study. Later, he traveled the world to teach and mentor others. I gues the correct term for Rene would be Renaissance Man. Truly, he is that.

Of Fire and Water: Alchemy and Transformation is the second volume of Rene's work I have been fortunate to publish. The first is a heartfelt book of modern prose poetry titled, *Ascension and Return: Poetry of a Village Taoist.* Like this volume, that work also relates stories of extraordinary people, places, and experiences. Taken as a set, these books show a man of passion for life, who has experienced more than most, and yet remains humble and continues to search for meaning in life through self-cultivation. Reading about Rene's upbringing in the Philippines, and given his personality, there is no doubt about his reasons for traveling path. Consider this passage:

> *Many Filipinos in the 1950s complained about our colonial culture and our Westernized way of life. But obviously they could not do much about it because, well, what and where was the alternative? (...) They called for a Filipino way both in private life and government policies, but their lives revolved around a colonial culture. Foreign policy was dictated from Washington, DC. Basketball was the dominant sport, Coke the most popular drink, English the most widespread language and the mode of instruction from the grades to college, Christianity the most widespread religion, and Western entertainment hugged the stages and airwaves. (...) In college I was into Hemingway, Shakespeare, Homer, Dylan Thomas, TS Eliot. I wrote in English, I joined oratorical and writing contests in English and won awards, I spoke and read English in the classroom and outside. I went to the Jefferson Library on the Escolta and the British Reading Room on Azcarraga Street for their books and readings. When I saw pictures of Hatha yoga postures, I thought they were weird. I was a perfect colonial!*

In an ironic twist of fate, it was in the 1970s when Rene relocated to the United States, that he learned about Asian culture, art, religion, and martial arts. The 'perfect colonial' came to burst through the colonial glass ceiling in the land of the colonizers. And the exposure he got to things "foreign" in America started him on the adventure of his lifetime. At 82, he has just returned from a teaching tour in the Philippines… the adventure never stops.

In the chapters that follow in this educational memoir of topic-specific essays, Rene takes the reader along with him on his journey toward self-cultivation in the Philippines, China, Thailand, America, Indonesia, Istanbul, Rome, Greece, Egypt, Cambodia, Mexico, Taiwan, and so many more places to meet extraordinary teachers and learn extraordinary things. You will meet Lao Kim, Johnny Chiuten, Jopet Laraya, Gin Soon Chu, Mantak Chia, Len Roberts, Amante Marinas, Xuan Kong, Ou Wen Wei, John Chang, and many other gifted teachers and practitioners.

I have known Rene for 30 years. He is godfather to my son Alex (named after my kung-fu sifu and our mutual friend, the late Master Alex Co). It's odd how we both move about but somehow end up living in the same area. After working in Tokyo for Charles Tuttle Publishing Company I was relocated to their Boston office. Guess who was also living there: Rene! I relocated to Baltimore and Rene was there for some reason and we spent time together. I had a family and moved back to the Philadelphia suburbs, and don't you know, Rene is living less than an hour away. From the grandmaster, I studied the traditional Yang Tai Chi form and Broadsword, Buddha Palm Qigong, and Lao Kim's Red Boy Prays to Guanyin and Dragon-Tiger forms and the Pole. So much to learn, so little time.

My 54th birthday was a few days ago, and a group of guests including Rene Navarro, were to come by my home tomorrow at 1pm for a cookout. But it's been raining nonstop and will continue through tomorrow, so I rescheduled the get-together for next week. Toward the end of the afternoon today the doorbell rang. And there Rene was, unexpectedly at my door with a gift bag in hand. I opened the door and he said, "I am sorry for being four hours late! Or am I early? I don't remember." We laughed and hugged, and he came in. He brought me some very nice Long Jing Cha (Dragon Well Green Tea Leaves) and we sat and sipped tea and discussed all things of interest. He paused the conversation and said, "If I had come tomorrow, we would not have had the chance to talk with so many people around." I smiled and said, because of the rain we rescheduled for next week. "Then it's good I came today." I agreed. Any time spent with such am amazing person is good… more than good, a blessing.

For those who have not had the privilege of knowing Rene Navarro, of learning from him or having tea with him, this book shall suffice. Boil some lotus flower tea (his favorite) and sit back and allow yourself to be swept into the stories of a lifetime. Then, seek him out and spend some time with him. You will love it. And I expect he will, too.

Respectfully,

Mark V. Wiley,
Publisher, Tambuli Media
April 29, 2023

A Man of Parts, A Master of Chinese Arts

by Ed Maranan

On Rene Navarro's website, www.ReneNavarro.org, there is a description of where his journey began:

> "Rene was raised in the shadow of the western mountain ranges of Luzon. His grandfather, Ingkong Poli, a raconteur and farmer and artisan, was the greatest influence in his early life. Ingkong Poli told him stories of powerful beings, warriors, monsters, fairies, from legends and corridos. It was in this idyllic world that Rene was first exposed to nature, storytelling, native herbs, craftsmanship, martial arts, poetry, and the mystical."

Rene was a law student, prominent Alpha Phi Betan, campus writer, and an articulate debater in UP (University of the Philippines) when I was still an undergraduate. The next time I heard about him, I was living in London, and I would be reading about his achievements in the US as a martial arts expert and a published writer. When he and another Fil-Am writer Patrick Rosal visited the UK, we arranged for a poetry reading at the Center for Filipinos in Hammersmith. After impressing the audience with a moving poem about the final days of his father, Rene proceeded to give a demonstration of Chinese spear and sword, annotating as he went through the graceful but powerful movements.

He invited me to his friend's house in Richmond, south London, where he cooked a gourmet meal for the three of us, and later the roof deck which had a magnificent view of the meandering Thames, gave another demonstration of his skill in Chinese martial arts and Filipino arnis.

A couple of years later, I wrote to him in Boston, inviting him to contribute an essay to a book I was editing with my daughter Len, *A Taste of Home: Pinoy Expats and Food Memories*. He came up with a terrific essay that did justice to the whimsical title: "Reflections on the Diaspora, Burung Babi, a Favorite Uncle, Malayan Fish Head Curry, and a Trip to the Mountains."

He visits the Philippines from time to time. Last year, he was here briefly to give a two-day seminar. The first day was on Zhan Zhuang (stationary postures and breathing exercises), while the second day, which I attended, was devoted to Tai Chi Chuan Tao Ren, the eight core movements based on the traditional Yang Family solo fist form. Only eight movements, but we sweated gallons through a full day of slow, deliberate motions done repeatedly.

As I write this, the boy from Tarlac who would turn into a Renaissance Man forever voyaging in the Filipino diaspora is in the mystical village of Ubud on the island of Bali for intensive training in Lei Shan Tao (Lightning and Thunder Path).

It is just one customary way station in a life-long journey of self-discovery, in search of the ancient secrets and methods of meditation and healing, the Taoist philosophy of going with the flow, as much as the cultivation of character and physical strength via the martial arts. For more than fifty years, Rene has trained under the best gurus, sifus, magi, teachers of the ancient arts. After obtaining a 3rd degree black belt from the Karate Federation of the Philippines in 1968, he became absorbed with Chinese martial arts and apprenticed under legendary teachers in Manila's Chinatown. He learned Shaolin kung fu from "the most complete master" Johnny Chiuten and grandmaster Lao Kim, and obtained mastery of the Chinese staff, spear, and sword under the tutelage of Lao Sigong. His first teacher of tai chi chuan was Chan Bun Te at the Hua Eng Athletic Association which was then in a Buddhist temple in Binondo.

Rene Navarro & Ed Maranan at the Carlos Palanca Literary Awards.

Immigrating to the United States after finishing his law studies at UP, he worked as a lawyer for indigent clients, but never let up in his pursuit of more arcane knowledge, obtaining a degree in acupuncture and a certificate in classical Chinese herbs, seeking out the masters of Chinese martial arts in San Francisco, Los Angeles, New Jersey and New York, gaining more expertise in martial arts, finally discovering the method of the Healing Tao under Mantak Chia in New York's Chinatown. It was also in New York where he reconnected with his Filipino roots, meeting up again with his former teacher in arnis de mano, Mat Mariñas. He resumed his training in Filipino stick fighting with enthusiasm, even coming home briefly after the EDSA revolution to renew his ties with old buddy and karate/kung fu teacher Johnny Chiuten who was by that time living in Bantayan, Cebu, perfecting his eclectic methods of Chinese, Japanese and Philippine martial arts.

Rene has gone to the source of this ancient knowledge several times. He traveled to Chengdu in Sichuan in 1983 to study various forms of wushu, such as northern spear, sword, monkey fist and cudgel. He was in China again a few years ago to teach English as a means of livelihood, but the main purpose was to explore further the ancient traditions of Shaolin kung fu in places where it is still being taught by venerable masters.

His knowledge of the ancient arts of healing, meditation, and fighting with bare hands or weapons is vast and prodigious, and this knowledge he imparts to students in workshops and seminars from the Catskill Mountains in New York to the shadow of the pyramids in

Egypt, from a sun-washed island in Cyprus to an executive suite in a Makati building, from a village green in England to a tranquil village in Thailand.

The fields Rene Navarro is considered an expert in and therefore qualified to teach includes acupuncture, dragon-well qigong, Xing Shen Zhuang rehabilitative therapy, Tai Chi Chuan Tao Ren and related forms, internal alchemy and spiritual practice, Chi Nei Tsang internal organs massage, Taoist philosophy, Shaolin kung fu or wushu, and arnis de mano.

An excellent chef, Rene's loves to serve up his two favorite dishes. One is congee with black chicken, herbs (ginseng, astragalus, He Shou Wu or Mr. Wu's black hair), red berries, and lurong or deer horn. The other one is pheasant or Cornish game hen with garlic, cloves, capers, olives, bay leaf, salted cod fish (bacalao), and chorizo de Bilbao.

I have hinted that he is an accomplished essayist. Rene is also a lyrical poet, with some of his poems appearing in various anthologies, and with three poetry collections reflecting his deep connection to the Chinese tradition: *Du-Fu's Cottage and Other Poems*, *Ascension and Return: Poetry of a Village Taoist*, and *The Weaver Girl and the Shepherd Boy*.

Here are some lines from his poem, "Dream in Baopu Temple":

As I pass the rock where we sat,
I catch a glimpse of you doing
the Immortal Sword Dance
in the moonlight.
There is a spark of lightning in the sky.
I hear the Golden Rooster
crowing among the pines
ready to fly.
I offer three joss sticks for you
and the Taoist priest
rings a gong that resonates
in the distance. Where
is Ge Hong, the alchemist,
can he do his magic
to bring you back
here among the willow
trees?

Table of Contents

Foreword ... vi

A Man of Parts, A Master of Chinese Arts ... viii

Author's Preface ... xiii

1. Self-Cultivation: Introduction to Chinese Culture ... 1
2. The Interface of Chinese Healing Modalities ... 18
3. Journey to the East: Wu Shu in Sichuan ... 26
4. Lao Kim: Mysterious Master of Kung-Fu ... 34
5. Johnny F. Chiuten: Fighter and Sage ... 45
6. Jose Santiago Laraya: A Lifetime of Dedication ... 54
7. Arnis: The Language of Combat ... 69
8. Gilas Arnis: Amante Marinas ... 78
9. Lapunti Arnis de Abanico: A Creative Synthesis ... 86
10. Looking for Yang Cheng-Fu ... 91
11. The Curriculum of Yang Family Tai Chi Chuan ... 101
12. The Mysterious Traditional Yang Family Chang Chuan Form ... 107
13. The Sword of the Immortal Lu Dongbin ... 113
14. Developing the Tai Chi Chuan Body ... 122
15. Tai Chi Chuan Insights of Vincent F. Chu ... 127
16. The "Mystery" of Master Cheng Man Ching ... 144
17. Mantak Chia: Modern Taoist Master and Alchemist ... 149
18. Of Fire and Water: Discovering Internal Alchemy ... 155
19. Thunder Path in Huangshan ... 166
20. Pilgrimages And Opening the Body to Nature ... 181
21. Letter From Cyprus ... 188

22. Dateline: Ubud, Bali, 2012 198
23. Jose Rizal: Zen Life, Zen Death 207
24. Jose Rizal, Alchemist 216
25. Haiyan Recovery Update: Healers on a Mission 221
26. Bringing Chi Nei Tsang Organs Massage to Homonhon 225
27. Thinking of My Friend, Uncle Rudy 228
28. Len Roberts: Poet 233
29. David Cortez Medalla 238
30. The Dragon at 75: Reflections on Growing Older 241
31. Encounters with Zhang Sanfeng 252
32. Reflections on the Diaspora, Burung Babi, A Favorite Uncle, Malayan Fish Head Curry, and a Trip To The Mountains 260

Afterword 274

End Notes 277

Acknowledgements 288

Photo Credits 291

Author's Preface

When I say my surname, strangers sometimes ask me where I come from. I tell them to make three guesses. Often, they are wrong. My Spanish name Navarro is a clue to the confusing history of my country: although an Asian country, the Philippines has a colonial culture influenced by the West, particularly Spain and the United States. There is a story in the clan that the Navarro ancestry could be traced back to a Miguel Navarro, portrayed as a Spanish noble man with a family crest but was probably a philandering priest who preyed on women in the confessional. A different version of the lineage points to a Chinese surnamed Chan in Batangas, a province four hours south of Manila. There is no documentation to establish which origin story is right.

Several of my relatives have traveled to this hometown called Balayan, famous for its fish sauce. My grandfather Paulino Navarro took my father Ricardo and me to meet relatives there back in the early 1950s. I vaguely remember that my grandpa shared the same physical features as his cousin: patrician nose, dark skinned, broad forehead, short. Nothing of Castillian descent. From what I heard then and later, my ancestor came from China, probably from Fujian, and carried the surname Chan. A Spanish Governor General issued an edict 200 years ago that certain barrios should adopt a Spanish name. Consequently, the Chans became Navarros. It was a common imperialist way of homogenizing the colonies and making their people forget their history.

The Chinese ancestry is what I follow in my imagination. I tell the story that 300 years ago, a Chinese pirate named Limahong fell in love with the Muslim warrior princess Urduja. She was promised to marry a Spaniard, but she was in love with Limahong. The two eloped on his ship and they plied the islands in southern Luzon, Philippines. They had several children who settled in Batangas and intermarried, some with Chinese settlers in the area, some with Indians, a few with the natives. To make a long story short, my great great great grandmother married into the Chan family. It was at this point that the Spanish colonizer issued a law that the residents of Batangas would use only Spanish surnames.

The joke is that there really was a Chinese pirate called Limahong and a Muslim princess named Urduja! But the two never met. It's the most ridiculous and impossible pairing imaginable. Limahong was never one to settle down and Princess Urduja never got married because as a precondition the man had to beat her in combat.

Many Filipinos in the 1950s complained about our colonial culture and our Westernized way of life. But obviously they could not do much about it because, well, what and where was the alternative? They called for a Filipino way both in private life and government policies, but their lives revolved around a colonial culture. Foreign policy was dictated from Washington, DC. Basketball was the dominant sport, Coke the most popular drink, English the most widespread language and the mode of instruction from the grades to college, Christianity the most widespread religion and Western entertainment hugged the stages and airwaves. During the decades the US colonizers ruled the country, they saw to it that their possessions were indoctrinated and "properly taught" — to borrow a phrase from the musical *South Pacific* — in the ways of the Americans.

In recent years the Philippines, like the US, has been undergoing a transformation of sorts as Eastern culture is becoming a part of the mainstream. Martial art of different styles, yoga, massage, acupuncture, meditation, even feng shui and astrology and a few others, are becoming more prominent. There are now healing centers operating under the law regulating them. Likewise, there has been a conscious effort by some groups to revive and promote old indigenous traditions and arts and to adopt Asian culture. At some events you'll see young men and women wearing indigenous clothes and playing indigenous music on indigenous instruments or doing Tai Chi Chuan and other Asian martial arts.

But back in the 1950s, largely because of our colonial education and upbringing, Filipinos did not have much connection to or knowledge of our Philippine culture. It was as if we were exiled from our own traditions and country — we consciously or unconsciously tried to mimic American ways and become Americanized. In many ways we even despised our customs and each other. We were also alienated from our Asian neighbors. I myself did not know much about Li-Po or Du-Fu until I heard Gustav Mahler's "Songs of the Earth" ("Das Lied von Der Erde"). I attended a Methodist Church, followed its rituals, believed the *Bible*, and sang with the choir at the Sunday services. On one Good Friday, I was one of those who gave a sermon on the Seven Last Words in church. At the university chapel, during Reformation Sunday, I used to recite Martin Luther's "Here I Stand" speech to the Diet of Worms. Others who were Roman Catholics joined processions, recited the Rosary, and took Communion, among other things. We all believed in the Holy Trinity, the Virgin Mary, Christmas, and the Resurrection of Jesus.

Back when I was in high school, I did not know any martial art. No hint of karate or kung-fu. Like many kids, I played basketball, I danced boogie and rock and roll. Believe it or not, when I was 14 or 15, there was a sports instructor who made a big group of us dance boogie while we were wearing cowboy outfits at an athletic meet. In college I was into Hemingway, Shakespeare, Homer, Dylan Thomas, TS Eliot. I wrote in English, I joined oratorical and writing contests in English and won awards, I spoke and read English in the classroom and outside. I went to the Jefferson Library on the Escolta and the British Reading Room on Azcarraga Street for their books and readings. When I saw pictures of Hatha yoga postures, I thought they were weird. I was a perfect colonial!

I was kind of thrust into training in Japanese Karate when my brother Florante found a teacher in my hometown and passed on the knowledge to me in 1962. Later Johnny F. Chiuten, another student in university and a martial art master, asked me to study with him. Still later, when he went back to his island home, he recommended me to the former Fujian temple monk, Lao Kim, jobless at the time, and the old man taught me kung-fu privately. At this point, as the essays that follow show, I became exposed to more eastern disciplines. My Chinese godfather, Chan Tek Lao, urged me to study Yang Tai Chi Chuan with his cousin Chan Bun Te in Manila's Chinatown. Later Chan sifu took me to enroll in a Tai Chi Chuan class taught by the Taiwanese master Lao Yun Hsiao. I learned about Rabindranath Tagore, the basics of Zen Buddhism and Hindu religion. But there wasn't any opportunity to learn more because the schools and centers for Eastern studies were not there. Our education was patterned after the system of the US. During my four years of college, I did not have a single course in Tagalog, our national language.

It was when I went to the US in late 1970 that I encountered Eastern training courses. Irony of ironies, for the first time, I started learning Arnis de Mano, a style of Philippine stickfighting called Arnis Lanada, with a young Filipino master Amante "Mat" Marinas in Elmhurst, Queens, NY. At LaMama ETC in the Bowery, as a member of a theatre group called Philippine Educational Theatre Arts League (PETAL) organized and directed by Cecille Guidote, I learned Philippine indigenous dances of southern and northern Philippines. I performed on stage as an Ifugao warrior wearing a colorful loincloth. I was the escort carrying the umbrella of the Muslim princess dancing the Singkil. I did a modern translation of the Tagalog prison poem, "Kung Tuyo Na ang Luha Mo, Aking Bayan" ("If Your Tears Are Dry, My Country") from the book *Isang Dipang Langit*, by the Philippine poet laureate Amado Hernandez. As an indication of my ignorance, I also saw for the first time Indian dances performed by a blind man (we called him Mr. Duth) and a monkey dance by a young woman who learned it in Bali.

I became passionate about learning the culture of Asia. For a time, I wrote haiku every day. I read the poetry and life of Basho and the *fu* (prose) poems of China. I studied Wu style Tai Chi Chuan with Master Leung Shum in Manhattan. I went to China to train in Wu-Shu in Chengdu, Sichuan Province in 1983; among the styles I learned was Monkey Boxing with the famous Xiao Yingpeng known as the "Monkey King," after the character in the epic *Journey to the West,* a book that took me two years to read. When I read about Mantak Chia's Healing Tao, I signed up for his courses in Chinatown, NY; later I attended week-long retreats and then trained and got certified as an instructor. I was also chosen as Instructor of the Year in 1989. Eventually I became Mantak's assistant and wrote and/or edited four of his books on neidan/internal alchemy and two on healing (Taoyin and Chi Nei Tsang internal organs massage). I studied different healing, meditative, shamanic, and spiritual methods. It was not enough. When I returned to the Philippines after the February Revolution of 1986, I studied Lapunti Arnis de Abanico in Cebu and became certified as an instructor. Johnny Chiuten, my teacher in Dragon Tiger Fujian Temple kung-fu, and I made a documentary film about the style on Mactan Island. Johnny took me around to meet Arnis de Mano

Rene Navarro, the young orator, in college age 19 (L) and in high school age12 (R).

masters, including the legendary Guiling Tinga of Bantayan Island. I observed Philippine healers in Cebu, Manila, Baguio, and Mount Banahaw. I refused to be like those Filipinos who wanted to cultivate and promote Philippine culture but paid only lip service to it and did not practice any of its traditions.

It was a serious way of intensive immersion in Asian culture. Perhaps it was a kind of rebellion against colonialism and the legacy of a western lifestyle. Perhaps I was making up for lost time or trying to get rid of my colonial life or finding a Filipino identity that was encrusted with centuries of meretricious Western influences, I cannot really say. But I had a great thirst for Asian traditions that could not be quenched, I just wanted more and more. And learning Chinese culture was like resurrecting my Chinese family's past that was obliterated by Spain and the US.

In 1989, I moved to Boston to study Chinese and Japanese acupuncture and Traditional Chinese herbology at the New England School of Acupuncture, and Classical Yang Family Tai Chi Chuan at the Gin Soon Tai Chi Federation in Chinatown. I passed the national exams, got certified as a diplomate in acupuncture by the NCCAOM and licensed in Massachusetts and later in Hawaii. I became faculty for NESA and as a senior instructor of the Healing Tao (now Universal Healing Tao), I pioneered a course in Inner Smile, Six Healing Sounds, Microcosmic Orbit, a meditation on the 12 regular meridians and Buddha Palm Qigong, and Tai Chi Chi Kung. I apprenticed to the Japanese master Kiiko Matsumoto and became her "moxa boy," applying and burning thread-like and sesame-size moxa on the indicated acupuncture points of her patients. I studied Pangu Shengong Qigong with Master Ou Wen Wei. I taught seminars in Eastern healing arts in the US, UK, Cyprus, Egypt, The Netherlands, the Philippines, and Thailand. I read the translations of *The Mahabharata* and the *Gita, Tao Te Ching, Zhuangzi, Upanishads*, Sunzi's *Art of War*, the *Yoga Sutras* of Patanjali, the Philippine epics *Aliguyon* and *Lam-Ang* and built a library of Eastern books. I listened to chants of the Heart Sutra and Upanishads on CDs and online, the recordings of sitar masters Ravi and Anoushka Shankar and the Indonesian gamelan.

My life has revolved around Eastern culture since then. I took lessons in Thai massage in Chiangmai, a few with the famous master Chaiyuth Priyasith. Later, I studied Thunder Path with David Verdesi in Bali, Thailand, Istanbul, Rome, and China. (David became the subject of the documentary "Superhumans" emceed by my friend, the famous Qigong master, Lee Holden.) David introduced me to the Magus of Java (John Chang) in 2006 and the hermits of Huangshan in 2007 and we sat at the feet of Hindu priests in Bali in 2012. While teaching English as a Second Language in Hangzhou, China in 2010, I took courses in Mandarin and Chinese calligraphy. I acquired rare statues of Shiva Nataraja and the Fasting Buddha. I followed the seminars of Taoist priest Jeffrey Yuen through Maryland, Massachusetts, New Jersey, and North Carolina and online. It was, well, immersion in Eastern arts with a vengeance!

The essays included in this book are literally attempts to show insights and samples of my studies over the years. They give a bit of the flavor of what I do and what I practice. Did I find what I was looking for? Yes, I did, and more. I discovered the incomparable and profound culture of Asia, the literary classics, and the transmissions of meditative, healing, energetic, spiritual methods that a Filipino could have been heir to if he were not constrained by the limits set in legions of ways by the colonial powers. How much richer the culture of the Philippines would have been if the country were allowed to grow on its own and not have been dominated by the West. I also realized that the human being has a great potential to grow and develop even beyond his accepted and traditional potential, that with certain disciplines consistently practiced he can develop powers beyond his imagination. I have seen this in my meetings with different masters and ordinary people and in my own practices.

Not only did the foreign colonizers rob us of our identity, but they also stole from us our own culture and our connectedness to our Asian family and their ancient heritage; they also inflicted their own culture on us and on our basically animistic traditions based on respect for and connection to nature and the environment. I believe how much richer our experiences would have been if we sat at the feet of a guru or a teacher and listened to the chanting of and commentaries on the *Heart Sutra* or the passages from the *Tao Te Ching*, how much more profound our lives would have been if we did martial arts in their original milieu. We survived the massacres and the indoctrination but barely and as confused little colonials we did not know where we were and what direction we were going. If we can disabuse ourselves of colonial mentality, we can now cultivate our own culture based on the remnants of our traditions and arts and what we have learned, especially from our Asian neighbors. China and India developed their culture over thousands of years; they had their own indigenous practices and beliefs and at the same time borrowed from their neighbors. In a real sense, the most advanced civilizations — like Greece and Italy — were eclectic, a synthesis of what they had and what they copied.

A last cautionary tale. The Western Procrustean Bed. The Eastern paradigm of the human being and the world includes not just the physical and material but also the energetic, mystical, intellectual, emotional as well as the spiritual.[1] But much of Eastern culture is often perceived and practiced through the framework of the materialistic West. Yoga has been reduced to an exercise for physical fitness and flexibility, meditation as a mode of relaxation, and nothing more. Martial art, a temple discipline among monks, has become just a system of fighting, sans philosophy, compassion, and virtues. Sunzi's *Art of War*, the classic of warfare, is just a manual for capitalist business and gamesmanship. Eastern disciplines often pass through the procrustean bed of the West. We have a long way to go to reach the heart of authentic Eastern culture.

Rene J. Navarro
Easton, Pa 18045
April 5, 2022

1.

Self-Cultivation: Introduction to Chinese Culture

Qi Bo to the Yellow Emperor, Huang Di:

> *In the past, people practiced the Tao, the Way of Life. They understood the principle of balance, of yin and yang, as represented by the transformation of the energies of the universe. Thus, they formulated practices such as taoyin (qigong), an exercise combining stretching, massaging, and breathing to promote energy flow, and meditation to help maintain and harmonize themselves with the universe. They ate a balanced diet at regular times, arose and retired at regular hours, avoided overstressing their bodies and minds, and refrained from overindulgence of all kinds. They maintained well-being of body and mind; thus, it is not surprising that they lived over one hundred years.*
>
> — *The Yellow Emperor's Classic of Medicine*[1]

TAOIST SELF-CULTIVATION

It is Autumn, just a little chilly now, with a soft breeze and occasionally a shower descending the Appalachian Mountains of northern Pennsylvania. Mornings I would wake up early, boil some tea, put on my black pants, sneakers, sweatshirt, and a vest, and carry a broadsword, straight sword, and sometimes a spear, to the park in Easton where I would practice. It is part of the regimen I try to observe every day when I am home.

When it is a little warm, a thick mist covers the Delaware River and much of the old bridge across it. It's not Wudang Temple, where Tai Chi Chuan was supposed to have been developed, or Huangshan, arguably the most beautiful mountain in all China and the legendary retreat of Qin Shi Huang Di, but it is a lovely setting for an aspiring Taoist.

I would face East in the direction of New Jersey where the sun would rise in a couple of hours. There are certain preliminaries I observe: quieting myself, clearing my mind, feeling the earth qi beneath my feet, activating certain energy points, breathing deeply, being aware of the environment. I would spend time just getting ready. And then I would do several rounds of the traditional Yang Family Tai Chi Chuan 108 movements solo form, broad-sword form, and the sword form.

Perhaps, I would conclude this part of my exercise with one or two of the Shaolin forms, the "Dragon and Tiger" set or "Plum Blossom Fist." When inspired and energetic, I would also walk through the complete sets of other Tai Chi Chuan forms of the system, and fragments of certain exercises like Zhan Zhuang and Ba Xian qigong.

There was a time in my early training in Boston in the '90s when I would do a form at least five times straight through, nonstop.

After my routine, I would sit on a bench facing the sun and spend time in meditation. It's just another practice in the large repertoire of Chinese qigong: absorbing the qi of the sun (or the moon) into the body through different points.

It's not always the same every time; I would include certain exercises that I feel are necessary or that inspire me in the moment. If it were raining or the weather is too harsh, I would stay inside and do other routines. When I am able to follow my program of practices, I usually sleep early, say, at 8 or 9pm and wake up at 4 or 5am. In between, I can wake up at 1am and do a qigong set, sleep, and wake up again at 2:30 to continue the practice, sleep, wake up again at 4 or 5am. At 7 or 8, I would usually have a breakfast of oatmeal, banana, and hot tea and toast with peanut butter. Well, it is not exactly a Taoist meal but because it's easy to prepare, that's what I usually have. In this area of Eastern Pennsylvania, that's the best I could do. When conditions allow it, I would usually have soup or congee with herbs.

There are many reasons why the Taoist practitioner would go to bed early and wake up at certain hours of the night. It has something to do with concepts like the Hour of Tzu and the circadian cycles of the body, the organs, and the qi. There is also a reason why the Tai Chi Chuan practitioner would face a certain direction — the Jade Emperor, the Green Dragon, the Sun all play a role in the matter — and why he would activate certain points in his body before he starts his form and breathe from the dantian/navel center. There is also a reason — or reasons — why he assumes certain postures and movements in qigong and why he eats certain food at a particular time.

SELF-CULTIVATION

It is all part of self-cultivation (associated with Yang-Sheng or a Nourishing Life regimen), a category of practices and disciplines that focus on the transformation of the body: physical, mental, psychological, energetic, and spiritual. It was mentioned in the *Yellow Emperor's Classic of Internal Medicine* more than 2,500 years ago. China is unique in that no other culture or country in history has such a complete repertoire of self-cultivation practices.

Over the years, possibly at least six-thousand years of evolution, self-cultivation practices were developed by the Chinese, primarily by the Taoists and secondarily by the Buddhists and Confucians, in pursuit of longevity, peace, tranquility, happiness, health, victory in warfare, and immortality.

There is no specific doctrinaire rule that says what these arts or regimens are, I don't think. But from tradition and the definition of self-cultivation techniques, it is possible to draw certain conclusions.

WHAT IT INCLUDES

To me, self-cultivation would include meditation, qigong, martial arts, movement, feng-shui, astrology, Tantric sex, massage, internal alchemy, qigong/taoyin and the healing arts of acupuncture, massage, and herbology. These are arts that are directed towards the development of the human being. These are activities that the Chinese would often do or have somebody do to them to develop themselves, they are arguably the earliest self-help methods of keeping healthy, being attuned with nature, losing weight, finding relaxation, having good sex; generally, living the good life.

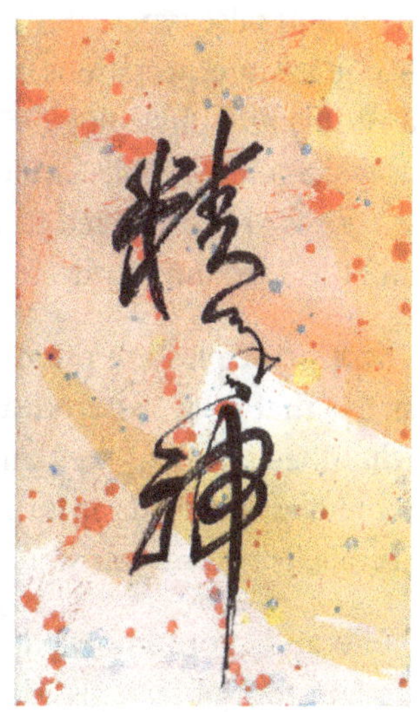

"Spirit" calligraphy by Tak Wah Eng.

What strikes me is the fact that these different arts, philosophies, and regimens are so intricate that they cannot possibly be mastered in a short period of time. It is usually used as a text for divination and not often as a guide to self-development, but the *I Ching* ("Book of Change") alone would take a lifetime, perhaps more, to understand. Confucius himself said that if he had another 50 years, he would devote them to its study. My teacher in Classical Yang Family Tai Chi Chuan, Sifu Gin Soon Chu, told me that a lifetime is not enough to master it, so why should one study other styles of martial arts?

It is puzzling therefore that there are practitioners who would claim the honorific "master" title, although they have not penetrated the deeper secrets of an art. Master of what, is a matter that would require a long, long explanation.

PURSUIT OF PERFECTION

Self-cultivation developed mainly due to the Chinese desire for improvement and perfection. In China, since ancient times, there has been awareness of the divine and eternal life and of the relationship between Heaven and Earth. A dominant concept is that the human being should pursue his destiny — the role he must play on earth — that Heaven has set out for him in this lifetime. Another concept is that although he is far from being a celestial being, he is touched by the divine and has the potential to become an immortal, a sage or a "righteous being" (or any class of enlightened person) through the development of virtues and the practice of internal alchemy.

In the heart is the residence of the *shen*, the Spirit that carries the purpose of life, the Spirit that keeps bringing us back to the course we are supposed to follow in this incarnation so that we will achieve our goal. To be able to achieve that goal or goals, we must learn different ways of prolonging life. This was basically a Taoist goal, but it has become widespread in China throughout most of its history.

Self-cultivation exercises are very often linked with principles and ideas like yin and yang (true and false types), Five-Elements theory, Qi, the Trinity (Heaven, Humanity, and Earth is one its interpretations), the Three Spirits and Seven Souls, Kan and Li (fire and water), anatomy and physiology, Heavenly Stems and Earthly Branches, Pa-Kua (Eight Trigrams), Magic Square, Magic Circle, Reversal and Return, and stillness and emptiness. Many of the exercises are connected to longevity, immortality, our relationship to nature, the Universe and the Tao, and our destiny and identity.

These principles are often hidden behind metaphorical language and numerology so abstruse that even experts can take a long time to decipher them. Especially for somebody who does not read the Chinese characters, ancient and modern, the search gets infinitely more daunting. It is as if the masters did not want the succeeding generation to know their secrets, which may as well be true.

More and more knowledge is getting lost because teachers are keeping it to themselves perhaps out of fear, greed, or distrust. In the course of time, practitioners get to learn less and less of the hidden transmissions and only the outer teachings are handed down. For the average student, what they learn may be enough. But for gifted and serious students, who are to be part of the lineage, it can be terribly frustrating.

There is indeed an Inner Tradition in much of Chinese culture, whether it is martial arts, acupuncture, herbology, qigong, meditation, sexology, internal alchemy. Different levels of knowledge — usually classified into the Trinity — have developed over the thousands of years of Chinese tradition. Frequently, what is popular is only the surface knowledge. In Tai Chi Chuan, for instance, the physical form is accessible and is practiced by millions of people. It is of course a good practice, especially if it is done correctly. But there are other levels too — esoteric and arcane — that are known only by a select few.

PRACTICE AND THEORY

As I review my practices, I realize how certain principles — religious, mystical, philosophical, energetic, cosmological, astrological — underpin the activities of my daily life. I don't even think about it now. After more than 50 years studying and practicing different aspects of Chinese culture, I have to some extent integrated these principles. At the same time, I feel humbled not only by the plethora of self-cultivation methods there are in existence, but also by the ideas and concepts that were developed by the sages, doctors, priests and priestesses, emperors, philosophers, and shamans in the course of Chinese history. These principles have permeated different facets of Chinese life.

Often, these principles are not obvious and clear to a non-Chinese. To mention just a few simple things: You bow three times, you face north, south, or east or you see different colors and flavors at a meal and of course there is a reason behind it. Through the millennia, certain ideas and philosophies and mythologies have informed the culture in different ways. Almost all areas of human endeavor in China have principles — or reasons, at least — behind them: from architecture to rituals, from relationships and hierarchies (both earthly and divine) to clothes, from ancestor worship to meditation, and much, much more.

Whether it is cooking or movement, fighting or meditation, funerals and births, weddings and initiations, geomancy or healing, there are principles that underlie them. With dietetics, you must know different correspondences: flavors, colors, balancing and proportion, seasons (as in Winter or Summer), scents, yin and yang; you need to know herbs, as well, because they are very much a part Chinese cuisine. In martial arts, possibly one of the most accessible of the Chinese disciplines, there are principles (or philosophy, if you wish) that one must learn if one is to achieve expertise in the field: strategy and tactics, breathing, qigong, point striking, yin-yang, meridians and Five Elements, etc. Martial arts, to the Chinese, are not just hitting, striking, and fighting. There are different levels of development which include different forms and principles, including at the higher ranks, circadian rhythm of the meridians.

Sifu Alex Dong Tai Chi Chuan Weapons.

So elaborate are the principles that it overwhelms me to think about them. As alluded to earlier, in acupuncture there are basic concepts about the human body and energetics that one must know. In the more advanced treatments, you must learn not just yin and yang, the names and uses of the 360 or so points, the different pulses and tongues, the relationships of the organs and meridians, and the manner of insertion and manipulation, but what to needle at certain times of the day or year as well. There are countless other considerations such as what the astrological chart of the patient shows. In certain cases, the acupuncturist may have to mediate the destiny of the patient or facilitate his demise when there is a struggle with death. It can of course be a mind-boggling labyrinth.

In feng-shui (literally "wind and water," or geomancy, the art of placement) different systems have been developed that involve the natal chart of the owner, the time the house was built, and the different directions of the Pa-Kua. It seems to be a simple straightforward approach, but it can be quite complicated. Black Hat and Flying Star are two of the more traditional styles of the art.

IT'S YOUR BODY

One of the major premises of self-cultivation is that you are blessed with a body — and its different manifestations — and you should be responsible for it. I believe there is an emphasis here on self-empowerment and human application: the ability of the individual to rise through his own effort. Plainly speaking, self-cultivation encourages people to engage in preventative regimen, i.e., do not wait for the body to break down. This is likewise the advice to healers from the *Huangdi Neijing Suwen*: waiting for disease to set in before they do a treatment is like digging for water only when one is thirsty or preparing for war when the enemy is already at the gate.

Another premise of self-cultivation is that you preserve and nourish the "Three Treasures," the trinity in the microcosm of the body: Jing, Qi, and Shen. These three form a hierarchy, Jing being the lowest and grossest (though not necessarily the least important), and Shen, the highest and most refined. Each one of them likewise has levels of refinement and subtlety. In the macrocosm of the external world, the trinity corresponds to Earth, Humanity, and Heaven. The trinity concept is likewise used in other fields: in architecture, in the arrangement of temples, and the hierarchy of deities.

The Three Treasures nourish each other and get transformed into each other through the techniques of self-cultivation. Roughly, Jing may be identified as sexual and creative energy and vitality, Qi as lifeforce and nutritional energy, and Shen as spirit or soul. At certain points, these three interface with each other and with the immanent Mind.

A common precept in self-cultivation is the "sealing of the senses" or some such version of protection from draining your energy or allowing the external world to enter your body. In Verse 12 of *Tao Te Ching* (translated by Jonathan Star), it says:

The five colors blind the eye
The five tones deafen the ear
The five flavors dull the palate
Racing, hunting, and galloping about
Only disturb the mind
Wasting energy to obtain rare objects
Only impede one's growth

So the Sage is led by his inner truth
And not his outer eye
He holds to what is deep
And not what lies on the surface

In Verse 56 of the same volume, it says:

One who speaks does not know
One who knows does not speak
Shut the mouth
Close the gates
Blunt the sharpness
Loosen the knots
Temper the glare
Become one with the dust of the world
This is called
"The Secret Embrace"
One who knows this secret
is not moved by attachment or aversion,
swayed by profit or loss,
nor touched by honor or disgrace
He is far beyond the cares of men
yet comes to hold the dearest place in their hearts

Other authorities from the Tao Zang (Taoist Canon) corroborate this concept.

The physical is important of course but it is on a low scale of development. That's why the martial, physical, and health aspects of training are on a lower level than energetic/qi development and the spiritual. The martial aspect trains the body for fighting, the health regimen improves the body's functions. Mental and spiritual are not their focus: these are cultivated in a different way and through different practices. What's more, war is something to be avoided anyway, according to a long line of Chinese classics especially the Laozi (*Tao Te Ching*) and Sunzi (*Art of War*).

A truly valuable practice is the preservation of sexual energy. Seminal retention in men is required in many cases. Indeed, before a student is taught anything, he (or she) may be required to observe celibacy for a certain period, often for at least two years. It is in a way the energetic equivalent of "standing in the low horse" for a several hours a day over a period of six months to a year. There is the famous quotation from Lu Tung-pin, the Sword Immortal: "The door through which I was born is also the Gate of Death." If the student cannot abstain from sex, he must learn the rules of engagement, basically a combination of breathing, muscular contraction, timing, and non-ejaculation.

What one eats, drinks, and breathes is also important. It is the foundation of nutritional energy and "postnatal qi." There are, of course, different nutritional regimens in China, what with regional, family, and temple cuisines. Vegetarianism is sometimes not mandated, except during heavy meditational practices and by certain sects. There are recipes required by Taoists and Buddhist groups for special occasions. For certain sects and practices, spirits and liquor are prohibited because they result in over-stimulation of the energy and the

Tai Chi Grandmaster Dong Zeng Chen with spear.

senses. Fasting may likewise be included in the regimen. As for this, there is a belief in the "avoidance of grains and cereals" that has something to do with eliminating worms from the body. "Bigu" is another related regimen: basically, giving up food and relying on water, mist, and the absorption of qi from the environment.

Breathing fresh air — especially in the mountains — may be advised for those with serious physical problems or those who have dedicated themselves to serious spiritual work. Different breathing techniques — divided roughly into "warrior" and "scholar" (or yang and yin) — are practiced for certain disciplines and at certain times.

There are also times when disciples will have to undergo a period of meditation in a dark cave. Doing the practices in complete darkness has been found to produce startling results in energy and psychic clarity. A person who has lived in isolation in darkness can experience a connection to past lives, recall childhood memories, encounter certain energies and spirits, or develop powers. It can of course possibly result in painful traumas as well.

GENOME AND YUAN QI

There is a belief in China that you inherit certain qualities at birth from your ancestors, Earth, and Heaven (to a great extent, through the alignment of the natal stars). These are the so-called prenatal qualities. Perhaps we can call them genetic predispositions today. Like DNA, these are imprinted in your life. They may determine your destiny. They are often compared to capital in the bank, your original deposit that can earn interest if you manage it well. In Chinese thought, they are termed *yuan qi*. Yuan qi is difficult to translate but it relates to the prenatal or original energy, something you have at birth: We are born with different amounts of yuan qi. One school of thought argues that, if you spend it, you can't replace it anymore. Another school of thought that is gaining currency nowadays believes that you can replenish it through food and herbs and certain practices associated with self-cultivation.

Yuan qi can determine your strengths and weaknesses, how much you have as part of your inheritance. Some people have strong lungs and weak digestion. Others have strong kidneys and weak lungs.[2]

In a simple way, the suggested approach in self-cultivation is that you should preserve and nurture what you were born with, develop and nurture what you have little of, and give birth, if possible, to what you don't have. If for instance, you have strong kidney qi, then you should not drain it; instead, you should nourish it. On the other hand, if you have weak lung qi, you should train not to make it weak by smoking; instead, you should try to make it strong by doing qigong exercises. If you feel your jing is failing or is absent to the point that you can't "get it up," then you should use a combination of treatments — qigong, herbs, and acupuncture — to let your sexual energy grow.

SELF-CULTIVATION METHODS

What makes 'a practice' a method of self-cultivation?

1) It is composed of a regimen that cultivates the physical, mental, energetic, and spiritual aspects of the human being separately or together.
2) The method is often directed or focused on: energy, emotions, parts of the body (tendon, bone, organs, etc.), spirit, sexual energy, etc.
3) It can be stationary or with movement (sitting, lying down, or standing).
4) It can be linked to breathing or breath and with the dantian.[3]
5) It can be synchronized with the time of the day or month or year and with the astrological and natal chart of the person.
6) It can be associated with the age or gender of the practitioner. Certain practices are age relevant. For instance, there are geriatric qigong exercises for old people. There are exercises for women and men.
7) The techniques are used for healing, but the emphasis is on the prevention of illness and the maintenance of health. The advice is, do not wait until you get sick.

INTERNAL AND EXTERNAL

There are generally two categories often used to classify self-cultivation techniques: internal and external or outer and inner. While these two interface in certain areas, they are different in their methods, emphasis, and goals. "Internal" techniques of self-cultivation usually employ visualization, meditative movements, breathing or postures, using the mind to go through "formulas" and procedures, or simply achieving stillness and "emptiness." "External" techniques refer to hard, vigorous techniques using the physical body, dynamic breathing, and in certain cases equipments.[4]

Each of the two has its own different levels, too, some more internal, or external than others.

We can say that arts like painting, calligraphy, poetry (the so-called "Three Perfections"), pottery, sculpture, dance, and music are self-cultivation practices, too, because they can influence the body, spirit, and mind of the practitioner and the audience but strictly speaking they are not the self-cultivation practices that the Chinese talk about. There is in self-cultivation an emphasis on the "self," (i.e., the practice is directed at yourself) as if you are cultivating a garden inside your body, seeding it, watering it, and making it grow.

You can have a hobby or a vocation like photography, fishing, car racing, collecting, and surfing but they are not self-cultivation practices per se. They are fine occupations, but you do not do them to transform yourself in the way that Tai Chi Chuan, for instance, does. Tai Chi Chuan has — or should have — the effect of internalizing the concepts of yin and yang, developing the yielding and emptying quality of the art, and bringing the mystical experience of the Tao on different levels, physical, energetic, spiritual.

SELF-HEALING: SELF-HELP

Self-cultivation is associated with self-healing. If you have emotional problems, you use self-cultivation techniques (anger, worry and fear are the usual emotions dealt with) that transform your psyche. If you have physical problems, you use certain specific self-cultivation techniques. (Many martial arts masters had physical problems before they started their training.) If you have spiritual aspirations, you use self-cultivation techniques that primarily work on the Spirit/Shen. There are many meditative formulas for developing your spiritual body.

Self-cultivation is also associated with transformation and self-improvement, as stated earlier. You can transform your emotions of anger and fear through qigong and martial arts. You can strengthen your tendons, too. Very often, a self-cultivation technique may be combined with another or with healing arts like acupuncture, nutrition and herbology. A child who is hyperactive is taught qigong. If a child has excess, uncontrolled energy, he can take martial arts to channel and transform it; he can be given an herbal decoction to support the treatment. In fact, that is the traditional solution to over-activity in children.

For a traditional healer, according to the medical classics, there are different levels of diagnostic skills: those who can see the problem by just looking, those who can see the problem by listening and asking, and those who can see the problem by palpation. A very good healer should be able to do an assessment by looking at a photograph of the patient. There are for instance people who are prematurely bald or are overweight and bloated, with sagging jaws and triceps and bags under their eyes, and sunken cheeks. There are others whose voices are weak or who are breathless climbing stairs or walking. Abuse of the body through overwork, sexual indulgence, overeating (or eating the wrong food), or emotions like worry, anger and anxiety can manifest in different ways. From certain symptoms, an excellent healer should be able to do at least a tentative analysis and a treatment protocol including qigong exercises, herbal remedies, and acupuncture treatment.

An elderly woman who has depleted energy can be given qigong exercises to do every day and herbal recipe to cook ("food cures"). A cancer or diabetic patient can be treated with acupuncture and herbs, but he must do qigong exercises as well. A habitual cigarette smoker may be treated with acupuncture to detoxify himself and qigong exercises to strengthen the lungs and kidneys. Sometimes, treating the symptoms — like dizziness, craving and restlessness — may not be enough; it may be necessary to get the commitment of the patient to give up his addiction and change his self-image and self-respect, and perhaps his "destiny." For a smoker willing and honestly committed to overcome his attachment to nicotine, acupuncture can help tremendously; if he is not willing, not even the gods can deliver him. Often, along with acupuncture treatment, he is taught meditation techniques to boost or nurture respect for his organs, especially the lungs, and improve his will. Needling the points along the Extraordinary Vessels (master and couple points, especially, which were first mentioned in the Ming Dynasty) can affect the emotional and constitutional make-up of the patient. In general, this approach may be prescribed for a patient who has some other forms of addiction, like alcoholism.

Pangu Shen Gong qigong Sifu Ou Wen Wei in New York City with Rene Navarro, Vincent F. Chu, and students.

METHODS

Self-cultivation is basically an ascetic approach. The student's goal is to live a healthy and productive life. To achieve it, he must give up a few things and transform his lifestyle. Smoking is, of course, a no-no; so is drinking alcohol (unless it is in moderation). You must give up the rich and greasy food, sleep earlier, avoid bad habits like unregulated sex. (The Chinese are big on preserving the jing.) You simply must make room for the different regimens in your life. You cannot stay up all night and do Tai chi chuan at dawn. You must learn to simplify so that you follow a schedule for your practices.

Simple self-cultivation exercises include Six Healing Sounds, Embracing the Tree, Frolic of the Five Animals (Bear, Monkey, Crane, Tiger, and Dragon), and Pa Tuan Chin (Eight Pieces of Brocade). These deal with developing healthy qi in the body and in the organs. Ou Wen Wei's Pangu Mystical Qigong, which has only three sets representing the energies of the sun and moon, is fast gaining popularity. There are more intricate exercises like Muscle and Tendon and Bone Marrow qigong, Wild Goose qigong, and Eight Immortals Qigong. As we move to the spiritual aspects of self-cultivation, we encounter regimens like the Enlightenment of Fire and Water, and Fusion of the Five Elements, and other methods of internal alchemy (*neidan qigong*).

Different self-cultivation techniques aim to achieve different therapeutic results. There are techniques that focus on the growth of the qi, tendons, bones and bone marrow, others the nourishment of sexual energy or the improvement of the organs or the clearing and transformation of emotions. Still other techniques develop one's ability to channel energies or develop powers.

EQUIPMENT

Sometimes special equipment is used: a bamboo or steel broom, crystal eggs, weights, a shot put, a steel bar, or weapons like the sword or spear. More and more of these devices are seeing the light of day. Teachers from Taiwan and Thailand are teaching the use of crystal eggs for women and genital weight hanging, along with external qigong like hitting the meridians and tendons with the bamboo or steel broom.

Perhaps, with the separation of the *martial* from the *healing* and *spiritual* practices, it is difficult to see the connectedness of the different disciplines. It may be that we see the sword, for instance, only as a weapon for fighting, but it is as well an instrument for maximizing and nourishing the healer's qi or the alchemist's spiritual transformation. Without the inner teachings, the practitioners will only see the outer application of their training: A martial artist will only be a martial artist and will not evolve into a healer or a realized being. That is why martial arts nowadays are basically stuck in that low level of evolution.

Rene (on far right) practicing the Tai Chi fan in Dalian, China in 2007.

Jeffrey Yuen, an ordained Taoist priest of the Jade Purity Tradition (88th generation lineage) and Dragon Gate Lineage, talks about how different arts of China — artistic, martial, healing, alchemical — are intertwined in such a way that they are one system of self-cultivation:

> *"... that's why calligraphy... is a very good adjunct if you really want to develop your technique of acupuncture... The unskilled clinician just uses the needle based on its form. A skilled clinician uses the needle based on its Spirit, so it is the Spirit of the needle that you are trying to capture, just like... in the Chinese martial arts, they say that's how you handle the sword. It is not just the physical thing you are hacking away at; it is the Spirit of the sword. That is what you are trying to capture. It is the Spirit of the sword. That means your Soul channels energy into it. That's what does the healing. That is why a lot of the qigong masters in China say that instead of touching you, they touch you with an instrument. Because their instrument, like a needle, is channeling Qi..." —Light on the*

Essence of Chinese Medicine: Huangdi Neijing Lingshu/Yellow Emperor's Book of Internal Medicine Spiritual Pivot, p. 16.

Different disciplines — calligraphy, swordsmanship, acupuncture, Tai Chi Chuan, among many — share certain practices aside from the philosophy: focus on and movement of the axis/center, stillness and quietism, balance, harmony, and the dantian (of which more later).

MUNDANE TO THE SPIRITUAL

The goals of self-cultivation can range from the most mundane to the most spiritual. The practitioner can seek to achieve peace of mind, control over one's temper and emotions, long life, happiness, relaxation, enlightenment, increased energy and stamina, ability to heal others and himself, channel, transform and project qi, give birth to and nurture the immortal fetus, and attain immortality.

Countless schools and styles and "paths" have developed over the years. Some of these lineages can be traced back to countless generations in the past. The Complete Reality School (North and South), Dragon Gate (Long Men) Sect, The Thunder Path (Lei Shan Tao), and others have been in existence in different manifestations since the time possibly of the legendary Fu-Xi.

Many forms of qigong and martial arts mimic the movements of animals, adhere to philosophical principles (like yin and yang), or name themselves after temples and mountains (Shaolin, Wudangshan), sages and immortals (Chang San-Feng, Lu Dong Bin, Lao Tzu, and Huang Di), or animals (Dragon-Tiger, White Crane, Monkey, and Praying Mantis).

CINNABAR FIELD

The dantian/cinnabar field is an important area to cultivate. Focusing on and breathing into the dantian is an indispensable part of many disciplines. It is believed that there are three dantians: lower, middle, and upper. Usually these are located in the abdomen, chest, and the head.

How important is it? Kristofer Schipper states in *The Taoist Body* (pp. 106-107):

> *"The Cinnabar Field is the root of the human being. This is the place where the vital power is kept. The five energies (of the Five Phases) have their origin here. It is the embryo's home. Here men keep their semen and women, their menstrual blood. Meant for the procreation of children, it houses the gate of harmonious union of yin and yang. Three inches under the navel, adjacent to the spine, the Cinnabar Field lies at the base of the kidneys.... Its location three inches below the navel symbolizes the trinity of Heaven, Earth, and Humans. One is Heaven; two, the Earth; three, the Human Being; four, Time. That is why the Cinnabar Field has a circumference of four inches... The Cinnabar Field is located in the region of clear water, in the village of the High Hill: it is called the Palace-that-keeps-the-Essence."*

What it is and where it is has been a bone of contention through the centuries. Some people believe that the main dantian is located behind the navel area (CV 6 to 8) and in front of the ming-men (L2-L3). Others believe that it is somewhere but nowhere at the same time. Says, Schipper:

> *"... Sometimes it is said to be the spot between the eyebrows, sometimes the mouth, or the heart, or a place under the navel, or the kidneys, and so on. Having spent time with the adepts of the practices to nourish the vital principle, I can say that according to them, the Cinnabar Field does not correspond to any exact place in the body, but 'must be found by each for himself during the meditation.' According to them, nothing more precise can be said about it."*

There are practitioners who nurture the dantian (elixir field) to be able to perform feats of strength and powers: eventually they may be able to propel their opponent across the room, break rocks or paralyze somebody from a distance, be able to generate some form of electricity in their body, perform levitation, set paper on fire, or project their spirit across time and space. These are not just folk tales, but phenomena that have been observed and documented by educated people. Development of the dantian is one of the most important practices in self-cultivation. There are teachers who consider the work so important that they will not teach you anything further unless your dantian is full.

HOW DO YOU STUDY?

For a variety of reasons, some of the techniques have been kept secret and have been shared only with relatives, close friends, and disciples. If a man or woman is ready, a teacher will appear, it is said. But it is admittedly not that simple. You would rarely find — and recognize — a master while you are walking down Avenida Rizal in Manila, Madison Avenue in Manhattan, or Leicester Square in London. No doubt the search for longevity is or can be difficult and expensive. You need to look for competent teachers in magazines, newspapers, on the internet and of course by word of mouth. Even when you find a teacher, you may not be accepted as a student, much less a disciple. Perhaps, the teacher does not like you, you are not prepared enough or there is no *gan ying* (resonance) between the two of you. You may have to fly long distances, get tested in the most painful and embarrassing way, spend money on hotels, food, and gifts. And after all of that, you are not even sure you'll be accepted.

And you must watch out for fakes. A legendary teacher in the US who was supposed to have been trained since he was a child in one of the sacred mountains of China was born in Brooklyn somewhere, according to one report. A man who sported a Taoist regalia complete with a topknot — we appeared at the same discussion panel at the same international conference at Harvard University a few years ago — and who claimed to be a Taoist priest could not produce his certificate of ordination from a temple in Taiwan, so it was reported.

The public can also easily be taken in by demonstrations of "powers." You can verify if there is a trick involved. Some of these may involve magic or illusions. Whatever, exercise a skeptical attitude whenever somebody claims to be able to move an object from a distance or levitate. These abilities take time to develop and are not acquired by just about anybody. In any event, you must ask yourself: Why am I interested in being able to perform these feats? Is it just an ego trip?

There are regular classes taught by teachers, but you must check their credentials because there is no certification system in China. Since there is a great interest in qigong and martial arts in the West, there seems to be coincidentally, a proliferation of "coaches" and "masters" in different styles. Tours are now common; you'll find many of them on the internet. For the serious practitioner in search of high-level training, it is necessary to take time to find a master with genuine credentials.

Masters from the high sacred mountains of China do not usually descend from their hermitages, except for a good reason. Before the outbreak of the Cultural Revolution, three Taoist hermits came down and appeared at a small village in China and trained a boy of eight or nine until he grew up to be a young man. He was Wang Li Ping. His life story is the stuff of legends. The saga is narrated in his biography *Opening the Dragon Gate*, written by two of his students. Another such rare happening has been documented in Indonesia where a young waif, a street kid, was adopted by a Taoist master of the Thunder Path Sect about 55 years ago. Identified as John Chang in the literature, he developed incredible powers after training in complete isolation in the mountains of Borneo for three years. His story is told in the book, *The Magus of Java: An Authentic Taoist Immortal.*

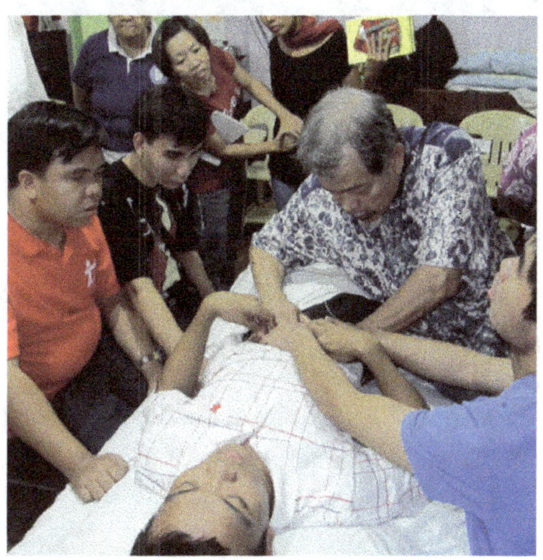

Rene teaching Chi Nei Tsang internal organ massage to four blind masseurs at INAM Philippines.

Perhaps such stories do not happen any longer? Well, take heart. On a different level, I understand, it is happening more and more. Jeffrey Yuen, who grew up in Harlem, NY, was trained by his adopted grandfather, a Taoist priest. Kristofer Schiffer, one of the most knowledgeable Taoist scholars, was ordained a priest in Taiwan. So was Michael Saso, another famous western scholar. A young friend, David Verdesi, who has been looking for a master in China for years now has been initiated into a Taoist sect, complete with rituals and ceremonies recently. He is a lucky one.

For those who do not belong to a school or lineage, there are masters in China who are now opening their classes to foreigners. Several Americans and Australians have been accepted as disciples in martial arts — Shaolin and Wudang — by famous masters. A Taoist from northern Scotland, Gordon Faulkner, is a lineage instructor in medical qigong.

For very good reasons, Shaolin Temple and Wudang Temple are two of the most sought-after destinations. There are classes being held all the time somewhere in their "campuses." Just recently, two of my friends — one from UK and the other from Texas — had spent a few weeks in Beijing and Wudangshan studying the *I Ching* ("Book of Change"), Tai Chi Chuan, and internal alchemy. I have another friend who organizes tours every year to the sacred mountains of China, especially Huashan. When I joined a Wu-Shu tour to Chengdu, Sichuan in 1983, it was one of the early ones.

Sifu H. Won Kim in Central Park, NY, in Tai Chi medium frame tiger style pose.

In the '60s, it was relatively difficult to get a Chinese master. I was one of the lucky few, I am sure. Sifu Johnny Chiuten was quite approachable and friendly, and even if I belonged to a different fraternity in University of the Philippines, he accepted me readily. His brothers were very friendly and accommodating, too, when I was practicing at their turf behind Johnny's house. His master, the famous and legendary teacher Lao Kim, accepted me as a private student without asking for remuneration. With Tai Chi Chuan, I was recommended by my Chinese godfather to his cousin, Chan Bun Te, a master at Hua Eng Athletic Club in Binondo. Dr. Jopet Laraya, Johnny Chiuten's fraternity brod, had almost a parallel experience with Lao Kim in the Philippines and James Lore in Canada more than three decades ago and with KK Chan in Hong Kong recently.

But then martial arts, whether internal or external, are just one of the areas of self-cultivation. Nowadays, it is not generally difficult to get tuition from a teacher. With acupuncture, herbology, massage, nutrition, feng-shui, sexology, and astrology, there are many schools and centers offering them in the United States. You basically need only eligibility and money to be accepted. It is in the other arts, especially authentic internal alchemy, and certain internal martial arts schools, that one can bump against a wall. Still, there are doors that have been opened, so all you must do to know where they are is to do research.

In the final analysis, what self-cultivation practice is worth devoting your life to? Are you going to spend all that time and money on something that won't mean anything much in the course of two or three decades? Can you actually sustain the discipline over a lifetime? Are you willing to sustain injuries and invest your energies on something you won't be able to do in middle age? That's the dilemma that many practitioners face, believe it or not. That's why to the Chinese, the internal arts are generally more important and valuable than the external arts.

SUMMING UP

Self-cultivation is an important and essential part of Chinese life. It is a preventative discipline for people who are healthy but can also be used by those who suffer from an illness or deficiency. At the same time, it includes quests that can take you to amazing mystical and spiritual studies and experiences. It is one of the most exhilarating journeys you can take anywhere, anytime.

The older civilizations developed different self-cultivation techniques. India and Egypt, possibly Greece, developed medicine, internal alchemy, martial arts, meditation, forms of yoga, and others. But it is China alone, I believe, that has cultivated its arts longer, continuously over thousands of years and with great variety and completeness.

Every day, the Chinese do their exercises at certain times of the day or night, but especially early in the morning. You'll find them in the parks, on rooftops, in their own living rooms, even on the streets and sidewalks. Some of them would be facing a tree or a lake. Many would be doing Tai Chi Chuan, the soft, slow form, or qigong. Some would be sitting quietly in meditation at home, on a chair or on the floor, or up on a mountaintop. It is all part of the ancient art of self-cultivation.

2.

The Interface of Chinese Healing Modalities

The following is the amended text of the remarks read at the Conference on the Integration of Traditional and Alternative Healing Arts Sponsored by the Department of Health/ PITAHC and the World Health Organization at Bayview Park Hotel on February 21-22, 2002.[1]

To get into my subject,[1] let me tell you a story. In the Chinese view of creation, there was Pan- Gu, the primal being, who was in the shape of the mythical egg. Pan-Gu was supposed to be a male, but I think he was really a hermaprodite, an androgynous creature. In the time before the beginning, Pan-Gu lay in the shell. In due course, within a period that is difficult to comprehend because there was no time or space, Pan-Gu grew. Stretching his/her limbs, Pan-Gu broke the shell. The coarse parts of the egg sank down to form the Earth or Yin and the subtle parts rose to form Heaven or Yang. To separate these two, Pan-Gu had to stand and push them apart. In the pressure of expansion, Pan-Gu shattered into a thousand million pieces. The hair became the forests and the trees. The bones became the stones and the mountains. The breath became the wind and thunder. The blood became the rivers and oceans. The parasites became the human race.

This myth of creation underscores the concept of the human being — and the universe — as a dialectic and as a process. We see from this story the ideas of yin and yang, the dark and the light, of the polarities of life. We see the idea of the five elements and the complicated nature of humans. We see the idea of Heaven being refined and of Earth being coarse. We see the idea that humans are just like the universe, and vice versa. What happens down here, happens up there. What happens up there, happens here too. We must just look inward into ourselves.

The Chinese, or at least the Taoists, consider the human being as a multi-faceted creature, a complicated being, composed of different aspects — material and physical, emotional, intellectual, energetic, spiritual. These different aspects of the human being interface into

Rene with students and members of the Philippine Academy of Acupuncture.

a whole. This paradigm of the human being is important in the development of Chinese medicine.

On the human level, one of the beliefs in Chinese medicine is that at a certain time in the life of the foetus, the Heaven (*tian qi*) enters the *ming-men* (door of vitality), Earth (*kun*) energy enters the navel through the umbilicus, and the two energies merge in the dan-tian or the elixir field. At this point Heaven is transformed into fire *(li)* and Earth is transformed into water *(kan)*. The navel area then is the center of transformation and potency. The eight extraordinary vessels open starting with the Microcosmic Orbit, the *du mai* and *ren mai,* which begin to activate and animate the unborn with new life-force or qi. In this pure state, the foetus represents the uncorrupted being, like the beginning. When the baby is born, the world does its work of corruption and the process of death sets in. To recapture that original state, the Taoists believe that it is necessary to follow the path of reversal. The *Tao Te Ching* says in chapter 40, *reversal is the way of the Tao*. Anyway, that is one view of this matter.

In the course of Chinese history, there was the idea that we could be like the gods — immortals. If only we knew what the gods ate or did to achieve eternal life — or at least longevity. To achieve immortality, the Taoists developed the regimen of alchemy — the transmutation of the base human material into the gold of eternal life. (It's like the Hermetic tradition in Egypt, India, Greece, and Europe, the search for the Philosopher's Stone that evokes the images of the pyramids, Thoth, and the Pharaohs, the Knights Templars, Merlin, the

Kim and Rene practicing Tai Chi Chuan in New York Central Park in 1998.

Rosicrucians, and the gothic Cathedral of Chartres.) There was external alchemy (*wai dan*) — the use of herbs, metals, and other objects. And there was internal alchemy (*nei dan*) — the use of the inner energies of the body and the universe, the fire and water, the metal and wood, and earth, sun and moon, the planets, and stars — transformed in the cauldron of the different dan tian of man.

This search for immortality influenced and impacted on the history of Chinese medicine. The Chinese tried to prolong earthly existence through a regimen of exercise and meditation and looked for an elixir that would bring eternity down to the finite human life. The different healing modalities grew and developed, influenced partly by the search for immortality and longevity, partly by the need for and demands of health.

In no chronological sequence, let me mention some of these healing modalities: Acupuncture, herbalism, qigong, meditation, feng-shui, martial arts, sexology, massage, stones and minerals, and internal alchemy. Sometimes, astrology is included along with movement.

Pardon me for adverting to my own journey at this point. I guess it is unavoidable since my understanding of Chinese medicine is linked with my slow discovery of its different branches and integrated nature.

In my own search for Asian culture in Manila, it was at first martial arts that I encountered. In the early '60s it was not readily available, but I was lucky that it was there for me. I studied with Johnny Chiuten, the famous master of Shaolin kung-fu. I went to Chinatown to study Yang style Tai Chi Chuan with Chan Bun Te at the old Hua-Eng Club in Binondo. I took private lessons with Grandmaster Lao Kim in Dragon Tiger Fujian Temple Kung-fu. Imagine a young Filipino walking down Ongpin early at dawn to study in one of the schools.

Martial art is probably one of the most misunderstood among the healing arts. It is often asked, "How can a discipline that entails hurting or killing somebody be a healing art?" The reason is simple — properly taught, the exercises of martial arts are health-giving, not only in a physical but also in emotional, psychological, and spiritual ways. Most of the martial arts practiced in China were or are part of the Buddhist and/or Taoist religions and contain deep philosophical and spiritual roots. A complete martial artist is not only a warrior but is also invariably a healer, often an herbalist and qigong practitioner, and sometimes an acupuncturist. In the Philippines, an *arnisador* (stckfighter) is often an *herbolario* (herbalist) and a *hilot* (masseuse).

When I went to China to study martial arts (monkey fist and cudgel, sword and spear, and Hsing-I Chuan) in 1983 I encountered for the first-time qigong, postures and movements which are a way of healing with energy. Qigong literally means the development of qi and is a comprehensive and fascinating discipline which includes different approaches such as growing one's energy, refining one's emotions, channeling chi from outside, projecting qi to a person or group of people, strengthening certain parts of the body, like the tendons or the bones or sexual energy, or developing one's shen or spirit.

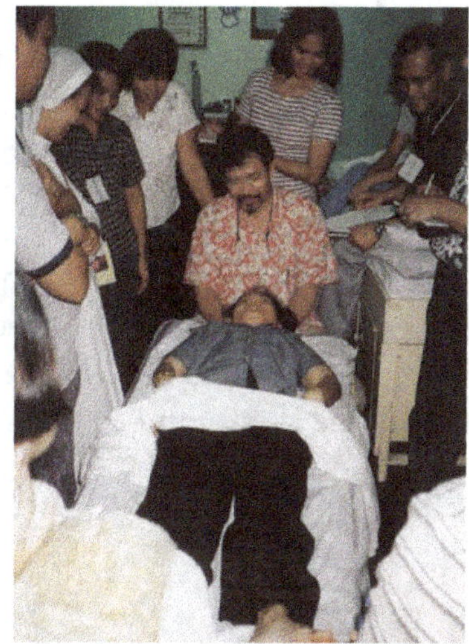

Rene demonstrating Chi Nei Tsang to students at INAM Philippines.

One summer in the early '80s I was in New York City and found two books by Mantak Chia. One was a book on meditation entitled *Awaken Healing Energy* which was an instructional manual on the "Microcosmic Orbit" practice; the other was a sexology text. Meditation and Sexology are of course the other healing modalities in Chinese medicine. Like martial arts, sexology is a misunderstood healing modality. Sexology from the Taoist perspective is the cultivation, preservation, and refinement of sexual energy for healing, longevity and spiritual discipline and growth. I began attending workshops on these courses and more, and studied qigong, *chi nei tsang* (internal organs massage), internal alchemy, feng-shui. There was so much to learn and ironically, I found them in the United States, the capital of Western culture!

Eventually, I left my job in legal services representing indigent clients. In 1989 I studied for three years at the New England School of Acupuncture and after passing the US national examinations, I studied herbalism for another three years at the same school. It was an entire world of experiences which I'll not get into at this juncture. In Boston, I also

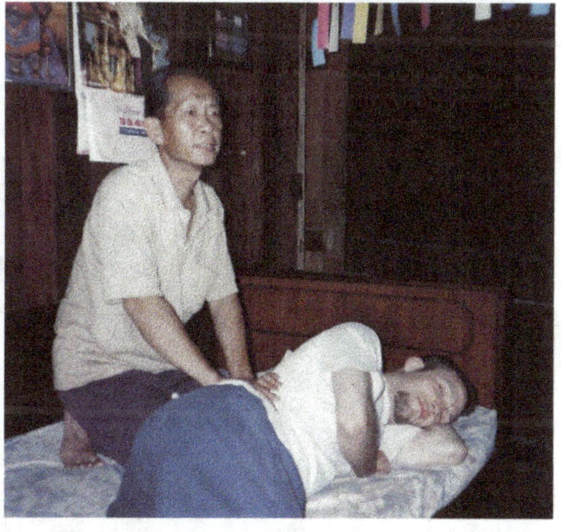

Thai massage master Chaiyuth Priyasith massaging Lee Holden, now a famous qigong master.

studied Yang Family Tai chi Chuan with the lineage master Gin Soon Chu, second disciple of Grandmaster Yang Sau-Chung. At his school I learned the 108-movement long form, two sets of the knife or broadsword, two sets of the straight sword, the staff-spear form, Chang Chuan, Tai Chi fast form, 2-person fighting set, and different forms of push hands. These are all transmissions of the famous Yang Family. I was probably the only Filipino crazy enough to devote all that time and money to this art.

When I started my acupuncture internship, I realized that acupuncture fits in with other healing modalities, that holistic medicine is not just holistic in diagnostics but also in therapeutics. We must integrate the various healing modalities for an effective treatment to take place. I realized that if real healing is to happen, the patient must be given an armamentum of treatment that will change his lifestyle and his environment. Many times, a client is treated and when he goes home, he through his behavior reverses the effects of the treatment. For instance, you treat somebody for high blood pressure and the next thing he does is go to the nearest McDonald's or order a plate of Crispy Pata. There must be healing through, for instance, acupuncture but through nutrition and qigong as well. A person must learn certain techniques to alter his lifestyle.

When I opened my clinic, I administered acupuncture and massage and qigong, I taught my patients how to cook, how to do tai chi and meditation, how to administer Chi Nei Tsang on their abdomen, how to transform their emotions and chi. Education became a part of the curriculum and services I offered. In teaching somebody, we also touch their

Rene performing the Kwan Tao at the Wah Lum Temple in Cohasset, MA in 1990, which he learned from Sifu John Loupos.

Rene with students of the Universal Healing Tao and Sifu Lao Kang Wan (standing second from left).

lives and the direction of their future. Let us remember that old chestnut that in teaching a man to fish we give him a livelihood.

In a culture that has been variously called colonial, hybrid, Westernized, even the deprecatory mongrel, where Philippine history has been dismissed as "300 years in a Catholic convent and 50 years in Hollywood," it is refreshing when I come back here (to the Philippines) to see the appearance and development of healing modalities that are eastern in origin and orientation. When I began studying Chinese martial arts in the '60s, there were very few of us Filipinos who were serious students. When I studied arnis de mano in the 1970s, I studied it not in the Philippines but in Elmhurst Queens, NY, Archie Bunker territory. At the time, arnis de mano, a popular exercise, was still in its infancy. Later, after the Fall of Marcos in 1986, I went to Cebu and Bantayan Island to study arnis or escrima and made a video documentary of one style.

In 1987 I taught a course in arnis de mano at the sports department of the University of the Philippines, probably the first if not one of the first to be taught at the state university. Out of the 12 or 13 college coaches who attended the intensive training, there was I think only one who knew arnis de mano. Now, there are so many practitioners of arnis de mano in the country. I heard that several colleges, like Ateneo de Manila University and De LaSalle University, are even offering courses in the art as a physical education requirement.

When you go to the parks, you'll see people practicing martial arts, Asian combative arts. There are now practitioners of acupuncture and massage in clinics, spas, and centers of healing. Massage, for goodness' sake, was done in the dark alleys of T. Alonzo in the '60s.

Society of Black Belts of America (SOBBA) meeting of masters at the Alex Co Memorial Gym in Lansdale, PA. Standing (L-R) Sensei Mark Nowak, Dr. Mark V. Wiley, Dr. Chris Viggiano, Dr. Juan Otero, Sensei Kenton Vanzant. Seated (L-R) Grandmasters Rene Navarro and Waikeung Lau.

I would like to see the development of a culture that is Asian and Filipino. It took India and China thousands of years to develop their cultures. Our culture is still growing and evolving. Who knows what role qigong and martial arts and the different forms of massage, including hilot, will play in our history? Even now, I can see people talking about integrated healing modalities. Not only Western but also Eastern healing, not only acupuncture but also herbalism and massage and Tai Chi Chuan.

We must be able to teach our people the regimen of self-healing exercises and empower our communities with accessible technologies. Ultimately, preventative and healing arts will be the cheapest and most efficient medicine in life. Not drugs, not acupuncture, not massage, but regimens which the patient can regularly pursue in his daily life.

I would like to see our indigenous healing arts researched and developed along with other foreign healing modalities. Although I grew up with herbolarios and hilots in Tarlac and got treated by them for injuries, I don't pretend to know much about our own native healing techniques. Mr. Bibiano "Boy" Fajardo, a PITAHC board member, would know much more, infinitely much more, than I do about it. He is a man who has devoted at least 30 years of his life to learning and practicing healing arts. Such a repository of knowledge but I heard he was not even invited to this conference.

I do know from experience that a Filipino healer treated my bum knee up in Baguio City last year. I was teaching in Amsterdam two years ago and I suffered from damp, wind and cold from the North Sea. Laser, acupuncture, moxabustion, massage, herbs failed to affect a treatment. This woman — Aling Rosa — made a startling diagnosis by slapping a piece of white paper with coconut oil on it and after looking at the squiggles said that I had *hangin* ("wind") and *lamig*, ("cold"). She also said that I needed to have my acupuncturist needle a point that she drew on a piece of paper. It was — for those who know acupuncture — the *ming-men*, a great point for knee problems.

What I'm saying is that let us investigate our own healing arts, let us develop a culture of healing that would give every modality, wherever it came from, whatever its name, a chance to prove itself in the market of competition. The issue is not the source or the name; ultimately, the only issue is the Filipino patient — he or she who would benefit from it.

In a country that is very poor, where as Professor Randy David said, the rich are like an oil slick in an ocean of poverty, we need an inexpensive, affordable, practical, accessible medical system, not prohibitive drugs, and services. Let us seriously look for an alternative. Keeping Rizal's *Noli Me Tangere* ("Touch Me Not") in mind, let us keep our house open to new ideas and thoughts wherever they may come from.

I was informed that I could not practice my profession in the Philippines because I am not a Western trained physician, though I am licensed to practice acupuncture in two states — Massachusetts and Hawaii. I am a Filipino citizen; I've held a Philippine passport for more than 30 years. But I cannot even practice acupuncture here. My friend Ed Tigulo, who studied acupuncture and herbs and tuina in Beijing (one of only two or three Filipinos in the world) and who has made so many sacrifices to heal and teach our people, cannot practice acupuncture here either. We have deprived him of his livelihood and his life. We have likewise deprived our people of his services and knowledge as an acupuncturist.

That, I think, is the worst kind of discrimination because we have discriminated against our own people. How many other acupuncturists have been disenfranchised by the system?

Let us correct this injustice as quickly as possible. Let us do it now.

Salamat po. Thank you!

3.

Journey to the East: Wu Shu in Sichuan

The poet Du-Fu's cottage.

Settling nervously into my seat in the China Airlines 747, I looked through the window. The heat shimmered on the tarmac below. It was in the high 90s in Shanghai. As the huge plane ascended slowly, banking at a steep angle, I glimpsed the geometric patterns of farmlands and felt a sinking sensation in my guts. I gripped the seat and closed my eyes. I discovered I had a fear of flying. I momentarily glanced at the wing. It was vibrating quite visibly.

Almost two months before, the tour landed in Shanghai. Due perhaps to the excitement, I did not notice my nervousness although on the same flight from San Francisco, a young woman, famous for her Kentucky Fried Chicken commercial, was in panic. She had a blanket over her head, Walkman earphones plugged into her ears, and a rosary clasped in her hands. Beside her was a young Buddhist convert from Berkeley, California, quietly chanting. I was, however, too preoccupied to share their fright. Indeed, I was too excited to bother with anything.

I was flying to China, birthplace of oriental martial arts, to train in contemporary wu-shu and traditional kung-fu. I was leaving family, home, and employment to undertake a predictably painful and expensive adventure. At 42, I was not young anymore; I learned later, I was the oldest in a delegation of 18 martial artists.

Why did I do it?

Quixotic and foolish it was no doubt. Crazy, too, I was emphatically and repeatedly told by friends and strangers alike (it didn't occur to me to check what my foes thought of it).

Rene in 1983 practicing Monkey style staff and fist forms.

No matter what everybody said, I felt no regret. In fact, I was shamelessly, unabashedly euphoric.

For me, it was a landmark experience and the consummation of a childhood dream. Although I had devoted nearly 20 years of my life to the theory and practice of martial arts, I had not studied in China before. I had not even traveled to China. As an adolescent in a small Philippine town, I nurtured dreams of walking the Great Wall and the Forbidden City. As a college student in Manila, I was intrigued and tantalized by tales of acquaintances and friends who had returned from a China visit (prohibited at the time). And as a kung-fu disciple in the '60s, I studied in Ongpin, the heart of Manila's Chinatown.

With my experience, I was not exactly a Johnny-come-lately in the world of martial arts. At the same time, at 42 (in 1983), married, with two teenage children (one 13, the other 17), it was perhaps a little too late to take the pilgrimage-cum-training? Whatever the arguments and complications, China became an idee fixe. I had to do it then or I would not have done it at all.

For three or four months before the scheduled departure, I trained hard to condition my body for the spartan discipline. Like a professional boxer, I woke up early for my daily workout. I walked/jogged a few miles with a weight on my shoulder (often a 20-pound steel bar) or in my hands (two rusty disc brakes from my old Volkswagen Dasher). I performed chi kung, Taoist and Buddhist breathing exercises which are supposed to transform sexual energy into psychic power and generate it from the dantian, the triangular area between the pubis and the navel. I stood in the horse posture for long periods of time until my legs felt like screaming.

My health habits went through a natural metamorphosis. I quit smoking without withdrawal symptoms. I started a water diet, culled from an apocryphal eastern manual, which required 5 glasses of spring water in the morning before I went to work. My diet tended towards vegetarianism.

To prepare for the dance-forms I wanted to study in China, I regularly performed special exercises. I learned to bend backward, sideward, and forward, and to fall on the ground four or five different ways for the "drunken" kung-fu Form. I learned to walk on my toes and mimic simian expressions for the Monkey dance. Drunkard and Monkey are two of the more famous pictographic styles in China.

Although my family was quite supportive, they did not find my antics amusing, especially when I began to sign off my letters with, "May the Force be with you." Shades of Obi Wan Kenobi! Other people thought it was a joke; they could not believe a man my age would do it. I could not believe it either, even when I landed in Shanghai.

At the airport, as we waited to go through immigration and customs, I felt the familiar tropics in my skin, the humidity, and the scent I had grown used to in the Philippines. I peered into the darkness and tried to soak images of the city as the van took us to a hotel. It was difficult to make out the scenery, but I noticed bicycles pedaling down the quiet streets. The chief mode of transportation within the city, it is to the Chinese what the car is to the Americans, except the bicycle leaves no toxic fumes in its wake and wastes no fuel to move itself.

Sichuan Monkey King, Xiao Yingpeng.

Xiao Yingpeng teaching Rene in Sichuan Sports College.

My roommate in Shanghai (and later in Chengdu) turned out to be the Buddhist convert on the plane. As we got ready to sleep, he requested permission to do his sutras — chants in Japanese which resemble the Tibetan rituals in my record collection. Bowed and on bent knees, he clutched onyx prayer beads while he mumbled in front of a sacred text. His voice sounded eerie and strange but relaxing and sometimes seemed to emerge from the depths.

There was certainly some irony in the encounter between a child-like American Buddhist and a middle-aged Filipino Methodist somewhere in Shanghai as they both pursued martial arts in the land of its birth.

Sichuan caves.

Shanghai wasn't much of a tourist attraction. There wasn't much to explore beyond the Bund. I did the obligatory Tai Chi Chuan in the park early in the morning and explored the hamlets (*hutong*) and open markets in the old Chinese section. I bumped into another Berkeley resident, a certain Richard who had a thin pigtail and an earring. He was stared at everywhere we went.

From urban Shanghai, a train brought us into the interior, past some of the most beautiful landscapes I have ever seen. Postcard-gorgeous scenery surprised us at every turn of our journey. There were caves built into the hills and mountains terraced with farms, and in the distance, towering blue peaks. Despite the harsh land, practically every inch of earth was planted. Like a Chinese scroll painting, the landscape unfolded, revealing new vistas as the train hammered along through tunnels and hills. At high noon, a tropical haze hung over the far horizon, as profound as a morning mist, feverish and gleaming in the hot sun.

We arrived in the capital city of Cheng-Du, province of Sichuan (also spelled Szechwan), after 2 days and 2 and 1/2 nights of travel. It was past midnight, too dark and too late to figure out our location. An air-conditioned minibus took us to our sleeping quarters.

The next day we were treated to a 15-course dinner by the Sichuan Wu-Shu Association at the city's largest restaurant. There was a generous supply of spirits to complement the generous supply of food. Toasts of *gan bei* were thrown left and right for every conceivable excuse. Towards the tailend of the banquet, almost everybody was sloshed. Well, most everybody, except the hosts who, most visitors to China have discovered, knew how to hold their drink.

Late that night and early the next morning, some delegation members spent time getting re-acquainted in the hotel. I do not know what happened in the bonhomie, I was then too inebriated to join. I noted in my diary however that, the morning after, nobody was too tired to attend the first of the rigorous training lessons at the local sports college.

Immediately I realized I was not in shape for the kind of training that was in store for the next few weeks. The pace was fast, the regimen demanding. Our first teacher, a 44-year-old woman, one of China's top experts, went through the routines with dispatch and gusto. It was all basic wu-shu drills for the first few days. Limbering, stances, hand maneuvers, fundamental kicks. Later, the training became more difficult and included aerials and floor work.

Every day, except Sunday, we practiced. At night I nursed pulled muscles and depleted energies for the next day's punishing rituals. Other trainees, much younger than I, I was happy to note, were not spared the exhaustion and soreness which seemed to be my unique fate.

Robin Shou of "Mortal Combat" movie, practicing Drunkard fist in 1983 in Sichuan.

Night life? There was really none. No bowling alleys, Broadway plays, singles bars, strip joints, bingo games, discos. No x-rated flicks, porno magazines, head shops, soap opera. There were in the area, Tai Chi classes in the park, kung-fu schools (run by families), acrobatic shows, painting lessons, Chinese movies, temples, parks, swimming pools.

I had also seen couples cozying up to each other in the park, but there was no evidence of heated clinches or osculatory probings. They were invariably positioned side by side, eyes staring into the darkness, the man's arm usually circling the woman's waist. Pretty innocent stuff. The Chinese do not kiss or hug in public. In any case, I did not see any display of eroticism.

It was the perfect atmosphere for boot camp or sainthood. Nothing to divert one's attention from the gruelling drills. Nothing to reduce one's energy. At night we were too exhausted and too sore to notice the stirrings of the flesh.

I would be derelict in my duty of honest reportage if I fail to mention an incident of East-West contradiction. A few members of the delegation protested the living conditions in the hotel. They made a big production of the "greasy food" (to me, it was excellent Szechwan cuisine), dirty toilets (they were clean by Third World standards), and the heat (it could not be helped, it was summer). The Chinese sports service company decided to move us to the Jing Jiang, an "American hotel" nearby, at their own expense, "for the sake of friendship."

Jing Jiang Hotel, which became our home for the rest of the tour, offered quite a few creature comforts. Bathtub in every room, a view of the gardens and the city, massage for a small fee, a penthouse and bar, gift shops in the lobby, Coca-Cola, and Budweiser at 1.60 yuan (about $0.80 US), American and Chinese meals, a telephone in every room, and air-conditioning (for a few dollars more).

Jing Jiang was a kind of way station for travellers en route somewhere — Tibet, Himalayas, Lhasa, Yangtze River, Kunming. There was a daily influx of tourists. The hotel would have tickled a novelist's creative fancy. Colorful characters, Greenwich Village types, Buddhist pilgrims, name the specification and into the proverbial revolving door the person walked, arrayed in the proper costume.

Tourists met, conversed over Tsingtao beer, and parted ways. I thought the hotel was a Kafkaesque metaphor for a place where people said hello and goodbye, people condemned to casual conversation and meeting. Note this interesting postcard left at the lobby simply addressed: "To Room # 666, Jing Jiang Hotel, Chengdu." It went on to say: "I am sorry not to have gotten your name and address last night. When I left your room, you were still asleep. But thank you for a very enjoyable evening." It was sent from Kunming Lake by a woman who should remain nameless here.

Sichuan. Coach. double knife. 1983.

Not one of us in the delegation was part of it, as far as I know. Kung-Fu Wu-shu was our constant preoccupation. However, there is a small caveat to this impression. At night, we would all gather in the penthouse, practice what we learned during the day, and eat the spicy Szechuan noodles and drink a tall bottle of beer. One time a bunch of Americans from our delegation held a Toga Party a la *Animal House* in the hotel penthouse. To date I have not sorted out my reactions to the spectacle of bored juveniles cavorting in bedsheets and towels secured with safety pins.

Sichuan. Cotton Boxing master.

As our training progressed, our classes broke up into smaller groups to study individual forms such as Praying Mantis, Monkey, Eagle, Snake, Pa-Kua, Hsing-I, Tai Chi Chuan, Chang-chuan, and Nan-chuan. Weapon sets were also taught (spear, broadsword, straight sword, cudgel, three-sectional staff, nine-section steel whip, double hooked sword, double daggers). Each of us managed to study at least five forms.

Sichuan. Cyndi Rothrock. 1983.

Among the forms I studied were Monkey Fist and Cudgel. The most famous Monkey King of China, a 68-year-old master, was our teacher.

Sichuan. Rene and teacher of Double Daggers.

On July 23, 1983, I wrote a letter to a friend, a Filipino writer based in New York City:

"We're almost at the end of our Wu-Shu Tour in Cheng-Du. Next week we pack up and leave this capital city. Some of us would go to Omeishan, the sacred peaks of the monkeys. Others to the Shaolin Temple at Loyang, and still others would proceed somewhere, destination unknown. I have chosen Shaolin, birthplace of classical kung-fu wu-shu. From there, I plan to proceed to Shanghai and, if money and wanderlust hold, to Beijing, the Forbidden City, and the Great Wall.

"It makes me sad to mention my departure. I have fallen in love with Cheng-Du. Now it's like an old friend. I have explored its sidestreets, the small stores, and open markets, the temples, and gardens. I feel safe here. I'm not afraid of mugging or meeting strange characters. I could leave by the stairway at dawn for a walk in the park or go to the penthouse at night for a drink. I'm almost sure no criminal lurks behind the next entryway.

"I have studied several forms, although the injuries are so painful. My ankle is swollen. There's a throbbing pinched nerve in my hip. I stubbed my toes doing a series of scissor maneuvers on the floor. I pulled a groin muscle while leaping with a spear. So why am I doing it?

"Whenever I study a form, I feel a surge of energy and inspiration, an almost sensuous high. It's this flirtation with grace and beauty that makes me forget the pain, even the isolation. Perhaps it's this glimpse of beauty that keeps us going, despite the meaninglessness of it all?

"The drills are mechanical and repetitious when we begin. Later, very much later, if we are dedicated and talented enough, these drills become elegant, things of beauty, forms without effort, 'artless art,' in the language of Zen."

Finally, we had to take our exams. I did only one short form, a soft internal style set called Hsing-I Chuan (translated as "Mind-Body Fist"). It was all my body could do after all the injuries. I was the first to perform before three of the most knowledgeable martial arts teachers in China. I was quite nervous, but I finished the form. Later, my teacher told me that I had no energy, no power. I became more nervous and anxious.

As we gathered to listen to the final verdict, I felt drained and nauseous. Our performances, it turned out, did not really matter. We all passed. While we were worried about making a good impression, the Chinese were looking for something else. To them, the examination was just part of a long process. We were told that what we do with the forms was our responsibility, that we should take the knowledge home with us and practice. It was probably the most important lesson of the whole trip. When we received our graduation certificates later in the day, we had a better understanding of our martial arts experience in China.

Great Wall at Badaling with Rene, Bill Cheung and Kurt Kraus.

As the huge 747 ascended slowly, leaving Shanghai behind, I reviewed the journal of my travel. My companions ("fellow travellers" I called them), befriended on the tour, had taken seats somewhere to be alone. We did not talk. A few hours into the flight back to San Francisco, it was night again and soon, we saw the dawn for the second time on the same day. It was a brief, brief dawn, the sun lingered on the horizon and then almost exploded in our eyes. We had crossed the international dateline.

Sichuan. Rene with Sword Teacher. 1983.

In the San Francisco Airport, my friends and I said goodbye. I confirmed my flight back to Allentown, PA. I heard yelling in the distance. There was a game show on TV in the airport lounge. I was back in America.

Sichuan. grad class. 1983.

4.

Lao Kim: Mysterious Master of Kung-Fu

The legendary Shaolin Temple in Loyang, Honan Province in South China, is the locale of many stories, some apocryphal to be sure, about warrior-priests who were trained not only in Buddhist sacred rituals and scriptures, healing, and meditation but also in kung-fu, combat forms mimicking animal movements. There were a few of these temples in China although the one in Loyang is the most famous.

It was in the Philippines in 1962 that I heard about a mysterious Shaolin master in Manila's Chinatown. He was discussed in reverential terms, a figure out of the mists of China's past, a master's master if ever there was one in Ongpin's competitive and shadowy kung-fu underworld. Lao Kim was his name. He was the private teacher of Johnny Chiuten, who was himself a master of great reputation and talent.

The first time I met Lao Kim was at a demonstration of Chinese martial arts in Chinatown. He looked deceptively frail, slightly stooped, almost completely bald, with a fair complexion and skin that looked like translucent rice paper. His face was often impassive, like a meditating Buddha. There was a tattoo on his arm of a woman and a coconut tree, if I recall, reportedly made while he was doing time in prison. He had disproportionately big hands, surprisingly large for his slender body, without any calluses or blemishes from his deadly profession. He was the resident master of a kung-fu club in one of the side streets off Ongpin Street.

I was Johnny Chiuten's student when I met Lao Kim again. He was out of a teaching job, dismissed I heard for being too strict with his students. Johnny followed him as a disciple and studied with him in private. For a while, Lao Kim worked as a bouncer in a gambling den. Then he spent a couple of years teaching in Baguio City, the Philippine summer capital up north, where the Chinese had built a temple.

A LEGENDARY FIGURE

I heard different, unverifiable stories about him. He was a master of *dim mak*, the secret art of maiming and killing with the thrust of a finger. He had light kung-fu, the ability to climb on vertical walls or somersault over the head of his opponent from a stationary position or deliver three flying kicks as he jumped from a sitting position. He was also an herbalist, an expert in *dit da* or traumatology, the art of healing internal injuries, with massage and herbs, and bone-setting.

Grandmaster Lao Kim (1970) patriarch of Fukien Temple boxing at Hua Eng in Binondo, Manila's Chinatown.

He was already in his '70s when I met him, but he was such a strong man — not in a muscular way but in the steeliness of his bones and tendons. He was like a crane — all sinew and bone.

It was said by those who knew him that he grew up in a small village in Fujian, south China, in the early 1900 or late 1800 during the Ching dynasty. I admit that this story seems apocryphal and could have been lifted out of a kung-fu movie; but anyway, I heard that Manchu soldiers raided the village and killed Lao Kim's relatives. The young Lao Kim was saved because he hid in a latrine.

When the massacre was over, Lao Kim came out and walked among the dead. Crying, the orphan boy of six or seven was noticed by a couple of monks who were begging at the time. He was taken to the chief abbott of the monastery on top of a mountain. He explained his plight, he was adopted by the temple and from then on became a part of the community of monks. There they trained in an ancient martial art. He also studied the sutras and joined the chants, but his consuming obsession was revenge.

I do not have the details of it, there is no verifiable information about the actual place, but in China of the time, there were rebels against the government. The legendary Shaolin Temple in Fujian, affiliated for a long time with the similar Buddhist one in Songshan, Hunan, was the refuge of dissident monks. Was this where Lao Kim and his fellow refugees escaped? We'll never know for sure — and I won't hazard a scenario — because the Fujian Shaolin Temple was supposed to have been burned and although three places claim it, nobody can prove where it was located or whether it even existed. I can imagine Lao Kim and his friends complaining to the chief abbott of the deaths of their loved ones. Being victims

themselves, the monks embraced the young refugees and trained them in the secretive martial art. After more than a decade of intensive workouts, combined with domestic work and Buddhist chanting and rituals, their hate still strong, Lao Kim and his group returned to the village and killed the soldiers in a campaign of vengeance.

When news spread that a monk had come down from the temple, Lao Kim attracted students from all over. The teachers at the schools where these students came from were upset and went to challenge Lao Kim. The fights ended with casualties at the hand of the young monk. The government soldiers came to arrest him. Now a hunted criminal, Lao Kim escaped to Hong Kong, hid in a cargo ship, and eventually ended up in the Philippines.

At the pier in Manila, still wearing his saffron robe, his only luggage was snatched by a thief. He ran after this man and killed him with a finger thrust to the heart. That's one version of the story, as narrated by my kung-fu classmate Jopet Laraya. The version written down by Karen Borla as narrated by Johnny Chiuten when she trained with him in Bantayan Island, is even more brutal: Lao Kim used a tiger claw technique and grabbed the intestines of the thief. What follows shows Lao Kim in jail. After a period in jail and since there was no charge against him, he was discharged to the Chinese community.

The stories I heard about Lao Kim's apprenticeship at the temple included playing with the tigers in the forest and, to develop speed, learning to avoid arrows. I could include some more details about his deadly training in the temple and the secret methods he taught his disciples like Johnny Chiuten, Dr. Laraya, and myself but I do not like to appear like I'm bragging or exaggerating the intensity and seriousness of our apprenticeship with the old master. All I could reveal for this piece is that Lao Kim had an unimaginably brutal period in the temple training under the monks.

From Johnny, I heard about secret training sessions with Lao Kim, of which the focus was no holds-barred fighting. They met late at night at a deserted place to spar. A participant in this realistic combat had to be on guard all the time — else he got hit with anything while in a friendly conversation during a break in the training. Foreign combat masters came around to challenge Lao Kim, but they had first to go through his disciple Johnny.

Sifu Lao was a formidable fighter with a repertoire of lethal techniques. Johnny demonstrated some of these occasionally: deadly and sneaky thrusts of the digits or holds and kicks that came from nowhere, footwork of great subtlety, movements that were shadowless. In sparring sessions with me, Johnny was quite agile, moving in, apparently without protection, but always in an area where he seemed to be beyond my range although he was so close, he could have disabled me anytime he wished.

Lao Kim in Kuanyin Twist: the hands, palms together, are held in front of the heart in a praying mudra and the legs are in a scissor or woman's stance. Red Boy was put under control and whenever he misbehaved Kuanyin recited the magic words that made the bracelets constrict on his head, ankles, and wrists. It was so painful, Red Boy put his hands together and begged for mercy.[3]

There were ground techniques, maneuvers from a lying down position, legs moving in unlikely kicks, which made Johnny's posture impregnable. He rolled around like a ball trapping you with scissor legs and then he would practically levitate from the ground and deliver three kicks at you. There were also bursts of simultaneous hand and leg attacks, three or four coming at the same time, without let-up until I was left feeling like an incompetent fool.

One time in 1966, during a furious exchange, Johnny even gave me a sample of a dim mak strike to the leg which created a bubble of blood which, I am sure, would have killed me if he had not administered a painful massage and awful tasting herbal wine. When I asked him why he nearly killed me, he said that I tried to kill him, too. It was the scariest moment in my more than 40 years of martial experience.

That fearful episode gave me an insight into another aspect of kung-fu. It was for combat, but it was for healing as well. The practitioner learned both sides of the coin. The best warriors were also healers — they knew the strengths of the human body, but also its vulnerabilities, and studied the ways to exploit and develop them both. This arcane knowledge was an index to China's ancient culture and the varied arts that developed and flourished,

Lao Kim in Tiger Pose.

Lao Kim with Guan Tao.

including acupuncture, herbology, martial arts, meditation, dietetics/nutrition, internal alchemy, painting, poetry, sexology, feng-shui, astrology, crystals and stones, massage, and others. Those who aspired to culture and refinement among the Chinese were expected to learn these arts.

FIVE ANIMAL SYSTEM

I consider it a confirmation of Lao Kim's mettle that during training with Johnny, I was never able to hit him with a solid strike. Still, while Johnny proved a formidable opponent, he never claimed that he beat Lao Kim in sparring. Lao Kim was always on top, although Johnny was not far behind. Johnny called the style "Hong Cha" or "Angka," depending on the dialect, the system based on the Five Animal pattern of external style boxing supposedly devised by a survivor of the Shaolin Temple in Loyang.[1] Chinese history, including martial arts, is replete with unverifiable legends and stories, perpetuated as unquestionable facts, so it is difficult to establish the truth about lineages and traditions. Many so-called "facts" are just guesswork and oral tradition, without credible evidence or documentation, embroidered by different families. Who invented Tai Chi Chuan? Zhang Sanfeng or the Chen Family or a wandering Taoist? Where did Shaolin Kung-Fu come from? Was it taught by the legendary Bodhidharma to the monks in Loyang? You can go down many of the different styles. My humble view is that we will never really know for sure. A number of styles in China and Hong Kong were supposed to have come out of this system and Lao Kim's version, I believe (although I am not sure), was of an older provenance. They had strong footwork, basically a low (not very low) horse, scissor and bow-and-arrow stance, with powerful fist techniques imitative of the five animals: Crane, Leopard, Tiger, Dragon, and Snake. Lao Kim's had all these ingredients plus sophisticated bridges (arm crossings), and transitional postures that shifted the body out of harm's way.

Lao Kim photo with students.

To me, the fist forms that stand out in his system are the ones known as "Dragon-Tiger," "Plum Blossom," and the "Fairy Child Praying to the Goddess of Mercy." The first is a long, yang, complicated, powerful choreography that takes the practitioner in all sorts of directions and demands tremendous stamina. The second is well, like a flower, with footwork and hands in intricate patterns. The third is a deceptively soft and simpler set with predominantly yin, open palm strikes. I have not seen the system anywhere, but I heard it came not from a family or individual master but from a Buddhist temple where Lao Kim trained somewhere in Fujian (Fukien).

Lao Kim with female students.

When Johnny left for Cebu to manage his family's business in the mid-'60s, I was without a teacher for a while. Kung-fu was very much the private preserve of the Chinese community in Manila and presumably in other parts of the world at the time. Filipinos managed to break into the school only because they assumed Chinese names or claimed Chinese ancestry. As such, it was through the intercession of my Chinese godfather, I was able to study Yang Family Tai Chi Chuan at Hua Eng Athletic Club.

Learning kung-fu was a tricky business. There were a few Filipinos who were studying in Chinatown, at Hong Sing, Beng Kiam, and at Kong Han. Even if you got a teacher, it was possible you were not getting authentic instruction. There were instructors who put together a mishmash of movements and passed them off as true Shaolin. I studied a couple of authentic forms (Dragon and Snake-Crane Combination) with Nel Maulit, one of my colleagues in the Karate Federation of the Philippines who had managed to train at Hong Sing Sporting Club.

Banner reads: When you enter this temple, the only thing needed is honesty and humility, three bows and worship to the God.

Lao Kim with the Farmer Hoe.

In one of his visits to Manila, Johnny recommended me to Lao Kim for private instruction. I studied with Master Lao and I learned several empty hand and weapons forms. On our first meeting I asked him through an interpreter how much I was going to pay. He replied that he took me as a student because of Johnny. I thought he did not like me very much, but I was not offended by his remark since it was quite unusual for a Chinese master to accept a student, let alone a non-Chinese, and a private one at that.

I was quite happy and proud to have had the chance to become Lao Kim's student. Later, another Filipino, Jose Santiago Laraya (nickname: Jopet or Dr. Joe), joined us and trained intensively with the old master. Jopet is an exceptional martial artist and was a fellow student at the university and Johnny's fraternity brother in the Beta Sigma.

I used to see Lao Kim at a carpenter's shop on T. Alonzo Street. There was no bed in the loft that served as his accommodation. One had to climb up a wooden ladder or a rope to get to it. On several occasions some young masters, who were themselves teachers, would come to ask him to teach them, but he consistently refused. Often there was an assistant, a cheerful and serious teenager named Ching See San who also served as a translator. Sometimes we practiced at the Hua-Eng Athletic Club, where I was studying Tai Chi Chuan, or at a warehouse somewhere in Caloocan, or on the rooftop of a hotel, and occasionally in Luneta Park by the Manila Bay.

Unlike workouts with Johnny, which were generally continuous skirmishes, Lao Kim's lessons had mercifully no sparring. But there were times when I foolishly showed Lao Kim a few fighting applications and he always surprised me with his responses. He moved in such a way that I couldn't hit him; worse, he came at me from an angle where I was most vulnerable. Lao Kim was quite awesome for his age. His stances were solid and grounded, his maneuvers were decisive, his hands vibrated like tempered steel. Whenever he demonstrated a movement and its fighting application, I seemed to suck in my breath because the technique was so lean, fluid, clear, and deadly.

Lao Kim performing a Kwan Tao form.

Lao Kim and students.

Lao Kim had a style that was aesthetically pleasing but also effective. And the footwork was simple yet profound, it was not just a straight, linear progression but multi-directional. It offered various deceptive alternatives in combat. (Later in 1986 on Bantayan Island, where I traveled from the United States, Johnny showed me an incredible variation of a technique he called positional sparring drawn from Lao Kim.)

One story illustrates Lao Kim's repertoire of techniques. It was in the late '60s, at a karate tournament sponsored by the Karate Federation of the Philippines of which Johnny Chiuten was the president. Lao Kim, Chang See San, and I had demonstrated Shaolin forms. See San did a sword form, Sifu Lao demonstrated a combination form, and I did the Dragon-Tiger form, the most advanced form in the system. Lao Kim and I stayed a while to watch the forms and the fighting. At our next training session, he taught me a form called Wat Let, which he said was excellent against a karate fighter. The form was linear with alternating attack and retreat patterns and diagonal footwork. I had already studied several forms — Dragon-Tiger, Plum Blossom, Fairy Child Praying to the Goddess of Mercy, Kang Li, Sword, Broadsword, Spear, and Hoe, among others — and Wat Let was a welcome addition.

QUINTESSENTIAL WARRIOR

Like Johnny Chiuten, Lao Kim was the quintessential warrior, a combat specialist in his craft. Although he enjoyed teaching a lot of complicated forms, he was at heart a fighter. To him, the final, ultimate test of martial arts was their effectiveness in combat. One time, he, his assistant See San and I paid a visit to Hong Sing to observe the class of the master. Lao Kim was quiet all the time the master was teaching (a form I recognized as Snake-Crane because I studied it) and was explaining the applications to his students. Afterwards,

Lao Kim. Ching See San.

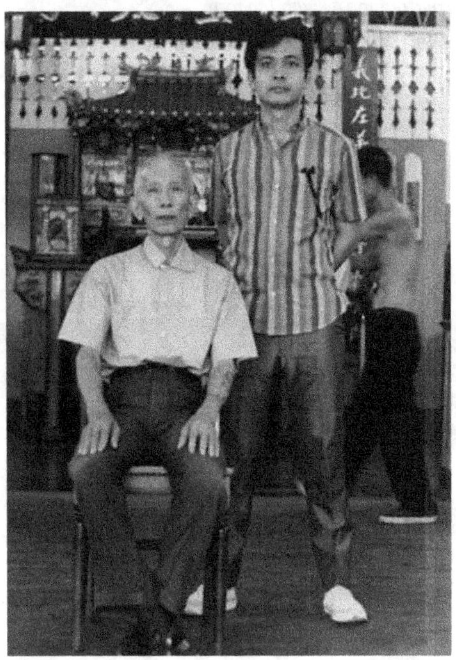

Rene Navarro in disciple photo with Lao Kim at Hua Eng Buddhist temple.

walking home, Lao Kim said through See San that the form was "flowery" and "won't work" in actual combat.

He was, like Johnny, contemptuous of dabblers, people who had no focus or dedication, and so-called masters who couldn't fight, dilettantes who collected forms and information. As Johnny often said, "You can have many forms but if you cannot fight, what's the use of all that learning?" I don't agree with that idea, since I believe in the health, aesthetic, and meditative aspects of martial arts; but when you are face-to-face with Johnny it is difficult to argue with him.

When I left for the United States in late 1970, I kept an intermittent correspondence with Lao Kim. He was hired to teach again in Manila (at the Sampaguita Athletic Club, if I remember) and had apparently drawn a lot of students to his school. He was busy, he said, through a translator, he had many students, he had to maintain the standards, the tradition. And then he was invited to Hong Kong to choreograph fight scenes in movies. He was back in the frenetic world of Hong Kong, where he taught some famous students and actors.

In the meantime, I had been observing masters. I saw quite a number from both sides of the United States. There were other Five Animal systems, but none like Lao Kim's. I saw a master in San Francisco teaching Hung Gar and watched the forms. I learned it was developed and systematized by Wong Fei Hung in the 1860s and was called Tiger Crane. Lao Kim's temple kung-fu was different because, although they were both based on the Five Animal system, his emphasized the Dragon and Tiger forms.

I travelled to China in 1983 to further my studies in martial arts. While the forms impressed me, I did not see anything quite like Lao Kim's Shaolin style there either. The forms I saw were beautiful, featuring graceful poses and acrobatic jumps, but they were not martial.

It wasn't until 1988 that I saw Lao Kim again, in Hongkong this time. Johnny had given me an address on the Kowloon side and a different name. I had a clerk in the hotel call him and make arrangement for a visit. When I went up to his place, a highrise apartment in a project called Ongsat House, I was surprised at how familiar it looked; it was like a development in any big city in the United States: impersonal, crowded. His one-room flat crowded with stuff, it had a wide bed, a small balcony, a couple of chairs. It was up on the 17th floor. There was an elevator marred by graffiti in English and Chinese. It was the kind of development that you entered with your reflexes on guard because if you were mugged by a gang, that was probably going to be the end of your life.

Disciple photo Lao Kim (seated), Standing (l to r) Chang See Sang, Johnny Chiuten, Rene Navarro.

Lao Kim's apartment had a steel gate. When I called "Shifu", he came to the door and said "Navarro" to my surprise. He let me in and I was saddened to see him wearing extraordinarily thick eyeglasses. I realized that even with those eyeglasses, he couldn't see very much. He showed me a diagnosis from an oculist. It showed something like "degenerative retinitis, inoperable."

We had snatches of conversation.

He gave me a Shaolin herbal formula with 36 ingredients. It reminded me of a bottle he gave me in the 1960s that said "External wash, internal drink," on the handwritten label. (He gave me one in the 60's which had 24 herbs. It was toxic: skull and bones were drawn on the bottle.) It was the same recipe that was used for the awful herbal drink Johnny Chiuten gave me. I had the prescription filled by an herbal shop on Nathan Road in Hongkong. I mixed the formula; it is sitting in a jar in my bedroom, still unopened.

1995 was the last time I went to Hongkong to see him.

He showed me an album, which I gave to him in the 60's, now full of photos — Johnny and his new wife Leonie, with Lao Kim in Baguio City; Lao Kim and his female students; Lao

Kim with Johnny and Lao Que Tong, a Hung Gar master in Hongkong; Lao Kim doing a tiger posture; Lao Kim with a KwanTao; Lao Kim and me in Binondo; Ching See San, Johnny and me behind Lao Kim smiling for the camera.

Rene Navarro and Lao Kim, Hong Kong 1992.

He told me that I could have the photo album. The woman who was there, whom I had never met before, was extremely crotchety. She made a lot of noise, apparently objecting.

For a long while we kept quiet. I recalled the times we shared, his expertise, the training sessions. I felt the continuum of life, of knowledge, of respect and affection. He complained of pains in his back. I lifted his shirt and discovered he had scoliosis. I massaged him for a while. I passed Chi to him and he acknowledged it with a smile and comment. As in two previous visits, I handed him a red envelop with Hongkong pounds.

Then it was time to go.

As I stepped out of the apartment, he slipped the album to me.

I took a few steps in the empty hallway and stopped. The steel gate was locked behind me. I felt quite sad to leave him. He had become an important part of my life in the Philippines: we had dinners with Johnny Chiuten; he attended the baptism of my son Albert; he had come to my house to meet my family. The old man had given me more than an album of photographs, more than memories. He gave me a discipline which to this day is a source of joy and meaning to me.

I heard from Johnny Chiuten that Lao Kim had passed away at the millennium. He was 114 years old.

GM Rene J. Navarro (seated) with disciples (L-R) Manny Maramara, Mark V. WIley, Karen Borla, at the Dragon Tiger Fujian Temple Kungfu Research Center.

5.

Johnny F. Chiuten: Fighter and Sage

I was in the Tao Garden, Doi Saket, Chiangmai, Thailand, last September 2010 attending the International Congress of the Universal Healing Tao to celebrate the 30th anniversary of the organization and Master Mantak Chia. I was scheduled to make a presentation on Taoist and Buddhist qigong. Recovering from jet lag, I received the first of many messages. One was from Ned Nepangue, a friend from Cebu, Philippines, asking me to call Johnny. Then another e-mail from Vic Ramos, a fraternity brother of Johnny's, came within a few minutes telling me that Johnny, my "old sparring partner," had passed away. Myla Salanga, his daughter, who lives in California, sent me the same message. So did Jopet Laraya, my martial arts classmate, from Hongkong. A few more messages came, confirming Johnny's demise.

The next few days, I walked in a daze. I taught a couple of classes at the conference, one of them a sequence called "Twin Dragons Chasing the Pearl," from the Shi Ji Kun form, the first set I learned from Johnny in Manila back in the '60s.

Johnny was my first Shaolin master. He was one of the constants in my life, a great influence on my journey. I met him back in the early 1960s. He was a large presence on the university campus, a respected member of the Beta Sigma Fraternity. He used to come to my dorm room to teach my roommate, a student of law like me. They practiced right there in the small space beside the bunk beds. I watched avidly as they performed techniques that I had not seen before, captivated as much by the ferocity of the execution as by the beauty and grace of the movements.

One day, I met Johnny at the law school cafeteria and sat down at the same table. He asked me why I was not studying with him. I said I did not know that I could. We made an appointment for a lesson right then and there. It was one of the most important decisions I had made at that juncture in my life.

Rene Navarro (R) sparring with his teacher Johnny Chiuten (L) in 1966.

Johnny with Praying Mantis master Chou Chi Man in Hong Kong, 1978.

On our first lesson, Johnny told me to stay in a very low horse-stance position when we began. What he did to me for the next three hours or so was incredibly graphic — and painful. He kicked me, pushed me, rode on my thighs and back, asked me to walk around, slapped me all over while I was in the horse stance. It was something I had not seen even in the kung-fu movies where the hero was asked to do 100 repetitions of a technique until he was bone-weary. Johnny's method, presumably transmitted from Grandmaster Lao Kim, was meticulously sadistic in a benevolent way. I mean it was meant for a purpose, and that purpose was to test my patience, endurance and determination, and inculcate in me certain mystical values, and to build me into a warrior. Well, I don't know if I became a warrior, but it certainly tested my patience. As for the mystical experience, I think I attained that, too, because at a certain point when I was about to collapse, I felt an enormous energy welling up, I saw a different reality, I reached a different level of awareness. I came back the next week and took some more of the same punishment and endured the other postures of Shaolin. By that time, the novelty was gone, and I was ready because I knew that to have a view of what it is at the top, you must climb the mountain, by yourself.

Johnny's climb to the top started when he was a kid. His father[1], himself a Shaolin master, sent him to Taisan in Guangdong province to study kung-fu with his grandfather, a lay monk from a Buddhist Shaolin temple. The boy trained but was not serious with the practice. Years later, his martial genes kicked in and renewed his interest in the art. He dabbled in karate and aikido but in the late 1950s finally found his master at Hong Sing, an obscure school in Manila's Chinatown: his name was Lao Kim (*aka* Goon Tiong and Lau Gam), a former lay monk who trained in a Temple in the Fujian mountains back in the 1880s.

Johnny Chiuten in Hong Kong with Lao Kim and Lao Kay Tong 1982.

Johnny was a new student at Hong Sing. According to him, a senior student named Shakespeare Chan, who was an assistant instructor, "made life difficult" (*binig pinahirapan ako*, in Tagalog) for him. Bullying was common and standard in martial arts schools at the time, the seniors taking on the novices, but the treatment was too much for Johnny, so he left the school. Lao Kim sent another student to look for Johnny and convince him to come back with the promise that Lao Kim himself will teach him privately.

So began this strange and probably unprecedented apprenticeship: the old Buddhist monk taking on the training of the young student, not in a school but in hidden places: warehouses, cemeteries, abandoned buildings. Many training rituals the disciple endured but one deserves mention: early on he was made to soak his right arm in a cold vat of herbs, after which Lao Kim lighted the fire; the water began to boil and got hotter and hotter ... This was done five times over a short period of time. There were other methods the disciple had to perform: strengthening the digits on hard objects and bags filled with beebees; hitting himself all over to endure the pain; flattening rolled pieces of paper; and standing for long periods on a narrow bench or ledge. Johnny also had to fight Lao Kim and other visiting masters from other countries in real no-holds-barred combat. Aside from the fist and weapons forms (like the nine-sectional steel whip), he learned ground fighting, *dim mak* (death touch), different kicks, bone-setting, how to make and apply *dit da jow* (herbal liniments), and massage.

Lao Kim and Johnny Chituen in Hong Kong.

Johnny. Rene. World Trade Center. 1987.

In a couple of years Johnny went back to Hong Sing. He and Shakespeare had a private confrontation. Asked about it, Johnny consistently refused to describe what happened. He would shrug his shoulders and say,

Johnny Chiuten at the Taoist Temple in Cebu, 2002.

Mabuti lang (It was just fine.) But what we know was that Shakespeare left for Hong Kong and trained with masters of Hung-gar (Lao Kay Tong), northern praying mantis (Chou Chi Man), and Tibetan white crane (Kwan Ren Fu) at the same time: one style in the morning, another in the afternoon, and the last in the evening. After three years of training, he returned to the Philippines. Meantime Johnny continued his training with Lao Kim. The two rivals met, I am sure, but neither of them said anything about these secret encounters. The last time I saw them together at dinner hosted by Shakespeare at a Chinese restaurant at Mega Mall, I sensed the undercurrent of tension but on the surface, they were laughing and chatting like old friends.

When he was a student, Johnny rented a small room in a cottage off campus, across from Balara. When you entered there was the scent of Chinese herbal medicine distilling slowly inside a giant jar in one corner of the minuscule room. A row of books on martial arts pressed against a wall — Tohei's Aikido, Nakayama's Shotokan Karate, a thick volume by Oyama, one of Tai Chi Chuan (Yang style I was told later), a few Chinese paperback manuals, a couple of texts, and a graph on acupuncture and sundry combat magazines from Hong Kong and America. A nine-sectional steel whip, rusting and ancient, was hanging from a nail. On one side of the spartan affair was a single bed, unmade and apparently just slept on. In one corner were a table and chair. One immediately noticed the carefully balanced photos under the clean glass top. Shots of martial artists in varied poses. One showed a stocky old man, silver-haired, a master of the white crane style of kung-fu, in a horse stance, his hands frozen into a pair of beaks. Another showed an even older man, bald and lean, almost ascetic, the famous Sifu Lao Kim, in a typical dragon claw hand, his eyes penetrating and intense. There was of course, the resident master himself, Johnny F. Chiuten, Jr., with a few of his disciples in the Beta Sigma Kung-fu Karate Klan of the University of the Philippines. I recognized Noli Nolasco, a tournament champion and the fraternity's senior instructor, and Jopet Laraya who was to become a close friend and classmate of mine under Johnny's and Master Lao's tutelage.

Johnny Chiuten with Shakespeare Chan, Rene Navarro, Noli Nolasco — Manila 2005.

Rene learning lessons in 1966.

A tiger stared from the scroll on the farthest wall. A crouched beast amid tall grass. A second look showed the feline's grace and the steady and deep black eyes. A hunter ready to spring at its quarry. The tiger reminded me of the master himself.

When he graduated with a degree in pharmacy, after shuttling from one course to another to prolong his kung-fu studies with Lao Kim in Manila, Johnny went home to the island of Cebu to run the family business.

The sparring continues...

On one of his visits to Manila, he introduced me to Lao sifu, then in his 70s, and asked him to take me

Johnny Chiuten training at the Taoist Temple in Cebu, 2002.

as a private student. The old man could not turn him down because Johnny was like his own son. It was a rare opportunity for anybody to be taught as an indoor disciple by Lao Kim, at the time considered to be the patriarch of Chinese Kung-Fu in the secretive world of martial arts in Manila.

Around 1968 Johnny and I began studying Tai Chi Chuan in Binondo. It was then I was really convinced that Johnny had that rare gift, that genius for martial arts. For he learned in a couple of lessons what I had tried to study in two months. He saw certain techniques where I saw only a pattern of motion. At the same time, he and I also learned pa-kua. But what was truly amazing was the phenomenal development of Johnny within that short period of training in the internal arts. In perhaps an excess of enthusiasm, he declared that many of the techniques of just a year back had become obsolete. Indeed, to me, that's how it looked. Striking and blocking, even weaving, techniques had significantly altered. Johnny, for instance, no longer blocked or dodged a punch; he yielded to it and used it to his advantage. His new techniques were even more efficient and frightening than the hard techniques he had learned and taught. Fingers pressured points, forearms pushed and probed, legs jammed and trapped techniques. Johnny also learned to bounce me off on contact, to propel energy as if there was force-field enveloping his arms. He seemed to be mustering air from somewhere, perhaps, from an internal source. At the same time, he managed to keep his breathing down, a discipline of utmost importance to those who are aware of the finer points of the art.

Johnny Chiuten demonstrating ground fighting techniques.

In late 1970, I migrated to the United States. I studied with Mat Marinas, an arnis de mano Philippine stick fighting master in Queens, NY. Meantime, Johnny began exploring the different styles of stick fighting (also called escrima) in Cebu. He became an instructor in the Balintawak arnis of Venancio "Ansiong" Bacon. Later he met Filemon Carburnay and the two of them reorganized and revitalized Lapunti Arnis de Abanico. Johnny and I filmed a documentary of the style on Mactan Island in 1987. Eventually he developed his own system called Arnis de Cadena Pronus Supinus.

Johnny Chiuten was an extraordinary man, a gentle, thoughtful, and serene person, one who would step in to reconcile opposing groups, but he was also a street fighter who never turned down any challenge. Perhaps the present generation of martial artists had not seen him fight or tested him. I personally vouch for the high quality of his techniques. In the '60s he would ask me to see him at five in the morning at his cottage in the university campus. I would arrive on time, but I did not like to wake him up. So, I would sit on the stairs and wait. When he woke up, at seven or eight, we would spend hours doing nothing but forms and sparring. Sometimes a martial arts master would come to issue a challenge and Johnny, as was the tradition, would ask him to spar a student like me first and then Johnny himself would take on the challenger.[2]

With Johnny, fighting had an uncommon agenda. He accepted challenges, not because of the ego thing, but because in his search he wanted to test himself against the best. And he openly taught his techniques because he believed that it's in sharing the techniques, both

Johnny Chiuten with Jenny Madamba (right) and American student Karen Borla (left) at Ogtong, Bantayan Island, Philippines.

external and internal, that the art improves. Many martial arts practitioners pursued him for his expertise and his instructions, but he never divorced martial arts from the energetic and philosophical aspects of self-cultivation. He was always looking for techniques that used the mind and qi without relying on the physical. He wanted to use qi to heal himself and others. Often when he taught me, he would quote passages from the *Tao Te Ching* or Sunzi: be like water, know the weaknesses of your enemy, be opaque like a pond. He was a fount of combat knowledge, but he was also a wise man, a very rare combination in the martial world that is inhabited by many violent types and rarely by refinement. He was always respectful of others, even those who were cross and rude. To Johnny, fighting was pursued with the detachment of Zen. He never fought anybody out of anger or resentment or personal issues. In this he was unique in the martial arts world, I believe. After a fight, he usually shared his techniques with his opponent. He had an open and benevolent nature. He had a generosity and wisdom that was beyond comprehension of the ordinary man. And he was always humble, never denigrating anybody, even those he had defeated in combat. He was a paradox in the martial arts world, gentle, thoughtful, hospitable, fluid. I could have sworn that he was a Taoist!

Over the years, Johnny evolved as a martial artist, a well-rounded warrior, somebody knowledgeable in various disciplines and arts. He restored or perhaps, gave a new meaning to the name martial artist. To refine himself, he learned many things even the occult, meditation, qigong, the 13-movement Tai Chi chi kung 1 (slow) form of Mantak Chia, Fusion of the Five Elements, kundalini yoga, silat and others. He studied with Han Ching Tang, the famous *chin-na* (joint locking) master from Taiwan. He filmed the Taoist forms of Mr. Sy (he gave me a copy), an instructor at Hua Eng. From his collection of videos, one could see the breadth of his studies. He was indeed into cross-training and mixed martial arts years before people had a name for them. Always, in his journey, he searched beyond the physical, and emphasized internal development and spiritual transformation.

I visited Johnny Chiuten in Bantayan Island in 1986, the first time in 15 years. I took a boat to Cebu, slept at his house, woke up at three in the morning, rode a bus to Hugnaya up north and took a ferry to Santa Fe. I stayed at his house on Bantayan Island for a month. During my visit, we trained together. He insisted on learning the Microcosmic Orbit Meditation (Xiao Tian Zhou), one of Mantak Chia's transmissions which, at the time, was probably only accessible to the Healing Tao (now Universal Healing Tao) students. We sat down and reviewed the materials. He even wanted to learn the secret "empowerment" segment that I studied with Mantak. It was somewhat funny at one time because I demonstrated the technique on Santa, the family maid! I guess I discharged too much Qi on her because she began to sweat.

The last time I saw Johnny on Bantayan Island, in 2002 — there was now a biplane that ferried passengers from Mactan — we reviewed materials on internal development in Ogtong Beach, where there was an underground freshwater lake. Needless to say, he and I sparred again. It was far from an equal exchange: at one point he nearly broke my right elbow and luckily, I managed to escape with a counter from the Yang Family *sanshou* (two-man set) form. The next day he and I left for mainland Cebu. He had an appointment with a cardiologist. In 1988 or thereabout he had a triple bypass in Texas, a problem he had to contend with since then. Nonetheless, martial challenges kept coming, non-stop. He said there was a delegation of martial artists from Australia waiting for him: a couple of their masters wanted to spar! I could not say don't do it because Johnny was Johnny, and I knew he would do it whatever obstacle stood in the way.

During the days before he died, he had OBEs (out of body experiences). He told his relatives that he was materializing in different places, some of them mysterious sanctuaries, and meeting spirits there. The master was not going gentle into the good night. When he passed away on September 10, 2010, I lost a friend, master, and guide.

6.

Jose Santiago Laraya: A Lifetime of Dedication

There were about 10 students of Johnny Chiuten who stood out back in the early '60s. One was Jose Santiago Laraya (Jopet or Dr. Joe for short), another was Noli Nolasco, and still another was Adolfo Pinlac. These three have made martial arts a significant part of their lives. And, as far as I know, they are still punching and kicking their way past middle age.

Jopet Laraya is probably the best, or among the best, of Johnny's students. A complete martial artist, an expert in the different arts that he has studied. He won't admit it, I know, but martial arts are his vocation. He is of course a veterinarian, but it is martial arts that he is dedicated to above everything else. His life, his journey, his destination. Other things are just preoccupations, some are simply just distractions to him.

Well, it is easy to understand that his studies of human and animal anatomy and physiology (A&P) have helped in developing his skills in martial arts. It is always helpful to know where the sternum, gastrocnemius, carotid sinus, inguinal ligament, among others, are and how the tendons, muscles and the whole skeleton are connected. I studied A&P and know for a fact how such knowledge can shed light on why certain areas and points in the body are ideal targets in combat and healing. But Jopet has a unique experience among martial artists because in his work, he admits, he has to apply holds and submission techniques to make some of his animal patients — from cats to bulls and horses — to keep still.

When I first saw Jopet, it was at Johnny's pad on Area 11 in the Diliman campus. He was among the youngest of Johnny's students. I recognized a few of them, but it was Jopet who made the biggest impression on me. Of all of Johnny's students at the time, it was Jopet who to me was able to do the forms the way they were supposed to be done. He did the Japanese katas and the Chinese fist forms very well indeed and caught their spirit.

With many practitioners, you find that they don't capture the essence of the style. One practitioner does a soft form hard; another does a hard form soft, or a practitioner does a Chinese Shaolin form as if it were a Japanese form. As if the form had a schizophrenic quality. With Jopet, he knew exactly how it should be done. No matter what the style. As if he was born into it. He is the best representative of what Johnny Chiuten, Lao Kim, and Jimmy Lore teach.

In Hong Kong posing with the Chinese lion head.

Jopet is also a fighter. He is soft-spoken but won't tolerate fakery or bullishness. He is the type who puts his fist where his mouth is, in a manner of speaking. He walks the talk. I have often said that if there was a street fight, I would feel comfortable if I had Jopet on my side. I have no reason to change that statement now.

Robin Young, Lion Head, Rene and Jopet.

Jopet and I have been in touch all these years, a span of more than 60 years through different countries and cultures. So, I know how he has developed through the years. Sometimes we met in Canada, in the US, Hong Kong, the Philippines. We studied with the same teachers. Although we belong to different (and sometimes antagonistic) fraternities in the University of the Philippines, he is in a very real sense a martial arts brother because we've shared many teachings and teachers in decades of searching.

Guests of Patrick Sifu in Hong Kong.

The first time we met outside of the Philippines was in the US in the early '70s. He had driven in from Oklahoma, where he pursued his veterinary studies, to New Jersey, where I lived, in his VW Beatle. Then I drove up from New Jersey and New York to meet him a couple of times in his home in Canada. We met a few times more in the US the last time when I lived up in Lake Harmony in the mountains of Pennsylvania; he brought his students with him. Mark Wiley, a famous martial artist and author, and faithful friend came to join us for dinner.

Jopet and I also planned to meet at Ray Galang's Bakbakan school for its inauguration ceremonies in Lodi, NJ. I was there, I waited for him, but he was teaching arnis and was held up at the martial arts school of one of my students in Nazareth, Pennsylvania.

Then we met 20 years ago in the Philippines; he picked me up at the Ninoy Aquino airport late in the evening, drove to UP, where we met up with GM Johnny Chiuten and Tetada Kalimasada pilati Ollie Jumao-as — for a week of fellowship, martial arts, dialogs, and qigong. We spent most of the time planning the book of GM Chiuten and meeting Johnny's many friends and colleagues.

Jopet and I met again in Hong Kong in 2005. It was the last stop on my China trip. Every night I would wait for him at my hotel, we would go to dinner at the restaurant across the street, walk to the park and practice Arnis De Cadena Pronus Supinus, the style our Grandmaster Johnny Chiuten founded. One or two of Jopet's students would be with him. We would go through the paces of arnis de cadena: one stick, two sticks, stick and knife.

We met again 10 years ago for the anniversary celebration of the International Fu Style Tai Chi Pa Kua Federation.

Dr. Joe as many know him has gone a long, long way from that young man at Area 11 in UP. He has honed his arsenal of martial arts, internal and external, and qigong. He has pursued a broad range of interest in different arts, not only Shaolin, but also Wudang softstyle like Tai Chi Chuan (both Chen and Yang), and arnis de mano, qigong, tetada kalimasada. How many practitioners can claim to have developed genuine expertise in these fields?

One art influences the others. Jopet's art was the richer for it. Eventually, I am sure, the Philippines will be the richer for it as well. Imagine arnis de mano, for instance, evolving into a total art with its own refined system of philosophy, energetics, healing, meditation, massage, and whatever else can be systematically added to it. That is how Chinese martial arts, for instance, developed: their masters synthesized different principles and movements from different fields, yin-yang with Five Elements, anatomy with qigong, meditation with combat, circadian rhythms with massage, point striking with the meridian system.

Like our GM Johnny Chiuten, Jopet never stops to rest. He is always on a quest for perfection. One wonders what he would become if he had another 50 years to work on these arts.

Sifu James Lore (Center) flanked by Jopet Laraya and Robin Young.

INTERVIEW WITH DR. JOE

RJN: Jopet, how did you start your martial arts training?

JSL: I can outline briefly my early martial arts life.

In elementary grades three-to-six in Tacloban City, Leyte, my dad belonged to the Masonic Temple (Scottish Rite Freemasons) and during their frequent parties with all the families together, my older teenaged brother and his friends would be taught some practical arnis (and another martial art which I think was like wrestling) by an arnis fighter and member of the Masonic Lodge (maybe the sergeant-at-arms). I remember just following what they were doing — hitting with the stick (I used a broken bamboo broomstick at that time), where to hit and how to avoid getting hit.

I also remember doing arnis (*espada y daga*) in P.E. with a female partner, but we did it to music (and then we did *tinikling* at the same time). All through those grades, I hung out with my classmates, and we used to make bows and arrows and *pana* with sharpened bamboo skewers. I did get involved very briefly in boxing when the father of my best friend, Boy Celeste (Mr. Juan B. Celeste, Ex-Commissioner of Customs) used to teach us boxing during the Masonic parties.

RJN: That's how many of us got involved in martial arts, too. We saw native plays called *moro-moro* and eavesdropped on arnis practice.

JSL: Well, I was the youngest in the family and so I had to learn to stand up to my *kuya*. You know how it is: if you are the youngest, eventually you end up doing all the errands in the house.

We moved to Ilocos Norte for my high school years, and I also learned to shoot the *paltik*, *pana*, and *tirador*. We engaged in a few "gang fights" during intramurals as I belonged to the Dragon Society, a one-speed bike gang of high school punks. Most of the guys I hung out with are now the top politicians of the Ilocos region.

Jopet and Rene with Buddha, Lantau Island, Hong Kong.

RJN: A typical childhood, isn't it? I am sure there was in the culture something that encouraged you.

JSL: As we had a big population of Filipino-Chinese classmates, I was able to acquire some rudimentary instructions in what I recognize now as White Crane and Tai Chi styles. I had more incentive to practice, plus they gave us extra money for the movies and to buy monay and *ensaymada*. Nothing formal, not streamlined — just basically fooling around killing time. I joined the YMCA that year, lifting weights and joining a few judo classes until I got on the receiving end of a shoulder throw and that was it. I quit soon after that.

A Polish priest, Father Tom Bilzak, taught me combat judo from third year high school to graduation and that would probably have been the more meaningful part of my early training as maybe I was a little bit more mature to appreciate the instructions.

RJN: When did you have your formal martial arts studies?

JSL: Moving to Manila for university was the main time frame where I really learned real martial arts. Johnny Chiuten was my first and major mentor in the martial arts in UP (University of the Philippines) while in the Beta Sigma frat. And then I was fortunate to learn under Grandmaster Lao Kim when Johnny moved back to Cebu.

RJN: Anything memorable during your Beta Sigma days?

JSL: Other than the fact that you went through the same thing I went through under Johnny's training, he did use me on a lot of occasions as a guinea pig to try some new techniques he came across or devised and wanted to try their effectiveness. And we did a lot of cross-training when we were with KaFePhil (Karate Federation of the Philippines) when

Johnny was its president. The tournament sparring matches were good training for actual fighting (not to mention the frat wars in UP).

RJN: How was your training in the frat?

JSL: In area 11, we started with warming up, then stances. After that we did katas, learned new ones then 1, 2, 3 or more step sparring matches before we did freestyle sparring (*walang pikunan* rule) and often we got ourselves bleeding, sprained toes and fingers, etc. We always got our asses kicked when we were "forced" to spar with Joe Liongson, Bal Villanueva, Titing Valdez, Banz Banez, Mario Pasamba, to name a few. I remember Norman Bituin, Ben Sto. Domingo, Drig Bayot, Noli Nolasco, Bart Gacad and I used to do the rounds of the clubs in Cubao challenging them to spar and Johnny would get mad and would just say, "Huwag lang kayong patatalo brod!" (Just don't lose, bro!). We really were troublemakers then!!

RJN: I recognize some of those names. They were some of the pioneers of martial arts in the university. Your group used to do demonstrations during the Lantern Festival. When I trained with Johnny, it was a lot of sparring, I remember. And it was on the ground, so that we all got muddy after a while.

JSL: Frat practice was always sparring until it came out of our ears, and it was always practical techniques with a few katas — just enough to whet our appetites. It was good *na nahasa ako ni*, preparation for me for the training under Lao Kim.

RJN: How was training with Lao Kim?

JSL: I trained at least five days weekly from anytime after 7pm to shortly after midnight. Saturdays I sometimes got a day off but Sundays, I would go to Lao Kim's place in the lumber yard, take the jeepney to Luneta, practice katas, learn new ones until sunrise, go back to Chinatown for special *lugao* (with egg). Around 1-2pm it was back to Luneta until 6 or 7pm then home — always katas, stances, the fine details of the sets, applications. The weekday training was always at the roof garden of a hotel in Ongpin (forgot the hotel's name now) — always stances, katas, practical applications.

RJN: I remember those days on the roof of the hotel in Ongpin. There were sometimes four of us, including James and Ching See San. Sometimes, my brother Flor showed up. The old man lived in that lumberyard in T. Alonzo. There were so-called massage clinics, possibly fronts for something else.

JSL: I was warned by Johnny never to ask Lao Kim to show the application of his movements as the old man used power to prove his point and I got hurt more than a few times. Luckily Lao Kim used his *dit dat jiao* on me — the liniment type and the one I drank (tasted like *lambanog*, a native wine) when he hit me on the chest with his palm and I vomited blood the following few days later.

One time I asked him why he wanted me to practice scraping my forearm with my palm, so he asked me to kick him — he palmed my shins and that was it. After practice, when I took my pants off, the pant leg was stuck to my shins, so I stepped on it with the other foot and yanked it only to find out that my shin was skinned almost down to the bone and the blood that clotted got my pant leg stuck to my shin — that smarted!!

RJN: Must have been quite an experience. I remember that Johnny had to soak his hands in a boiling herbal bath when he started. And he had to drink that awful decoction, too, like you and I did.

JSL: Lao Kim had also broken the bridge of my nose with the tiger claw, broke a few eyeglasses with the same technique, hit my nerve points under my nipples, in the pectoral area above the nipples, on the forearm, above the elbow on the inside part, the inguinal (groin) area, the inside of my knee about two inches above the knee, on the back of my leg in the middle of the gastrocnemius (calf) muscle. These were all poked by Lao Kim with his fingertips. Johnny also has grabbed me on my abdomen with his tiger claws during initiation in the frat (Welcome to the Kungfu Karate Klan!).

Jopet and Rene, Mt. Poconos, PA.

RJN: I used to attack Lao Kim, too. But he always had a great, surprising maneuver.

JSL: I must have worn out the soles of at least a pair of tennis shoes every three or four sessions practicing sweeping techniques in the roof garden.

Lao Kim taught by experience, i.e., you must feel the pain to know how much pain you will be inflicting on your opponent. And he was a perfectionist insisting on repetition until each and every move was to his satisfaction — in technical detail and power!

RN: When he had something to teach or correct, he would get up. Sometimes Ching See San would be with us.

JSL: Other than Emilio, James Kuan, and another guy whose name I don't remember, I remember Ching San and you dropping by the roof garden for some brushing up on techniques. All that mattered to me was that I had to learn as much as I could learn from Lao Kim before I left for Canada and before he decided to not teach me while Johnny was relocated in Cebu. So I took every chance to learn from him as much as I could.

RJN: I remember that Lao Kim gave you a thorough training and he liked you very much. So, what happened after you left for Canada?

JSL: When I moved to Canada in 1969, Lao Kim saw me off at the airport with my cousin and I promised to visit him each time I was back, and I did.

As soon as I landed in Toronto in September 1969, I was already in Chinatown the following day looking for a kung-fu club. I found Mr. Tom Locke, a pharmacist, who referred me to see Mr. Jimmy Lore at a certain place. I did and eventually found Mr. James (Jimmy) Lore, chief instructor of Jing Mo Kung Fu Club of Toronto.

GM Johnny Chiuten with his disciples Jose Santiago Laraya and Rene Navarro.

RJN: James Lore has been featured in *Asian Martial Arts Journal* as a master who trained his students in the lion dance.

JSL: The first thing Jimmy asked me, was if I knew kung-fu, so I said yes. He asked me to demonstrate, and I did (with my Italian leather shoes and tight pants).

I did the Dragon-Tiger set, ripped the crotch of my pants while landing in the horse, but finished the set, nonetheless. After I finished, Jimmy told all the students that they should all do their stances and sets with the same stances I used — very solid, precise, and purposeful. What a compliment. I was with him until I left in 2002, becoming one of his closest students and colleagues.

RJN: What did you learn?

JSL: I learned weapons, empty-hand sets and fighting sets from him including the old style lion dancing. Jimmy taught the arts taught to him by the Chinese Freemasons in Vancouver and several other instructors, each one specializing in different weapons. Jimmy eventually trusted me and gave me freedom to do whatever I wished to do in his club after proving unquestioning loyalty to him.

RJN: It's great that you studied lion dancing, too. I consider it one of the most beautiful arts developed in China and it is based on martial art movements. There are many symbols there, just like Tai Chi Chuan, and they hide some esoteric meaning. I guess the readers would be interested in some of your adventures in a foreign country.

JSL: I remember one "Double Ten" parade while doing the lion dance, one other club raised the lion head at our lion. Jimmy saw this and asked another assistant instructor to take over. This guy refused as he said it would not be proper for him. Jimmy got mad. At that time, I used to smoke heavily. Jimmy asked me if I wanted to take over and accept the "challenge" of the other team and I said yes. I ran to the guy in the lion head, tapped his shoulder to signal I was taking over, and I proceeded to attack the other lion. We had more than a few minutes of elbowing, kicking, etc., which the Westerners thought amusing and exciting to see "lions playing" not knowing that we were actually fighting. My horse stance training paid off and after landing a few good blows on their lion head and his knees, the other lion started backing away while I kept pursuing until I felt a tug on the head and Jimmy's hand on my shoulders saying — "It's over, let him go."

Jopet Laraya with espada y daga of Lapunti Arnis de Abanico.

RJN: I remember you mentioned that episode sometime back. It must have been quite a scene. I don't know how many people in martial arts developed an expertise in the lion dance. Some of these arts are now lost.

JSL: That night at the banquet, the Taiwanese consul approached Jimmy's table and asked him if it was his lion that was involved in the altercation and Jimmy said yes. The guy said, "I knew it. Who was under the head?" he asked. Jimmy pointed to me: "Dr. Joe was the head." The guy shook my hands, offered me a drink which Jimmy instructed me to accept, and they spoke in Cantonese. I gathered that the guy was happy with the club performance during the lion dance. Shortly thereafter, a guy (the other lion head) approached our table, and I grabbed a bottle of whiskey getting ready to hit him in case he wanted more trouble. Jimmy stopped me and said just to watch. The guy poured some tea, offered it to Jimmy which Jimmy after a few seconds hesitation drank. Then the guy poured another cup of tea which he pushed in my direction. Jimmy instructed me to drink it and not knowing then what it meant, I drank it. Then the guy gave the salute to Jimmy and Jimmy told me that it's over, they have apologized for challenging our club and they recognized the club's position in the Toronto Chinatown circle. We were the top fighters. And I have been given the chance to prove myself and gave the name "Dr. Joe" respectability in the martial arts circle in Toronto. Up to now, my name still has a nice ring to it.

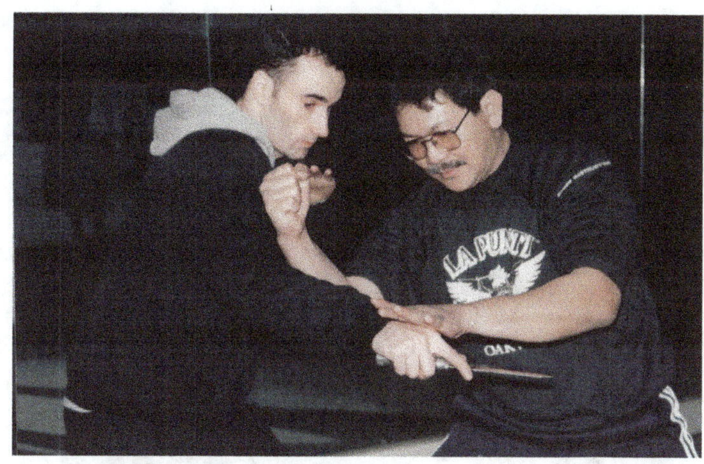

Dr. Joe demonstrating the start of a knife disarm.

During the photo shoot for Rene's segment in Edgar Sulite's book, Masters of Arnis, Kali and Escrima, (L to R) Edgar Sulite, Alex Co, Rene Navarro, Christopher Ricketts, Alfonzo Co.

Another incident occurred during the Tiananmen Square massacre vigil in City Hall. Some troublemakers were disrupting the memorial, so Jimmy punched the guy, and he went down like a light while holding a cup of coffee while we were talking in the sidelines. Another club took the credit for it, and it was the Tai Chi club practicing in the same community center as we did. They even started to badmouth the club saying we did nothing. Some of the students told me about this and so they asked me if I could do something about it, so I did.

RJN: Can you give a background about James Lore?

Dr. Joe demonstrating the stick trapping technique.

JSL: Jimmy was born in Victoria, BC in 1915. His dad was the official translator of Dr. Sun Yat Sen and was also the head of the Western Canadian Freemason Society. His first instructor was his dad after which he was trained by the Freemasons.

His style is reminiscent of the Plum Blossoms style, Hung Gar, and Choy Lai Fut styles. Most of his handsets had a cross pattern, including his weapons sets. He also taught several fighting sets (staff vs. spear; bench vs. staff/spear; empty hands, butterfly knives, and shield vs. trident, staff vs. staff).

RJN: I read about James Lore's extraordinary teachings of the lion dance. It is the kind of thing that can round off Shaolin training.

JSL: The most extraordinary thing he taught was his awesome original lion dance routines incorporating traditional low, solid stances, not the "prancing" stances often seen now. It was always a great pleasure for the senior Chinese citizens watching Jimmy's Jing Mo guys doing the lion dance as it reminded them of the real lion dance way back in China! And the lion dance routines were so unique that it is rare to see the same routines being done nowadays.

RJN: What did you do in the club aside from learning different fist and weapons forms and the lion dance?

JSL: The only thing Jimmy did not approve of was sparring in class as he did not want any of the students getting hurt and developing ill feeling towards one another. He was truly a father figure. He taught everybody and anybody willing to invest time and sweat to learn, and it only cost $10 monthly. It was way back in 1970 and that was what we charged as recently as 2002.

He was criticized by the Chinese community for teaching kung-fu to the "white people" but he reasoned that that was the best way to teach other cultures the real culture of the Chinese. Besides, if anybody did have any problem with that, they were more than welcome to stop him from teaching.

Jimmy always stepped in to protect his students. His club was a second family, so all the students were treated as family although you had to be someone special to belong to the "inner fold" of students, those closest to him.

The club was the official bodyguard of the Nationalist Chinese citizens in Toronto and each time that group had a gathering, the club was always invited to either do a lion dance and kung-fu demonstration and/or make sure the "other side" did not cause trouble for them.

Because of his background, Jimmy was and still is a man with a big reputation in Toronto Chinatown. Everyone knows him or knows of him and his Jing Mo Kung Fu Club.

He used to run a Chinese grocery store and at an earlier time collected tong from the gambling joints in early Toronto Chinatown (circa '50s). At one time or another, students did their stint helping with the unloading of groceries from the store van and/or delivering goods to customers.

A lot of students have gone through the training halls of Jing Mo, good and not-so-good ones. And a lot of them were very thankful for their training and a lot of them used the club and their association with the club for selfish personal reasons. And unfortunately, the latter type of students was directly responsible for the demise of the Jing Mo kung fu Club in early 2003. His teachings are luckily enough being carried on by his loyal students who have only Jimmy's teachings and his legacy in mind.

RJN: Any other stories, Jopet?

JSL: Other incidents. The club got challenged by the top student of a Wing Chun instructor from Toronto who came to our club in Oakville and wanted to do "sticky hands" with me.

Jopet Laraya and Mark V. Wiley, at Rene Navarro's home in Lake Harmony, Pocono Mountains, PA.

I reminded him of the proper protocol in kung fu — he had to go through my top student first. Inasmuch as we don't do *chi sao* the way they do, he couldn't dispose of my student, so I gently reminded him to come see me anytime he wanted to — just give me enough notice as my vet clinic then was getting too busy, and I needed enough time to make arrangements for the clients and their pets. After all, kung-fu was only my secondary love next to my profession — plus it was my profession that paid my bills to subsidize my passion for the martial arts. After that I was invited to the opening of his club (they teach Tai Chi and Wing Chun) and we have remained good acquaintances.

We were also asked to spar with the students of an Okinawan Karate club in Oakville. All my students sparred with their top students, and everyone got hit in the groin. They thought that was unfair and complained (the instructor included). I explained simply — I taught self-defense, not tournament competition stuff. That was that! We never got invited to spar with them again!

RJN: What else did you study in Canada?

JSL: I also learned Yang style Tai Chi from 1977 to 1981 from Sam Ho, a HK Chinese who lived in Pretoria, South Africa and relocated to Toronto. He taught me in exchange for teaching his three kids Johnny and Lao Kim's style.

I also opened the Oakville Martial Arts Club (renamed the Dragon-Tiger Kung Fu Club) from 1976 to 2000. I incorporated arnis into the curriculum and brought the first Canadian delegates to Bantayan to learn lapunti arnis de abanico. Together with you, Rene, we brought the Lapunti style out of Cebu and introduced it to the Western world, something which we never got credit for!

Working with guro Manny Bueno, I conducted several arnis seminars from Vancouver to Prince Edward Island, New Brunswick, and Nova Scotia, including Toronto.

RJN: You took other courses at the time, didn't you?

JSL: While in Toronto, I got involved with Mantak Chia's Taoist Esoteric Yoga for about three years, learning the basics of microcosmic orbit and inner smile plus the energizer breathing (packing).

RJN: Where do you live now?

JSL: I moved to Hong Kong in 2002, got involved with Chen style Tai Chi unde Sifu KK Chan and started teaching him and another student, Pronus Supinus. In addition, I write articles for several martial arts magazines and am currently organizing material for arnis de cadena, the stickfighting aspect of Johnny Chiuten's Pronus Supinus style of fighting.

KK Chan, my Chen Tai Chi instructor, is a topnotch student of Master Zhu from Singapore, a direct student of the Chen family. A great forms tournament champion and competitor, now one of my Arnis Pronus Supinus students. He's enjoying arnis especially Johnny's arnis

Circa early 1980's — with GM Lao Kim at his residence in On Yat House, Kowloon, HK.

because of the kung-fu and Tai Chi principles incorporated into the style. I just have to make him aware of these principles as applied in Pronus Supinus.

I am currently involved in learning tetada kalimasada, an Indonesian martial art and energy generating system. That's the end of my training.

RJN: You have studied with a lot of teachers and associated with many groups and people over a lifetime. Can you mention something about your influences?

JSL: Last, but certainly not the least, I would not have been able to develop my comprehension of all the martial arts skills I have learned if it weren't for the kind advice, encouragement, explanation, and demonstrations of Lao Kim, Johnny Chiuten, Rene Navarro, and Jimmy Lore.

RN: Thanks, Jopet, to be put in the same category as the other three is a great honor for me. So, what is going on now?

JSL: As of the end of 2020, I have been spending most of my time practicing Fu Style Pa Kua and Tai Chi at home because of the pandemic. Whenever the restrictions are lifted and congregation of people of a certain number is allowed, we resume practice — forms, weapons, Pa Kua push hands. Sifu Patrick Lee, the designated representative of Fu Style Pa

Kua and Tai Chi by Gen. Sun Paul Kong, a direct student of GM Fu Chen Song, has been spending more time with me explaining the different principles involved in Pa Kua. The intricacies of this style (Dragon style) — the coiling, undulating movements, and contortions involved in the sets are making more sense to me. Predictably, Gen. Sun was an engineer, and he applied his knowledge of physics to improve the efficiency of the dragon-coiling movements of this style. I'm glad that my physics background (I took Physics twice as I flunked the first time in UP) helped me understand Sifu Patricks' explanations.

My first eight years with Sifu Patrick was mainly learning sets, performing in demonstrations during Chinese holidays, banquets, or invitations to other clubs' anniversaries. From 2018 to the present, the focus was on dissecting the sets and applying the movements. Sifu Patrick has also taught me how to build special training equipment and different exercises using them, special training technics (he has incorporated the technics from Mi Tsung Law Horn — Huo Yuan Jia's style — the founder of Chin Woo).

In addition to trying to master these things in Pa Kua, I have been busy trying to continue writing the manuals (J.C.'s Pronus Supinus Arnis de Cadena, History of the UPBS Kung Fu Karate Klan, a "coffeetable booklet"). Last but not the least, I am trying to finish writing the book on Veterinary Surgery (geared toward the Filipino practitioner) which I hope can be endorsed as a required textbook or complement the surgery textbook currently in use by Philippine vet schools.

The biggest project I have, in collaboration with sifu/sihing Rene Navarro in documenting the Dragon-Tiger style of GGM Lao Kim and GM Johnny Chiuten. I must really dig in deep to reconstruct accurately everything I learned from both of them. I am thankful for the Taoist breathing exercises I learned in Toronto from Mantak Chia's system. It somehow triggers my subconscious to help me in the reconstruction process.

Since 2017, we have been successful in establishing and spreading Fu style Tai Chi and Pa Kua in Canada and in the Philippines. Every moment we have, Sifu Patrick Lee, Sijie Teresa Chung and I discuss the contents of our other ongoing project — training manuals in Fu Style Tai Chi and Pa Kua.

To date, most of my contemplation time is spent on reviewing, dissecting, analyzing, applying, and justifying the movements of these different martial arts disciplines I have been lucky enough to have learned. Hopefully, I will be able to pass on this knowledge to deserving students.

RJN: Anything else you can say to the readers?

JSL: My quest has given me many things. I have been gifted with an art. The training was rigorous and painful, but you have to eat bitter to develop and grow, not only as a martial artist but as a human being. I can say that I have lived a full and exciting life.

7.

Arnis: The Language of Combat

Consider different words translated from an original language into English. Very often, the meaning is lost because the English equivalent does not quite carry the import of the original word. To convey the connotation of a word, it may be necessary to go into an extended footnote. It gets worse when, as in acupuncture or arnis de mano, a mere number is assigned to designate a needling point or a stick strike.

In acupuncture, numbers are often used in the West to designate the meridian points. Stomach 25 is lateral to the navel, known as Conception Vessel 8. That does not say much really. But if we look at the original name of Stomach 25, we realize that it is termed *tianshu* and that Conception Vessel 8 is really *shen que*. Tianshu is the "Axis of Heaven" — meaning the North Star, thus alluding to the macrocosm and the division of the body into Heaven and Earth. Shen Que is the "Spirit Gate" — the place where the spirit makes its entry to the foetus. Now that no doubt implies so much more than "Conception Vessel 8." Knowing the meaning of the original name is indeed important in understanding its meaning. We can go on with many more examples in acupuncture, but that is not our focus here.

In arnis, the same problem exists. For example, in the Tagalog region, "Tagang San Miguel" means the sword strike (*taga*) of Saint Michael (San Miguel). It is basically a diagonal downward strike from right to left, usually with the left foot leading. It's often given the number "1" in the numbering of strikes. The different implications of the name are lost because the number is not adequate to carry them. True, "1" may refer to "1 o'clock" and using the pattern of man, it is the left shoulder. But "Tagang San Miguel" refers to more than that. It refers to Saint Michael as well and the posture he assumes in Philippine iconography. It is in short, a strike that describes not merely the trajectory of the blade or stick but also the dynamics of the body, the way the shoulders are angled, the way the whole movement flows in a powerful fusion of different elements. Saint Michael is also, as every Filipino knows, on the logo of the leading street drink called, well, Ginebra San Miguel, not the popular beer but a potent gin also called *cuatro cantos* or "four corners" referring to the square shape of the bottle.

Grandmaster Guillernmo Tingga in action.

Guillermo Tingga — empty hand defense against weapon.

Another example: "Tagang Buhat Araw" means a strike (taga) coming from (*buhat*) the sun (*araw*). It is, in the system of Arnis Lanada of GM Porferio Lanada, strike number 8 in the sequence; in the system of Balintawak arnis of the late Venancio Bacon it is number 12. It is also number 12 in Lapunti Arnis de Abanico, the system founded by the late Filemon Caburnay and Johnny Chiuten. But "Tagang Buhat Araw" implies a whole world of meaning. It is not only that it is a vertical downward strike coming from above, but also a strike that requires that the sun be behind the practitioner; and the opponent should not see it because he gets a glare from the sun that's directly shining on his eyes.

Still another example: "Sungkit." This word describes a movement that includes a poking gesture, but not merely a poke, it's really a flick of the wrist, that imitates the act of pulling down a fruit with a hook. I don't think there is an English word that is the equivalent of the original here. Perhaps "pluck" may be used, with an asterisk of course. Most of the popular systems of arnis do not include it or many other names in their *abecederio* (alphabet of numbered strikes).

"Panastas" has an affinity to "Sungkit" in that the tip of the stick or the blade is the focus of the trajectory. "Panastas" however refers to an entirely different technique. It mimics the act of unravelling a thread from a cloth with a knife or blade. Therefore, the target is not the eyes; it could be any other part of the body, but the direction is usually upward vertical.

"Panastas" likewise suggests that it is not really a stick technique but one for a bladed weapon such as a knife or a bolo.

Grandmaster Porferio Lanada and Rene Navarro.

"Sungkit" is different from "Saksak" which is a thrusting movement. "Saksak" means not just a flick of the blade which would blind or nick but a deep forced entry into the body or face using the tip of the weapon. We can go down a long list of words that graphically depict the concept behind the strikes.

Rene's punyo defense against Alfonzo Co. Image was taken for Rene's inclusion in Edgar Sulite's book, Masters of Arnis, Kali and Eskrima.

Imagine if numbers were employed in Tai Chi Chuan to represent the movements in the form. It is difficult enough to conceive of "Peng" as "Ward-Off," but say, we refer to "Peng" as number 1. Or "Rollback" as number 2 and so on down through the eight core techniques. It's even worse if we just numbered all the movements in sequence, from 1 to 108. In the sword form of the Yang Family, we can appreciate the imagery and allusiveness of "Monkey Presents the Peach of Immortality," of "Seven Stars of the Big Dipper," and of "Immortal Points the Way." There are limits to translation, as many experts have realized. "Yin-Yang" will always be "Yin-Yang," Tai Chi Chuan will always be Tai Chi Chuan, not "Grand Ultimate Fist," its ttranslation, qi will always be qi, not simply "energy" or "vitality."

When I studied arnis with the legendary Amante "Mat" Marinas in the early 70s, it was at first basically learning the "numbers" of the different strikes. Dan Inosanto and Porferio

Daga with Kris and Balisong.

Arnis Strike — Adlabis sa Ilalim. A sweeping movement from the left to the right.

Arnis Strike — Aldabis sa Itaas. A sweeping movement from the right to the left.

Arnis Strike — Aldabios sa Ilalim, Kaliwa (left).

Arnis Strike — Panastas.

Arnis Strike — Bulusok Ng Dalawang Kamay at Sandata.

Arnis Strike — Tabas Talahib.

Arnis Strike — Tagang San Miguel.

Lanada were likewise using "numeros." Each of the 12 strikes had a corresponding number. Every now and then, Mat would tell me the Tagalog names, apparently drawn from the Luzon region, including Manila, Bulacan, Batangas, and Quezon. I learned later that he was giving the names used in the book, *Mga Karunungan sa Larong Arnis*, by Yambao and Mirafuente, the first book written on arnis de mano.

The book is written in Tagalog. At this writing (June 2004), no English translation has been done on it, as far as I know. Mat gave me a few pages of the book when I wrote an article about him in 1973. (Much later, in 2022, Mark Wiley gave me a scan of his original copy that was given to him as a gift from his kung-fu teacher, Sifu Alex Co).

Later, I asked my father to get a copy of it in the Philippine National Library. With the description of Mat and my own background as a guide, I began studying the different techniques from the book. I analysed the different names and how the techniques were

Mark V. Wiley simultaneous check and strike -1997.

Guillermo Tingga — Doble Baston.

applied in an actual fighting situation. To me, it was a revelation to understand the names and descriptions of the strikes and movements.

I realized how different the techniques are when one studies them in the language that they were originally described. Even the counting — *isa* (one), *dalawa* (two), *tatlo* (three), etc. — was different. It had a different cadence and rhythm to it. Like a Philippine dance, arnis assumed a beat, a syncopation. "Bulusok ng Dalawang Kamay o Sandata" and "Indayog ng Katawan" gave me ideas that a mere numbering system would not have.

When I studied Lapunti Arnis de Abanico in Cebu and Bantayan Island in the Philippines, I pressed my teachers to use the original Visayan names of the strikes. It took more time to study the names and write them down, but it was a satisfying endeavour. Certainly, more than a number, *witik* has a nice rhythm to it that conveys a certain panache.

How then do we translate the original words into English? Since some words are almost impossible to translate, possibly the best solution for some practitioners is to study the art in the original language. But since not everybody can spend time in learning Tagalog or Pilipino, Capampangan or Visayan (one of the languages in Central Philippines where arnis is extensively practiced), the second-best step is to study the different names of the strikes in the original language along with the closest English translation. Besides how many instructors are there who speak the Philippine language of the arnis style that they are teaching? Many instructors of arnis, even unfortunately Filipinos, often do not even know the native names of the techniques. The foreigner learning arnis in the Philippines will be surprised to note that many Filipinos teach arnis in English!

Which brings us back to the question: In practice, is it really necesssary to know the original names and meanings?

Placido Yambao — Tigpas.

Placido Yambao — Hulipas.

I have seen quite a number of practitioners who did not learn the original names, some of them seem to do quite well in practice, others don't have have much idea of what they are supposed to do. There are also those practitioners who have learned the original names of the arnis strikes who seem to have more clarity and information in their teachings. There are also those who have been able to understand and adopt the techniques despite lack of knowledge of the original names. In practice of course, there are factors that come into play such as physical dexterity, tactical instinct, kinesthetic gifts, etc. I have played sparring with practitioners who have no idea of the names, whether in English or in the original language, but I have a strong respect for their abilities.

As a Filipino, I take pride in the beauty and symbolism of the arnis names. It gives me joy to see somebody teaching the art in my own language. It makes me feel that s/he cares deeply not only for the enlightenment of the student but also for the art and my culture.

Learning the original language of the art likewise deepens one's understanding of the culture and may ultimately bring the practitioner to the deeper spiritual content of arnis de mano. Many of the names used, for instance, allude to environmental conditions and Filipino imagery. "Tagang Buhat Araw" is not just a downward overhead strike. It suggests nature (the sun). So does "Tabas Talahib" (cogon grass). In short, like the Chinese, Filipinos

Placido Yambao — Aldabis sa Ilalim.

Placido Yambao — Tagang San Miguel.

picture their movements in terms of their living conditions and cultural milieu. Movements are not just numbers or hours on the clock. As in Tai Chi Chuan and qigong and other Chinese arts, the names are poetic and carry meanings that cannot otherwise be conveyed with numbers.

"Tagang San Miguel" is an allusion to Michael, the revered Saint who occupies a high position in Christian heraldic iconography, along with Raphael. Here we are treading on some of the mystical and religious aspects of Philippine martial culture. For arnis de mano is not just a fighting system; it is not just scoring points or bashing heads. It is imbued with a mystical tradition — with *orasyon* (prayers/meditation), animism, respect for nature and reverence for the spirits who live there, healing, occult, magic, search for connection to the divine, etc. Certain movements, even the sound of the sticks, are a means of communication — conveying for instance an invitation to an opponent or a friend. The amulets and talisman or *anting-anting* that the *arnisadores* carry in their person or tattooed on their bodies (like the late Antonio Illustrisimo) contain prayers, exorcism, and symbols.

The arnisador who is steeped in the Philippine tradition is usually a *hilot*, a healer who knows energetics, herbs, and massage, and is connected to the nature spirits of his homeland. One such arnis master I studied with was the late Guillermo "Guiling" Tinga of Bantayan Island who as a healer used herbs, anting-anting, and orasyon to heal his patients. He carried the Philippine martial artist's amulet which has a crucified Christ on both sides of a brass metal cross. The hilots in my hometown who treated me with massage and herbs in my childhood for a sprained elbow or ankle were likewise arnisadores, although they did not announce it. I did not know it at the time, but I realised much later that the prayers they muttered

Professor Florendo "Vee" Visitacion Attacks Mark V. Wiley — 1995.

were probably a mishmash of Latin and possibly Hebrew and Aramaic, Jesus' original language.

When acupuncture was brought to the United States from China in the '70s, it was almost divorced from its cultural foundation. In many schools, it was taught as an independent, free-standing course. But later, it was realised that it could not be practiced optimally without the other arts like qigong, meditation, nutrition, massage, and others, that acupuncture has principles, that it was not just a mechanical needling of "points."

To fully present it, arnis should be learned and taught along with its related cultural foundation. Learning the language of the art can be a good beginning.

Mat Marinas said, "Arnis is communicating with sticks." Here he was not referring to verbal language or nomenclature but to techniques. What he meant was the practitioner's use of the stick to convey a repertoire of meaning through rhythm/beat/*kumpas*, deception, strategy, and tactic. Language here refers to the sum total of his postures, intention, agenda expressed through movement, speed, sound and whatever else can contribute to victory, including the way the stick cuts the air or hits the opponent's stick. At this point, we progress to the world of mastery.

8.

Gilas Arnis: Amante Marinas

Caveat: This article was published in the Ningas-Cogon magazine in October, 1974 and is based on information that was available at the time. Much of the scholarship has since been revised.

Like a guitar in the hands of a master, the arnis stick must come to life, assume a personality of its own so at the instant it hits the air, one forgets the hand that wields it. Gilas is the closest Tagalog word for it. Mind, body, and spirit as one, incarnate in the movement of arnis. Japanese martial artists call it muga. Total union of the conscious and unconscious, action and thought, makes a movement spontaneous, effortless, instinctive, natural, explosive.

It is not easy to reach that state where a simple exercise becomes imbued with mysticism and ritual. Legions who come to the martial arts despair of the regimen and drop out fast. And very few of those who persist ever achieve mastery. Disciples working their way toward the ultimate must pass a rigorous road that may take years or, as in Tai Chi Chuan, decades to travel. Patience, zeal, talent must combine in generous proportions if a student is to reach mastery at all.

Not quest of mastery but plain curiosity drove Amante Marinas to arnis, the Philippine art of stickfighting. His teacher, Porferio Lanada, accepted the novice 10 years ago, without the customary ceremony, without the harrowing tests for patience and character.

SECRETS OF THE ART

Acceptance into the martial arts is usually not that easy though. Expertise is treasured, like family heirlooms, and taught only after a thorough initiation, reminiscent of the wu-shu families in ancient China who had the tradition of handing down the lethal secrets only to the favorite student. Behind the mystique of secrecy is the master's belief, among others, that he is responsible for his students. A deadly art is to be transmitted not to every Mary and John on a silver platter but to those who have demonstrated a good character and ability to use the techniques only when truly justified.

Amante P. "Mat" Marinas, grandmaster of Pananandata

Lanada himself spent years trying to break into the training camp of his closest relatives. His grandfather and his own father denied him entry. Practicing in the banana groves of the family estate, the elders gathered in secret, under a full moon. Meantime, the 10-year-old enthusiast ate his heart out, hidden behind the banana trees, as he watched the ancient ritual. Like Yang Lu-Chan, the legendary master of tai chi chuan fame, he surreptitiously memorized the drills and practised them alone. At 15, he finally became an initiate.

Marinas did not start formal training that early. He recalls having played with sticks as a child, like many other young Filipinos, probably in imitation of the sword-fighting heroes of old Tagalog movies or the corridos heard at the feet of his grandfather, but he was in his early 20s when arnis beckoned to him. Like many a Filipino who looked down upon a native art, he took lessons skeptically at first.

Early on, having been awarded a black belt in aikido and karate, he discovered that arnis was comparable to the most sophisticated martial arts. True, the foremost masters were and are illiterate peasants or provincial laborers. (Lanada, his teacher, was a taxi-driver and cargador.) But so are many combat teachers. Grandmaster Lao Kim, Philippine Chinatown's kung-fu patriarch at 76 and master of a Hung Gar style and the mysterious art of tien hsueh (dim mak) was a carpenter.

A MISSION

Out of pride in his native heritage, Marinas decided to embark on a mission. To propagate the art in America. Not an easy job for anybody, especially in the presence of hundreds of masters, true or false, who are only too eager to give any new arrival the usual once-over.

It was in mid-'72, armed with two rattan sticks and narra daggers, he landed with his young wife Cherry in New York City. Within a month's time, like one who had a job to do, he was asked to prove his mettle at a popular club. For a whole week he was tested by an unusual reception committee of skeptical instructors of varied manners, questions, competence, and disciplines. The kind of welcome most everybody does not get, even in America. Needless to say, Marinas proved his point, with a vengeance. He was accepted as an instructor — of instructors. Soon, three black belts, apparently impressed, sought him out as their teacher and followed him after he opened his own school.

Amante Marinas in 1973 with doble baston — arnis double sticks.

Today, over year after that trial and baptism, he has two classes, one on Lexington and 78th Street, and the other in Paterson, New Jersey. He has also come out with the first in a series of manuals of arnis, co-authored with his teacher. Three more manuscripts are scheduled for future release. He has been featured in a ten-page spread by one of the more prominent self-defense magazines distributed worldwide.

Unfortunately, he has not found an audience among Filipinos for the art. So far, at this writing, only four have taken interest to seek instruction. "Aside from the *sayaw* (Filipino dance) and the *kundiman* (love song), arnis is perhaps the only art in America that is truly Filipino," he says. "It is something that we must study, not only to perpetuate our own culture, but also to keep ourselves in shape — mentally and physically — in this age and time. We must retain an awareness of ourselves and of the reality around us."

Marinas is not one to drop words out of a sociology textbook, but he does describe situations and moods academicians would unhesitatingly call anomie and alienation. He confesses to having encountered the spectrum of characters who inhabit the martial arts world — people who take to the martial arts as an ego trip; physical culture buffs who mistakenly regard the martial arts as a mere physical exercise; devotees who pursue their regimen doggedly in rain or snow or sleet; the revolving door type who come in and go out of the scene with embarrassing regularity; the Wyatt Earp superhero who thinks he is the best and dares one and all to prove otherwise (invariably, as in the classic stories, he gets his comeuppance from, believe it or not, the quiet artist.)

A FILIPINO ART

"Arnis," he says, "is our own. It is Filipino. But we tend to downgrade our own culture — our own handicraft, scientists, artists, intellectuals, martial artists. When it is a Chinese martial artist who speaks, or a Japanese or Okinawan, we listen. We recognize the value of our art only when we have seen it arrive in America."

The reprimand hits home. For in a kind of poetic justice, I discovered arnis de mano rather late in life, only after a long, meandering trip to the other martial arts — wado karate, at first, rather halfheartedly; then, kyukushinkai; finally, external, and internal systems of kung-fu wu-shu, with undisguised celerity. The uncle who was an expert in arnis was ignored. The classmate who rhapsodized about it was secretly scoffed at. Not until I encountered another friend, Guillermo "Doc" Lengson, a dentist who held a high-degree black belt in karate and an expert rank in arnis, was I finally converted. But it was a little too late to take more of the free lessons offered for I was leaving for America. Not too late though to be awed and overwhelmed by his impressive arnis techniques.

And now, four years later in 1972, somewhere in Elmhurst, Queens, NY I find this young master halfway across the globe from home, and seek his views about the relatively obscure Filipino art.

ORIGINS OF ARNIS

So little is known about arnis, even among Filipinos, it is thought to have been introduced to the Philippines by the Spaniards. The name of the art is Spanish, a corruption of harnes, a contraption worn by moro-moro performers and waved about during festivals. Unknown to the Spaniards, these deceptive motions of the harness were in fact rituals of the underground art of arnis.

How arnis developed in the Philippines is not known. A martial arts historian claims that its origins are Indonesian, but he must have been thinking, not about arnis but about silat and kuntao. A comparison of the nomenclature, weaponry and patterns of the current styles obtaining in the Indonesian archipelago and the Sulu area confirms the kinship. And the kris, bow and arrow and spear are weapons shared by both. However, arnis as its name implies is a different art: it was apparently derived from fencing because many of the names used in its techniques are Spanish: larga mano, corto, medio; fraile, abanico, pluma, cinco teros, doce pares, enganyo, etc.

In pre-Spanish times, barangays propagated arnis in secrecy. Schools known as bothoan were established where a core of select students, usually in their early age, were sworn to silence (under threat of death) and subjected to the spartan drills. In some barangays, martial arts were part of the school curriculum, something like the equivalent of physical education but deadlier, and included wrestling, the use of bow and arrow, blowguns, spear and sword, darts, herbal medicine, and military tactics.

Probably contemptous of native skills in war, the Spaniards did not suspect that even in the Battle of Mactan, the islanders showed combat expertise learned in the tribal schools. Lapu-Lapu, a martial artist, employed certain strategems one can find in battle texts.

BATTLE OF MACTAN

To lure the Spaniards, Lapu-Lapu advised Ferdinand Magellan not to attack at night "but to wait until morning, so that they (the natives) would have more men," according to Antonio Pigafetta, Magellan's chronicler. Lapu-Lapu "said that in order to induce us to go in search of them; for they had dug certain pitholes (probably with stakes — author) between the houses in order that we might fall into them." Magellan, himself an old warrior, did not fall for the ruse and attacked instead at dawn. Lapu-Lapu's men were ready — with bows and poisoned arrows (for long distance assault), spears and "lances tempered with fire" (for intermediate and close-range encounters) and kampilans or kalis (for infighting).[1]

In a touch of generalship worthy of Sun-Tzu himself, Lapu-Lapu did not attack while the Spaniards were disembarking from the ships but waited until they had landed on the beach. Thus, the enemy was placed in a position of weakness — unable to use his cannons on the boats; with the sea behind him; without protection in front; no means of reinforcement; and on a terrain chosen by Lapu-Lapu himself. Pigafetta narrates that "when we reached land, those men had formed in three divisions to the number of more than one thousand five hundred persons (probably a bloated estimate — author). When they saw us, they charged down upon us with exceedingly loud cries, two divisions on our flanks and the other to our front... When our muskets were discharged, the natives would never stand still, but leaped hither and thither, covering themselves with their shields." Magellan then ordered his men to "burn their houses in order to terrify them. When they saw their houses burning, they were roused to greater fury."

The exchange from a distance lasted about an hour. Lapu-Lapu's men directed their arrows on the bare legs of the Spaniards, whose bodies were protected with armor. Magellan was hit in the right leg with a poisoned arrow. At this juncture, Magellan ordered his men to retreat, but it was difficult to negotiate the way to the boats.

Magellan was hit in the face with a bamboo spear. He managed to kill his assailant with a spear, but as he was drawing his sword, a spear hit him in the arm and a kampilan wounded him in the leg, and he fell, on his face. Finally, he was killed with spears and kalis. Humabon wanted to buy off the body, but Lapu-Lapu refused, saying in typical martial art gallantry that he would not surrender it "for all the riches in the world" and that he preferred to keep it "as a memorial" to a courageous man.

Legaspi, who followed the ill-fated Magellan expedition to the Philippines, was entertained with kali dances by different barangay chieftains. He remarked that kali was not just a sport or for fun but a preparation for war.

Indeed, with arnis' warrior code similar to Japan's *bushido*, arnis developed in its disciples a martial outlook and stoicism, an ability to face death for a cause, a high sense of duty, respect, control and what the Japanese call "mushin no shin" or "mind of no-mind. " Practitioners who broke their oath were expelled or punished severely. Ancient kali was studied not merely as an initiation into adulthood but as a training for war, a kind of selective conscription — barangay style.

Today arnis is getting a revival in the Philippines, most notably in the schools. Unfortunately, the members of the military and police have been studying it also, ostensively for use against the civilian population. As one recalls the barbarity with which the club was used by the "forces of law and order" against students in the Philippines in the last five years, one cannot

Amante Marinas demonstrates a counter against a thrust.

Amante Marinas demonstrating a technique with the staff (pingga).

but lament this development — a development which is no doubt contrary to the spirit and history of arnis as a weapon of freemen and as a symbol of Philippine resistance against oppression and tyranny.

STYLES OF ARNIS

Many styles of arnis have evolved in different areas and barrios. Marinas' style is a distillate of four, namely, Lapu-Lapu (doce pares), sinawali, Balintawak, and espada y daga. Lapu-Lapu, reputedly the style descended from the hero of Mactan, is a close-range combat, replete with disarming and grabbing techniques, which uses a 24-inch muton. Sinawali is named after the Filipino mat because of its intricate patterns, and uses not one, but two sticks which are swung in wide, continuous circles around the body. It is considered by many experts to be the deadliest and most aesthetic of the different native stick fighting styles.

Balintawak comes from Central Luzon and is reported to have been the style known by Andres Bonifacio, the hero of the Revolution of 1896. It was popular among the viajeros of Pampanga, Batangas and Pangasinan who used the sharpened anahaw rod to protect themselves from brigands as the itinerant peddlers and merchants of ancient China employed the staff, a 6-to-7-foot pole, to fight off marauding bandits who plagued their route.

Espada y daga employs a long stick and a short one in a complementary way. With the popularization and integration of styles these distinctions have blurred. An adherent of one style may be using two or several in practice. There is even a style of recent vintage that claims the name of "modern arnis."

UNSEEN PRESENCE

As in all traditional martial art schools, death was an unseen presence in the ancient kali training camps. An initiate was trained to focus his attention on the forehead of his opponent without blinking for a long period of time because, in an actual encounter, failure to do so could be disastrous. Progressing from sticks to steel blades, he had to learn the routine: Kata — the "dance of death." One-man and two-man sets, exercises that involved repetitive figures. Multiple attacks. Until the technique became so refined, its desired effect, disarm, main or kill — was inevitable. It was indeed the life-and-death struggle itself choreographed in the drills.

Don Simeon de Anda y Salazar decided to proscribe arnis in 1764 when he discovered that the native revolts were being led by kali masters. Filipino ingenuity, however, found a way of concealing the art behind ceremonial dances. Sinulog and binabayani for instance were actually dances, are in fact used as training forms to the present. The prohibition likewise forced the Filipinos to use sticks, usually rattan instead of steel blades.

Until the turn of the century, many Filipinos were heirs to this dying martial arts tradition. Gen. Gregorio del Pilar, Antonio Luna, Andres Bonifacio, to name only a few, were avid adherents of arnis. Dr. Rizal, himself, started studying arnis when he was barely 10 years old. He was one of the best in his hometown, as a series of bouts during a town fiesta proved. "My hand is shaking," he wrote a friend, "because I have just had a fencing bout; you know I want to be a swordsman."

A MODERN WARRIOR

Seeing Marinas cross sticks with an opponent, one understands why arnis brought Magellan and his band of conquistadores to their knees at Mactan. So refined are his movements, so impeccable his techniques, one has no doubt at all he will emerge as the most famous of modern arnis masters. Fighting like a guerrillero, he offers no solid front to hit. He converts defense into offense with ease. He seems remote as to be unreachable, but when he attacks, he is right there with his adversary. He advances, retreats, side steps, crouches, fakes without pause, yet each movement has a meaning, however elusive it may seem to the tyro.

LIKE SUN-TZU

Listening to him, one finds Marinas' principles of combat akin to Sun-Tzu's. Feint to the north (head) and attack to the south (groin or shin). Encircle to the east and march to the west. Pretend weakness and vulnerability to keep the enemy off-guard. Entice the enemy to attack a supposedly weak position and then trap him with an unexpected blow. These are implicit in the kali techniques as they are in other martial arts schools, but Marinas like a true heir of the early Philippine warriors articulates and applies them with startling clarity and results.

It does not take long to realize Marina's commitment to arnis. And his mastery of the art. A high school valedictorian, college scholar, topnotcher (3rd place) in the chemical engineering exams a professor of chemistry and mathematics in Manila, Marinas has given to arnis the same devotion, intelligence, imagination, and attention to details he has displayed in his other pursuits.

As his arnis stick draws a figure, whistling as it travels, it assumes a power of its own as if the air itself has come to life. Suddenly, one feels the presence of gilas or muga, wedding of mind, body, and spirit.

9.

Lapunti Arnis de Abanico: A Creative Synthesis

It doesn't happen all the time, but when a master studies two martial art styles, he can develop a third style. Lapunti Arnis de Abanico is one such third style of martial art that was born of the mating of Chinese southern Shaolin kung-fu and arnis de mano. In this case, it wasn't one master but two — Filemon Caburnay and Johnny F. Chiuten, both of Cebu, Philippines — who created the style.

TWO MASTERS

Filemon Caburnay was the grandmaster of Arnis de Abanico (which is the Spanish word for fan), a style that was basically a close-quarter system common among the stickfighting practitioners of Cebu. He studied with several masters and incorporated their techniques into his system. Like many martial artists in the Philippines, he was also proficient in karate and judo. For a long while he was affiliated with the Doce Pares Club of Cebu and trained as the sparring partner of Filemon "Momoy" Canete, the patriarch of the famous Canete clan.

Caburnay split from the Doce Pares Club in the '60s to start his own school with an emphatic martial curriculum. He called it Arnis de Abanico style and included a wide variety of techniques — an abecederio (alphabet) of twelve strikes, formas (forms), combination attacks and defenses with single stick, double stick, dagger and stick and dagger. There were auxiliary techniques as well, among them, *trangkadas* (locks) and *tapi-tapi* (block, tap and strike). Caburnay, a quiet and pleasant man who was retiring, was the yin part of the union.

Johnny F. Chiuten, the other master in this unprecedented alliance, was more outgoing and vocal. He tended to mix it up with fellow martial artists and was active in martial activities. He studied Japanese karate, aikido, Chinese martial arts, including Tai Chi Chuan Yang Family style and pa-kua chang, but his forte was a Fujian five-animal style he studied with Lao Kim, the famous Kung-fu master of Manila's Chinatown. He also studied arnis with several masters, among them, Venancio "Ansiong" Bacon, the grandmaster of the Balintawak system and one of the founders of the Doce Pares Club.

GM Filemon Caburnay (R) and Ondo Caburnay (L).

Chiuten was already a legend in Philippine martial arts at the time the Lapunti Arnis de Abanico was organized. He was a street fighter who had proven his mettle in fighting masters who were willing to take him on. He was also the former president of the Karate Federation of the Philippines (KaFePhil), chosen by his peers in a so-called "election by combat," in the words of Erwin Castillo, the only known case of a candidate who announced his willingness to fight anybody who opposed him or doubted his competence.

Ondo Caburnay applying a disarm.

Johnny Chiuten was also known in the '60s as the instructor of several famous fighters — among them, Noli Nolasco and Nelson Guerrero, both karate tournament champions, Jopet Laraya, Adolfo Pinlac, and Guillermo "Doc" Lengson.

Doctor Lengson, a dentist, also studied arnis de mano and was one of the stick instructors of Remy Presas. He also studied Japanese karate. He took over the Karate Federation of the Philippines after Chiuten's term and was effusive about the lessons and sparring sessions with him. Using Filipino words to describe his experience, he said, "Sinagasa ako ni Johnny." Translation: Johnny ran me over (with his non-stop offensive style of sparring) like a truck.

Chiuten admired the arnis de mano styles he had seen and sought different masters for instruction. Along the way, as he became more steeped in his training, he began to see certain "weaknesses" in the styles. Ever the courteous master, Chiuten wasn't exactly dismissive of the prevailing arnis de mano styles that he had studied but he had ideas for improving them. He thought that because of their stand-up posture, they tended to be static, slow,

GM Johnny Chiuten with Doble Baston (Double Sticks).

GM Ondo Caburnay and father Felimon in Tapi-Tapi (checking and trapping techniques).

GM Felimon Caburnay with espada y daga (sword and dagger) in scissor posture.

The Caburnays, father and son, training in their backyard in Cebu, 1987.

and mechanical. There was a noticeable absence of footwork, especially the lateral. Note, however, that like Dr. Lengson, Chiuten was using Filipino words which conveyed restraint and finesse of language. Certain Filipino words can be critical without being blunt.

When we discussed his experiences, Chiuten lamented aspects of training and fighting. Without naming names, he observed that some practitioners just stood up, their feet planted firmly on the ground. He thought the techniques were deadly, but he also believed that there were a few missing techniques that could make the style more lethal.

Caburnay and Chiuten met in 1972 and combined the existing techniques of Arnis de Abanico — solo baston, doble baston, daga and espada y daga, along with the subsidiary techniques of tapi-tapi, palakaw, arko, contadas, and trangkada — and the deceptive footwork and locking techniques of Southern Shaolin. They also added long-distance techniques and moved away from the defense-oriented techniques of their close-quarter system.

The reverse scissor stance of Lapunti Arnis de Abanico.

In sparring, Johnny introduced the outside attacks, *lastico* (rubber), ground fighting, and the *engano* — (from the Spanish *enganar*, to gain, baiting techniques). He had other innovations in mind, but he stood aside to watch the new style evolve.

The third style that was born, Lapunti Arnis de Abanico or Lapunti, as the style is often called, stood for the three barrios outside of the city proper where the style was created — *La* for Labagon, *Pun* for Punta, and *Ti* for Tisa.

SCISSORS STANCE

The focus of the new system was the cross-legged scissors stance (sometimes called *equis* or X). It is an easy enough posture, but it completely transformed an already effective style into a dynamic, elusive system. Used as a bridge, this posture added the necessary flexibility and mobility to the style that Chiuten was looking for. Later, in the last decade, practitioners of arnis de mano caught on with the innovation and began incorporating the scissor stance in their styles. Two young arnis masters in the Philippines — Rolly Maximo and Christopher Rickets — demonstrated their version of the scissors when I was in the Philippines.

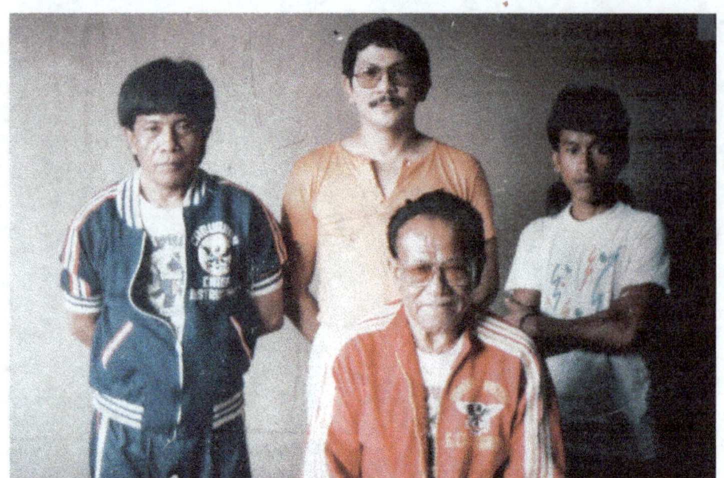

Grandmaster Filemon Caburnay (seated). Standing (L to R), Ondo Caburnay, Jopet Laraya and student.

An instructor of Lapunti Arnis de Abanico in the west is Dr. Jopet Laraya, a veterinarian who is also master of Hung gar, with a strong background in Tai Chi Chuan and other martial styles. He wrote a book about Lapunti Arnis de Abanico and taught the system in Canada for several decades, before relocating to Hong Kong.

When I was in Cebu in 1986 and 1987, I studied Lapunti Arnis de Abanico and made a documentary video of the system on the Island of Mactan, where Ferdinand Magellan was killed in a battle with Lapu-Lapu. Along with this information, Chiuten gave me other videos of masters performing. He also gave me a video showing Lapunti Arnis de Abanico in different stages of its evolution.

A NEW SALUTATION

In 1987, I had found the original *saludo* (salutation) of the Lapunti Arnis de Abanico to be incongruous, because in my mind, it belonged to the era of General Ver, the right-hand man of President and dictator Ferdinand Marcos. I explained to Grandmaster Caburnay and his son Prudencio (Ondo) that the era of Marcos was over and that there was a new president (Corazon Aquino) and a new regime of democracy, and we had to develop a new saludo. With the permission of Grandmaster Caburnay, I choreographed a new salutation which incorporated a scissor posture and a double downward fan strike. This bow is still used by Lapunti Arnis de Abanico practitioners.

With the demise of Filemon Caburnay, his son Prudencio "Ondo" was chosen as the new grandmaster. However, after GM Felimon Caburnay's passing there was a disagreement with the new head of the organization, Johnny F. Chiuten broke off from Lapunti at the millennium. GM Chiuten started his own system called Arnis de Cadena Pronus Supinus. Dr. Jose Santiago Laraya leads Arnis de Cadena.

10.

Looking for Yang Cheng-Fu

You open the door and walk to the second floor of the old building at the corner of Beach and Harrison, the crossroads of Chinatown, Boston. When you enter the school, you see the paintings — peach blossoms in Springtime, bamboo in Summer. As you walk further, you see the photographs of the masters of Yang family Tai Chi Chuan and brush calligraphy on red silk cloth. Looking down from one wall are photos of Yang Lo Sim, Yang Cheng-Fu, Yang Sau-Chung, and Gin Soon Chu, the resident master. This is the new location of the Gin Soon Tai Chi Club, the oldest Tai Chi Chuan school in Chinatown. Up until 1996, it was located near the turnpike, at the corner of Tremont and Tremont, in a much smaller space. The club has been around for more than 28 years.

If there is a class going on, you'll see students doing different routines — empty hands and weapons, solo and paired forms. The classes are small. Earlier, you'll see a student being taught alone or a couple doing push hands, or a group doing the solo form. In one corner two or three students will be going through a knife form again and again. Then, later, the whole class assembles for the solo form led by one of the senior students. Afterwards, there's push hands by beginners and advanced students. It's a long way from the late 1960s when I first studied Tai Chi Chuan.

Studying Tai Chi Chuan in the Philippines in the late '60s, I saw a form, slow, smooth, flowing, hypnotic, elegant. It did not look like it had any power, but I saw and felt in the movement an energy that seemed to vibrate into the bones. A strange sensation to me who, at that point, had been steeped in the hard, vigorous, and physical southern Shaolin Temple style. The leap from hard Shaolin to soft Tai Chi was difficult for me to understand, so was the idea of deriving power from gentleness and the mystical Chi.

MULTIFACETED SYSTEM

Tai Chi Chuan is an ancient Chinese discipline, one of the priceless treasures of Chinese civilization, along with calligraphy, painting, and acupuncture. It is an internal system of healing and energy work, a dance, a philosophy, a meditation, a spiritual quest, a way of centering, and a therapy.

But Tai Chi, as the art is commonly called, is a martial art as well. It is therefore not an ordinary dance, or a relaxation exercise. It is indeed, despite its deceptively harmless movements, a sophisticated fighting system. It can be used and was designed to immobilize, maim, or kill.

The basic movements must have been invented at least two thousand years ago but the system itself was developed sometime in the 13th century by Chang Sanfeng, a legendary Taoist monk in Wu Dang Mountain in China. It was said that he learned the dance in a dream (shades of Tartini!); another story showed him devising the movements from the fight between a crane and a snake that he had seen in his backyard. True or false, these are myths that have been perpetuated in the media and by disciples of the art. Perhaps there was no Chang Sanfeng. It is also possible that if he existed, he did not dream or see the fight between a snake and a crane but just visualized them in different forms like dragon and tiger or yin and yang. Who knows?

Tai Sigung Yang Cheng Fu.

Whatever happened (or not), different systems grew, some in temples (Wu Dang Mountain and the White Cloud Temple in Beijing are the most prominent) and others in families (Chen, Wu, Sun, and especially Yang) around China.

YANG FAMILY STYLE

Yang Family style Tai Chi Chuan is the most wide-spread system. Its origin, like ancient Tai Chi, is shrouded in mystery and legend. One story (considered apocryphal by authorities but perpetuated in the popular literature) says that Yang Lu Chan studied it by disguising himself as a servant in the Chen family household and spying on the practitioners at midnight (this version has a couple of variations, one of which has him as a servant who could not speak and the other that he joined the Chen family as a servant when he was a child).

Another story has it that he was already an accomplished Shaolin Long Fist martial arts master who joined the Chen family to learn their system. Still another story (not necessarily the most reliable) has him studying, not the Chen family style (a southern Shaolin style known as Cannon Fist Boxing which later became known as Tai Chi Chuan), but another

Sigong Yang Sau Cheung.

style taught by a mysterious boxing master who was visiting the Chen's. A story that crops up occasionally in the literature is that he also studied with a Taoist monk.

Whatever the truth behind the confusing claims, the Yang Family style as it is known today was developed by Yang Lu Chan's grandson, Yang Cheng-Fu, who revised the family style to make it simpler and more accessible to the public. In the '20s and '30s up to his death in 1936 Cheng-Fu propagated it as he traveled around China. Among the masters who learned the style from him were his oldest son Yang Sau-Chung (now deceased who was 28 years old when his father died), Tung Ying-Chieh (deceased), Chen Wei Ming (deceased), Tin Shao Lin (Shanghai) and Cui Yi Shi (Beijing).

I studied a version of the Yang style Tai Chi Chuan solo form at the Hua Eng Athletic Club in Manila's Chinatown. It was Yang style handed down through the famous master Han Ching Tang who was visiting from Taiwan in the early '60s. (I later visited his daughter Han Linlin who teaches martial arts in Cambridge, Ma.) Han, who taught Tai Chi Chuan and northern Shaolin Boxing at Hua Eng Athletic Club in Binondo, Manila, reportedly studied the art with Yang Cheng-Fu in Shanghai, possibly in one of those workshops in the '20s and '30s. There was no formal teacher when I joined the school in 1968, but there were veterans who helped. A few advanced students studied the sword form with Han Ching Tang. I don't remember seeing Han or any of his students doing any other form of Yang Family Tai Chi Chuan aside from the solo form and the sword. Han's interpretation of the solo form modified the original in a few places — the opening (his is similar to the Hsing-I), the 'Wave Hands like Cloud' and 'Needle at Sea Bottom,' among others.

You went to the morning class and followed the movements. If you had a problem with the sequence, you asked one of the other students. There was pushing, stationary one hand and two hands, and moving two hands. Chan Bun Te, who managed the school, made occasional but excellent corrections. After a couple of years, the class thinned out as many of us took Tai Chi lessons with Liu Yun Hsiao, the grandmaster from Taiwan, who was in town for a year or so teaching internal systems. I also went to Luneta Park by Manila Bay and joined a group of practitioners who met at dawn almost everyday. A few times I led the group, perhaps the only Filipino who ever did.

Like many practitioners, I learned only the long empty-hand form, basic Push Hands, and read the classics of the art. At the time, there wasn't much information about Yang Family Tai Chi Chuan. Johnny Chiuten, who studied the solo form with me, became a serious practitioner of the art when he realized the possibilities of the style. What I learned and read was enough to give me an idea of the depth of the internal style. I was tantalized beyond belief. I fantasized about studying with Yang Cheng-Fu, who was said to be able to emit power from his body without the slightest movement. I thought if I learned with a real master for a few years.... The idea of receiving the secret Transmissions from an heir of Yang Cheng-Fu, of learning what the art is all about.... From that time, I tried to keep an eye open for such a master.

Gin Soon Chu with Tai Chi Spear.

Gin Soon Chu with Tai Chi Gim.

Newly arrived in the United States in late 1970, I had no teacher. But I did the Tai Chi Chuan long form on a regular basis. I observed the famous Cheng Man Ching who had a school at the foot of Manhattan Bridge on the Bowery in New York. He had a reputation as a formidable fighter. His short form of 37 movements was derived from the Yang Family classical fist form of 108 movements. It was said that he studied with Yang Cheng-Fu. As far as I know, nobody has been able to reliably establish what forms Cheng studied or how many lessons he took with Yang Cheng-Fu. There seems to be common agreement among those who know Cheng, however, that the two times he pushed hands with Yang Cheng-Fu, he was knocked out cold. There were articles that said he studied with the legendary Yang for a decade. Later, a researcher estimated it was three years. More recently, Master Alex Dong of Hawaii quoted his grandfather as saying that Cheng studied only for six months. Whatever the truth behind the different claims, back in the 1970s, Cheng was the most popular and impressive master of Tai Chi Chuan in the West.

Cheng's students did the short fist form, stationary push hands, and sword play. I would stand on one side and watch the players do the form or push hands. I did not talk to anybody, I just watched. Most of the lessons I saw were apparently given by his senior students. Later, Cheng wasn't around when I went to watch; he went back to Taiwan.

Leung Shum, the Ying Jow Pai Eagle Claw master, impressed me. I studied Wu style with him for several months. He was an excellent teacher, but I never did finish the form possibly because I thought it was the same as the Yang form. I dropped by to see a few other Tai Chi masters in New York. In San Francisco I observed a couple of instructors doing their forms. I went to China in 1983 to take intensive training in contemporary wu-shu. I saw a number of Tai Chi Chuan masters, but nobody made a strong impression on me.

TAOIST ARTS

I started studying with Mantak Chia of the Healing Tao in late 1983 and learned his Tai Chi Chi Kung form, a still more abbreviated version of the short Tai Chi form. It was a version of the original 13 movements. Chia put a lot of emphasis on analyzing the internal mechanism of the Tai Chi movement. His was a compact form but very difficult to master. I also learned a short fast form from him.

In the summer of 1986, I visited Boston. I called up Gunther Weil and Rylin Malone, friends from the Healing Tao who were teaching at Harvard, for dinner. I had not seen them since

Chan Bun Te.

Cheng Man Ching.

In this technique the arms or the shoulders are engaged and then without visible movement the partner of GM Gin Soon Chu is bounced off through the discharge of jing.

In this technique, one of the 28-35 advanced fa jing methods, there is no physical contact. Chu Sifu manipulates the Qi of his opponent from a distance.

the last Healing Tao Retreat in North Andover, Massachusetts, in 1985. We agreed to see each other outside the Copley Square Hotel. They took me a short distance in their car to a building near the Chinatown exit of the Mass Pike to a Tai Chi school. Another Tai Chi Chuan school, I said to myself.

There were students practicing earnestly in the courtyard behind the school on the first floor of the Mass Pike Towers. Sword and saber, two-person set, staff, long form, fast form, and a type of stationary two-hand maneuver that included grasping, pushing, and trapping, much of which I had not seen before.

A KARMIC ENCOUNTER

I was introduced to the teacher, Gin Soon Chu, who smiled a lot but did not speak much. At the time I had read widely about Tai Chi Chuan, but I did not see anything about him. He was, as far as I was concerned, just one of the many teachers that I had to include on my list. I sat down to watch the proceedings. Although the sequence of movements was similar to the solo form I had studied at Hua-Eng in Manila, theirs looked stilted, awkward. I was wrong; I realized that they were doing the postures differently. It was the first time I had seen Tai Chi postures done that way anywhere I had been — in the Philippines, Hongkong, China, California, and New York.

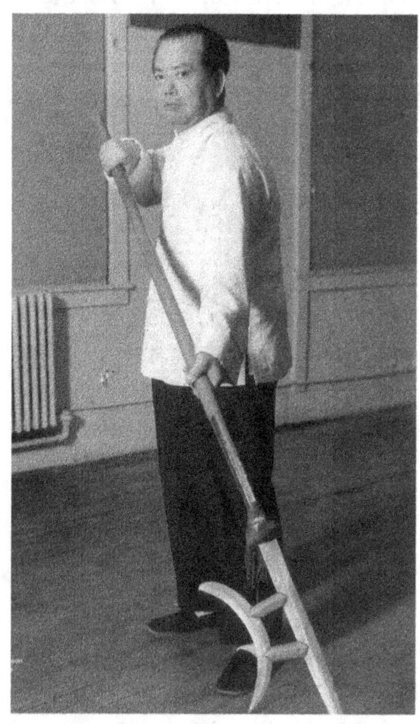

GM Gin Soon Chu with the rare Tai Chi halberd of General Lubu of "Romance of the Three Kingdoms".

Afterwards there was a kind of Push Hands, using a maneuver that was basically stationary, from a 'press' position until somebody was uprooted. It was called 'Dynamic Push Hands' to distinguish it from its soft, yin counterpart. The teacher pushed, too, showing an incredible strength that belied his age and size. He was bouncing people back to the opposite wall, 20 feet away, or up in the air with no visible effort. I was impressed. It was a power I had not seen before. I wondered if it had something to do with the postures of Tai Chi Chuan that I had found awkward.

I knew instantly that he was the Yang Family Tai Chi Chuan master I was looking for, as good a manifestation as any of the spirit and abilities of Yang Cheng-Fu, the father of modern Tai Chi Chuan. Later, I learned that Gin Soon Chu studied with Yang Sau-Chung, the first-born and heir of Yang Cheng- Fu, in Hongkong. A lineage instructor, he knew the curriculum of authentic forms handed down by the Yang family and had been authorized to teach. I decided I was going to study with him. But it was a long drive from Pennsylvania to Boston, some six hours one way. Gunther offered his sofa for me to sleep on while I was in town. Nothing came of it though because I had too many things to do at the time.

STUDYING WITH A MASTER

It was three years later that I finally had the chance to study with Gin Soon Chu. When I decided to study acupuncture, he was the reason I chose to relocate to the Greater Boston area. He was even more impressive when I saw him again in 1989. He was not only bouncing people, but he was also tying them in knots or stopping them cold WITHOUT TOUCHING them! I asked the advance students how this felt, and they really could not explain, except to say that it was like something erupting inside or the muscles get stiff, or a wall seems to have materialized in front. Just like that. You'll never know unless you experienced it, they said. I was told it was pushing on the level of Ching, beyond Chi. It was a release of vital energy. The alchemical change from raw Chi to primal Ching.

Sifu Fang Ning.

At the time of this writing (1998), I've been through four corrections of the solo form and finished several other forms, including the Chang Chuan (Long River form), stick, two sets of the broadsword (knife), the sword (gim), and have been working on the two-man set. I am still receiving corrections to my forms, especially the solo form and the sword form; there doesn't seem to be an end. These forms are like heirlooms to me, received from a teacher who received them from his master, and on through the ancestral line. It has been a productive and happy education for me.

During the six years that I was studying acupuncture and herbology, the lessons with Gin Soon helped give me a center, a sense of wholeness and focus. I have likewise felt a great improvement in my energy. The Tai Chi Chuan students and Vincent, Gordon, and Chu shifu were my family.

The different forms emphasize and reveal different aspects of the art. Each form also sheds light on the form before it so that as one progresses, the different techniques acquire a deeper and larger dimension. While it is true that the solo form is a self-sufficient form for some people, it is also true for me and many practitioners that the other forms complement it and bring it a step or two further.

Gin Soon Chu has been a joy to study with. Completely childlike. Very gentle and serene. And unbelievably awesome. When he does a form, almost everybody stops to watch. His school, founded in 1969, is observing its 29th anniversary, the oldest Tai Chi Chuan school in Chinatown and in the Greater Boston area.

Some of his students have been around for several decades and they still come to study. A number of them, like Linda Sugiyama, Sarah Freed, Hwon Kim (who has opened his own school in Manhattan), and John Conroy (who has been teaching for some time in Providence, Rhode Island) have developed powerful techniques too — one can see it in the way they do their forms and in the impact of their techniques. To me, they represent the potential power of Tai Chi Chuan of which many so-called masters are embarrassingly clueless.

Yang Sau Cheung — Push Hands.

I am still a child learning the rudiments of an art. Pushing 60[1], I don't know how much time I have to learn all the forms Sifu Gin Soon teaches and how deeply I can go into them. There are still the Yang Cheng-Fu's personal sword and the spear forms, among others. And there are, I heard, the secret Yang Family forms — reportedly the basis of the modified solo form that Yang Cheng-Fu introduced in the 1920s to make Tai Chi Chuan popular by being easier to learn.

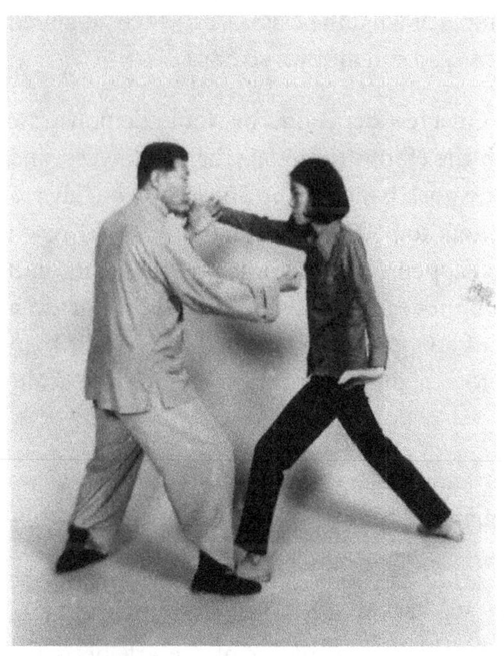

Yang Sau Cheung inside defensive movement.

Yang Sau Cheung outside defensive movement.

GM Yang Sau-Cheung, his wife, his first disciple Ip Tai Tak, and second disciple Gin Soon Chu in a rare photograph in Hongkong.

I see the other students, especially the veterans, and I wonder if I'll ever be able to develop their abilities. A couple of them would often give me advice on my movements or general Tai Chi Chuan development. The training is quite tough and demanding, the push hands routines especially so. With Vincent Chu, Sifu's son, or Fong as we fondly call him, who is a master in his own right, push hands is a serious business; it is the crucible for developing high level techniques. Fong subjects most everybody to an unforgettable treatment that goes right to the bones.

The push hands training is no doubt the most difficult of all. The Yang Family techniques as transmitted by Sifu, are the most varied and most challenging I have seen in my long search. A combination of yielding and power, softness and hardness, the techniques include a wide repertoire of energy discharge. It is a perfect example of what the classics call "steel wrapped in cotton" because it is so effortless but so explosive, so soft and yet so hard.

Chu Sifu has an obvious mastery of push hands. On a few occasions, he would demonstrate different aspects of it, including maneuvers with the elbow, shoulders, hands, fingers, and chi manipulation from a distance. I've seen him do push hands many times and I am always fascinated by it all. Often Sifu ties me up in knots too. While pushing, he would reach one or other parts of my body and something happens, a burst of energy it seems, and my breathing pattern changes. Something inside moves me to assume a posture or do a movement. I twitch, I feel like choking, a rush of energy moves through me. When I am asked how it feels, all I could say is, it is difficult to explain; you must experience it to know it.

Both father and son have incredible Jing power and the legendary "empty force" that we often associate with the Yang Family Tai Chi Chuan masters.

Gin Soon Chu is Sifu to his students. I never heard anybody call him a master and he never demanded it, although he is definitely that. You'll find him at his school, eyes shining brightly.[2] He is childlike and playful and gentle. A genuine master of the art, he is the fulfillment of a personal quest that began 30 years earlier 10,000 miles away on another continent.

11.

The Curriculum of Yang Family Tai Chi Chuan

"The Tai Chi Chuan curriculum consists of hand forms first (i.e., empty hand), such as Tai Chi Chuan and Tai Chi Long Boxing. Next comes One Hand Push Hands, Fixed Position Push Hands, Push Hands with Active Steps, Ta Lu, and Free Sparring. Last comes weapons, such as Tai Chi double-edged sword, Tai Chi broadsword, Tai Chi spear (i.e., thirteen spear), and so forth." —Yang Cheng-Fu[1]

When I was studying Tai Chi Chuan Yang family style in Manila's Chinatown in the late 1960s, I saw only three forms — the solo form which we later called the long form to distinguish it from the short version; a sword Form; and push hands (if we can call it a form). The master who taught Tai Chi Chuan where I studied, at the Hua Eng Athletic Club, in Manila, was Han Ching-Tang, the famous teacher from Taiwan. Han Sifu wasn't around when I started studying, but Chan Bun Te, an impeccable stylist who had studied the form with him, was.

I studied the Solo Form and Push Hands but not the sword form, although there were students who were practicing it when I was at Hua Eng.[2] I learned a few movements from the man who was teaching it then, whose name I can't remember now but was probably called Mr. Sy. But he left and nobody took his place. Johnny Chiuten gave me a video of this talented man performing several forms: solo form, sword form, a type of Chen style solo form, and Pa-Kua Chang — apparently most of them, if not all, he had learned from Han Ching-Tang.

I understand that Master Han studied the solo form from Yang Cheng-Fu in the Sports College in Nanjing in the early '30s but I do not know for sure. Han had revised it in many ways. The opening, for instance, looked like the beginning of Five Element Fist of Hsing-I. In other places, he had changed the movements too, but fortunately not the names.

Chan Bun Te at Hua Eng, in Binondo, Manila's Chinatown, in 1969.

I later learned another version of the Yang family solo Form from Grandmaster Lao Yun Hsiao (also from Taiwan), when the master was visiting the Philippines in 1970. He did not teach us any other Tai Chi Chuan form. At the time, like many people, I thought these three forms were what constituted the whole Tai Chi Chuan curriculum of the Yang Family.

When I moved to the United States in August 1970, I saw a few teachers. Their curriculum covered the solo form plus push hands. Sometimes they taught a sword form; often not. I observed Tai Chi Chuan masters on both East and West Coast.

From what I had seen at his school in New York City, the legendary Cheng Man-Ching taught his abbreviated 37-movement solo form, push hands (sensing hands), and sword. I haven't found any other evidence that he taught any other form. It is possible that he also taught Ta-Lu (translated at the Gin Soon Tai Chi Club as "great pulling"), which is really part of sanshou (two-person sparring form), to a few students.

In 1986, I was taken by Gunther Weil and Rylin Malone to the Gin Soon Tai Chi Club in Boston's Chinatown district. For the first time, I saw a more varied curriculum that included not only push hands, solo form, and sword but also staff-spear and chang-chuan (long fist). It was quite a pleasant surprise not only to see a genuine master in Gin Soon Chu, the second disciple of Yang Sau-Chung, but also to come upon forms I had not seen before — and he was teaching them openly.

There are two possible reasons why only one or two Tai Chi Chuan forms of the

Yang family became widely disseminated. One reason might be that the Yang family did not teach the other forms — or taught them only to a few people, mostly their close disciples or children. Another reason is that most students are inclined — for lack of time or motivation or opportunity — to study only one or two forms.

When Yang Cheng-Fu was alive, it appeared that only two or three forms were taught in public — the solo form (large frame, crane style), simple push hands, and the first sword form. The other forms — like those mentioned above and perhaps others — were usually not taught. Which makes me wonder: What did the famous masters like Dong Ying-Jie, Chen Wei-Ming, Fu Zhongwen, and Cheng Man-Ching learn from Yang Cheng-Fu?

H. Won Kim and Rene Navarro.

From the curriculum that he taught, Chen Weiming learned the solo form, first sword, push hands, and chang-chuan. What the others learned I won't even bother to guess. A sensitive subject this, and I don't like to step on anybody's toes. Students can get temperamental when they are told that their teacher or the system they studied has certain, well, deficiencies. It is possible that these masters learned some or all their forms from Yang Cheng-Fu's son Yang Sau-Chung, who from age 14 to 18, became his father's assistant.

Rene with Gin Soon Chu Sifu and his eldest son Vincent Fong Chu.

I could be wrong because there are no eyewitnesses of, or films of classes from, that time. In the Yang family tradition, except for the times when Grandmaster Yang Cheng-Fu taught in public, usually he taught only one, perhaps two students at a time. As a result, a student may not know what other students were studying unless he talked to them. Moreover, one student can claim to have learned a form or everything from Yang Cheng-Fu himself and only Yang Cheng-Fu would know the truth, and he is dead.

With Grandmaster Yang Sau-Chung (1909–1985), many of the lessons were taught in a small apartment in Hong Kong. There was really no room for a big class. Each student took private lessons. As far as I know, there were no public announcements of workshops or classes.

What Yang Cheng-Fu was talking about in the epigraph above is that there is indeed an extended curriculum of fist and weapons forms. It is not just one or two forms, there are several; apparently, some of them were secret forms taught only to a few disciples.

In the list, Yang Cheng-Fu mentioned the Tai Chi Chuan form. This probably refers to the solo form, the revised form that was popularized in China to help the people improve their health. I say "probably" because there are different versions of it, and I won't presume to know what the great Yang was referring to. With that caveat, I would like to speculate that many of the masters who studied the solo fist form in the 1920s and 1930s learned the revised form that Yang Cheng-Fu taught in many cities. It was large-frame, straight back and high.

Master Yang also referred to Tai chi Long Boxing. Was he being redundant here, since Tai Chi Chuan also refers to Long Boxing, or was he referring to another entirely different form? I conjecture that he was referring to another form, specifically the Chang Chuan (long fist) form, which is often considered the long form in the Yang Family. Chang Chuan is also

A thrust from the Tao (knife) form #1.

Single whip posture from the 108 solo fist form.

Sifu Liu Yun Xiao (7th from left in front row) and the Tai Chi Chuan class in 1970, Chinatown, Philippines. Rene is in the 2nd row.

sometimes referred to, rightly or wrongly, as the 'fast form' (because of its fast movements) or the fajing form (because of its explosive techniques).

I have not seen the Chang Chuan form mentioned in the literature. But, according to Vincent F. Chu, the son of Gin Soon Chu, he heard that there are books in China about it written by students of Chen Wei-Ming. Chen Wei-Ming himself listed the moves of Chang Chuan in his book on the Tai Chi Sword published in the 1930s. A translation of this book into English by Barbara Davis omits the list.

Chang Chuan is a beautiful and rare form characterized by alternating slow and sudden, dynamic, and explosive movements. The movements are similar in name to the solo form but there is variation in the sequence and in the technique and execution.

There is also a complete form called two-man sparring set. It is a form that enables the practitioner to learn the deeper application of the different movements in the solo and Chang Chuan forms. The student must study both sides (A and B) to learn the form.

Push hands in the Yang family tradition as transmitted by Yang Sau-Chung is a complicated discipline. There are at least seven different facets of it, some involving stationary postures with hand movements and positions that are intended to develop internal structure, sensitivity, receiving and explosive energy, softness, and dynamism; others involving manipulations of the qi; still others involving movement of the hands and feet (like Ta-Lu). Basically, it was a training method that incorporated the 35 or so techniques of fajing.

GM Gin Soon, his wife, Masters Vincent F. Chu and Gordon Chu and the senior disciples including Linda Sugiyama, Jean Young, and H. Won Km.

From the curriculum offered by the late Gin Soon Chu, I learned there are indeed these fist and weapons forms handed down in the Yang family. There are even three versions of the broadsword form (one of them, a vigorous and fast version known as Yang Sau-Chung's favorite, another with a jumping inside crescent kick) and two versions of the sword form (one of them called Yang Cheng-Fu's form). There are other forms that Gin Soon Chu knows, but I can only guess what these forms are. One of the lineage transmissions of Grandmaster Yang Sau-Chung is called the "tiger style." This is different from the popular crane style in which the spine is vertical, and the movements are wide and flowing. In the snake style, the posture is much, much lower. These different animal styles can be varied depending on the frame.

Yang Cheng-Fu's "and so forth" in the quotation above leaves much to the imagination. He was obviously referring to other forms, but he did not elaborate.

12.

The Mysterious Traditional Yang Family Chang Chuan Form

In the presence of knowledgeable Chinese martial artists, I recently mentioned the traditional Yang family Tai Chi Chuan Chang Chuan form. Nobody recognized it. Not even the master who had studied many systems.

Yang Jwing Ming, the famous martial arts author and teacher, does not appear to have studied or heard about it himself. In his book *Tai Chi Theory and Martial Power*, published in 1996, he does not mention it. He does say, however, that:

"Chang Chuan (Changquan): ... Long Fist or Long Sequence. When it means Long Fist, it is northern Shaolin Chinese martial style which specializes in kicking techniques. When it means Long Sequence, it refers to Taijiquan and implies that the Taiji sequence is long and flowing like a river." (p. 255)

In his list of Tai Chi Chuan forms in the same book, nothing is mentioned about Chang Chuan long boxing; which seems to show that he did not know of the existence of the Tai Chi Chuan Chang Chuan form when he wrote the book in 1996. Jou Tsung Hua, author of the book, *The Tao of Tai Chi Chuan*, one of the most comprehensive books on Tai Chi Chuan, also did not mention it.[1] Neither did Cheng Man Ching, the legendary "Master of the Five Excellences," or martial art authority Robert W. Smith, who studied under and collaborated with Cheng. Wayson Liao's *Tai Chi Classics*, which is probably one of the best books on Tai Chi Chuan, also has no mention of it. It is only one of two books I know of that list the 34 or so types of fajing (the other is Yang Jwing Ming's cited above). More than any other book I have read, it lays a program for the development of fa jing (transfer or discharge of energy). Sadly, it does not mention the Chang Chuan form, although it suggests auxiliary training like weapons and especially the sword.

What Yang Jwing Ming also said significantly is, "... the modified form of Tai Chi became today's Tai Chi Chuan, or the so-called Tai Chi exercise. This is the Tai Chi practiced publicly in China today; it is the Tai Chi dance, also called the Chinese Ballet by some Westerners. In these modern times, a person may receive instruction in and practice the art of Tai Chi for years, and, regardless of which style is being taught, still stands a very good chance of learning only 'public Tai Chi.' In other words, most of the Tai Chi practiced today is not the original Tai Chi, and it is devoid of meaning... It is when a person becomes serious in the study of Tai Chi that the search for the authentic art, the temple style, begins. One can only then appreciate the courage and dedication of the masters who have preserved the line of temple Tai Chi down through the centuries. This is our heritage." (pp. 14-15). I wonder what he would have said about Traditional Yang family Tai Chi Chuan Chang Chuan.

Golden Rooster posture from TCC Chang Chuan.

Chen Wei-Ming, who studied with the legendary Yang Cheng-Fu, mentioned the form in his book on the Tai Chi Chuan sword and gave the names of the postures, but he did not explain or illustrate them.

The Traditional Yang Family Tai Chi Chuan[2] curriculum is composed of many varied forms — standing postures (zhan zhuang), fist sets (for solo and partner training), push hands (one-hand, two hands, single step, double step, broken flowers, etc.) and weapons (three broadsword forms, two sword forms, two staff forms). There are also varied ways of doing the forms depending on the frame (small, medium, and large) and levels (snake, tiger, and crane). What became popular was the slow solo form in different versions, especially the large frame, crane level, which Yang Cheng-Fu taught publicly. In the public perception, this slow form became identified as the Yang family Tai Chi Chuan (or the Yang style, for short).

In the book *Tai Chi Touchstones: Yang Family Transmissions,* translated by Douglas Wile, Yang Cheng-Fu is quoted as saying that there are fist and weapons forms. Among the fist forms, he mentions the Tai Chi Chuan solo form and long boxing. I claimed in Chapter 11 that the solo form is the 108-movement set while long boxing is Chang Chuan. Depending on the lineage, different schools call the Chang Chuan form differently. Sometimes it is called small frame form or fast form.

Sifu Ip Tai Tak, the first disciple of Grandmaster Yang Sau-Chung, referred to Chang Chuan as long boxing during his interview with Robert Boyd.[3]

Rene. Central Park. Fist Under the Elbow posture from the traditional Yang family Tai Chi Chuan Chang Chuan form.

ITT: Tai Chi is like a tree. If you nurture it, it will grow. But it is only a potted tree without Chang Chuan. It can be knocked over. If you plant the tree in the ground, it will take root and cannot be pushed over.

That is what qigong training does for your Tai chi. Chang Chuan training brings your qi down to your feet. Tai Chi brings the qi up and circulates it around. Push hands teaches one how to release it through your hands.

RB: And that is the combination that brings Tai Chi from health exercises to martial art?

ITT: It will allow the tiger practitioner to apply some of the moves. But it is not the true Tai Chi combat way unless you also practice the long boxing form.

RB: The long boxing form you speak of is different from the Tai Chi form?

ITT: Yes, the Yang family long boxing form is a martial form different from Tai Chi Chuan. It can be done at varying speeds and can be modified to meet a master's individual martial standards.

My form differs somewhat from Grandmaster Yang's form. You can be creative with long boxing form, but not with the traditional form.

RB: So the four components of martial Yang style Tai Chi are...?

ITT: Tai Chi, long boxing, Chang Chuan and push hands. Without this combination you cannot master Tai chi for self-defense.[4]

Among the children of Yang Cheng-Fu, it was the oldest son, Yang Sau-Chung, who mastered the curriculum of the family. He was only 18 or 19 when he was regarded as a master of the art and taught on his father's behalf. The other children learned but not as extensively since they were still small when their father died, and they learned from each other and from older relatives. Yang Zhendo, the third child, and the most popular, promotes not the traditional Yang family forms, but the wu-shu style competition forms. It is probable that the two older surviving children may have learned the Tai Chi Chuan Chang Chuan form, but we have no way of verifying at this point. According to Vincent F. Chu, one of the surviving children, Yang Zhen Ji, claimed to have studied the form; he also said that there are a couple of books on the Chang Chuan form in Chinese.

Master Gin Soon Chu of Boston, Massachusetts, second disciple of Grandmaster Yang Sau-Chaung, teaches the Chang Chuan form in his school. It was directly from him that I learned traditional Yang family Tai Chi Chuan Chang Chuan in the early '90s. Chu sifu teaches Chang Chuan when the student is ready for it. When it is taught at all, it often comes after at least five years of training, i.e., after the solo form, push hands, staff-spear, knife, sword, and sometimes the two-man sparring set.

Here is the list of Tai Chi Chuan Chang Chuan postures per Sifu Vincent F. Chu:

1. Beginning Tai Chuan Chung Chuan, 2. Diagonal Left Hand Warding Off, 3. Diagonal Grasp Sparrow's Tail, 4. Left Hand Warding Off, 5. Brush Knee, Twist Step and Push Right Hand Forward, 6. Play Guitar, 7. Shoot the Goose, 8. Step Forward, Parry, Intercept Punch, 9. Seal Tightly, 10. Cross Hands, 11. Embrace Tiger Return To The Mountain, 12. Grasp Sparrow's Tail, 13. Diagonal Single Whip, 14. Diagonal Lift Hand, 15. Fist Under Elbow, 16. Step Backward Drive Away Monkey (3 times), 17. Brush Knee Punch Down, 18. Right Foot Kick, 19. Brush Knee Punch Down, 20. Step Forward Grasp Sparrow's Tail, 21. Fish Tail Single Whip, 22. Back Fist Punch, 23. Fair Lady Work on Shuttle/4 corners, 25. Grasp Sparrow's Tail/Ward off, Rollback, Press, Push, 26. Part Wild Horse's Mane (3 times), 27. Lower the Snake Body, 28. Golden Rooster Standing on One Leg (l and r), 29. Step Backward Drive Away Monkey (3 times), 30. Diagonal Flying, 31. Lift Hands, 32. White Crane Spread Its Wings, 33. Brush Knee, Twist Step and Push Right Hand Forward, 34. Pick Up Pearl from Sea Bottom, 35. Fan Back, 36. Back Fist Punch, 37. Step Forward, Parry, Intercept Punch, 38. Step Forward Grasp Sparrow's Tail, 39. Single Whip, 40 Waving Hands Like Cloud (7 times), 41. Single Whip, 42. High Pat Horse, 43. Separation Kicks, 44. Turn Around Light Foot Kick, 45. Left Brush Knee, Twist Step and Push Right Hand Forward, 46. Right Foot Kick, 47. Hitting Tiger, 48. Hit Ears with Fists, 49. Left Foot Kick, 50. Turn Around Right Foot Kick, 51. Brush Knee and Punch Downward, 52. Step Forward Grasp

Rene. Snake Creeps Down, 1969 Philippines.

Rene. Snake Creeps Down, 2000 USA.

Sparrow's Tail, 53. Single Whip, 54. Waving Hands Like Cloud (5 times), 55. Single Whip, 56. High Pat Horse, 57. High Pat Horse Palm, 58. Single Lotus Kick, 59. Brush Knee Punch Downward, 60. Step Forward Grasp Sparrow's Tail, 61. Single Whip, 62. Lower Snake Body, 63. Step Forward Forming Seven Star Stance, 64. Retreat to Ride The Tiger, 65. Lotus Kick, 66. Shoot the Tiger, 67. Step Forward, Parry, Intercept Punch, 68. Seal Tightly, 69. Closing Tai Chi Chuan.

Note some of the names like "Shoot the Goose" and "Fishtail Single Whip." These postures are like "Shoot the Tiger" and "Single Whip" respectively but with some variation in the speed and the trajectory and form of the hand.

Although the names of the Chang Chuan postures are the same as in the solo form, they are different in the execution. So much so that the two sets appear to be from different schools. In the Chang Chuan set, one version of the single whip has the right hand open, that's why it is called a "fishtail"; in the "Shoot the Tiger" posture, the strike is upwards, that's why it is called "Shoot the Wild Goose." There are other differences.

It is true that the Chang Chuan form is shorter than the 108-solo form, but because of the fast movements alternating with slow movements, the Chang Chuan is more difficult and tiring. There has never been a time when one performance of the Chang Chuan did not leave me breathless.

What is it in the Chang Chuan form that makes it an essential training for martial art? The Chang Chuan form is not the solo form done slow and fast. it is an entirely different set. I have no information as to when it became part of the traditional Yang family Tai Chi Chuan curriculum. But unlike the solo form, it seems to have undergone the least change throughout its history.

The form is unpredictable. One time the practitioner is moving slowly and then suddenly, without warning, goes fast and back to slow. Unlike the solo form that's done slowly throughout, you can change the speed of the Chang Chuan form as you wish. Sometimes the person doing it begins to look like a cartoon character or a clock that's been wound up.

There are many explosive martial techniques in the form. You can picture the slow movements gathering qi and the fast movement discharging it. There are also kicks and movements in Chang Chuan that are not in the solo form.

As Master Ip said, you can be creative with the Chang Chuan form. What he meant by that is subject to different interpretations. He probably referred to the changes in speed, but in my experience, you can also adjust the frame and the level. Since the practitioner who does Chang Chuan has already passed different stages of training, one can begin to improvize.

It is always a pleasure to watch a good performance of the traditional Yang family Chang Chuan set. Of the different versions I have seen among the students of Chu sifu the best are H. Won Kim's and Tony Chu's. The former runs a traditional Tai Chi Chuan school in New York City with a complete fist and weapons curriculum. Tony Chu, a cousin of Vincent Chu, is a computer programmer.

This unique set is a real heirloom. No wonder the Yang family taught it only to their close relatives and trusted students. We are fortunate that the faithful practitioners of traditional Yang family Tai Chi Chuan like Sifu Gin Soon Chu of Boston and Ip Tai Tak of Hong Kong have rescued the Chang Chuan form from obscurity and shared it with their students. Now, like the traditional solo form, Chang Chuan can be a gift to the Tai Chi Chuan world.

13.

The Sword of the Immortal Lu Dongbin

Its ideal length is often measured as the distance between ground and the navel or alternatively the tip of the middle finger and the ear. Indeed, a manageable short weapon, but the Tai Chi Chuan sword is the most difficult weapon I have ever tried to study. It is more difficult than the spear, which is the "King of Long Weapons," or the nine-sectional chain, the "King of Flexible Weapons," or the kwan Tao of the legendary Three Kingdoms.

Oddly enough, from its appearance, the sword is a deceptively simple weapon. It has a handle and a blade. The handle has a pommel at one end topped with a tassel, on the other end there's a guard. The straight blade has a sharp tip, a ridge in the middle running down most of the shaft, and two supposedly sharp edges. At its thickest, it is only about six millimeters, tapering down to a point of about three millimeters. The more elaborate versions of it, usually for ritual and exorcism, are designed like works of art, the blade etched with ancient scripts and patterns such as the dragon and phoenix and the Seven Stars of the Big Dipper, the handle and scabbard embossed with raised dragon designs.

The traditional Yang family Tai Chi Chuan sword set is simple. Like the sword itself, the form has nothing complicated about it. Even when stylized by contemporary practitioners, there's no difficult posture. The form is simplicity itself, nothing flamboyant or intricate. From the list of movements, there are only 54 postures, a short form compared to the solo fist form.

THE YANG FAMILY SWORD

When I first saw the Yang family sword form in the '60s, I was impressed by its economy of movement. There was nothing dramatic, nothing theatrical about it. I did not know at the time what the postures were called and did not ask. I was impressed by its simple grace and beauty.

The man whom I observed doing the form at the Hua Eng Athletic Club in Binondo was, I think, Mr. Sy. He was serious but open and friendly; a smile seemed permanently etched on his face. I did not know how old he was, just that he looked youthful like one of those Taoist sages in plain clothes. He practiced Yang style Tai Chi Chuan regularly, and we followed him, mimicking his movements in class. Later, I learned that he also practiced Chen style Tai Chi, Pa-Kua Chang, and northern Shaolin. Not a mean feat for anyone, I am sure.

Immortal Lu Dong Bin nd His Sword.

Of Sy's forms, however, it was the sword that I recall most vividly, which he probably learned from Sifu Han Ching Tang of Taiwan, who (as mentioned in the previous chapter) taught at Hua Eng in the early '60s. He was the strongest presence in the school at the time and I think the most talented, except for my teacher, Sifu Chan Bun Te, whose advice on Tai Chi he sought often.

I learned Grandmaster Lao Kim's wonderful southern Shaolin sword form in the late '60s but it did not impress me as strongly as the Tai Chi sword of Mr. Sy. I also studied a beautiful wu-shu sword routine, northern style, in Cheng-Du, Sichuan Province in China in 1983, but I did not get interested in it either. It was the Tai Chi Chuan sword form that fascinated and obsessed me for many years. I decided I was going to look for somebody who could teach it to me.

It was, I guess, one of my idiosyncrasies that if I wanted to study something, I made a commitment to look for a qualified teacher and study with him. For instance, after reading the epic *Romance of the Three Kingdoms*, the kwan Tao became one of the weapons I wanted to learn. I saw an exciting version done by a student of Master Chan Poi of the Wah Lum Praying Mantis school at a tournament in Long Island, NY where I was a forms judge. Through a series of synchronicities, which took many years, I met and befriended John Loupos, a fellow Healing Tao instructor, who learned the form from Sifu Chan. John taught me the Green Dragon kwan Tao set in Cohasset, Massachusetts, in 1990 in exchange for lessons in arnis de mano.

I had the same but stronger commitment to the Tai Chi Chuan Sword. I studied it in the early '90s with Master Gin Soon Chu. He had two sets of the sword, a basic form and an advanced form sometimes referred to Yang Cheng-Fu's sword form. The two sets are actually very similar but there are distinctive differences. They have the same names for the different postures and the same sequence, but some postures are different. There are also movements and gestures that are added in the second set.

I conjecture that it was the first set that the famous master Chen Wei-Ming learned from the Yang Family, probably from Yang Sau-Chaung, first son and heir of Yang Cheng-Fu, who was teaching on his father's behalf at the time. The second set was probably not taught in public, but I could be wrong. In his book, *Taiji Sword and Other Writings*, Chen Wei-Ming gave a description and illustration of the first set, along with the solo form and the names of the Chang Chuan movements. Other authors have likewise basically presented the first set.

ORIGINS OF THE FORM

Where did the Yang Family Tai Chi Chuan sword form come from?

GM Gin Soon Chu in the Shoot the Wild Goose sequence from the traditional Yang family Tai Chi Chuan sword form (#2). The movement occurs a couple of times towards the conclusion of the set. The sword hand thrusts while the sword moves back simultaneously pointing down and the body leans forward and twists. Another version of the movement has the sword parallel to the ground. It is one of many names in the form that mention different animals: the White Ape, Dragon, Rhinoceros, Great Rock, Phoenix, etc., that are really allusions to legends in Chinese mythology.

It is often said that Yang family Tai Chi Chuan was derived from the Chen family style. I am skeptical of this claim, along with the other that the Chen family invented Tai Chi Chuan since I haven't seen any credible evidence for it. From Yang family oral tradition, Yang Lu-Chan, the Yang family first patriarch, studied with Chen Chanxing, it is true, but what Yang studied with Chen was not the Chen Family style (a Shaolin style, I believe) but an internal Taoist style, the predecessor of the Yang family system. (This, I submit, may account for the many differences between the Chen and Yang family styles fist and weapons forms, including push hands.)

Several masters are mentioned in this lineage, although there does not seem to be a continuity in the chain. Before Chen Chanxing (1771–1853) there were Chiang Fah and Wang Tsung Yueh (both 16th century). The lineage is apparently and understandably vague and murky but eventually (so the tradition goes) it is traced back to Wu Dang Mountain Temple and the Taoist Immortal Zhang San-Feng ("Zhang of the Three Peaks") who was supposed to have lived in the 12th and 13th century.

There were movements or styles similar tor almost identical with Tai Chi Chuan before Chang San-Feng, but he is credited with choreographing the original Tai Chi Chuan 13 Movements form after seeing — or dreaming about — the fight between a snake and a crane. He is also credited with being the author of Tai Chi Chuan, longevity, sexual, and immortality texts in the Taoist canon. I don't know if he existed (although many famous authorities like Eva Wong, Thomas Cleary, Douglas Wile, Livia Kohn, and Michael Saso mentioned him) or whether he founded Tai Chi Chuan or authored all those transmissions. However, all I can say at this moment is that different Taoist temples in China, including Bai Yun Guan (White Cloud Temple) in Beijing, developed their own versions of Tai Chi Chuan — or what we may consider versions of the art — probably many centuries ago. I believe that the temple styles of Tai Chi Chuan preceded the family forms. (The issue here may revolve around the question of who used the name Tai Chi Chuan first.)

HEAVEN, HUMANITY, AND EARTH

One of the important concepts in Chinese culture, expressed in many books but especially marked in *Tao Te Ching* is the principle in verse 42: "one splitting into two, two becoming three, and three multiplying into the ten thousand things." This has been translated to mean, among others, that wu chi became yin and yang, yin and yang became heaven, humanity, and earth, and these three became the Myriad Objects.

As applied to many disciplines, the rule of three can refer to the human microcosm. In this case, the rule of three refers to "jing, qi, and shen," the so-called "three treasures." In martial arts, it refers to the levels of practice: mastery, competence, or refinement. On the macrocosmic, there are also three levels — heaven (spirit), humanity (physical), earth (energetic). This is one interpretation. In his book *The Tao of Tai Chi Chuan*, Jou Tsung Hwa has listed these three levels also and has his own definition of each.

GM Gin Soon Chu — gim (sword) vs. Tao (knife) technique.

For now, it's all that I can offer without going into the extended explanation. It is difficult to separate these three into boxes. What we should remember is that there are different levels of achievement in Tai chi chuan.

TAI CHI CHUAN CURRICULUM

I have not seen any information as to when the sword form became a part of the Yang family curriculum. Has it been there before or since Yang Lu-Chan? Or was it adopted later? From where? I don't know if we have a way of knowing. Much of martial arts history is a mishmash of rumors, half-truths, and self-serving claims with only a tiny kernel of truth. To me, the origin of the Yang family sword is as mysterious as the Yang family dragon halberd form or the genesis of Shaolin Temple boxing.

Rene executing spear thrust.

The monks on Hua Shan, Bai Yun Guan, Wu Dang, and other holy mountains are known to practice their own versions of the Tai Chi Chuan sword form. I do not know if the sword form of the Yang family came from one of the temples; but how did the sword become a part of the Yang family curriculum?

It is said that the sword form is independent and separate from the Tai Chi Chuan solo fist form. If we analyze the movements of the sword, we will see that they are different from the solo form. On the other hand, the movements of the knife (broadsword) are like the solo form.

A larger question: How did a profound art like Tai Chi Chuan become a family martial system?

Whoever made the claim that their family invented Tai Chi Chuan is, I think, merely boasting and should not be believed. The Yang family learned Tai Chi Chuan from Chen Chanxing, Cheng Chanxing learned his style from Chiang Fah — or was it Wong/Wang Tsung Yueh? The Wu family developed their system to a great extent from the Yang. So did the Sun. One style built from another, and so on.

In my view, it is almost inconceivable for an ordinary individual, no matter how brilliant, to invent such an art. It would take a sage, an adept, over a long period of studies. For a Tai Chi Chuan system like the Yang family's is not developed overnight but over decades of intensive contemplation and work. It is a series of extended choreography by somebody who

Rene Tai Chi Gim Shoot the Goose posture.

probably knew elements of dance, meditation, centering, internal alchemy, astrology, warriorship, shamanism, the *I Ching*, Feng-Shui, and meridian energetics, among other things — elements which are apparently parts of it. And he or she, or they, put it all together.

Tai Chi Chuan is not just learning how to use a weapon to cut down an opponent: that requires expertise in fighting with a blade. Tai Chi Chuan is not just moving with grace: that requires knowledge of the dance. Tai Chi Chuan is a whole lot more. It is not just going through the motion or mimicking a movement or fighting or knowing meditation and stillness. To discover its many facets the practitioner must have studied and integrated many aspects of Chinese culture.

Wherever the sword form came from, or whatever date the Yang family included it in their curriculum, it is intriguing that the names of the postures suggest a provenance that seems to be a mixture of high Buddhist and Taoist concepts and ideas.

What is it that makes the traditional Yang family Tai Chi Chuan sword form so demanding?

SWORD AND KNIFE

The weapon used to compare with the sword is the Tao (knife/broadsword), the willow-leaf sword. We may agree or not, but the knife is said to be the weapon of the foot soldier while the sword (gim/jian) is called the weapon of the general. The implication is that one is for the common practitioners while the other is for the nobility or the adept, people of the higher status or rank.

The sword has been described as a dragon or a phoenix in flight or a graceful woman. That is, it is not for ruffians or ordinary warriors, but for high-ranking dignitaries or enlightened individuals. Its techniques are supposed to be refined and subtle.

There is a long poem by Du Fu, the consummate poet, describing a sword dance in almost ecstatic terms. Here is a short version of it[1]:

Her swordplay moved the world.
Those who beheld her, numerous as the hills,
Lost themselves in wonder,
Heaven and Earth swayed in resonance
...
Swift as the Archer shooting the nine suns,
She was exquisite, like a sky-god
Behind a team of dragons, soaring.

Tai chi Jian Black Dragon Wags its Tail.

The sword works on 13 different techniques — slicing, piercing, thrusting, cutting, intercepting, among others — that's why it is also called 13 Sword. Like the numbers eight and nine, 13 is magical in Taoist numerology. The Tai Chi Chuan sword, like the fist form, does not meet force with force but neutralizes, redirects, listens, uses the force of the opponent, and like the proverbial water, seeks the weakest spots of the opponent. The eight different positions of the hand holding the sword correspond to the Eight Trigrams just like the eight different core techniques of Tai Chi Chuan.

When a red or yellow tassel (long or short) is attached to the sword, the techniques take on a different emphasis. The tassel, like the tail of the dragon, must move in circles. It must whip back and forth, clockwise, and counterclockwise, upward, and downward. Special training from an expert teacher is necessary to learn the tassel movements. Very often, if the practitioner does not know how to use it, the tassel can get entangled on the sword or on the wrist. But if the practitioner is good, the tassel can be a graceful and impressive addition to the sword. Ancient warriors used a special tassel that had sharp edges in it, making for an effective weapon complementing the sword.

SWORD QI WORK

As a general rule, in the Yang family tradition, a fist form essentially grows the qi within the body while a weapon like the spear or the sword is meant to extend the qi of the practitioner to the tip of the weapon and beyond. This part is the energetic aspect of sword expertise. Since Tai Chi Chuan is an internal, not an external art, the qi aspect of the training is important, otherwise how can we call what the practitioner is doing Tai Chi Chuan? The aim of sword qi work is not just to build the qi within, a difficult attainment, but to be able to project it the length of and past the weapon itself.

Tai chi Jian Yaksha Searches the Sea.

Note, however, that the word chi (qi) in Tai Chi Chuan (Taijiquan) is not the same word and does not have the same meaning as the qi in qigong, which refers to vapor rising from rice. The "Chi" in Tai Chi refers to something bigger, the breath that animates the universe as the characters indicate or the Tao. The Chi in Tai Chi Chuan is not just the life force we develop in practice or from nutrition; it is the immanent divine authority that powers everything. You'll see a mouth (breath), a tree, woven together, etc. between heaven and earth. Tai Chi is symbolized by the yin-yang pattern. The radical for Tai includes big, large, or great (da) and perhaps its rendition into "Grand" is not farfetched (太), but at the same time, the dot in the pictograph for man suggests a center or a precious object[2].

SPIRITUAL SWORD

What's truly amazing is that the sword is not just a weapon for fighting or an equipment for exercise and qi development. It is extremely effective for fighting, to be sure, and it is highly conducive to energy building and projection. What puts it above other weapons is its association with spiritual ideas and practices. From the names of the postures, it is a qigong or meditation routine that is also a shamanic, spiritual, and immortal dance or choreography. No offense meant when I use "dance" because many of the rituals in Buddhism, Taoism, and Shamanism are dances. There are dances of immortality focused on the Seven Stars of the Big Dipper or the Magic Square. The martial arts are dances, too.

Consider a few of the postures such as "Immortal Points the Way," "Three Rings Around the Moon," "Stallion Jumps Over the Mountain Torrent," "Carp Jumps over the Dragon Gate," "Light an Incense to Heaven," "The Big Dipper," "Falling Flowers," "Presenting the Tablet to the Jade Emperor." These images are allusions to a quest as the practitioner searches for enlightenment and immortality. "Immortal Points the Way" initiates and closes the search, "Falling Flowers" indicates an experience of nirvana while "Holding the Tablet," showing the act of presenting the scriptures or the record of one's life, culminates the journey of the spirit. Note likewise that many of the techniques have the sword aligned to the Navel, which is the Gate of the Shen or Spirit.

Here we move into the ethereal, metaphysical, spiritual realm of Taoist martial arts. It is this aspect of the sword that prompts me to call the Tai Chi Chuan sword the "Sword of the Immortal," after Lu Dong Bin, nicknamed Ancestor Lu, considered the "Sword Immortal" and the "Man Who Returned to the Tao."

THE KNIFE (BROADSWORD)

On the other hand, compare the nomenclature against some Tai Chi Chuan knife postures: Beginning; Handover the Knife; Step Up to form seven stars; Retreat to ride the tiger; Step forward the handover knife; step aside and cut; Push Knife horizontally; Underhand cut; Jade Maiden flying to the moon.

Except for "Jade Maiden Flying to the Moon," an allusion to the legend of the Jade Rabbit mixing the elixir of immortality, and Seven Stars, an allusion to the Big and Small Dippers, regarded in Taoist cosmology as gates to the Polestar, there is really nothing to associate the Knife with spiritual practice. Like many weapons of the same design, they are essentially for fighting, health, occasionally for ceremonies, and not much else besides.

The solo fist form has such allusions, too, but most of them refer to the original concept of Tai Chi Chuan — i.e., the primordial struggle between Snake and the Crane (Earth and Heaven?). Here and there, you'll have the monkey in a gesture of repelling something or offering the peach of immortality, a "Golden Rooster Flying to Heaven," or hands etching patterns like clouds.

It is a staggeringly demanding task to learn to wield a sword that has all these varied qualities and attributes and transcendental aims. You may be able to whip through the Tai Chi Chuan sword form itself or use it for fighting, you may feel the vibration of qi, but how do you learn its spiritual side? How do you, like Lu Dong Bin, Ancestor Lu, or the monk practitioners on Wudang Shan, use it to cut through the illusions and darkness? How do you use its postures and choreography to reach enlightenment? There are certain requirements to achieve that apotheosis: you need to complete your destiny perhaps or attain emptiness, reach mastery of the different elements — breath and chi, and union of the body, energy, and spirit.

It is the challenge of a lifetime.

14.

Developing the Tai Chi Chuan Body

Several of Gin Soon Chu's secret transmissions are difficult to describe. I do not think there is any material out there that explains them. They were new to me when I first encountered them at his school. I asked myself, Why is he doing this, why is he doing that? I struggled for clarification. Several years into my training, I realized that they were part of the curriculum to develop a Tai Chi Body. The technique described below was one such method. Truly a rare method, but it was just a daily occurrence at the school when Chu Sifu was teaching. Most everybody went through it at least once a week, especially those who were just beginning. It was foundational to his style.

I am not sure, but I believe that Gin Soon Chu created his Tai Chi Chuan based not only on what he learned from Yang Sau-Cheung but from other masters as well. True, the core forms belonged to the Yang family style, but it was more than that; it was actually a synthesis of a lifetime that included other "keys" from other schools and went beyond the teachings of a single master or a family. The other methods — also intended to develop the Tai Chi Body — included training to attain the 28-35 fajing techniques, some of which a few students have achieved at Gin Soon's school.

With your hands in a "press" position, Chu Sifu would lean on you with his shoulder or forearm. It is a simple gesture. Nothing seems to be happening. To somebody looking, there does not seem to be anything special about it. Just another exercise, one would think. There's only a subtle shifting that's not visible to the untrained eye. Sifu does not say anything. Every now and then, he would look at you. But most of the time, he is looking down at the floor. At first you can feel pressure on your arms, then your shoulders, down your spine and finally to the legs. The inexorable force. Both of you are kind of stuck in this position of nothingness and impasse that takes maybe 5–10 minutes. But to you it seems to last an eternity because it can get excruciatingly painful.

That is how it feels when you meet an immovable object. Your whole body seems to stretch and anchor, even vibrate. If you are fully conscious, if you listen to what is happening to your body, you'll know that Chu sifu is doing "something" to you. No language, no word, is necessary. He does not have to say anything because you can feel it in your bones, in your tendons and muscles, in your *qi hai*, the "sea of qi". You can feel certain parts of your body responding, becoming aware, getting liberated, energized with qi. Your qi hai is receiving some pressure, a slow "ballooning" and expansion. Your tendons are being filled with energy. Your heels are sinking into the floor at first but later into the earth and then the gravity "recoils" up your leg into your spine, shoulder, and arms. It is a magical feeling. When Chu sifu is done, he tells you to stay in a Zhan Zhuang posture, stationary stance, both feet flat on the floor, with the hands in the "press" position, and you stay there for maybe 30 minutes or until your sweat begins to pool on the floor.

Gm Gin Soon Chu: the inexorable force.

GM Chu in push hands with Rene in 1994.

I have not seen this teaching device anywhere, except at the Gin Soon Tai Chi Club. It is in fact one of the ancient and secret methods of the Yang family. You can learn forms and you can spend years practicing the forms but if you are not exposed to the direct methods of transmission, you may not progress very much. The technique described here is one of the techniques for developing the Tai Chi Chuan body.

Some people do not understand what they are going through during this exercise because Chu sifu does not say anything. Many want him to say something, *anything*, but English isn't his language. At one time a few of his American students in a school in the Northeast United States dismissed Chu as being incapable of transmitting the essence of the teachings because of his lack of proficiency in English. This small group of disgruntled students simply misunderstood the ancient method of transmission. It was a tense period that embarrassed

Chu Sifu demonstrating Ling Kong Jing.

Gin Soon Chu shoulder strike.

the master, but he did not say anything public about it. Actually, he did not have to say anything. The fact is that when Chu sifu looks like he is leaning on the student, he is conveying a secret, a non-verbal lesson. What he is doing, the apotheosis he wants you to reach, is beyond language: words can only desecrate it. Silence and stillness are the bridge to the gong, the high achievement and goal of the Path. You don't reach it through words but through a connection to your qi hai and eventually to your so-called dantian (the mystical Elixir field).

The profoundest teachings — ancient, huge, deep, and elusive like quicksilver — aren't conveyed with words but with movement and subtle gestures. If you do not have an inner ear, a deep sensitivity, or a capacity for silence, you'll miss a whole lifetime of transmission. Even a teacher who has a mastery of English cannot capture the inner teachings. What is missing is the ability of the student to receive the true transmissions. Even if the student understood Chinese, he will not be able to "embody" the distillation of Tai Chi Chuan classics unless he has the qualities required to reach mastery. The teachings, whether verbal or intuitive, are just the "finger pointing at the moon."

Sometimes you may have to understand the paradigm of the elusive human body from an Eastern point of view with all the elements that go into who you are: physical, mental, emotional, energetic, spiritual. You must understand different concepts, too — dantian, the energetic cauldron that holds the mysterious jing (distilled qi); san bao (three treasures); the meridian system; Yin and Yang, and Tai

Chi; the different energy centers that can receive and emit qi; the structure of the bones and the marrow and their relationship to the different organs; the shamanic nature of the movements.

Chu Sifu: parry and punch sequence.

As Laozi wrote, "The Tao that can be spoken is not the Tao." And yet, most people demand explanation. They require words to clarify what is happening when what is happening is beyond words. If you are a teacher and you are conveying something magical and ethereal, it is ridiculous for a student to ask you to explain. The experience of the ineffable is private and personal. A connection, between teacher and disciple, attained on the level of energy, is simply not captured with words because it has its own inarticulate language. There is that elusive epiphany or satori: you have a rare insight into a magical and miraculous phenomenon.

There are those who will probably get frustrated and resentful because they demand instant knowledge and expertise. But "gong" requires conscious and countless repetitions. The Chinese character showing the radical for strength and a carpenter's T-square means time and work as a measure of achievement. If you are gifted, you may get "It" faster than others. But if you are like most people, you may have to plod along; if you're lucky, you'll get a glimpse of It. Most people don't: they'll get the movement in Tai Chi Chuan by mimicking the teacher. They are like monkeys. The deeper lessons will just pass over their head and get lost. I have seen many practitioners who have spent years practicing forms, they will nurture their health and develop a level of proficiency, but they will remain at the foot of the mountain. Or if they climb the mountain of forms, they will not see the beautiful landscape. They will, in a manner of speaking, miss the forest for the trees.

The training that one undergoes at the Gin Soon Chu Tai Chi Club not only covers a whole repertoire of forms — fist and weapons, solo and paired, external and internal — but each form is connected to the next, one form strengthens and clarifies the previous one. For instance, the two-man sparring set reveals the fighting application of the solo fist form, the double staff form complements and improves on the single staff form. Obviously, the solo form is good, but it is self-limiting because while it can provide a level of expertise and experience, it does not, for one, connect to the application aspect of the art. Very often the practitioner who translates the solo fist form movements into a combative technique often frames them within the context of a Shaolin or an external system, therefore losing the inherent principles of Tai Chi Chuan.

The qi development is another matter altogether. When Chu sifu pushes against you with his shoulder while you are in the stationary posture of Press, he is not only aligning your physical body, but also "feeding" you qi and cultivating your qi. You become aware of how you should adjust your legs, your feet, to be able to hold your position because if you don't your structure will collapse. It is like the training in certain Zhan Zhuang postures where you are pushed from different sides to get you to be aware of a center and to root.

Chu Sifu assisting student to develop the Tai Chi body.

My own experience with this facet of the training may be different from others. But essentially, the purpose is the same. Chu sifu trains you to be aware of the different aspects of your body — physical, mental, and energetic. In short, the paradigm of the human body. When you were studying the movements, you were not much conscious of the different "inner" components of your body — the skeleton, the tendons, and muscles (sinews), your connection to a partner and to the earth, the alignment of the heel, leg, spine, scapulae, and the arms. With the push that he gives you that starts gently and then becomes an inexorable force, you begin to learn how to develop the Tai Chi Chuan Yin-Yang body — soft but solid, empty but full, "steel wrapped in cotton." Later, perhaps much later, you begin to be aware of the dantian, that mystical cauldron behind the navel. It is one of the first stages in the development of the Tai Chi body.

The Tai Chi body is not just a physical, material body. It is the totality of who you are and more. It is your optimum potentiality, what you are capable of when you have combined the different elements — physical, material (muscle, tendon, and bones), emotional, energetic, meridian, mental, and intellectual. How do you comprehend the mind and spirit? How do you explain the extra-sensory being that you can emanate from the ordinary dimensions of your physical self?

I have seen Chu sifu demonstrate aspects of the 35 Fa-Jing (discharge of energy). It is incredible. He can grab your qi even when he does not touch you and you become immobilized or get bounced away as if an invisible palm has trapped you or smashed into your body. You ask yourself, where did *that* come from?

15.

Tai Chi Chuan Insights of Vincent F. Chu

I do not remember meeting Vincent Fong Chu in June of 1986 when I first dropped by the Gin Soon Tai Chi Club. I do not remember the first time I met him either. Fong, as Vincent is fondly called, is a self-effacing man. He blends into the room with his quiet voice and quiet presence. He seems to be listening and watching all the time. Even when he teaches and pushes.

When Fong teaches, you'll notice his sense of details, his meticulous eye, his knack for pointing at the root of the postural problem. Even if you don't know Tai Chi Chuan, you'll appreciate the lessons because they are worded with such clarity and demonstrated with the precision of body language. If you know Tai Chi Chuan, you'll appreciate the knowledge of this relatively obscure master.

When Fong pushes, everybody watches. I have seen many masters (both personally and in videos) and read many books about pushing but only Fong and his father Gin Soon Chu have the repertoire of push hands techniques that I have only read about in the Classics. Fong, who has a facility for English, can also explain what he is doing in terms of the variety of Fa Jing techniques that are mentioned in the Tai Chi Chuan Classics.

I've studied traditional Yang family Tai Chi Chuan in the Gin Soon Tai Chi Club since late 1989. The school is small. Ten to 20 students usually come. It is not rare to see only a handful of students. You don't have the standing room only classes that are common in other schools. Each student is privately coached for 10 to 30 minutes by Chu Sifu, Fong, or one of the senior students.

When I began studying Tai Chi Chuan in 1968, in Manila's Chinatown, the students arrived at the club and followed the form. There wasn't much correction done. Somehow, we were able to memorize the form. It was the same practice in the Luneta Park in Manila and, I noticed, in the other parks in China.

But at the Gin Soon Tai Chi Club, there is a close attention to the execution of the form. When students finish the solo form, they are subjected to corrections, at least two, of the entire form before they start pushing or moving on to any other form.

Much more than any instructor I've seen, Vincent is very particular about alignment and postures. He is quite knowledgeable about Tai Chi Chuan, especially Traditional Yang family style. He rarely talks but his knowledge is deep and various. During our private discussions, he would show me certain forms which I thought were lost.

How did the old solo form of the Yang family look? I would ask. He won't answer immediately, but a few days later, he would do a form I haven't seen before.

Vincent "Fong" Chu emitting Qi from a distance.

What is the sword form for? I would ask. It is for fighting somebody who has a weapon, he would say. But nobody carries any weapons around, I would protest. He would say, it helps you extend your qi.

How do I learn the applications of the solo fform? Through push hands and Fa Jing.

He doesn't provide much explanation. His answers come in short, pithy statements.

When he was a child, Vincent began studying the Traditional Tai Chi Chuan of the Yang family from his father, Master Gin Soon Chu. He is now 63, so he has been studying Tai Chi Chuan for over 50 years. He has also studied with Grandmaster Yang Sau Chung and several other masters in China. He trained in the traditional way, through repetition of the forms and techniques. Often, he would stay in one corner and repeat a technique several times. Or he would do the left side of a form.

He studied different forms from the old repertoire. At first, I was surprised to see certain forms that I had never seen before. He would say he was just improvising but later he would say that he was doing a Yang family form. I should not have been surprised because Fong belongs to the lineage of the Yang family. He is not your run of the mill teacher, but a real master of the lineage. He isn't your one- or two-form instructor teaching that it's going to take the student 20 years to learn what he teaches. It is better for Vincent to tell us his experience in his own words. Below is an interview I conducted with him on xxx date

INTERVIEW WITH SIFU VINCENT F. CHU

RJN: Can you say a few words about yourself?

VFC: My Chinese name is Kwok Fong Chu. My parents called me Fong for short. Over the years, I saw that many people had a hard time pronouncing my Chinese name, so I have an English name, Vincent. I am the middle child of Gin Soon Chu and Chok Lan Lee, born in 1960.

RJN: When did you first begin studying martial arts?

VFC: I started my basic training from my father when I was very young. It is difficult to say exactly when I began. My father is a disciple of Yeung Sau Chung, the oldest son of Yang Cheng-Fu of the Yang family Tai Chi Chuan.

RJN: What was your earliest recollection of your first lessons?

VFC: I recalled he asked me to stand still. In his own words, "Stand still and don't move until I ask you to!" Much later, I realized he asked me to practice the wu chi posture.

RJN: How long did you stay in that position?

VFC: Like any young person, I had no patience to stand still as a child. Over the years, I can easily stay more than one hour without any difficulty walking afterward.

RJN: What is the posture supposed to teach?

VFC: Later in my life I understood from my reading that wuji posture is the qigong technique practiced by ancient Chinese. It has many functions but the most obvious is working on the practitioner's nervous system to integrate the physical and spiritual body.

RJN: Who are your other teachers? What style do they teach?

VFC: My second major teacher is Professor Fang Ning, He is a 5th generation Yang style practitioner. I also have some instructions from my father's classmate Mr. Ip Tai Tak and his teacher Yeung Sau Chung.

RJN: Where did Professor Fang Ning study? Can you give us a background about his teacher?

VFC: Professor Fang said he began his Tai Chi Chuan training in 1944 when he was at St. John College in Shanghai City. Later, when he moved to Beijing in 1953, he studied under Master Tsau Li Shu. Master Tsau was one of Yang Cheng-Fu's senior students in Beijing.

RJN: What did you study under Professor Fang Ning?

VFC: Professor Fang taught me the system of Yang Style Tai Chi Chuan that he learned from his teacher.

RJN: Can you trace the lineage of the martial arts you are teaching?

VFC: I am the 6th generation practitioner of Yang Style Tai Chi Chuan. My teacher, Gin Soon Chu, Fang Ning, and Ip Tai Tak are the 5th generation practitioners. My father's teacher, Yeung Sau Chung, and Fang Ning's teacher Tsau Li Shu were from the 4th generation. Yeung and Tsau's teacher, Yang Cheng-Fu was the 3rd generation. Cheng Fu's father, Yang Chien Hou was the 2nd generation and Chien Hou's father Yang Lu Chan was the 1st generation.

RJN: If a person is looking for a teacher of Tai Chi Chuan, what are your suggestions?

VFC: First, one must look for a knowledgeable teacher, not a famous teacher. Today, with magazines, books, and the internet, it is easy to be famous. In the United States, there are many people teaching Tai Chi Chuan. It is necessary to find out what one is teaching. As in medicine, it is good to look for a specialist because this doctor trained extensively in a particular field. The same thing can be applied in Tai Chi Chuan. It is better to find a teacher solely teaching Tai Chi Chuan. If a teacher included Tai Chi Chuan as one of the styles in the curriculum, this teacher knows very little about Tai Chi Chuan because one cannot master all styles.

RJN: For a person beginning Tai Chi Chuan, what are your suggestions regarding the exercises and routines?

VFC: First, one must remember all the movements. Second, one must do the movement correctly. Yang Cheng-Fu's 10 points is good guidance.

RJN: Of all the Tai Chi Chuan forms, what are the most important? What do you yourself practice?

VFC: It is documented that the Tai Chi Chuan creator Chang San Feng learned the Shaolin system in his youth and later after he studied Taoism, he incorporated his martial art with Taoist philosophy to create a new art known as the internal martial art system. The basic characteristic of this new martial art system is that it emphasized training as well as application. There is only one Tai Chi Chuan solo form, but it has many variations to condition the practitioner's body. The variation I selected to practice on any particular day depended on my objective at that time.

RJN: What are these variations? And what do they aim to accomplish?

VFC: In Yang Style Tai Chi Chuan, there are two types of bare hand solo forms. They are the Tai Chi Chuan solo form and Tai Chi Chang Chuan solo form. Most of the time people see Tai Chi Chuan solo form demonstrated in public. Based on Taoist philosophy, Tai Chi Chuan solo form has two functions — as a cultivation art, as well as a martial art. Its primary emphasis is as a cultivation art and secondarily as a martial art. Over the years, the Yang style Tai Chi Chuan solo form developed into the large frame form, medium frame form, and small frame form. The goal of the large frame form is to open the joints to issue power. Since the movement is large, it often issues long jing (power) during application. The medium frame form is to channel the power to the feet so one can issue power without any obvious movement. It is a form to develop martial art skill. The small frame form is to stretch the muscles better for qi circulation. It often issues short jing or sudden power during application. It is also known as an application form. Tai Chi Cheung Chuan solo form is rarely demonstrated in public. It is mainly practiced as a martial art. It is for this reason that not many people know and practice it today.

RJN: What is the role of qigong in Tai Chi Chuan and martial practice?

VFC: Chinese martial arts highly emphasize internal and external harmony training. When speaking of internal training, it refers to qigong. This is training to energize the body so it is possible to execute a powerful strike.

RJN: Can you give us some important principles of Tai Chi Chuan?

VFC: The waist is in the midsection of the body. The Tai Chi Chuan Classics say that if one does not have balance in movement, seek out the problem in stance and waist rotation. The classics also say that if one practices Tai Chi Chuan movements without rotating the waist, one is not practicing Tai Chi Chuan. It is the most important area in physical activity. Anyone who has lower back pain can tell you how important it is to have a healthy back in movement.

RJN: What can you say about qi?

VFC: It is the most important substance in Chinese culture. We see people apply this qi in many daily practices and writing. People's understanding of the world is based on what they see. Since qi is invisible, it is difficult to explain what this is. With the advancement of scientific technology and research, qi is understood today as energy and power. It is like many types of energy that we know of today based on their function, such as electricity and gravity.

RJN: What is the role of qi in Tai Chi Chuan?

VFC: Practicing Tai Chi Chuan involves three steps. They are external posture, intent, and qi. As I said before, qi is power. It fuels all physiologic functions. The external movements of Tai Chi Chuan are based on the qi circulation internally. Strong qi yields a healthy body, good and proper body alignment, and posture.

RJN: How is qi developed in Tai Chi Chuan?

VFC: The Six Harmony Theory and Tai Chi Chuan Classics indicate the relationship and importance of intent, qi and power. In the three steps of Tai Chi Chuan training, the intent guides the qi circulation, and the qi circulation controls the external movement. Qi is invisible. It is difficult to tell when it is present. We can understand its presence by fee ling. The qi development is based on the correctness of movements. If a posture is correctly aligned, it does not inhibit but support and encourage qi circulation. Therefore, qi development in Tai Chi Chuan is based on the correct execution of the movement.

RJN: How did the Yang family choose their disciples?

VFC: In the Chinese martial art community, accepting a disciple is like adopting a child. It is very serious business. In the past, Yang family members selected their disciple very carefully. My father said Yeung Sau Chung checked out the members of my family two generations before him. Ip Tai Tak said Yeung Sau Chung observed his character and personality four years before he was selected. From this, one can better understand the quotation: "If looking for a teacher is difficult, looking for a disciple is even more difficult."

RJN: Is there a ritual when a student is accepted as disciple? Please explain.

VFC: I don't know the specific detail of the ritual. It has four elements. An intermediary introduces the prospective disciple to the teacher. A prospective disciple gives the teacher a written document listing his family information. The new disciple pays respect and bows to the altar which lists all the former lineage members, and a party is held to which are invited all the members of the martial art community. My father said when he was accepted as a disciple, he held a party so Grandmaster Yeung could introduce my father to the Hong Kong martial arts community.

RJN: What do you think of the "Temple" style?

VFC: With the open policy in China, I read from magazines that there are many Temple style Tai Chi Chuan. In comparison to the common styles, such as Yang, Wu, Sun, Chen, and Zhao Bao, Temple Styles emphasized more on exercising the body and the common styles emphasized the martial application more.

RJN: How is training conducted in the Gin Soon Tai Chi Club? Can you describe the progression of teaching, how a student starts and develops from the beginning to the advanced level.

VFC: In our school, all students begin with the solo form. After they master the solo form with two corrections later, students begin dynamic push hand training, as well as other push hand exercises. One year or six months into push hand training students begin to learn weapon forms. Generally, students learned the Tai Chi Staff first and continued with the Tai Chi Knife, Tai Chi Sword, and later the Tai Chi 13 spear set. After the weapons training, students begin to learn the Tai Chi long form, sometimes also called the fast form, and the two-person Set.

RJN: Can you clarify the differences between small frame, medium frame, and large frame? What frame did the Yang family members do?

VFC: As I replied in your previous question, it is a variation of the solo form. Today, what people call Yang family style Tai Chi Chuan refers to the Tai Chi Chuan form standardized by Yang Cheng-Fu. Traditionally, there was only one form in the Yang family. That form had small circular movements and high stances. For that reason, it was called the "small frame" form. It was a very difficult form to master in martial application, so Yang Chien Hou reformed it. He made it easier for students to learn by adding another larger circular movement to a small circular movement with lower stances. This became a transitional form or the "middle frame" form. Although more people were practicing with this new version, it was still not popular. Yang Cheng-Fu reformed the form again to make it still easier for students to learn. He changed the form by removing the small circular movements and keeping the large circular movements. This form is known as the "large frame" form. This form was so popular and easy to learn that the Chinese government based the creation of the "simplified form" on this version in the 1950s. The "88 form" from the '60s was based on the "large frame" as well.

Vincent Chu demonstrating a rare Yang family Tai Chi Chuan form at a banquet in Boston.

RJN: What are the advantages of the medium frame?

VFC: There is no advantage from one frame to another as I described. Each version serves a particular purpose. The Medium Frame from Yang Chien Hou is to build martial skills by further training the body, especially the lower body. The medium frame by Yeung Sau Chung is for application. He believes that it is better not to have the hand reach out too far or come too close to the body. Maintaining the hands midway is better for the hands to move quickly.

A FOLLOW-UP INTERVIEW

This interview followed the passing of Grandmaster Gin Soon Chu in 2019 and covers many details previously unknown to the general public.

RJN: Can you provide the date and place of birth and the date and place of death of your father?

VFC: Born in Nam Fun Lane Village, Taishan Country, Guangdong, China on September 1, 1933. Died in Hebrew Senior Life, Boston, Massachusetts on March 18, 2019

RJN: How about the names of parents and siblings with dates of birth, if possible.

VFC: Older sister: Ngan Oi Chu. Older brother: Gin Sin Chu. Mother: King Fong Wang. Father: Hing Leung Chu.

RJN: Name(s) of wife and names of children with dates and places of birth?

VFC: Wife—Chok Lan Lee. Three sons: Kwok Shing in 1954 in China, Vincent (Kwok Wing) 1960 in China, and Gordon (Kwok Chung) 1976 in Boston.

RJN: When did he migrate to the US? What work did he do?

VFC: He came to the US in 1969 and worked as a cook in Song Hee Restaurant full time until it closed in 1976. Teaching Tai Chi Chuan part-time one week after he came to the US and then taught full time since the restaurant closed in 1976.

RJN: When and where did he start studying?

VFC: He had three Tai Chi Chuan teachers. They were Lee Kwok Wing, Lai Hok Soon, and Yeung Sau Chung. My father's roommate Kwan Chop told me my father's health was very poor. Everyone recommended that he study Tai Chi Chuan. My father and his best friend Chen Ping Tim studied nine months with Lee on the Wu Style Tai Chi Chuan in Hong Kong. Next, they began with Master Lai (Lai studied from Yang Cheng and Yeung Sau Chung in Gangzhou, China) in 1956 until his passing in 1963. He continued his Tai Chi Chuan with Yeung until he immigrated to the US in 1969. He made several trips later back to Hong Hong to continue his training with Yeung. When my father studied with Lai, my father was Lai's only assistant. He said Lai had many private students. These private students (all women) had money and they sent their drivers to pick up Lai to teach at their homes every morning (they don't want to be seen in public). The last student's driver takes him back to the out-door teaching location (he had several locations) and my father then goes to work and trained with Lai after work in the evening. When Lai died, my father inherited the school and continued his teaching until he immigrated to US in 1969. Students called him Young Sifu due to his age. Eddie Lee's uncle was one of the students who studied with my father, and he informed Lee about my father's immigration to Boston. This is why Lee was looking for my father at Song Hee Restaurant a week after my father arrived.

My father studied bone setting Chinese medicine from two people, Liu Wei Yu and Lee He Ping. Liu Wei Yu was his main teacher.

My father said he studied the Emei 13 Stances, internal martial art eight postures, Micro-Orbital Meditation, Dim Mak (death touch), and talisman from him. He was a famous Republic of China military doctor, and the mainland Chinese government used his son to ask him to return to China in later 1950s and early '60s. Liu specialized in difficult to treat diseases.

RJN: What did he teach? What forms were included in the curriculum? What forms and techniques did he emphasize?

VFC:

a. Micro-orbital Meditation. My father learned this from Lee He Ping in the 1950's. Lee was already in his 80's at the time, my father said. He was a military doctor in the Republic of China. His son from mainland China wrote to him said the country needed his service and he returned home around 1958. His tai chi chuan was known as the Wu style's head and the Yang style's tail. I don't know what it means.

b. Emei 13 Stances Chi Kung. My father learned it from Lee He Ping. Chen Ping Tim told me it is also called the Gu Yang Tzu's 13 techniques Yi Jin Gong.

c. Medium Frame Solo Form. My father learned it first from Lai Hok Soon and corrected by Yeung (Yang) Sau Chung.

d. Tiger Form. It is the medium frame solo form inner practitioners called it tiger form.

e. Dynamic Push Hands Exercise. My father learned it from Yeung (Yang) Sau Chung as a method to develop internal power. I named it "Dynamic Push Hand Exercise" to separate it from Single and Double Hand Stationary Step operations, Single and Double Hand Dynamic Step operations and Da Lu Exercise.

f. Two people Pre-arranged Sparring Set (San Sou). My father learned it from Lai Hok Soon. I personally think Yeung (Yang) Sau Chung forgot this form without a partner to practice. Ip Tai Tak told me he saw Yeung did the first several movements.

g. Tai Chi Staff. My father modified it from the halberd.

h. Tai Chi Knife: A/B/C. My father learned A/B forms from Lai Hok Soon and the C form from Yeung (Yang) Sau Chung.

I. Tai Chi Sword: A/B. My father learned the A form from Lai Hok Soon and the B form from Yeung (Yang) Sau Chung

j. Tai Chi 13 Spears Set. My father learned it from Lai Hok Soon. My father told me he saw Ip Tai Tak practice it as a solo form and explained to Ip that 13 Spear set is a partner form.

RJN: List the forms (Tai Chi Chuan fist and weapons, meditation, and chi-kung) he studied with GM Yeung (Yang) Sau-Chaung and other master(s).

VFC:

A. Chi Kung or Gong-Exercises

   a. Center Harmony Chi Kung
   b. Three Circles Exercise
   c. Yi Jin Jing
   d. Ba Duan Jin (Eight Piece of Brocade)

e. Circular Standing Qigong
f. Internal Martial Art 8 Postures
g. Tai Chi Small Knife
h. Dragon Claw
i. Tai Chi 13 Stances
j. Micro-Orbital Meditation

B. Traditional Tai Chi Chuan Solo Forms

a. Medium Frame Solo Form
b. Large Frame Solo Form
c. Small Frame Solo Form
d. Crane Form
a. Tiger Form
b. Snake Form
c. Tai Chi Chung Chuan
d. 108 Techniques Tai Chi Chuan

C. Push Hand Exercises

a. Stationary Step Single Join Hands
b. Stationary Step Double Join Hands
c. Dynamic Stepping (Stepping on the flowers)
d. Dynamic Step Single Join Hands
e. Dynamic Step Double Join Hands
f. Great Pulling (Da Lu)
g. Opening and Closing
h. Four Corners and Four Directions
i. Dynamic Push Hands Exercise

D. Weapons

a. Tai Chi Knife: A/B/C/D
b. Tai Chi Sword: A/B/C/D
c. Tai Chi 13 Spears Set
d. Small Flower Spear
e. General Lu Bu's Halberd

RJN: Who are his disciples and advanced students?

VFC: John Conroy and HW Kim are the disciples. Eddie Lee, Joe Lee, Reggie Wong, Winston Yee, Ronald Goon, Phillip Wong, Warren Wong, Alfred Lee and Bill Lee are some of the senior students.

RJN: Where can a student study GM Chu's curriculum?

VFC: Gin Soon Tai Chi Chuan Club in Boston, MA; John Conroy's Rhode Island School, RI; HW Kim's School in New York, NY; Dimitris Mougdis' School in Stuart, FL; Patrick Loisel's School in Rennes, French; Valerie Daniel's School in Lamballe, French; Karel Nuhlkicek's School in Zlin, Czech Republic; Gianpiero Farina's School in Milan, Italy; Stephan Hagan's School in Hamburg, Germany; Bob Boyd's School in South Burlington, VT; Lik Choi's School in New Jersey; John Toy's School in salem, NH; Nicanor Snow's School in Salem, MA and Tom Tam's School in Quincy, MA.

RJN: List the forms (Tai Chi Chuan fist and weapons, meditation, and chi-kung) he studied with GM Yeung (Yang) Sau-Chaung and other master(s).

VFC: Microcosmic orbit meditation, wu chi posture, 3 variations of the bare hand solo form, tai chi Chang Chuan form, 13 emei qigong stances, 13 characters form, yi jin jing, ba duan jin, three circles exercise, 3 tai chi knife forms, 2 tai chi sword form, halberd, small flower spear, staff, 13 big spear set, two person set, circular standing qigong, etc.

RJN: What forms did Chu sifu study with Yeung (Yang) Sau-Chaung and what forms did he study with other masters?

VFC: As far as I knew, my father studied the medium frame solo form, large and small frames variations and Chang Chuan from Yeung (Yang) Sau Chung. The medium frame, Chang Chuan and two- men set from Lai Hok Soon. 13 characters form from Lee He Ping.

RJN: Please explain (a) 3 Circles Exercise; (b) Internal Martial Art 8 Postures; (c) Tai chi small knife; (d)Tai chi 13 Stances; and Dragon Claw.

VFC:

a. Three Circle Exercises is a group of exercises involve the upper body, middle body and lower body to lubricate the bodily joints.
b. Internal Martial Art 8 Stances is a standing exercise with 8 positions of bird, snake, tiger, dragon, heaven, earth, wind and cloud.
c. Tai Chi Small Knife (dagger) is a technique to apply the thumb as a weapon.
d. Tai Chi 13 Stances is an exercise divided into static and dynamic with 13 positions. The static condition is to condition the body and the dynamic condition is for fa jin exercise.
e. Dragon Claw is a grasp technique by applying the fingers. Any part of the body can be a target, not the bodily joints only as in the eagle claw.

RJN: What did you study with your father?

VFC: I studied from my father the following: Microcosmic Orbit meditation, Wu Chi posture, 3 variations of the bare hand solo form, Tai Chi Chuan Chang Chuan form, 13

Emei qigong stances, 13 characters form, Yi Jin Jing, Ba Duan Jin, Dragon Claw, Tai Chi Dagger, Three Circles Exercise, Push Hand exercises, 3 Tai Chi Knife forms, 2 Tai Chi sword forms, Halberd, Small Flower Spear, Staff, 13 Big Spear set with a 10 feet in length and a diameter from duck egg to duck egg yolk in size, two person set, circular standing qigong, etc.

RJN: How about with other teachers/masters?

VFC: From Yeung (Yang) Sau Chung, I obtained the bare hand forms, weapon forms corrections, and the features of the variations of the bare hand solo forms. I studied from him in September 1984.

From Ip Tai Tak (1929-2004), I obtained his practical experience. Push hand exercises, Dragon Claw application, Tai Chi dagger application, internal martial art Eight Stances and Hitting Tiger and Press Push hand operation. He shared with me his understandings about the solo forms, weapons forms, supplementary exercises, and a copy of his diary. I studied with him from 1992 to 1999. From Ou wen Wei, I learned Pan Gu Shengong (Pan Gu Mystical Qigong) from him and how to become a better person. I studied with him from 1994 to present.

From Fang Ning (11/27/24-9/23/21) (a student of Cui Yi Shi), I obtained Wu Chi posture, Center Harmony qigong, 3 bare hand forms, Chang Chuan form, Fast Form (also known as the Opening and Closing Tai Chi Chuan), Push Hand exercises, Tai Chi Sword form, Ba Duan Jin, Jin Ba Duan, 13 Big Spear set, 108 bare hand form (also known as Yang Family Tai Chi Chuan Solo Form), 5 Animals Frolics, 13 Animals Form and San Feng Yi Jin Gong. I studied with him from 1993 to 2021.

From Liu Xi Wen, I obtained the small circle solo form, Yang Shao Hou's fast form, push hand exercises, information about Yang Shao Hou and his teaching curriculum and the differences between Shao Hou's 108 movements form and Cheng Fu's 108 movements form. I study with him in 2006, 2008, 2014, and 2016.

From Chan Ping Tim, I obtained the Gu Yang Tzu's 13 techniques Yi Jin Gong in 2018.

From Tang Shan Fu, Fang Ning's senior student, I learned some of the abstract Tai Chi Chuan principles incorporated with his personal experiences from the time I study with Fang Ning.

RJN: What forms, techniques, etc. do you teach at seminars?

VFC: Bare hands forms, weapons forms, and some of the supplementary exercises.

RJN: Privately?

VFC: I conduct no private class.

RJN: What forms/techniques are important in the Tai Chi Chuan curriculum?

VFC: The 108 movements bare hand solo form.

RJN: Who choreographed the Tai Chi Chuan Chang Chuan form?

VFC: No idea who choreographed the specified Chang Chuan. However, from my research, the name Tai Chi Chuan began much later. It began with 13 movements, 13 postures or 13 principles, later it was called Chang Chuan and much later, it was called Tai Chi Chuan. At Yang Lu-Chan's time, it was called Cotton Fist or Soft Fist, not Tai Chi Chuan yet. Wu/Hao Style Li Yi Yu (1832-1892) wrote an essay that mentioned Chang San Feng was the creator of Tai Chi Chuan and later he corrected himself on the same essay and wrote that the Tai Chi Chuan creator was unknown. In an article that I read several years ago, Tai Chi Chuan traced all the way back to the Yellow Emperor. It was he who saw the fighting between the bird and snake in Chang Mountain to inspire him to develop the philosophy of soft overcoming hard and come up with the idea that Tai Chi Chuan, not Chang San Feng as written in Dong Ying Chien's red book. People who came after him added content to enrich the form. The person who contributed the most was Chang San Feng. Therefore, people in Wu Dang Mountain called him as the patron saint of Tai Chi Chuan.

RJN: How many Tai Chi Chuan forms are there?

VFC: There is but one bare hand form with many variations. Each variation is based on the objective. It was Gu Liu Xin in his book *Tai Chi Chuan Research* published in 1963 who called each variation with a name such as Large Frame Solo Form, Middle Frame Solo Form, and Small Frame Solo Form.

RJN: Please give a short history behind the 108 solo fist form.

VFC: Traditionally, Tai Chi Chuan has one form. It is known as the 108 movements form. It does not necessarily mean the form has 108 movements. Number 108 has special meaning, it is associated with traditional Chinese culture and there are other martial arts that have 108 movements form as well. There are many ways to practice this form based on one's objective. It has large circular hand motion to stretch the bodily joints, small circular hand motion to stretch the body and sinews, medium circular hand motion for offensive and defensive applications, low stance to work on the lower part of the body, medium stance for martial application, and high stance for mobility, fast and slow transitional movements, etc. All the different Tai Chi Chuan forms available today are derived from this form. Different practitioners have different interests and personalities that developed their practice into many forms. The result of their forms is mainly different in executions of the physical movements, but the principles are the same. Therefore, it does not matter how different in execution the movements are, all the forms are called Tai Chi Chuan. Yang Cheng-Fu modified the bare hand form throughout his life. There is a clear difference of the form he taught before and after he moved south to Shanghai. Most of his students followed him in Shanghai, Guangzhou, and Hangzhou learned the modified form or the standardized form. It had 85 movements as he demonstrated in his book. Fu Zhong Wen called this the 85 movements

Vincent Chu. NY Chinatown. Elbow and Shoulder Technique.

Vincent Chu. Parting the Wild Horse's Mane.

form. For those students who learned from Yang Cheng-Fu before he moved to Shanghai in 1928, the form he taught was the longer and more complex movements. It was called the 108 movements form. The number of movements between the two forms is the same.

Today, although most people practice the 85 movements form from Yang Cheng-Fu's lineage, since it is derived from the 108 movements form, it still called the 108 movements form by many people. However, many people don't pay any attention to the number of movements. They simply called it Yang style Large Frame form. Depending on how one counts the movement, the number can be higher or lower.

Speaking of the spear in Yang style Tai Chi Chuan system. It is referred to as the 13 big spear set. It is a partner spear set composed of four adhesion techniques and four counter techniques, four free techniques and four counter techniques, four application techniques and four counter techniques, and one coiling techniques. Yang Cheng-Fu's student Li Yan Xun (1894-1976) arranged each of the eight adhesion techniques, eight free techniques, and eight application techniques plus the beginning and closing techniques into three big spear solo forms to practice and choregraph a 41 techniques big spear routine based on the techniques from the 13 big spear set. It is truly a brilliant innovation. To some people these 10 feet in length 13 big spear set is also known as the Big Staff without the metal spear attached. Due to its size, people applied it as a tool to develop internal power. It was told that Yang Cheng-Fu practiced shaking the staff 400 times a day to develop his internal power.

Yang Lu-Chen was famous for his Tai Chi Chuan and the Small Flower Spear. Today, there are many people practicing the Tai Chi Chuan transmitted from him, but nobody knows about his Small Flower spear. In 1977, When my father showed his interest to learn the halberd. Grandmaster Yeung told my father that the halberd came from General Lu Bu. An important general in the Three Kingdom (220AD to 280AD). Grandmaster Yeung apologized to my father that the halberd is kept for the Yang Family member only. However, he gave in only after my father promised him that he will teach it to his sons and nobody else (I have written an article about it and posted on our Tai Chi Chuan website: www.gstaichi.org). A year after my father learned Lu Bu's halberd that he was taught the Small Flower Spear and my father realized it has the same techniques.

RJN: Can you say something about the staff form?

VFC: Yang style Tai Chi Chuan does not have staff form in its curriculum. The staff form that is transmitted in our school is the form my father modified and transformed from General Lu Bu's halberd. It has practical techniques without any flowering movement. This is why it does not have many movements. Yang Cheng-Fu's student Cui Li Shi (1890-1970) in Beijing choregraphed a 42 techniques staff form with his daughter in 1964 for wu shu long weapon competition.

RJN: And the Tao or Knife form(s)?

VFC: There are several variations of the knife form available today. Yang Cheng-Fu made changes to the knife form just like the bare hand form throughout his life. There were two forms from Lai Hok Soon and a form from Yeung Sau Chung involved more with speedy circular stepping my father taught me. Fang Ning told me the knife form has many circular motions and it caused him to become dizzy, so he does not like to practice and forgot how to practice it now. He confirmed that the knife form has several variations. Because the Tai Chi knife (broadsword) uses a narrow blade and not a broad blade, as commonly see outside China today, there are many movements executed as sword movements.

RJN: And the sword forms?

VFC: Many years ago, I read an article published in Wu Dang magazine. It mentioned that the Tai Chi sword came from Lu Dong Bin's Heavenly Dragon sword form. Lu was one of the Eight immortals in Chinese mythology and lived during the Tang Dynasty. In 1992, when I visited Beijing, I ventured to the White Cloud temple and met a Taoist priest named Wang Li Ming. After many conversations, he told me he does not know any Tai Chi Chuan but he can demonstrate a sword form for me. He called it Lu Dong Bin's sword form. I recognized several movements at the beginning of the routine that are similar to the Tai Chi sword movement.

Yang Cheng-Fu made changes to the sword form and the bare hand form and knife form throughout his life. His early students learned the form with some variation compared to the form later students learned. The form I learned from Fang Ning has some movements slightly different from the form my father learned from Lai Hok Soon and Yeung Sau Chung. The form you know came from Lai Hok Soon's teaching. Lai was a student of Yang Cheng-Fu and Yeung Sau Chung in Gangzhou City, South China.

Fang Ning told me the changes in the bare hand form began from Yang Chien Hou (Yang Cheng-Fu's father). He realized that the small frame form of Yang Lu Chan is difficult for practitioner to attain skill. Chien Hou enlarged the circular motion from the bare hand form movements with larger motion and sometime repeat the same motion multiple times to make it easier for the student. Cheng-Fu continued his father's changing idea by keeping the largest motion in each movement. Liu Xi Wen told me the traditional 108 Movements has many techniques in each movement. For example: It is like from movement A to B, there are many a, b, c small unit in between and these smaller movements are individual techniques. How Yang Cheng-Fu changed the form was by removing all these smaller movements from each bigger movement. Overall, Yang Cheng-Fu and his father changed only the technical element and not its internal power, so the martial art value remains. We see this change from his bare hand form and weapon forms. All the bare hand forms or weapon forms from his early day are more complicated to practice technically than his later day. Because of his modification, people find it easier to learn and Tai Chi Chuan became a popular art. Yang Shao Hou on the other hand believed that what he learned was what he taught. He does not believe in making it easier for the students. Therefore, he does not have many students. It is not that he does not want to teach the students. It is that the students are not able to learn from him. In Chinese martial art, external system emphasizes technical training and internal system emphasizes on refining the body or internal power training. Believing that a movement is fueled by internal power, it will become a powerful technique.

RJN: What are the characteristics of the Tiger, Crane, and Snake? That is, what are their similarities and differences?

VFC: Crane form has the high stance. Tiger form has the medium stance and snake form has the low stance. They are named by inner practitioners. Generally, they are called high stance, medium stance, and low stance forms. A posture or movement involved with the legs in a stance, the hands move in circular motion and body positioning. Leg stance has high stance (40% and 60% weight distribution on the legs), medium stance (30% and 70% weight distribution on the legs) and low stance (20% and 80% weight distribution on the legs). The hands have large, medium, and small sizes circular motions. For example, on the size of the circular motion, in the Brush Knee and Push forward movement, in the large circular motion, the push forward hand is positioned higher than the shoulder and the brush down hand is positioned lower than the knee. In the medium circular motion, the push forward hand is positioned level to the shoulder and the brush down hand is positioned level to the knee. In the small circular motion, the push forward hand is positioned below the shoulder and the brush down hand is positioned level to the hip. The body positioning has straight upright and leaning forward. With three components involved in a movement, 3X3X2=18 possibilities. The solo form has 18 variations.

Crane form involves all the movements done in high stance, small hand circular motion with the body positions upright. Tiger form involves all the movements done in medium stance, medium hand circular motion with the body positions leaning forward. Snake forms involves all the movements done in low stance, large hand circular motion with the body positions leaning forward.

As I said before, based on one's objective, one can practice the solo form in many (18) variations. Crane form has high stance. It is for mobility. Tiger form has medium stance. It is for practical application. Snake form has low stance. It is for training.

RJN: I believe this is important because many people confuse the three. Also, many people think there is only one form in the Yang family. What did your late father, Gin Soon Chu sifu teach in Boston?

VFC: As I said, there is one form with many variations. We teach the tiger form. I think different masters sometimes share the same forms. They also teach different forms they learned from other teachers. Generally, people teach the form they learned and incorporated their experiences and understanding. No one person is teaching the same form. Otherwise, it is but copying without any original input.

RJN: When I was studying with Mantak Chia, I learned a list of transmissions, including the Microcosmic Orbit. I also learned the Microcosmic Orbit from Taoist priest Jeffrey Yuen and Tai Chi Sifu Chan Bun Te. Chan Bun Te was the younger cousin of my Chinese godfather Chan Tek Lao, who was my adopted father.

VFC: If you learn the same subject from different teachers. It is no different as you stay in the same grade but keep changing school. There is no progress in education.

16.

The "Mystery" of Master Cheng Man Ching

There are many mysteries in martial arts history that may never be settled because they are so remote, there is no record or reliable witness to a fact or simply that nobody who knows has come forward. Where did Tai Chi Chuan originate? Who invented Shaolin Temple boxing?

One of the strange mysteries in contemporary martial arts involves the famous Cheng Man Ching, and the origin of his legendary push hands prowess. Strange because Cheng is arguably the most famous Tai Chi Chuan master of the 20th Century. A multi-faceted man, Cheng is one of the most admired and influential Tai Chi Chuan masters of all time. Much has been written about him by his students and disciples and researchers. There should be nothing or practically nothing important unknown about the master.

Asked about the source of his powerful push hands, he attributed it to Yang Cheng-Fu, one of his teachers. Robert w. Smith found it difficult to believe that Yang Cheng-Fu taught him Push hands because Cheng himself said that the two times he did push hands, Yang knocked him out cold. Mr. Smith himself, who has written about the master and probably knows more about him than anybody else alive, says: "It remains a mystery."[1]

Apparently, Mr. Smith did not consider credible Cheng Man Ching's statement that his Push hands expertise came from Yang Cheng-Fu. If Cheng did not learn his Push hands from Yang Cheng-Fu, then from whom? Robert Smith himself raised this question and had apparently been chasing after a credible answer for years. In a few articles, Mr. Smith has posited the hypothesis that Cheng studied push hands with a few masters.

I would like to offer some light on this issue and narrate how I got interested in the matter.

When I was looking for a Tai Chi Chuan teacher in the early '70s, I observed the classes of several masters. One of them was Cheng Man Ching himself, a master whom I had admired since the '60s. I first read about Cheng in a martial arts magazine, probably *Black*

Belt, in the 1960s in an article about his famous student William Chen of New York. And then I read Robert Smith's writings about him. I read other literature about him. When I moved to Brooklyn, New York, I took the time to see Cheng's classes. He had apparently a large following and was very much loved by his patients and students alike. He had a great reputation, made partly from his fine books, partly from reports of actual fighting with other masters, and partly from push hands with his students.

I saw students practicing push hands from a stationary position, doing the short 37-movement Tai Chi Chuan form, and sword sparring with Cheng. Cheng went around giving pointers or sat at a table taking pulses and prescribing herbal formulas. I did not see him do push hands, so I have no direct knowledge of the quality of his push hands techniques.

Master Cheng Man Ching

But he had a reputation for powerful push hands techniques. Robert Smith, Wolfe Lowenthal, and Bataan Faigao, a Filipino now teaching Tai Chi Chuan, among others, have spoken or written glowingly of Cheng's push hands prowess. From what they reported, Cheng had an incredible softness, a trait he probably had even before he studied with Yang Cheng-Fu. He had the ability to bounce his students "off the wall" without showing any sweat or exertion. Mr. Smith has described Cheng's push hands as being "mystical."

In both Smith's *Chinese Boxing* and Smith and Cheng's co-authored *T'ai Chi: The "Supreme Ultimate" Exercise for Health, Sport, and Self-Defense*, Cheng is shown bouncing somebody. It was one of the things that impressed me early on. Recently, I also saw a film strip of Cheng Man Ching doing push hands and propelling his partner a distance backward.

From what I have read, early on Cheng discounted the ability of Tai Chi Chuan masters to propel an opponent backwards without touching. He believed "the trick will not work against an equal or a superior."[2] Wolfe Lowenthal however says, "At its highest level, receiving energy enters an ineffable realm, where as a result of what Professor (Cheng) calls the practitioner's spiritual enlightenment, he is able to repulse an attacker 'with a look.' The old man stressed that this level of attainment is not magic; it is real and something we can achieve."[3]

Cheng is reported by Smith to have the ability to do tian *xue*, or meridian point striking to injure or kill, but apparently, he did not learn it from Yang Cheng-Fu. As an acupuncturist, masseur, and martial artist, I am inclined to believe that Cheng probably had this technique, although I have not seen any proof that Cheng had used it on anybody. Robert Smith reports that Cheng admitted to not learning the healing part of the art.

When I first read about Cheng Man-Ching, there was no information on how long or what forms he studied with Yang Cheng-Fu. Later on, in the late 1960s I read in the book co-written by Cheng Man-Ch'ing and Robert W. Smith, that Cheng "learned personally from Yang for nearly a decade...."[4] I did not think much about this matter until mid-1996 when I read an article in *Journal of Martial Arts* (Vol. 5, No. 2), titled "In Search of a Unified Tao: Zheng Manqing's Life and Contributions to Taijiquan," by Barbara Davis. She said in a footnote that "there is some confusion about the precise dates of Zheng's study with Yang Cheng-Fu... Zheng himself wrote in his preface to Yang's 1934 book, *Taijiquan Tiyong Quan Shu*, that he was introduced to Yang in Renshan Zhengyue (February 1932) by a Mr. Po Qiucheng. That would place Zheng's period of study with Yang from 1932 until 1936, when Yang passed away. Cheng Weiming's calligraphed preface (dated 1947) to *Zheng's Thirteen Treatises* states that Zheng studied with Yang for six years."[5]

Intrigued by the subject raised by Ms. Davis, I pulled out the other books I had on Tai Chi Chuan to see what they said about this issue. Here are the relevant parts:

> ***" ...friends had introduced him [Cheng] to the great T'ai Chi Ch'uan master Yang Cheng-Fu and he became the last disciple of Master Yang. For six years he studied with Master Yang everyday and his body became healthy and strong."*** —Madame Cheng in her introduction to the book *Cheng Tzu's Thirteen Treatises on T'ai Chi Ch'uan.* The same book says: ***"I [Cheng] followed Professor Yang for seven years..."*** (p. 204)

Mr. Smith, an avid Tai Chi Chuan practitioner and researcher and admirer and student of Cheng Man Ching, seems to have revised "nearly a decade" by saying, about thirty years later, "When Zheng Manqing began learning Taiji from Master Yang Chengfu in Shanghai during the early 1930s...."[6]

In a recent interview in *Tai Chi International* (London), vol. 1 # 3, Master Dong Zheng Chen said, "...my grandfather (Dong Ying Jieh) told me that Cheng Man Ching only trained with Yang Cheng Fu for six months."

Reading the available materials this time around, Mr. Smith's "mystery" statement came up again. I asked myself, If Mr. Smith himself doubts that Cheng studied push hands with Yang Cheng-Fu, then who did he actually study with in the Yang Family? As every martial artist knows, a student does not always study with the head teacher; there are assistants who take over the teaching. Did Cheng learn his push hands from Yang's assistants? It is not a remote possibility, for Yang reportedly had a number of assistant instructors and disciples — among them, Chen Wei-Ming, Tung Ying-Chieh, and Fu Zhongwen, who unfortunately are all dead. I used the word "reportedly" since I do not know the positions of these famous practitioners, who appeared in photographs with Yang Cheng-Fu, in the Yang Family lineage.

There was of course the reclusive Yang Sau-Chung, firstborn and heir of Yang Cheng-Fu who was in his 20s at the time. A quiet, private man, not much is known about him. He is often overlooked by people writing about Tai Chi Chuan, although from his background, he should have been quite a celebrity. He started his Tai Chi Chuan studies when he was seven or eight and finished the curriculum — empty hands and weapons forms and apparently including the old Tai Chi Chuan solo form and secret family techniques — when he was 12 and began assisting his father. When he was 18, he began teaching on his own. Yang Sau-Chung was the primary assistant of his father, and it was he who actually taught a number of famous masters. He was about 29, already a recognized master, when his father died.

Vincent F. Chu, chief instructor at the Gin Soon Tai Chi Club in Boston, and son of the late Gin Soon Chu, who gave me the foregoing details, has perhaps provided a possible clue or perhaps an answer when he quotes Yang Sau-Chung as saying that: (1) it was an influential person, perhaps the mayor of Shanghai, who asked Yang Cheng-Fu to teach Cheng; (2) actually Yang Cheng-Fu refused to teach Cheng; (3) Cheng's father said that Yang could assign somebody to teach Cheng; (4) whenever Cheng approached the older Yang for a lesson, Yang would say, "Song;" and (5) it was he, Yang Sau-Chung, who was assigned to and taught Cheng.

I believe Yang Sau-Chung made these statements. And I have no reason to doubt that he was telling the truth. It is easier to believe that Cheng Man-Ching studied with Yang Sau-Chung instead of Yang Cheng-Fu because from the reports Yang Cheng-Fu appeared to have disliked Cheng Man-Ching. (Else why did Yang knock him out not once but twice?) Besides, from the contradictory statements of the people who knew him, Cheng did not seem to have had a long time to study with Yang Cheng-Fu who died sometime in 1936. Was it between three to four years? Admittedly, a relatively short period of time in an art where training is not in terms of years but decades. (If Cheng did study with Yang Sau-Chung, the training could have continued after Yang Cheng-Fu's death.) And it appears from the reports that during the last years of his life, Yang Cheng-Fu had gained much weight and did not like to teach.

However, from the above statements of Yang Sau-Chung, there is nothing that specifically says that Cheng Man-Ching got his push hands prowess from him. Both Cheng and Yang Sau-Chung are dead. Was there a communication or contact between the two after Yang Cheng-Fu died? Did Cheng ever mention anything about Yang Sau-Chung? If Yang Sau-Chung was Cheng's teacher, has there been any public acknowledgment of this relationship either by the student or the teacher?

Whether or not these statements attributed to Yang Sau-Chung are credible, the fact is that they are worth looking into since the issue of where Cheng studied his legendary push hands technique, raised by his students themselves, is unsettled. Is there anybody out there who can shed further light on this issue?

Like his father, Vincent F. Chu himself studied with Yang Sau-Chung in Hongkong. I understand from Vincent F. Chu that Yang Sau-Chung did not come out with these pieces of information because he was secretive.

Where Cheng Man-Ch'ing learned his powerful Push hands is an interesting historical issue worthy of a treatment in a detective novel. It's an issue that should not diminish the great reputation of Cheng Man-Ching whose contributions to Tai Chi Chuan are enormous. But certainly, the man who taught him the Yang family Tai Chi Chuan should be given credit, too, for helping produce one of the giants of Tai Chi Chuan.

Did Cheng Man-Ch'ing get his Push hands prowess from Yang Sau-Chung?

As Mr. Smith says, "It remains a mystery."

17.

Mantak Chia: Modern Taoist Master and Alchemist

It was nothing much, just a crude little sign with a Buddha image and the words Healing Tao Center and a 3rd floor Bowery walk-up, a small room above a hair salon. When you entered the street entrance and as you walked up, you got a whiff of the chemicals and singed hair.

After I read the books *Awaken Healing Energy through the Tao* and *Cultivating Male Sexual Energy*, I called Mantak Chia, and his secretary directed me to this place in New York's Chinatown for a weekend workshop.

That was the beginning of my involvement in the Healing Tao (now called Universal Healing Tao). It was the early '80s. I had just come back from training in China, and I was not happy with what I learned there — wu shu, which was largely competitive forms with impossible (to me) acrobatic maneuvers and fancy stances. When I saw the two books — now the classics of Taoist yoga in the West — I knew immediately that they were the keys to the new area I wanted to learn, the energetics of the human body, the level of spirituality that I had only read about.

I was not aware of any master teaching it, not in the west, nor in the Philippines where I had studied Shaolin kung-fu, Tai Chi Chuan, and Pa-Kua Chang in the 60s. Microcosmic Orbit Meditation and Taoist Sexual Yoga were considered esoteric subjects not to be taught in public, not even in private, except to a few trusted in-door students. They were not in fact mentioned in the literature that I read in English. In his teachings, Mantak did not allude to any sources in the Taoist canon; apparently, his lessons were direct transmissions from his masters.

Like most everybody, I took the basic courses — Microcosmic Orbit Meditation, Inner Smile, Six Healing Sounds, Healing Love, and Iron Shirt Chi-Kung 1 (Zhan Zhuang) and

3 (Bone Marrow Neigong) at that center. It was the progression of learning that led to the most mystical and secret methods of the Enlightenment of Kan and Li.

A year later, Mantak asked me to join him in a weeklong retreat in northern Massachusetts. From the basics, I proceeded to learn the three levels of Fusion of the Five Elements, Iron Shirt 2 (tendon stretching), and the Tai Chi chi kung 1 (slow form).

In 1985, in one of the workshops in Chinatown, NY he asked me to join the Teacher Training to be held in Big Indian, the Catskill, upstate NY.

Grandmaster Mantak Chia

I did not know much about this young teacher at the time, except that he had studied with a lot of masters whose names appeared in his brochures and books. Some of the teachers were not mentioned because there were too many of them. He boasted of having bought some techniques. "This secret was bought with a house," he would say. What he meant was that it was worth a house. Much of what he was teaching was inaccessible at the time, rare knowledge that was being disseminated publicly for the first time in the West.

Mantak had a unique approach to teaching and learning. He spoke of the energetic centers in terms of their location in the physical body — he was discussing anatomy and physiology, something that nobody perhaps had done before. For the first time, a Chinese master was combining the knowledge of East and West in meditation and chi-kung and spiritual practice. There were illustrations and graphics that clearly defined the anatomical locations of the meridian points he was talking about.

It was a cozy organization with people doing volunteer work or getting study credits for working on the computer or the kitchen. There was a family atmosphere. Early followers of the Healing Tao were Gunther Weil and his late wife Rylin Malone, two Harvard graduates, who added respectability to the operation; Juan Li, a quiet scholar and practitioner, who with his art background, drew the remarkable illustrations of the Transmissions; Michael Winn, a journalist and explorer and scholar; Ron Diana, an extraordinary healer who was grounded in spirituality.

Mantak and Maneewan lived in Huntington, Long Island. Later, they moved to a big ranch house with a large basement annex for office space. Writers and instructors would come and visit and do some work on the manuals and books. Sometimes, they would rely on information from workshops; often also on the notes of Mantak Chia.

There were sleeping quarters adjacent to the office. Mantak himself answered the phone when he was around and answered questions from around the world. It was a surprise to many who did not expect the master to be accessible. He also did computer work, was proud of his know-how and was quite happy to teach.

Writers were hired to produce his manuals. There were likewise volunteers who did writing and editing. Manual after book, book after manual, were written and edited and published.

GM China demonstrating the simplified version of the Heart Sound in the series 6 Healing Sounds that also include the Lung, Kidney, Liver, and Spleen along with various techniques to heal the body and the Shen.

At about that time, Chia began teaching Chi Nei Tsang internal organs massage (it wasn't called massage but chi transformation at the time) and internal alchemy — Lesser Enlightenment of Kan and Li (water and fire).

The student usually started with Microcosmic Orbit meditation, a discipline opening and bridging the two primary meridian channels of the body, the Ren/Jen in the front and the Tu/Du in the back. As practiced in qigong and meditation, these two channels are different from the acupuncture meridians of the same name. Since acupuncture basically addresses the superficial energetic lines, it does not usually go deep. But since qiqong-cum-meditation goes into the profound energy channels and centers, its perception of the Ren and the Tu is profound. Moreover, the terminal and beginning points are different. Ren goes deep in the perineum and probably loops inside the genital organ and the terminates in the tip of the tongue. Tu begins in the perineum and anus area and terminates in the upper palate. I suspect that it loops around to connect to the central channels of kundalini. In the Microcosmic Orbit meditation, these are deliberately bridged and linked when the tongue touches the upper palate and when the perineum and anus are contracted.

GM Mantak Chia with instructors in New York City at the millennium.

From the Microcosmic Orbit, the student may study Taoist Sex/Healing Love Tai Chi Chi Kung 1 (short and slow Tai Chi form emphasizing the internal structure) and Tai Chi Chi Kung 2 (fast form qigong set). Mantak Chia's curriculum includes the Yi Jin Jing, levels he called Iron Shirt 1 (Zhan Zhuang), Iron Shirt 2 (Growing the tendons and sinews), and Iron Shirt 3 (Bone Marrow Neigong). And yet, while the curriculum is clearly set and openly taught, there is always for Mantak Chia a craving to know more. For the man is never content with what he knows. He is always searching for something, always seeking beyond the mystery. During the years that I've known him, he was always studying with a master or testing the effectiveness of a technique or transmission. The master lived in the total darkness of a cave, observing life: Mantak had to know how it was done. So he built his own darkness retreat and practiced Taoist fasting!

The next step is usually Fusion of the 5 Elements (there are three levels of it). Further are the areas of Kan and Li, of which there are also three stages, representing the two cauldrons in the Navel and the Solar Plexus and an intermediate Cauldron in the Heart Center, and Sealing of the 5 Senses. Internal alchemy usually refers to the Kan and Li (Water and Fire) but may indeed include Fusion because internal alchemy involves the mixing or "cooking" process inside the body to transform the basic elements of nature.

As its name implies the Healing Tao emphasized healing — the practices of meditation, qigong, Tai Chi, massage, and nutrition are facets of traditional Chinese medicine. But at the same time, it was slowly moving toward and offering the immortality practices of internal alchemy. The opening of the different channels was just a preparation for the advanced practices of Kan and Li (Water and Fire, Hexagrams #63 and 64, *I Ching*), Sealing of the

Five Senses, Congress of Heaven and Earth and Reunion with God. These teachings were transmitted to Mantak Chia by Yi Yun, One Cloud Hermit, a breatharian and a refugee from the mountains of Central China who had to move to Hongkong to escape the Japanese bombing during World War II.

GM Mantak Chia and students at Rudi's in Big Indian, Catskill, NY in 1989.

Nonetheless, people had a choice of curriculum. For some, the hard chi kung training was a chance to toughen the physical body for martial arts. For others, there were healing techniques — massage and qigong — and spiritual practices.

Mantak and Maneewan Chia with students at Big Indian.

After spending several years in New York, the Healing Tao moved its operations in 1994 to Chiang Mai, Thailand, on a large spread below a dam about 30 minutes northeast from the city. It was a reasonably priced farm, with fruit trees and rice and a stream flowing through it fed by the waters from the dam uphill. It was called Tao Garden.

It is as a teacher that Mantak stands out. His method of creating blocks of information and formulas in a systematic and progressive manner from the most basic to the most complicated, from the foundation knowledge to the high spiritual practices, has become a model in teaching eastern knowledge.

Rene teaching Tai Chi Chuan TaoRen and basic sword to a group from Amsterdam in Chiangmai, Thailand.

While many teachers of Tai chi chuan, for instance, limit their curriculum to its forms, Master Mantak Chia includes significantly substantial materials like sexology,

Grandmaster Mantak Chia of the Universal Healing Tao having dinner at the Tao Garden with guests James McConnell and Rene. James is a disciple of the legendary Grandmaster Wang Liping, hero of the book "Opening the Dragon Gate."

anatomy, Microcosmic Orbit, Yi Jin Jing and Dantian Chi kung, subjects that improve the Tai Chi Chuan forms in terms of power, aesthetics, and qi.

What makes Master Mantak Chia different from many eastern teachers is that he has not projected himself or claimed to be a "spiritual leader" but simply as a master of a technology — a system of formulas and practices that anybody can use for healing, self-realization, and spiritual development. He seems to say, "Here is a curriculum of practices. This can be the road to self-mastery, spiritual independence and perfection." His system embraces different facets, from the simple qigong to the esoteric formulas, addressing the whole human being in a step-by-stem progression. Everything was openly discussed and openly taught. They are transformative: through the alchemy of practice, they can change the serious practitioner physically, energetically, emotionally, intellectually, and spiritually. They are accessible and surprisingly easy to learn. Without exaggeration, I believe they are the backbone of my own practices and life. Whatever it is I am doing, I always return to these transmissions as my dependable friend and companion.

18.

Of Fire and Water: Discovering Internal Alchemy

Early morning in Doi Saket, Chiang Mai, Thailand. Nobody around. At the bridge to the Meditation Hall, I put down the broadsword and the sword and wore my Tai Chi Chuan practice shoes. I could see bats flying over me. Fish were jumping for air in the lake. Reflected on the waters was a full moon. From a distance, I was able to make out the mountains silhouetted against the northern sky. Two years before, I usually heard monks chanting sutras at a temple on a hill nearby. I did not hear them this time. It was extremely quiet. Above me, I could see the Great Bear, the Big Dipper and the Polestar (its equivalent in the physical body is Tian Shu — #25 of the stomach meridian, two inches lateral to the navel, along the edge of the rectus abdominis). I planted my feet on the wooden floor, focused my attention on my Dantian, the Bai-Hui and Bubbling Spring. I breathed slowly and softly from my nose, from my skin, from my bones, my feet, until I established a kind of rhythm. It was the start of my day at the Tao Garden. Alone in the dark, I did my usual routine — several sets of the solo form, staff, broadsword/knife, sword, and Tai Chi Chuan Chang Chuan.

And then the important Taoist meditation-cum-qigong practices of Fusion of the Five Elements and Kan (Water) and Li (Fire). It was primarily the reason why I travelled all the way from New York to Thailand. Mantak Chia was offering the course in Sealing of the Five Senses for the first time at the Tao Garden.

According to Chia's teachings, there are nine stages of immortality practice, from *Greatest Kan and Li: Gathering the Cosmic Light* by Mantak Chia and Andrew Jan.

1. The Inner Smile, 6 Healing Sounds, the Microcosmic Orbit and Chi Kung
2. Sexual Practices including Dual Cultivation
3. The Fusion Practices and the Macrocosmic Orbit (Fusion of 5 Elements 1, 2, and 3)

4. Lesser Enlightenment of Kan/Water and Li/Fire
5. Greater Enlightenment of Kan/Water and Li/Fire
6. Greatest Enlightenment of Kan/Water and Li/Fire
7. Sealing of the 5 Senses
8. Congress of Heaven and Earth
9. Reunion of Heaven and Earth

I don't know exactly when my search for Taoist spiritual practices began. I am not even sure now if I knew, at the beginning, what I was looking for. To put an exact date on the start of my Taoist spiritual quest is impossible. I can say that I took a palpable interest in Chinese culture back when I met Master Johnny Chiuten in the early '60s. His expertise in martial arts and his personal interest in my development awakened and nurtured my growth. That was when I began to read the different literature relating to martial arts. Of course, there was nothing about Kan and Li or the spiritual practices of the Taoists that I can remember coming across.

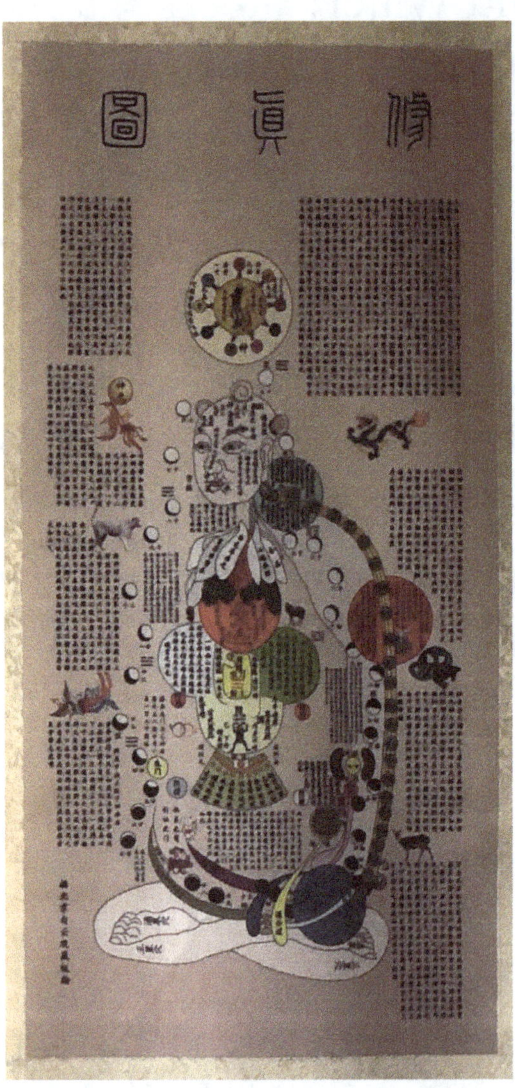

Xiuzhen Tu ("Chart for the Cultivation of Truth or Reality") could be found in the White Cloud Temple in Beijing. It is used as a guide by practitioners of neidan (internal alchemy).

At the Hua Eng Athletic Club in Binondo, where I studied Tai Chi Chuan Yang Family Style in the late '60s, there was an altar, but it was I think Buddhist. Except for lighting joss sticks and kowtowing three times before I practiced, there were no religious liturgies or rituals. I came across the literature later, probably in the late '70s. It must have been Lu Kuan Yu's *Taoist Yoga*. That, as far as I can remember, opened my eyes. I was warned against practicing from a book, but I did, apparently with good results.

Later, back from a martial arts training in China in 1983, I came across the two early books of Mantak Chia — *Awaken Healing Energy Through the Tao,* a manual on the Microcosmic Orbit meditation, and *Taoist*

Secrets of Love and Sex, a book on Tantric practice. I called up the Healing Tao and signed up for the first of my numerous workshops with Mantak Chia. These early workshops were held at a third-floor walk-up on the Bowery, NY Chinatown. It was about a two-hour drive, one way, for me from Pennsylvania.

I would come into the city early in the morning on a Saturday and drive back home late at night. I would do the same thing on Sunday. I came across a description of Kan and Li practice in a catalogue of the Healing Tao, but I was not particularly impressed. I had just dipped my foot in the waters, and I steeped myself in the basic teachings. In 1986, invited by Mantak Chia and Maneewan, his wife at the time, I joined the Teacher Training in Big Indian, New York, and after an intensive examination, was certified to teach Microcosmic Orbit, Inner Smile, Six Healing Sounds, Tai Chi Chi Kung I, Iron Shirt I (Zhan Zhuang), and Healing Love.

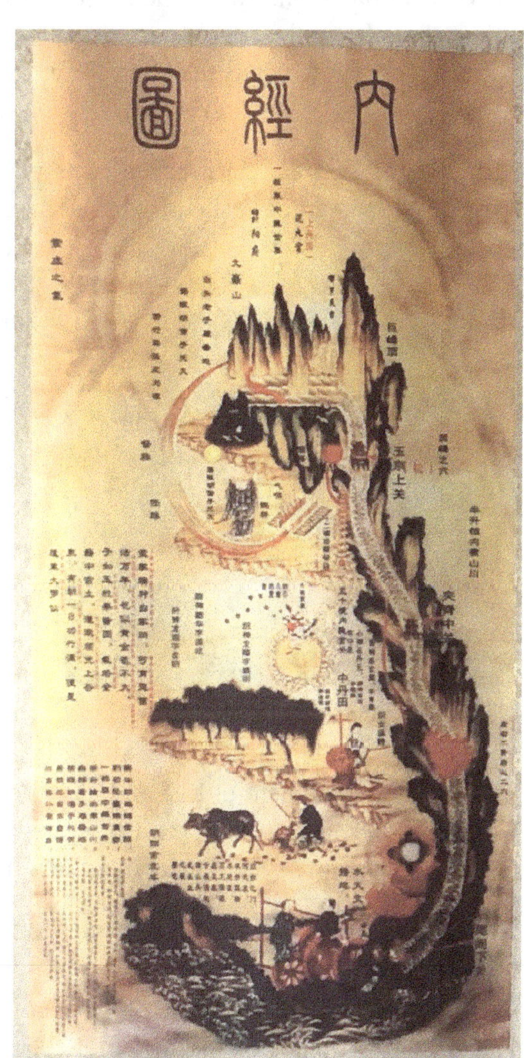

Neijing tu ("Chart of the Inner Landscape of the Human Body or Cosmos") is a guide for practitioners of neidan. Rene was gifted with both the Ziuzhen Tu and the Neijing Tu by his friend Eric Baculinao, former NBC bureau head in Beijing.

It was at this time that I began to seriously consider practicing Fusion of the Five Elements (1, 2 and 3) and then studying the Enlightenment of Kan and Li, the secret and esoteric Taoist formulas of internal alchemy. These transmissions were handed down by Yi Eng, One Cloud Hermit, a refugee from the mountains of Central China to the young Mantak who was studying high school in Hong Kong. Sometimes called White Cloud, he was a Breatharian, one among a few, who did not eat anything, except possibly pine needles and nuts and avoided grains, and who survived on pure mountain air.

When I began to take an interest in Kan and Li internal alchemy practices, there was already existing scholarship about the esoteric practices: Richard Wilhelm's translation of a highly redacted version of *The Secret of the Golden Flower* (with a profound but misleading introduction by Carl Jung), Joseph Needham's encyclopedic *Science and Civilization in China* (Book 5 has a chapter on Kan and Li), and others in French. Later, more translations of the materials from the Taoist canon were made by Thomas Cleary. Still later, more scholars and practitioners began to mention Kan and Li: Eva Wong, Livia Kohn, Kristofer Schipper, Isabelle Robinet, Michael Saso, Nathan Sivin, et al.

WHAT IS KAN AND LI?

In internal alchemy, Kan and Li refer to the polar forces processed in the body. They could refer to sexual energy (water) and heart (fire) or moon (yin) and sun (yang), etc. But on a different energetic plane. (Caveat: My description here is rudimentary and is not meant to be precise and complete). The internal alchemy practice of Kan and Li refers to the union and dissolution of opposite elements in the cauldron within the physical body which aims ultimately to bring the adept to immortality. It follows an almost parallel development as external alchemy, which is the quest for immortality using herbs, minerals, elements, and others.

Each level of Kan and Li practice takes place in a Cauldron. Lesser Enlightenment of Kan and Li (sometimes called Sexual Alchemy) takes place in the Navel Center, Greater Enlightenment of Kan and Li (also called Sun and Moon Alchemy) in the Solar Plexus Center and Greatest Enlightenment of Kan and Li (or Inner Heart Alchemy) in the Heart Center. Each level requires the mixing and dissolution of different ingredients — from the basic sexual energy to the planetary and stellar qi resulting in a higher consciousness and spatial perception.

Among the rice terraces in Bali, Indonesia.

Other alchemical schools practice the three cauldrons or dantian in the navel area (lower), heart (middle), and the head/cryptic room (upper). They do not have a dantian in the solar plexus. From the microcosm of the body in Lesser Enlightenment of Kan and Li, which engages among others the heart/wood and kidney/bladder, and opens and nurtures the meridian pathways, the practitioner moves to the middle dantian / solar plexus and draws the energy of son and moon and others.

The Greatest Enlightenment of Kan and Li (in the Heart Cauldron) is a powerful meditation, achieving purifying and cleansing transformation before the practitioner moves to the Upper Cauldron for further work on the Shen/Spirit. The fourth level takes place in the Crystal Room where the pituitary and pineal glands are located behind the Third Eye. It is at this point that the practitioner draws in the stellar forces — North Star, Big Dipper, 28 Constellations, etc. — and does the practice of Sealing the Five Senses (the thieves — eyes, ears, nose, tongue, and body). It was the last retreat I took in the Tao Garden in Chiangmai. At the time, I was retired and had more time for practice. I had a house in Lake Harmony in the Pocono Mountains in Pennsylvania, and I had started to spend more time there alone. Friends and students visited when invited but I was by myself most of the time doing the practice especially in the dark and outside at night even in Winter.

As I was editing the manual on the Sealing of the Senses, I found a passage in Zhuangzi:

In the stone circle of Mull, an island in the Hebrides in Scotland.

> The emperor of the Southern Sea was Lickety, the emperor of the Northern Sea was Split, and the emperor of the Center was Wonton. Lickety and split often met each other in the land of Wonton, and Wonton treated them very well. Wanting to repay Wonton's kindness, Lickety and Split said, *"All people have seven holes for seeing, hearing, eating, and breathing. Wonton alone lacks them. Let's try boring some holes for him."* So, every day they bored one hole, and on the seventh day Wonton died.[1]

While the senses are valuable in perceiving the outer and inner worlds, the Taoist canon is replete with passages that advise the avoidance of abusing the senses. The senses are considered the gateways to the body and death. If they get abused and weak, they cause the diminution and draining of the organ energy and life. It is then the role of the Taoist practitioner, who seeks longevity and immortality, to seal off the senses and return to the original state of Wonton/Huntun — without holes for the senses. In the Taoist canon, this is part of the Reversal that the Tao Te Ching speaks of in Chapter 40 — the return to the Tao. For the mythical Edenic beginning is associated with Huntun or Pangu — in an egg- or gourd-shaped existence, one whole being, who grows but doesn't age, before everything divides into yin-yang, Three Forces, Five Phases, and the myriad objects (*Tao Te Ching*, 42).

If we can dissolve the polarities and contradictions that are the destiny of every infant's postnatal existence, then we can revert and be born again in a deathless form — as a drop of Spirit in the Ocean of Energy or as an Immortal. The Sealing of the Five Senses formula is based on the Taoist belief that the senses can indeed cause death, that a return to the Tao requires strengthening and sealing them. The idea of Reversal underlies Taoist practice. It was the search for immortality that, most of all, informed all efforts at longevity. In the healing and longevity modalities, it was necessary to balance and harmonize the polar energies of the body. In the immortality practices, it was necessary to dissolve the polarities.

The process of Reversal began with the very first meditative formulas — Inner Smile and Six Healing Sounds, insight meditation that aims to bring to the practitioner stillness and quiet, a dead-wood kind of state that connected the practitioner to himself and the reality of an energetic body. We move from the external world to the inner and learn the continuum and parallels between them. Then it proceeded to the opening of the Microcosmic Orbit and the other channels of energy — conduits of our energy body that were basically wiring the body. Fusion of the Five Elements dissolved the contradictions in the Pa-Kua while Kan and Li dissolved the contradictions in the Cauldrons.

Rene receiving his Kan and Li (Neidan-internal alchemy) instructor's certificate at the Meditation Hall of the Tao Garden in 1997. Left to Right: William U. Wei, Rene, Mantak Chia, and Maneewan Chia.

This is an elegant formula that tries to recapture the Huntun/ Pangu consciousness — a return to a mythic time of innocence. Where did this practice come from? It was one of the inner alchemy transmissions of White Cloud Hermit, according to Mantak Chia. A piece in the Nine Secret Formulas that start with Inner Smile, Five Healing Sounds and Microcosmic Orbit Fusion of the Five Elements and culminates in the Return to the Tao.

The experience of many practitioners underscores the wondrous universe traversed in the journey.

The different disciplines and formulas cover many areas — insight meditation, ecstatic flight, internal alchemy, qigong. These are often combined in practice. Different practitioners include different combinations. How do the alchemy formulas work for Healing Tao students who live in society, working a 9-to-5 job, maintaining a family, doing a myriad odd thing that distract from the practice? To the many practitioners I have talked to who have taken these courses, there is one particular concern and strategy: the development and refinement of the energies — the subtle body — and the nurturing of virtues and our connectedness to each other on this planet.

The practices are basically pursued by Breatharian hermits in the mountains who have no commitments, no relationships, no mundane cares, no jobs; what they have is silence, the earth below and the heaven above, and their single-minded quest of immortality. At this stage for many practitioners, the most important work is on this earth — our evolution as human beings; our relationship with one another; our growth as Taoists; the cultivation of that inner landscape that is the human spirit.

There are two other higher formulas in the spiritual practices of Immortal Tao — Congress of Heaven and Earth and Reunion of Heaven and Man — which Master Chia has not taught at this date. If my experience is any help, the blurb description of the courses in the catalogue cannot do justice to the actual practice.

These formulas are difficult to describe. Even when done in writing, they are hard to follow. That is why they are not explicitly described in the literature. At best, they are concealed in alchemical jargon. The literature is so couched in esoteric terms that, unless you have studied with a master, it is almost impossible to learn the practices from books. Needless to say, a qualified teacher is needed to traverse the dangerous terrain of Kan and Li internal alchemy. There are many hazards along the way.

One of the aims of Kan and Li is to give birth to the Immortal Fetus through the copulation of Yin and Yang in the body of the adept. The Immortal Fetus is nourished with energies from within the body and without, grows, attains its own consciousness, and becomes capable of independent existence — it is an indescribably intricate process. Each step is fraught with risks, thus needing a master guide. The practitioner can get lost along the way — or the Shen can drift away from the moorings of the physical body during ecstatic flight or star travels.

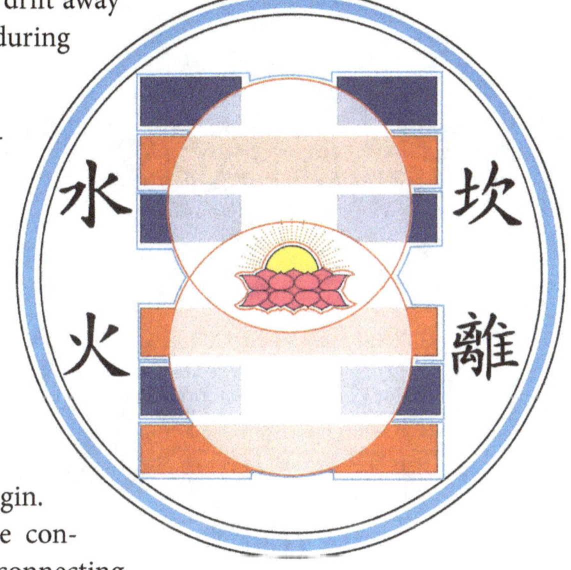

Fire and Water Trigrams

Always, it is obligatory to refine the energies, dissolve the polarities, cultivate the emotions, and educate the senses in discrimination and detachment. Strictly speaking, much of the work happens in the microcosm of the human body but, like coitus in dual cultivation, it could transpire on the upper plane above the Bai Hui/Crown.

Some of the techniques are shamanic in origin. They involve ecstatic flight, blending the consciousness with nature and the Universe, connecting to guardian spirits and animals, and going beyond the physical body. In the Taoist canon and in paintings, there are Taoist immortals flying on the back of dragons, Taoist breatharians (like One Cloud Hermit) on mountain tops subsisting only on air and pine needles, Taoist monks seated in meditation while their Spirits are wandering in the space above them.

In 1987, Master Chia asked me to write the manual of the Greater Enlightenment of Kan and Li. It was both flattering and humbling to be so chosen because Kan and Li is one of the most abstruse and important practices of esoteric Taoism. Internal alchemy formulas have been well -guarded secrets in the long tradition of Taoism. I attended the 2-month retreat in Big Indian, Catskill Mountains, NY, which included Basic Practices, Chi Nei Tsang, Fusion of the Five Elements, Tai Chi Chi Kung, Lesser Kan and Li, Greater Kan and Li. and Greatest

Kan and Li. There were about fifty students. Mantak Chia said that there was the Healing Tao stage — disciplines that helped students to heal themselves or others and to promote longevity. Now, he wanted to emphasize the Immortal Tao stage — the spiritual practices that travelled the road to Taoist immortality.

When I studied the materials — many videos, notes, lectures, illustrations — I realized that in Kan and Li one of the central practices and at the heart of the system was the concept of reversal or inversion. That is, since Fire is above Water in the human body, it is necessary to reverse their positions. This is suggested by Hexagrams #64 (Wei Chi/Before Completion) and #63 (Chi Chi/ After Completion) of the *I Ching*. (There are other hexagrams in the *I Ching* as well as trigrams in the Early Heaven and Later Heaven Pa-Kua that play a crucial role in internal alchemy). Reversal is likewise suggested or mentioned in many sections of the Taoist canon. There are several paradoxical chapters in Lao Tzu that indicate the Taoist concept or reversal — not just philosophical of academic concepts but actual yogic, meditative and qigong work. Among them:

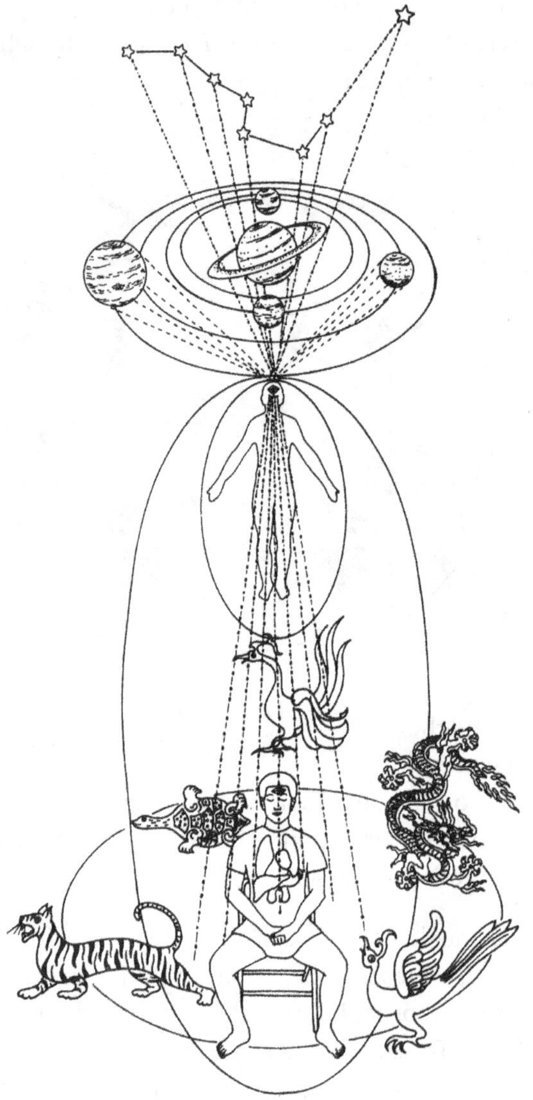

Chapter 6

The Valley Spirit never dies.
It is the Eternal Female.
In being used, it is not exhausted.

Chapter 40

"Reversal" is the movement of the Tao.

Chapter 42

The Way gave birth to the One.
The One gave birth to the Two.
The Two gave birth to the Three;
And the Three gave birth to the ten thousand things.

Many of the disciplines of the Taoists reverse the usual direction of nature. We can see it in the tantric practices, for instance, where Ching (sexual energy) is not allowed to drain but is

Maintaining awareness of all sources of energy

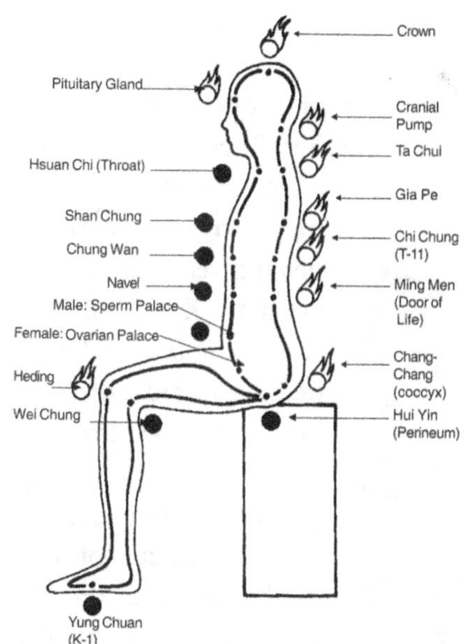

Pathway of the Microcosmic Orbit

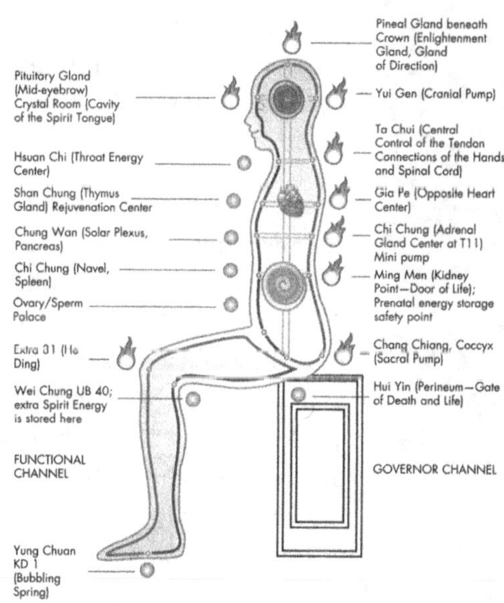

Energy circulating in the Microcosmic Orbit

re-directed upwards to the organs, senses, and the brain or in qigong, where the breath is sealed or inverted.

In Sealing of the Five Senses, we reverse the process again. We revert to the state of Hundun and attain primordial consciousness, the Uncarved Block. Sealing the Senses, the opening of which (in Chapter 7 of *Chuang Tzu*) resulted in Hundun's death, is necessary for the Spirit/Shen to Travel unobstructed in Space. There is so much more in the internal alchemy practices that I haven't mentioned. Suffice it to say for our present purpose that the work is indescribably wonderful and ethereal. Much more than Tai Chi Chuan, qigong, and meditation, internal alchemy is to meet the ultimate experience in life. It is the apotheosis of the whole Taoist search.

*****

I've heard so many commentaries about Taoism, lectures, and writings by scholars.

What they offer can help interpret Taoist literature from a philosophical and academic viewpoint: but it is not complete. It is the Yin of Theory without the Yang of Practice. With respect to scholars and academics, the problem with an intellectual reading of Taoist materials is that practice is the foundation of the literature. Taoist study requires actual application, you must work in the internal universe of the physical body — balancing this and that chi, controlling this or that energy, seeding this or that organ. In certain instances, you follow the Pa-Kua or the cycle of the Five Elements or the seasons. Much of what the writings say has a corresponding meditative and qigong formula. For instance, when the *Tao Te Ching* speaks of the Eternal Woman being the gate of heaven and earth in Chapter 6, it refers to a long tradition of yogic practices. When Zhuangzi speaks of the butterfly and dreaming, there is likewise a practice that is alluded to. There are many examples from the literature. That is why words in Taoism do not count for much.

In my experience and research, I realized that a quest can go through a process of development and evolution, perhaps defining a hierarchy of studies. There are the foundation disciplines — physical and energetic exercises, nutrition and dietetics, martial arts — which may also be meditative and/or healing regimen. Then, there are the higher healing and fusion formulas. And at the top of the pyramid are the spiritual practices — whatever they are called — involving the growth of virtues, the transformation and refinement of energies, the balancing of the different qi in the body, the cultivation of the Shen, and ultimately the mystical Return to the Source as the formulas " dissolved" the polarities in the body. It is a long, difficult journey requiring commitment, openness, and dedication to practice and study.

Supreme Unknown Alchemy

Like the quest of an art, internal alchemy is fraught with uncertainty demanding many years of lonely Work and may include solitary existence and ascetic life as a renunciate. There is a tremendous amount of standing and sitting that require patience and stamina; that may be the reason why Zhan Zhuang (standing post postures), stationary yoga-like postures done for a long time, are taught as a foundation. But there are ineffable moments of light and beauty, many of them coming almost every time one practices.

My colleagues, like Michael Winn and Andrew Jan, who have done the work longer than I have, describe their experiences with wonder and amazement. They travel through space like the adepts we read about. They come back from their meditation with bright eyes and auras. I practice slowly and deliberately. Unlike many practitioners, I prefer to stay close to earth and within the boundaries of my physical body. I am very careful and reverential when I approach the higher spiritual materials. It is sacred ground. Often, I am happy just to work on basic and foundation regimen — Inner Smile, Six Healing Sounds, Microcosmic Orbit, Circadian and Eight Psychic Channels and Fusion of the Five Elements, qigong, and Taoyin exercises.

Some people study martial arts — often the fighting aspect of it, sometimes it is healing and meditative aspects and go no further. Others start with healing and energetic practices and move on to the spiritual. Still others begin with spiritual practices and then pursue martial and qigong practices.

Many just dabble with the basic regimen and are satisfied with it or perhaps they would hop from one discipline to another never quite commit themselves to anything. There is no fixed route. I've seen the varied lot of humanity. Everybody takes his own road — to the top, sometimes, or not at all.

I don't like to sound ungrateful or arrogant. I wish to acknowledge that there are scholars who are actually practitioners. To list a few:

1. Kristofer Schipper, author of *The Taoist Body* (originally in French), is also an ordained Taoist priest in Taiwan. I met him at Harvard University during the international conference on Ecology and Taoism, where he was the keynote speaker and I read a paper on Taoist practice.
2. Michael Saso, a former Jesuit, is likewise a practitioner, and author of *Taoist Master Chang*. He spends his time travelling in China visiting Taoist temples and monasteries. He has written a few books about Taoism.
3. Eva Wong has a doctorate in oriental studies, is a famous practitioner of internal alchemy, who has written the best book on Feng Shui and translated internal alchemy materials.

19.

Thunder Path in Huangshan

Huang-shan!
Huang-shan!
Huang-shan!

—after a Japanese haiku

There's more in the rabbit hole! David Shen Verdesi

October 31, 2007, Hangzhou:

We've come down from the Autumnal climate of Huangshan/Yellow Mountain, Anhui Province, China, where for two weeks we trained in the foundations of the Thunder Path under David Shen Verdesi and his Xing Shen Zhuang Fa assistant the Turkish model, Gonca Denizmen.

We came here to celebrate with other students from Singapore, Russia, and US. They had just arrived in the ancient city of Hangzhou from Tienmu Mountain, celebrated by Li Po in his farewell poem. In the intermittent rain of a Chinese Indian Summer, almost like an incipient fog in its softness, we made a pilgrimage to the temple dedicated to Gou/Ge Hong, the Taoist alchemist, military strategist, and author of *Pau Po Tzu* ("The Master Who Embraces Simplicity"), and in dreamlike euphoria, we just had a great time, despite the damp, in the restaurants and cafes on legendary West Lake.

You should see the hundreds of practitioners doing their routines in the mist amid the willow trees at dawn! From my room at the Hyatt, the view was striking, the kind of scenery that Du-Fu would have romanticized in his poetry.

Hangzhou was the retreat of emperors, poets, artists, officials, and generals because of its landscapes and quiet, but it is now like a beehive, buzzing with cars and tourists, and commerce, with daunting constructions all over town. The only good time to see the famous lake is late at night or at dawn when you'll see a solitary man doing his Tai Chi Chuan routine in the dark.

November 11, 2007, USA:

Now, after a week at David's pied-a-terre in Dalian, China, I am back in the US, and I am looking in retrospect at that mystical period on Huangshan. I told David I would write about him, but he said he's still young, wait until something more happens, and so I decided to write about the journey itself as I saw it.

My wife, Lolit on our first day at Huangshan, arguably the most beautiful mountain in all of China. We climbed different peaks, posed for photos, and loved the too brief time there.

A truly astonishing surprise was that two hermits (they'll remain nameless here to preserve their privacy and anonymity), Buddhist masters, descended their cave and joined us for a few days in our hotel. One was the Grandmaster who was 118 years old and the other — "Uncle Master" we called him — was 100. The GM, we heard, had been living in caves for the last 80 years. His teacher died two years ago at 180.

We visited them in their summer mountain sanctuary about an hour by car from our hotel. From the paved highway we entered a stony road negotiating a long ascent to the top and parked in front of a solitary house. We walked to a waterfall up to the entrance on which was carved the Chinese characters for "Cave of the Immortals" I believe. I recognized the character for "xian" — a man and a mountain — which is translated usually into "immortal" in English. The long dark passage was lit with hundreds of candles like a scene from a Hollywood movie. Immediately, even without the theatrical effect, you knew this was a power vortex. At the rear of the cave, we saw the GM and Uncle Master meditating on a rock ledge in front of a wall with Chinese inscriptions.

After the amenities, everyone gathered in front of the house. We were given a sample of the root the hermits ate: it was like a yam but inside it had the consistency of a rope, all dry pulp and fibers. The GM and Uncle Master posed for pictures with the group and a solo one with David. It was the fourth time David had met the GM.

A few years ago, the GM told Jiang sifu (age 43) that a westerner will come and should be accepted as a disciple in the lineage. David wrote to me a long e-mail about his acceptance into the fold, about the different masters who came down from the mountains and temples to attend his initiation led by the Grandmaster, and the different feats that were exhibited at the ceremony.

David Verdesi and Rene after practicing the Dragon Tiger Fujian Temple Kungfu form "Red Boy Praying to the Goddess of Mercy" outside the Meditation Hall of the Tao Garden in 1997.

It was also the Grandmaster who predicted a month before our training in Huangshan that David will succeed this year in achieving Yin Yang Gong, the ability to emit "electricity" in his body like John Chang, the legendary Magus of Java.[1]

I am ahead of myself in the chronology of events. On our arrival in Huangshan, tired from our long journey, we were welcomed by Jiang sifu, disciple of the Grandmaster and David's immediate teacher. It was the first time most of us had met him. He was also tired and had just come from Malaysia and had driven four hours from the airport. He wanted to perform an empowerment and blessing ceremony for us. He asked us to sit on the floor, with our palms facing up. He cracked his fingers, grunted a few times, and made some movements that looked like a sequence from a Tai Chi Chuan form (Brush Knee and Push). Nothing much seemed to happen, but in an instant, we tasted a honey-like secretion (ambrosia) in our mouths and throats. The ordinary bottled water turned into a sweet drink (speaking of holy water!). Our fingers were coated with the same sweet substance. It was all done from a distance with Jiang Sifu's powerful qi. Believe it or not, just to prove it wasn't a fluke, we licked somebody's finger to his embarrassment. I was naturally skeptical, so I went to the bathroom: My urine tasted sweet too. I told Philip, a British hypnotist: when he came back from the bathroom, he said his pee tasted sweet. Even the next day, after we showered and washed our hands, the sweet taste remained. Jiang sifu did the ceremony a few times during our visit and even sent us off with a few bottles each.[2]

To see to it that everybody was fit to undertake the training, Sifu also gave us regular treatments with qigong, Chinese acupuncture, and herbs. It was the most sophisticated and well-rounded Chinese medicine practice I had ever seen anywhere in my years of Oriental medical studies. The skills that we had found awesome were being used for healing: Sifu was drawing blood without lancets, just with his qi, diagnosing illnesses and deficiencies with his Third Eye and his "electricity" and moving qi with his palm. He would hold your hand and send his qi into your body. If you have stagnation or blockage, he will tell you and suggest a treatment. He prescribed herbs and dan/pills/elixir and herbal tonics to students who needed them. I had five special dan/pills in one session.

At the hotel, on the second or third day of our training, the two ancients did some awesome demos — pyrokinesis, telekinesis, etc. —moving objects, projecting heat, burning paper, withering a plant, among others — from a distance of 10 to 20 feet. I can't believe that these Immortals/xian — perhaps that is what they are called in China — exist.

Like other skeptics in the group, I tried to see if there were any tricks. It was as close to laboratory conditions as one could make out. Other skills were shown, and I can see their healing and spiritual purpose, but I do not think I should spend any more time describing them here because they were so mind-boggling, they can distract from their real goal.

As the Grandmaster predicted, David passed his test for Yin Yang Gong by demonstrating his ability on 12 of us. Yin Yang Gong is considered in the tradition as a significant step towards mastery and immortality.

It was a very touching, and dramatic, moment for David, perhaps the crowning achievement at this point in his more than 15-year search that started when he was a young teenager looking for masters among the waiters and chefs in the Chinese restaurants in Rome. Seeing David succeed in passing Yin Yang Gong, the past flashed in front of me: I recalled times he and I spent together over the years, his search for the authentic masters, the focus he committed to his journey, the obstacles he had to encounter and overcome, the heartbreak of rejection, the cruelty of skeptics, the loyal support he received from his friends and students.

I had known David since he was 16 in early '90s when he used to join me at dawn for martial arts practice at Healing Tao retreats in upstate NY, and later, at the Tao Garden in Chiangmai, when I knocked on his door at 4 or 5 am to wake him up to work out on a Shaolin form called "Red Boy Praying to Guanyin." It wasn't the form he really wanted to learn; he asked for "Dragon Tiger", but I told him "10 years." Over the years we met in New York or in Chiangmai, always training together with materials we had learned from different masters. He shared techniques he had learned such as Drunken Qigong, Empty Force, Ba Shen Qigong, Jin Shui, and Xing Shen Zhuang Fa, among others. I showed him

Shaolin forms from Sigong Lao Kim and Sifu Johnny Chiuten (from my training in the 60s) and Traditional Yang Family Tai Chi Chuan forms I studied with Master Gin Soon Chu of Boston (in the 90s). David and I shared some parallels in our search for authentic teachings, and we did not even realize that we were both dragons.

I had attended David's seminars and retreats as his guest in Chiangmai several times. The first lessons in 1999 were from the period of his encounter with Da Zhen, a hermit in northern China, the second in 2000 was on Xing Shen Zhuang Fa. Once it was with one of his teachers Professor Wang Ting Jun, covering the subject Xing Shen Zhuang Fa, too. In Istanbul (2004), he covered neigong aspects of the Thunder Path. I had seen photographs of his masters on his altar in his home along the Bosphorus in Turkey and was impressed. I was invited to attend his seminars in Yunnan, Bangkok, Denmark, and Koi Samui. I wanted to go, but for one reason or another, mostly financial (retired pensioner in 2002), I could not make it. Come to China and stay with me, he said, be my guest, I have a room for you, he e-mailed from Shanghai.

When he mentioned Huangshan, I perked up: I toured the mountain two years ago in late summer or early autumn, explored the peaks and panoramas during the day and night, at dawn I watched the magnificent sunrise, and practiced qigong and Tai Chi Chuan in isolated spots and fell madly in love with it. There weren't any visible temples but there were caves and huts for hermits. It was another power vortex with the high, but different, vibration I had felt in the pyramids and temples of Egypt, Stonehenge, Mount Banahaw south of Manila, and the Iao Valley in Maui, among others. You enter the frequency of the spot, and you are swept into something powerful and mystical and unforgettable. There are contradictory stories, but the legendary Yellow Emperor/Huangdi was supposed to have ascended in broad daylight on one of the peaks. Huangshan was the most exhilarating journey I had taken in my years of traveling in China, which included a three-day train ride down from Shanghai to Cheng-Du in 1983, a cruise down the Yangtze from Chongqing through the three Gorges in 2005 to the Great Dam, the Great Wall, and Beijing, Hangzhou, Shanghai, Suzhou, Chengdu, and Xian are mythic cities of my imagination. So, when the invitation came, I said yes without any hesitation.

David Verdesi, Rene, and Lee Holden at the Tao Garden in Chiangmai, Thailand in 2002.

It turned out when we arrived in the city that it wasn't the same place that mesmerized me before in an earlier incarnation. It was in Anhui Province, true, but it was on one of those foothills that ringed the mountain range. The small city had one hotel, a post office, a hospital, an internet café, and the usual outlets for goods — clothes, sneakers, jewelry, arts, and crafts — and a park in the process of renovation. There was little traffic (mostly motorcycles) and pollution, dogs roamed looking for food. We often went to a restaurant where they served venison, rabbit and lamb, good protein for our intensive training program. There was the occasional saffron-robed Buddhist monk wandering the streets. There was noticeably the absence of western tourists because there was really nothing much to see. It wasn't the place we all had expected, it wasn't even close.

Magus of Java photo with family.

We were all puzzled to be there because we had expected high, cloud-covered peaks, dangerous cliffs, and gnarled pine trees — and isolation from the known world. There was a reason however why Jiang sifu chose the place: its proximity to the mountain cave of the Grandmaster. It was just slightly more than an hour away by car.

Under the guidance of David, we practiced Sheng Zheng Gong every day together as a group (there were 13 of us from different parts of the world). He guided us through different aspects of the meditation for several hours each day. David covered many subjects, regaling us with stories of the masters he had met and studied with, and introduced us to the foundations of the Thunder Path. Gonca led us in the contortions of Xing Shen Zhuang Fa, a series of isolation movements that were meant to open energy centers on the "lightning path" of the Ren and Du Mai, the ancestral channels, create the condition for the development of the dantian and combined with the internal Sheng Zheng Gong, lead to the experience of the Golden Flower and with grace, to the Cultivation of the Heart. The training covered a very simple procedure on the surface, but to me it was a surprising way to, among others, a deep song… a word invariably translated as relaxation, but means much, much more, a combination of letting go, surrender, wu-wei and faith.

Early in the morning or late at night, I practiced alone or with David and Gonca on the rooftop of the hotel or in a park. David and Gonca practiced routines of their own. We were planning to work together on some forms. We brought our Tai chi swords from Shanghai but I was able to teach them only the introductory movements of the Yang Family Tai Chi Chuan sword because so many exciting things were happening at the same time. I did the personal Tai Chi Chuan sword form of Yang Cheng-Fu that choreographs the search for immortality — shades of Taoist Immortal Lu Dong Bin!

David reminded me, "Dragon Tiger… it's 10 years now." I remembered the promise I made in Chiangmai, and we started the form, but so much was happening, and I felt he had so much on his plate — Shaolin kung-fu forms did not seem to be the most important on the list.

GM Xuan Kong, as he came out of the Immortal's Cave where he lived and walked to the join the group led by David Verdesi in October 2007. The hermit initiated David as a disciple sometime after the millennium in Shangrila, somewhere in Yunnan, China.

Gonca, a professional model in her early 20s, is from Turkey. The first time I met her was on my second visit to Istanbul. I taught her movements called Plum Blossom 8, Twin Dragons Chasing the Pearl and White Crane Stretches its Wings at the time. It was gratifying to see her practicing them in Huangshan every day, three years later.

David was given several dan/pills, the size of a *da zhao*, a red date, and herbal tonic every day during our training. His qi was locked by Jiang sifu in a procedure that snapped the tendons and looked painful. At the end of our training, his dantian was locked too: he was warned not to do anything that would use his gong for a period of 6 months at which time he will be tested again for the next, higher stage of his training. It was all a very elaborate grooming for a young disciple of the Thunder Path.

I do not think much is known about the obscure, mysterious and secretive tradition of the Thunder Path, sometimes called Lei (Thunder) Shan (Lightning) Tao (Path). The Chinese god of Thunder is called Lei Kung (half-man and half-bird) perhaps derived from an Indian avian god. Oral tradition reveals different threads running through much of Thunder Path's unverifiable history. We hear about Mo-Tzu as the founder and Damo of Shaolin, and the author of the monkey epic *Journey to the West*, or Zhang San Feng, the legendary creator of Tai Chi Chuan, being associated with the Thunder Path.

The lineage (or lineages for there are several different schools) seems to disappear and go underground, and then reappear as the transmission is revealed through a mysterious manual, a strange master, an epiphany, or a mystical experience.

One of the last public manifestations I think is John Chang of Java, who studied as a child with Liao Sigong, an old, mysterious and superhuman Chinese master who was supposed to have given him a book of the 72 levels of expertise! This tradition calls its lineage the Mo-Pai, after Mo-Tzu, who lived about 2500 years ago, a contemporary of Confucius and Lao Tzu.

In the early 90s or late 80s, a couple of documentarians (Lawrence and Lorne Blair) traveling through Indonesia chanced upon John Chang (not his real name), filmed his demonstrations, Kostas Danaos wrote a book about him entitled, *The Magus of Java: The Teachings of a Taoist Immortal*, and the rest is, well, history.[3]

There are other masters of the tradition, I discovered, but they are anonymous, preferring to stay in the background. According to David, Lei Shan Tao is one of at least six paths to immortality which include, among others, Jin Dan Tao, Yang Shen Tao, and Tong Ling Tao. Jiang Sifu's lineage is traced back to Damo, the legendary Indian monk-priest who was supposed to have settled in the Shaolin Temple, faced a wall for 10 years, received the manual of the teachings from an ancestor and left the transmissions of the Muscle and Tendon Changing (Yi Jin Jing) and Washing the Bone Marrow (Xi Sui Jing) neigong (internal work) and the Golden Bell Qigong *(Jin Zhong Zhao).*

I had read the book, *Magus of Java*, an admirable pioneering work in the field, several times. It was as much a book about John Chang as it was about Kostas Danaos, the author had interjected himself into the story so much, it was close to being tedious. I was not exactly dismissive of the story, but like many people I was skeptical. I thought, how can anybody set a ball of newspaper on fire with his qi, stop a bullet from an air gun with his palm, thrust a chopstick into a two-inch board, or talk to the spirits of the ancestors, among other unbelievable things? It defied rationalization and science. I had finished reading *Magus* while I was teaching in Amsterdam at the millennium. In 2005 I was in Istanbul as a guest of David Verdesi when I heard him saying, "Sifu, Sifu," on the phone. I asked him, Who is that? He said, "The Magus of Java." I want to see him, I said.

In 2006, David invited me to Java to meet John Chang, the Magus and Thunder Path master himself. I thought it was a chance to verify the truth for myself. The day before my departure, my granddaughters and I got caught in the Winter rain during the Chinese New Year celebration in New York City. I fell sick with the flu the next day as I left for Indonesia via Frankfurt and Singapore.

I was terribly depleted and feverish when David picked me up at the airport. For several days, I tried to recover with doses of Yin Qiao but it was futile against the bug that had penetrated the interior. David introduced me to the Magus. The Magus suggested I should see a western physician. A friend took me to his uncle, a doctor, who prescribed a regimen of antibiotics.

Almost every day we went to see the Magus. There were always people waiting, some just to be there, others to get treatment, a few stayed for lunch. I was astonished to meet a thoroughly unassuming man my height, perhaps even with my looks, who was wearing rubber flipflops, a white tee-shirt and shorts. It was as if another man materialized in front of me. He was not what I had expected. I had fantasized about somebody else for almost 10 years, somebody with extraordinary energy and presence. Now, for the first time I looked into the deep, gentle, and imperturbable eyes of this master. He was not different from you and me. He smoked, had a large family, attended a Christian church, ran a prawn farm, got sick like any of us (but recovered fast).

Upon David's request, the master demonstrated his gong/expertise to me. He asked me to touch his forearm and I was shocked: electrocuted is probably the most accurate way to describe it. I had never seen — or felt — anything like it in my more than 40 years of searching. An electricity-like vibration shook me to my core.

I was instantly convinced. Out of fear perhaps I did not seek any other proof. He said it was only 5% of his power. He told me to touch his Chi Hai/Sea of Chi/CV 6 and I felt the same electrical jolt. He put his forefinger on my Chi-Hai, and I felt waves of electricity going through my whole body. When he tested my dantian, he said it was 20% full. I did not know if I should be happy or embarrassed.

The Magus' powerful skill, as far as I know, has never been used by him to harm or injure anybody (although I have, like others, thought of the possibilities and consequences in a fight) but to heal. (Well, there are stories about his exploits when he was very young.) Many patients from around the world have entered his clinic. During my visit, the next few weeks, he treated me — successfully — with acupuncture for a serious rotator cuff injury and a painful ankle. When Chang sifu manipulated the needles, the pain was so excruciating, it was like somebody stuck my finger into an electrical socket, even though somebody (Ana, David's girlfriend) was standing barefoot holding my arm to ground me. I have honestly never seen anything like it in my life as an acupuncturist. I asked about payment; I was told the master never did charge for his acupuncture services or his teachings.

During my stay in Java, the friends of David — students and relatives of the Magus — showed me their martial art called Pa Lei Chuan (Eight Thunder Fist), a part of Lei Shan Tao, and I found it very economical and effective. I was a dinner guest at their home, I did not expect such hospitality, and I was even more surprised to witness this secretive style.

Meantime, David continued teaching me the basic foundations of Thunder Path — the different strains of the lineage, the vocabulary of the practice, trajectory/pathways of the work, the essentials of establishing the dantian and stillness, timetable for the different techniques, among others — lessons which started when I attended his seminar in Istanbul earlier. I took notes, practiced the pieces he gave me, and promised to pursue the art into the rabbit hole in the years to come!

Before we left Indonesia, David and I went to the Magus to say goodbye. We sat at his clinic, a small one-room affair, with a treatment table on each side, acupuncture diagrams on the wall, and a wooden bench with holes — purportedly bored with chopsticks by the master. There was something I had wanted to ask him, a question that had been playing on my mind since I read about him in Amsterdam about 14 years ago. I begged permission and asked: How do I start? His answer was quick and final: Sit down and meditate. That's it? I said to myself. I was disheartened. No technique, just sit down and meditate. Here I was at the threshold of probably the most powerful and promising transmission I had ever seen

Rene and friends at Huangshan, Hangzhou, China.

David, Rene and Gonca with other students in Tiandi/Heaven and Earth in Xihu/West Lake, Hangzhou.

in my 40-year journey through many masters and systems and countries, and the master told me to sit down and meditate. What did I have to do? What did I have to meditate on? I thought I was grasping at straws.

David had seen many of the Magus' powers and concluded it was not just "magic" or illusion. The man was real. I trusted David because I knew he was like me, willing to go out of the way to find true knowledge. Sometimes, when he heard about a "master," he would check their reputation and verify what it was they had. He would pay tuition and seriously study. He would test if they had "gong" or if they had spiritual development or whatever their skills were. Needless to say, he was disappointed often ... and it cost him money and time. Imagine traveling to a distant place, spending on fare, food, hotel, and gifts, waiting for days to see a master one has heard of, and being told that you have no *shen* and to come back in a year or two. He went to see a famous master in Southeast Asia, paid his tuition, took the lessons, and later asked for a demonstration. "There was nothing there," David sadly said about it. But there were other astounding experiences — of masters who could walk through walls, leave the imprint of their palm on concrete, or manifest their *yang shen* in the real world. "There seems to be no boundaries for these masters," David commented.

I am not surprised that through his persistence, he found the authentic master teachers — like Jiang sifu, the Grandmaster and his younger companion, and Grandmaster Wang Liping, the subject of the biography, *Opening the Dragon Gate: The Making of a Modern Taoist Wizard*, and others.

After the two-week intensive in Huangshan, everybody dispersed, some went to Beijing, others to Tienmu Mountain. David, Gonca and I took a taxi to Hangzhou, a 5-hour ride, to fly back home. Jiang sifu was with his assistants in the other car and we followed them. When we said goodbye, it was a moment of mixed emotions. Jiang sifu and David embraced, one seeker from the East, the other from the West, two links in a continuum of tradition, brothers belonging to this mystical lineage that goes back perhaps a thousand years or more but is only beginning to attract disciples from outside of China. Through the rest of the route, we fell into a profound quiet as we dwelled on what had happened, what perhaps was a milestone in the history of the East-West relationship.

Just as we arrived at our destination, David broke the silence and said, "Rene, why don't we spend the night in Hangzhou to celebrate?"

Rene got a sample of the root that the hermits ate in Huagnshan: it was almost all fiber. We were told they ate nothing else. Xuan Kong was a Breatharian, i.e., he drew his sustenance from the pure mountain air around him.

December 21, 2007/Winter Solstice:

It was an incredible journey for me. I learned many new things, met a bunch of wonderful people — searchers all — from different parts of the world, and of course saw those awesome masters.

It is clear from what I have seen and read that the secrets of China are still around, kept in hidden spots, perhaps in caves by hermits, that what we see in the parks, temples and training halls is only the tip of the iceberg, that there are masters out there who carry the real transmissions. Maybe one day, perhaps in the next incarnation, we will be lucky enough to have a glimpse of and understand and learn the awesome powers and spiritual achievements of these exceptional beings.

At the same time, it is important for me, as well as for others, to take those astounding demos not so much in terms of power but in the context of healing, spiritual development and transformation, and the potential of the human being. As David said, we should see beyond the obvious impact of the demonstrations: they are meant partly to satisfy the need for concrete proof of human possibilities and partly as a basis for scientific verification of a person's attainment. I do not know if I am quoting David correctly, but he did say that we need something more substantial than claims of mastery and achievement.

In passing, it should be mentioned that, during the two weeks, we witnessed only about two hours of demonstrations. One healing session up in the mountain took the old masters about three hours (including interruptions) transferring Qi from 14 bulls to three of us. It was the most unusual and most talked about and controversial healing technique I have ever seen, and I was one of its lucky beneficiaries.[4] The healing sessions with Jiang sifu must have taken at least 10 hours at different intervals while the training took at least 6 to 7 hours a day.

Demonstrations usually bore me. Still, I cannot deny I was impressed with the exhibitions. Who wouldn't? These after all were not your break-a-bottle-with-the-fist or lift-200-

pounds-from-your-genitals type. They are not your everyday feats of strength done in a circus atmosphere. For me, at my age, what I want to pursue is training in — stillness and clarity — perhaps, in the cultivation of the heart. I don't know what it may entail, I do not know its consequences, I am still at that stage when I am exploring the different paths. Searching for peace and quiet within is probably the most difficult quest in the world because the senses and the mind are always picking up something, always being ambushed by desires and thoughts. The way to emptiness is full of obstacles because the world is teeming with temptations and the inner self is itself a constant battlefield.

GM Xuan Kong (in red) with Master Jiang Feng (to his left) and students just outside the Cave of the Immortals.

Of course, power is important — imagine what a person with a pure heart can do with it — but it can also fall into the wrong hands. Responsibility goes with skills. Love — and healing — should be the foundation of life. There is too much meanness and cruelty and egotism, even in everyday life, not much patience, acceptance, forgiveness, and accommodation. Like success, fame and fortune, power can distract us from our intended and true goals — our destiny — on earth. We have seen masters who have been derailed from their intended mission because they were blinded by the blandishments of the world or misled by their own greed; and those who seek power often get bogged down in showing off and blatant exhibitionism. Either way, the route of power, unless guided by a pure intention, is invariably vain and corrupting.

David emphasized the need for "prayers," or an attitude of reverence and wonderment for the sacred in our lives. Whatever it is we believe in, he said in Huangshan, we must honor the divine. We are indeed just like the shamans in the Chinese character for ling or spirit—we can only mediate between heaven and earth to bring down the blessings and grace from above.

I don't know if I can describe the journey completely. The amazing talents of the masters, the hospitality of the people, the camaraderie of the students, the incomparable training. All I can say is that it was much, much more than I expected. It was both humbling and enlightening, a great gift to this writer on his 67th (68th in China) birthday!

Sometime late in 2008: After I finished the article, David wrote his reflections on what happened in Huangshan:

I'm not sure where to begin, so I guess starting from the end make sense.

It was October last year when Rene and I were together in Hangzhou, and it was then the beginning of the end.

Grandmaster Xuan Kong as seen through the hole he literally burned by emitting Qi from his Sword Hand at a distance of 7 to 10 feet. He had also demonstrated other feats like making a lighter bounce on the floor from a distance of 5-7 feet with Qi from his palm while he was positioned in a posture similar to Brush Knee and Push in Tai Chi Chuan. He also emitted electricity from his hand. It made me wonder at the time if these techniques — pyrokinesis, telekinesis and Yin Yang Gong (or the mating of the Yin and Yang in the dantian) — were originally a part of the Fa Jing (disharge of Jing) methods of Tai Chi Chuan.

Rene Navarro, teacher, and good friend, and I sat in the hotel smoking a good cigar and we spoke of the oddest realization: after 15 years of hard trying, to experience the power of the Yin Yang Gong even if only at a primitive stage, left me... with nothing.

No permanent transformation in the core of my being, not even the sense of fearlessness toward death. Having reached a form of immortality really did not make any difference, actually the opposite. The strong sense that the "me" who should feel different is not there to be found.

I thought of Rene breaking bricks with his bare hands and imagined how similar it must have been, a skill, applied concentration and controlled power, but did it make us better people?

Obviously not, for we carried all our self — our ego — imperfections, separations and illusions, attachments, sorrows, and fears along, we did not realize liberation from suffering, nor unbound joy and participation in the divine.

Most of all none of these achievements seem to grant even the bare benefits most people expect, like superior health, rejuvenation, and buoyant energy. Both myself and the great masters I met were and are subject to the banal seasonal cold once in a while, a flu or the aching of age as anyone else coupled with aging, and by looking at the masters who achieved higher level I saw nothing, but the same pattern repeated.

The only thing which made a difference has been the clarification of Xing -self nature- attained years before, and having fulfilled Ming destiny, actualized potential- made Xing and what is before Xing to come forth.

In the months which followed Huangshan I went through a major "walking dead man" state as it's called in Taoism (but will keep it for another time), which was in its own right a great lesson leaving me with the very same impression, the development of incredible skills at the level of the Shen rather than the Qi but ultimately just skills which nothing contributes to happiness, and true fulfillment.

Furthermore creating the illusion of a crystallization of the sense of "I" and "self" doing a practice, the deluded but reinforced perception that there is an "I" achieving, an "I" fearing death, an "I" to be "immortalized" leading to nothing but a greater separation from the divine which is seen as unreachable if not through hardship and self-denial, losing the great gift we all have to actually know God immediately by looking in the nature of Love.

Magus of Java photo with family.

As the months passed the questioning became stronger, and it was July when Sifuji, one of the only real enlightened masters I know, appeared in a vision calling me to see him in Korea... when I got there, that was the end and a new beginning, finally after 11 years I was ready to let go and drop everything ready for his teachings, to finally "jump" as he likes to say since I met him in the 90s. He passed the transmission of the Miao Tong Tao, and made me a free man, a man who loves, who lives in god's grace, he took away my burning desire, he quenched my thirst, fulfilled my hunger, was a small awakening.

He then told me I was not to go back to China and in fact no matter how hard I tried I was not able to go back. Coming back to Italy was magnificent, I wonder why I left in the first place 16 long years ago.

Imagine that shortly after coming back, friends from the Chinese community invited me to meet a Chinese gentleman visiting who turned out to be among the highest Lei Shan Tao masters I ever met so far (he leaves prints on rocks making well above level 36, Magus is 20, Jiang is 10) right here in the heart of Rome! Life is ironic.

Problem was that having lost all illusion about practice and spirituality, having quenched the thirst and having found that which is not to be found, leaving nothing undone, and nothing else to do really but being, have been really looking for a way out from teaching and just disappear in silent anonymity, till last week when the chance actually came and...God's hands guided me toward teaching again, this time to teach and show others the power of Love, the most simple and great practice of all, from where the fulfillment of Sifuji words, to go and teach the Miao Tong Tao till the time is right....as for what the teaching of the Miao Tong are about, is direct experience and what Sifuji passed to me is the ability to bring people in to direct experience, beyond words, forms, concepts. Simple, magnificent.

After you experience you know.

This I have been teaching since the beginning really, so nothing new, I realize it now.

Therefore, remember practice is practice, nothing more, nothing less, in itself does not lead to liberation, yet like anything is a tool toward it, and dear to the Chinese tradition the media, the expedient and experience of Qi and Shen is the base of choice toward the great breakthrough.

Lao Zi said the Tao I teach is the Miao Xuan Tong Tao, the Tao of the wonderous, ineffable, and mysterious breakthrough leading to Xi Ming or penetrate enlightenment.

20.

Pilgrimages And Opening the Body to Nature

One of the things I missed during the Covid-19 pandemic was traveling to distant countries. Not only remote countries but sacred places. Every now and then I would look at my archive of photographs and revisit them: Borobudur in Indonesia, Angkor Wat in Cambodia, Glastonbury in England, Lake Titicaca and Machu Picchu in Peru, the stone circles of Scotland, Mount Banahaw in the Philippines, the stone house of Mother Mary in Ephesus, the Oracle of Delphi in Greece, the basilica of the disciple Lazarus in Cyprus, and the pyramids of Giza in Egypt.

I am not a good travel writer. I do not bother to point out ordinary places no matter how attractive or give directions to tourist spots. I am more interested in places of pilgrimage where I could feel a special energy, discover the divine presence, an insight into myself or life, or find an extraordinary experience that will transform me. There are many such places in the world.

But it requires a special kind of listening, patience, and curiosity to "connect" to the special energy of a place. Perhaps, if you've done meditation, Tai Chi Chuan, or an art like painting or poetry or you have a religious calling or love history, you'll be able to feel the frequency or vibration or if you have the ability to keep quiet and allow the atmosphere to enter, you may be able to access the "heart" of the place. You have to leave most everything behind and be open to a new experience. In the phraseology of Zen, you must empty your cup to get it filled. That is a precondition almost of how you build an energetic relationship with a place.

Often you have background knowledge of the place you are going to because you have read about it in your research. But it could also be that you do not know where you are going because a guide has it all planned for you. This was what sometimes happens when only an outline of the tour is provided. It has happened to me more than once. On a trip to Myanmar, my companion and I were picked up from the hotel by car and were taken to a boat. We did not know where we were going. After an hour, we arrived at our destination. We walked

In one of the stations in Mount Banahaw, the most sacred mountain in the Philippines located 3-4 hours south of Manila. The pilgrim stopped and lit a candle along the way of the Cross. The shirt Rene is wearing shows the trigrams for Fire/Li and Water/Kan, the symbol of Taoist neidan (internal alchemy).

to an old temple built into a cliff. It had a small, bare altar inside, hardly big enough to accommodate 10 people. There were two monks. And then the guide took us for a walk to a white temple. We had the same kind of experience when we were in Laos: a guide took us from the hotel, put us on a boat on the Mekong, and after two hours, we clambered up a ladder to the Temple of 10,000 Buddhas.

In other counties it was different. We had no guide to lead us. During a pilgrimage to Delphi, I took my two granddaughters Ava and Isabel with me. They were a great help with navigating the mountain: My primary doctor allowed me to join the Mediterranean tour although several tests showed I had symptoms of a heart condition, and a cardiac procedure was considered a possibility. I let Isabel and Ava go ahead of me when I reached the plateau. I sat down and did my qigong overlooking a breath-taking landscape. It was Summer Solstice, June 21, and there were women in white tunics chanting probably in honor of Gaea, the Goddess who was the original Oracle before, as in many other places, the patriarchy installed a man — in this case Apollo — in her place.

Sometimes the destination is not the place but a master. This was true on my visits to Bali, Java, and Huangshan. I was with my friend and teacher David Verdesi; we went to see "King" (I do not like to disclose his name to preserve his privacy) and a 93-year-old Hindu priest famous for his ability to change into a monkey right before your eyes. King gave us a rather strange initiation — passing a red-hot chisel on our tongues. It was a cleansing and kundalini ritual. Another master David took me to was the Magus of Java, the legendary John Chang who could project electricity from his body. And of course, we went to Huangshan to meet with GM Xuan Kong and Jiang Feng sifu, both wonderful healers with powerful energy and generous spirits. Important to remember: Whenever you meet a master, it is important to be humble and sincere. The master invariably can "read" your energy at first sight and it's possible you'll be ignored or told to return in five years.

One time at the Abbey in Glastonbury, I had what may be called an OBE (Out of Body Experience). While meditating at the altar in the ruins of the old chapel, I found myself in the same place several centuries before. I saw soldiers killing priests and nuns while children were crying. I woke up when I heard somebody announcing, "We are closing." I realized I had been dreaming for the last 2 hours. When I got back to the house where I was staying, I read in a book that indeed nuns and priests were massacred by the soldiers of the King.

At the "basement" of the temple at Dendera. What are these etchings shaped like eggplants? Note the figures seated in a kind of yoga asanas. We were told these were drawings of ancient batteries.

I've done my meditation rituals or, when possible, Tai Chi Chuan in different places: Avebury (an even larger and more extensive stone circle than Stonehenge), Temple of Karnak (where Jesus spent some years studying with the priests), several places in Scotland, and Besakih (Mother Temple) on the slope of the volcano Mount Agung in Bali.

Prambanan in Java. The temple is located along the Ring of Fire, the circle of volcanoes from Hawaii to Indonesia to Japan and the Philippines. The area is also associated with the Lost Continent of Lemuria. If you are lucky, you'll see mystical powers demonstrated by extraordinary people: shape-shifting shamans who could change into a monkey, healers who could do "psychic surgery" or produce "electricity" or fire from their hands or move objects from a distance.

It is difficult to explain the experience that is spiritual and mystical. There is a kind of transfiguration, a heightened sense of wonder, a departure from the ordinary and mundane. You leave the place transformed and you are aware of the possibilities of life and travel. This experience is totally different from mere tourist travel. In the latter you are just a casual visitor, you see things — however beautiful or impressive — but they do not affect you in

A break at Delphi, the Oracle of Apollo, in Greece. I took my granddaughters Ava and Isabel there on June 21, Summer Solstice. There were women in white singing and performing rituals.

The omphalos, the symbol for the navel or center of the world in Greek mythology. It is associated with the pineal gland because of its shape.

a deep sense, you are not transformed emotionally and psychically, you do not establish a profound relationship with the place or the person you are seeing.

When I walked up the Tor in Glastonbury, I felt myself on some kind of initiation, walking along not just a path but a Path. Step by step, I was being suffused with energy of the place and its history, I was moving into the past or the mystical, beyond the geography or the location, beyond into the mystery.

That is the apotheosis of a pilgrimage. You are touched on a soul level, and you are not the same again.

OPENING THE BODY TO NATURE

In my travels, I have often done qigong and Tai Chi Chuan in power vortices — in the pyramids at Gisa and the temples in Upper Egypt (Karnak, Dendera, Abydos), in the Tor on Glastonbury, and the Stonehenge in England, in the peaks of Huangshan in China, in the stone circles of Scotland, Iao Valley in Maui, Hawaii, and Mount Banahaw in the Philippines. I have done qigong even in enclosed spaces like the Egyptian section at the British Museum and the Egyptian Temple in the Metropolitan Museum in New York City.

Imitating the postures at the temple of Karnak in Luxor. If you do it right, you would feel a strange vibration that is similar to the experience of Qigong or Tai Chi Chuan.

It is essential, even critical now, to harmonize our lives, culture, and lifestyle with the world around us because we are at risk of losing the earth to deadly pollution, severe exploitation, and extreme climate changes. The situation is dangerous for the world, humanity, and the different species, an issue we'll have to address sooner than later. But in the meantime, there is a very simple way of connecting and harmonizing with nature and speaking the language of ecology in our daily lives. Since the body itself is naturally constructed with energy points like the earth in feng-shui, it is quite easy to align to the world around us. It is just a matter of:

- ✓ Standing still
- ✓ Keeping quiet and listening.
- ✓ Avoiding distractions from the senses or the mind.
- ✓ Allowing the body to settle down. If you need to breathe, make it soft and gentle like a tiny ripple on a lake.

Here's what to do: Plant your feet shoulder-width apart and straighten your back. Remember to slightly bring your chin down towards, but not touching, the manubrium. You may not be aware of it in the beginning, but this act stretches the cervical vertebrae and opens Governor Vessel 16 (Fengfu) and Governor Vessel 20 (Baihui) and Esoteric Hall (Yintang). Next, bring your hands down, palms either facing the outer thighs (to align Pericardium 8 (Laogong) to the Gallbladder/Wood meridian running down from the head to the feet) or the palms facing to the back (to feel what's behind you). Put your tongue up to the hard

A stone circle in Scotland, one of many that were built thousands of years ago along with Stonehenge and Avebury. If you assume an attitude of silent prayer or meditation, you could possibly tap into the energy vortex of the place. Pilgrims sometimes speak of seeing ancient priestesses in white performing rituals in these sacred places.

upper palate or just behind the teeth to create what is indicated in the *Neijing Tu* as the "Sacred Ground."

A lot of people ask, are there any techniques? Yes, there are techniques. You can do Tai Chi Chuan or Eight Precious Brocades or a series of Qigong or Taoyin movements. But you can reduce them to the most basic and simple ones like what is listed above. Just quiet down, close your eyes, and it helps if you feel grateful for who you are. There is always something special or even magical that happens when one feels a sense of gratitude for the blessings of life.

When one is positioned for standing meditation as described, one does not have to do anything else. It is that simple. It is wonderful if you are in the Parthenon or in Huashan. But you do not have to be. You do not need to be in the King's Chamber in the Great Pyramid, or in Haleakala Volcano on Maui. You can just do it in your rural backyard or in your own living room. You do not need any extra equipment or any elaborate accoutrement. If it is necessary to focus, you can light an incense or a candle or play soft meditative music or breathe softly. But these can be distracting for some people. So, find what you are most comfortable with. Minimize distractions and movements.

As you practice more, you will possibly realize that there is a subtle activation of the Bai Hui (GV 20) at the top of the head, Qi Hai (CV 6) and Shenque (CV 8) area in the belly, and Yongquan (Kidney 1) at the bottom of the feet. These are four of the most prominent points in the body that are the easiest to activate. There is also the Laogong (PC 8), the power point of the palms. Often, the vibration of qi starts at the fingertips or Jing (Well) points, collects at Laogong and travels up the arms.

Stay in position for 30 minutes to an hour. In the beginning, it is usually difficult to be still for more than five to 10 minutes, but with regular practice, you will feel comfortable doing it for longer and longer periods of time. You will feel different experiences. The energy of the feet sinking into the ground, for instance. Or the Jing (Well) points of the fingers feeling vibration or some meridians opening. Or, in the best times, the body itself seeming

Rene with Huayna Picchu Dragon at Machu Picchu in Peru

to become transparent or porous as if its boundaries have dissolved. The whole body would seem to be breathing after a while. There is a sense of opening to the outside world. The body and the earth in incredible alignment and harmony. It is the path of stillness that is suggested in Chapter 16 of the *Tao Te Ching*.

At the end of your work — call it meditation, call it qigong, whatever name you may use — be sure to make a gesture of closing. Put your palms over your navel. Imagine the energy collecting in your lower belly (often associated with the navel center) and resting there in sturdy container. A closure is necessary in a ritual so that you can connect again to the mundane and return to the ordinary world and time.

Blessings to you!

In Sillustani Circle, the last stop on my Peruvian pilgrimage. There's an Inca cross in the center where I did my Tai chi form. Close by were an ancient graveyard and the Altiplano, a flat hillside where extraterrestrials are said to land, according to my guide.

21.

Letter From Cyprus

Dear Nadine,[1]

It must have been the slow passage of tiny Venus across the face of the Sun. The usually sedate waves of the Mediterranean crashed heavily on the shore. A blustery wind, unexpected at this time of the year, whistled through the date palms, eucalyptus, and fig trees. The sea raised white horses on the waves as I followed the transit of the planet across the sky on the internet.

Outside the flat the pomegranates are flowering, red petals staying on the vine pod as the green fruit grows. The lemon trees are bearing green fruits even as the mature fruits ripen: these trees seem unaware of the changes in the seasons. The jacarandas are in their last bloom: you wonder how such beauty is possible on earth, and if we deserve it.

I've been waiting for May, a young Filipina who works in a health spa doing massage in Lemesos, to call. She was supposed to provide information about a group of kabayans who are interested in learning arnis de mano from me. She thought some Philippine stickfighting would add flavor to their usual off-day of volleyball and basketball. The Filipinos meet at St. Catherine's Roman Catholic Church on Sunday or at Boracay, a disco-cum-restaurant run by a Greek Cypriot and his Filipino wife, but nothing has apparently been decided. (The latest from the grapevine is that the kainan building literally collapsed because a neighbor removed a retaining wall, so the Pinoys had to look for another meeting place.) Like immigrants from Sri Lanka, many Filipinos are in Cyprus as "domestics," but they also do extra work as nannies or in their employers' restaurants, cafes, hotels, waiting on tables, cooking or housekeeping. There are four Filipino men hired as chefs in a Japanese restaurant at the Four Seasons. A Tagala from Quezon often works long hours in a bakery in Omodos, a village famous for its excellent wine. Her friend and roommate, also a Filipina, runs the cafe next door serving coffee to silver-haired card-playing patrons; another woman just arrived from the Philippines is being trained as a waitress at another cafe across the street. V. from the Visayas takes care of a 90-year-old Greek Cypriot around the corner in Potamos Germasogeia.

The stories they tell. Just today, I heard about a Pinay who collapsed in tears in a telephone booth when she heard that her husband, whom she was supporting, had taken a lover back home.

I'm new and only intermittently visiting here but wherever I've traveled I've met many of them, women who left their homeland, families and often husbands and children to face a difficult and uncertain future.

You ask a Pinay, "Kumusta ang buhay?"

She invariably answers, "Okey lang."

Somebody should archive the stories of courageous and determined Pinays here in Cyprus and across the water in Greece. I heard there are Filipino men too, but I haven't seen them.

At the ruins of a Christian abbey in Bela Paix, Northern (Turkish) Cyprus. I was commuting between North and South (Greek) teaching Tai Chi Chuan and Qigong. I attended a recital at the church performed by British cellist Matthew Barley who played pieces from Bach's Unacompanied Cello Suite.

There are Russians here, too, but they have quite a different reputation. From what I read in the newspapers, many young women from the former Soviet republics — all of them seem to be blonde — are in Cyprus as "artistes" working in "cabarets." There have been frequent reports of "indecent acts" and "compromising positions" whenever the police raid these places. In one block on the other side of the Rialto, a reputable theatre here, there are at least four such places of "entertainment."

My 12-day trip to Egypt was surprisingly hectic. I heard that there was a bad desert sandstorm with the temperature at higher than 110 F. But when I arrived the storm had dissipated, and the temperatures had gone down to a comfortable level. I had anticipated a quiet time, teaching a short Chi Nei Tsang (CNT) internal organs massage and qigong workshop in Cairo, and then spending a few days at Sharm el Sheik in Sinai, perhaps a day at the pyramids in Giza, a few hours to view the archaeological digs at Saqqara. But it turned out that many patients had signed up for treatments and consequently the trip to the desert and the Red Sea had to be cancelled. A few of the women I treated were veiled, indicating a conservative Muslim background; one wore black, but they were willing to receive acupuncture and CNT, some of which was focused on the area of the dan-tian in the abdomen.

I did not usually sleep until after midnight because of dinners on the town almost every night. The expat community and the rich Egyptians in Cairo seem to gather either at the Nile Hilton or the Marriott Gardens to meet friends, develop a network or negotiate deals.

It's like Manila, where the rich and famous and the almost-there go to the Intercon or Manila Hotel for their night out, to see and be seen.

My guide and host, an Egyptian homeopath and western doctor from the outskirts of Cairo, whom I first met and treated at the Tao Garden in Chiangmai, Thailand, took me to the famous and classy Mena House for breakfast. You can see the pyramids from the Khan el Khalili restaurant, named after the shopping district in Cairo, similar to Divisoria in Manila, where you can haggle endlessly in hopes of a good bargain. You can take your time over pita bread with hummus, or the varied cheeses and olives while chatting over coffee. The waiters in their immaculate uniforms hover around you unctuously. Very few people in the restaurant — and most of the few probably tourists — are poring over the English newspapers for the latest casualty report from Iraq. Through curtains made of onion-shaped wooden beads, one can see the three pyramids sitting in the sun, tourists being disgorged from buses, and camels for hire.

The pyramids at Giza were not crowded. Japanese tourists, with their ubiquitous cameras, were not in sight. I posed for a photo riding a camel for my grandchildren in the States. We wandered around the sand dunes outside the second pyramid, supposedly Khafre's, which was closed, looking for a place to sit. The pyramids have been fenced off with barbed wire for the last two years or so. When I visited in Winter of 2003, I asked an Egyptian colleague who also teaches Taoist Yoga to get me a taxi-driver who could take me to the pyramids early in the morning. David, an Italian who spoke Arabic and sported the Egyptian name Daud, meandered around the city at dawn to a poor village on the edge of the fence. We clambered up the rocks through a gap in the fence to a promontory where we could view the sunrise over Cairo. A uniformed guard threatened to put me under arrest. A companion cautioned me not to make sudden moves. Were it not for the timely intervention of David, perhaps I would have landed in jail for trespassing?

At Giza. One day I hired Daud, a taxi driver, to take me to Giza at dawn. He picked me up at 4 in the morning and took me to a small village just within sight of the pyramids. I clambered up the rocks and jumped over the fence. Just before sunrise, a guard in uniform detained me for trespassing. Through Daud's intervention, I was discharged. I walked away feeling relieved, but took a photo of the guard anyway.

Last year I had been inside the first pyramid — Khufu's reputedly — including the King's and Queen's chambers. In the King's Chamber, it was for at least an hour, although tourists were herded out every 5 or 10 minutes. The so-called sarcophagus, believed to be the King's burial coffin, I believe, is probably part of initiation ritual paraphernalia. It is cut so precisely; one wonders how the ancient Egyptians could have invented a saw or a drill that

Two of the pyramids at Giza. Note the size of the people standing beside the Great Pyramid in the foreground. It is difficult to imagine that there are more than 2 million blocks of stone in this one.

could achieve that degree of exactness. If you hit the side firmly with your fist, you'll hear a vibration of stunning frequency that resonates in the hall. There are several huge 20-to 30-foot-long granite blocks of rectangular shape sitting above the chamber that seem to serve as a tuning fork. How and why, they were installed there and with what instrument are things I can't imagine. Was the chamber an acoustical device? What was its purpose? I did Chinese qigong in several spots to test the energy in the place. When the tourists were gone, a chant astonishingly went up, filling the premises with a mystical sound. It gave one goose bumps because it seemed to penetrate the bones and the marrow and lift one to a level of unbelievable exhilaration. It seemed to have been made by a choir, but by a couple from Rome — Roberto and Andrea — who had been unobtrusively meditating in one corner undisturbed by the guards and came up with a soaring OM. They introduced themselves to me later outside because they wanted to know what I was doing with all those qigong postures.

The Queen's Chamber accessible at the bottom end of the stairway from the King's Chamber was closed to the public. But Egyptian guards are not immune to gratuities — bakshish in Arabic — so through the intervention of a friend, I was able to go in for 30 minutes of meditation. There is an air shaft aligned to a constellation like the shaft in the King's Chamber, giving rise to the belief that the pyramids, like similar constructions in Mexico, Cambodia, and Peru, were part of a religious cult that worshiped — perhaps journeyed — to the stars!

From my readings of the literature, I tend to agree with this interpretation. There's a cove, a niche, on one of the walls which looks like an altar of some sort.

There are many unanswered questions—who built the pyramids, what for, how and when did they do it? How were the multi-ton stones carved into precise proportions? How were they adjusted in place? How were they aligned? There are, of course, many speculations. What was the purpose of aligning the Sphinx to the solstices? Were the pyramids arranged in a pattern that mimics the stars? I have read many of the books offering answers. The research materials are not your "Chariot of the Gods" genre, but scientific explorations substantiated by educated studies from scientists and savants. I am filled with continuing wonder. The calculations and measurements that I've read are so incredible that I believe there's something in these speculations.

Where did those constructions come from? They seem to have been put in the desert and then abandoned. What advanced civilization built them?

As I sat on a large crystalline stone that probably fell from the facade of the second pyramid, I went into a deep contemplation and surrendered myself to the palpable silence and energy. But hardly five minutes had passed when a man in burnoose (headgear) and galabeya (gown) materialized with a camel and touted a ride. Nobody leaves you alone here. Always, as in many tourist destinations around the world, there's somebody selling something — chilled bottled water and soda pop, film for cameras, mementos of ancient pharaonic times. And they are persistent. You can never say no. Badin, badin, you would say. Later, later. Knowing certain Arabic expressions indicates you are not a tourist. English will not do.

Last year, at Luxor in Upper Egypt (strange geography here because upper is down south on the map) I also felt a strange, powerful energy in certain spots in the Court of Ramses, the Colonnade of Amun and especially the Peristyle Court, which, according to R.A. Schwaller de Lubicz, was supposed to be the navel of the Temple. More mystical experiences in the temples of Karnak, Dendera and Abydos!

The figures on the massive walls and pillars show pharaonic postures. Were these positions like Chinese qigong? Was their purpose to heal? Were there secret messages behind the postures? I mimicked them, and it might just be me, but I felt a strong energy! A kind of heaviness, a reverberation in my body, a gravitational magnetic pull. Two of my friends in the Healing Tao Center also saw in the carvings parallels to the acupuncture points of Chinese medicine!

I should not fail to mention the felucca (sailboat) rides on the Nile at sunset under the able guidance of Captain Ahab (his real name, I heard from the hangers-on in the dock) or the caleche rides of driver Makmoud on the Corniche. The Sunset on the Nile is arguably the most beautiful in the world; it's not just from one direction but a 360-degree bowl of colors (as Juan Ramon Jimenez described in Moguer, Spain, in a poem in *Platero and I*). If you are a nostalgia buff or have a weakness for romance, the felucca and the caleche are the vehicles you should not miss for they represent the old Egypt. But be prepared to haggle and pay the exact fare because Akmal will surprise you by keeping the change with a nod to the boat or horse, that it needs bakshish! You'd like to get upset of course but he does it with such charm and humor, you let him get away with it.

There were always people touting camel rides. When I hired one, the camel knelt down but when I went up on it, the camel stood up but wouldn't budge. A lost photo op!

Egypt holds a powerful and continuing fascination for me and many other people. I'll probably return again and again to those ancient monuments. There is an invitation to teach Tai Chi Chuan and meditation in the White Desert and Siwa Oasis this year. The awesome silence and emptiness make for an ideal place for going inward. The pyramids have been there for thousands of years—several studies reckon 10,000 BCE—appearing defaced, plundered, incongruous now. Perhaps someday, the Department of Antiquities will find the Hall of Records among the sand dunes near the Sphinx, which will reveal the secrets of the pyramids. Meantime, the mysteries defy reason and analysis.

An Egyptian woman whom I treated in Cairo came to Cyprus to get a week's worth of treatments. Her father was a diplomat to the Philippines when she was a teenager. Yesterday she sent me a long effusive e-mail with a poem about her experience of acupuncture and moxa, a Japanese style influenced by Kiiko Matsumoto, my teacher in Boston, and lessons in Heaven and Earth qigong.

Over tea, we talked about the culture and civilization of Egypt. The pyramids and temples, mathematical principles, mythology, astronomy and astrology, medicine, internal alchemy (the word came from Alkemia, the ancient name of the country), etc., and how they influenced western civilization, from Greece to Italy to North America. This influence is not usually acknowledged, of course. You look at the architecture of the old buildings and churches, especially the Gothic like Notre Dame and Chartres cathedrals, and the geomancy of cities like Washington and Paris and Philadelphia, and you'll find heavy Egyptian influences. How about the search for the Philosopher's Stone? You read the mythology of Italy and Greece, much of it Egyptian. Even Dante's Divine Comedy clearly bears the footprints of ancient Egypt.

The other night I read my love and war poems at the Curiosity House in Larnaca, a city in Southeast Cyprus. Joseph Blessingson (that's the English version of his name), a Muslim healer and poet from the North, and I shared the stage. It was meant as a bi-communal event to make a statement about reconciliation, acceptance, and unity in this divided country. I was surprised at the enthusiastic reception. Aphrodite's pervasive myth notwithstanding, Cyprus is very conservative, influenced strongly by the Greek Orthodox Church. I read poems on Hiroshima, my childhood during the war, also some confessional love poems and Su-Mi, a near-erotic prose poem. The small intimate audience asked for more, and I ended up reading two love poems from Pablo Neruda (whose 100th birthday we celebrate this year) and "Turn the Page," one of my works-in-progress.

I sometimes wondered if this man vending scarves in the marketplace in Luxor held ancient secrets in his head. In Karnak there was a guide who turned out to be a Guardian of the Temple. He took two of my friends and I to the smaller temples that were closed to the public. When the guard asked for tip, this man who materialized from nowhere said, No bakshish! No tip.

Larnaca is the town where Lazarus was supposed to have been buried in the temple where he served as a bishop for 20 years after the resurrection of Jesus. Thousands come for a pilgrimage to the church and his sepulcher under the impressive altar. The apostle Mark who wrote the first gospel went to Cyprus, later to Egypt, where he apparently founded the Coptic Church, in Alexandrine. Their cross is the ankh—meaning life—in the shape of a sandal strap. John the Apostle left Israel and was exiled to Patmos where he wrote the Revelations. Subsequently, he went to the neighboring island of Ephesus with Mary and started a church there, too. There's a basilica named after him that's in ruins. Oral tradition says Mary went into seclusion on a mountain. A small, solid stone chapel was built in her honor—a place of pilgrimage for worshippers around the world. Paul evangelized in the Mediterranean — Cyprus, Corinth, and Ephesus—and died or was killed in Rome. Mary Magdalene sailed on a boat to France; a basilica holds her relics there. Thomas travelled to India and built a church there. Cyprus is mentioned in the Bible, probably the earliest outpost of Christianity.

Next week I intend to go to the Turkish North for a couple of days. I've been there a few times, once with a colleague to demonstrate Chinese qigong and T'ai Chi Chuan swordplay to an audience of 60. (How I transported the weapons back and forth across the border is another nerve-wracking story for later.) It's not yet known how long travelers are allowed to stay across the Green Line, the border of Greek and Turkish Cyprus, guarded by United Nations troops. As a Filipino, a holder of a Philippine passport, I am always wary of visa requirements. For one reason or another, many countries in Europe and Africa grant visas at the border to almost all nationals except for Filipinos, so I typically have to apply for visas well in advance.

I've wanted to walk again around Kyrenia/Girne Harbor and the Venetian Walls, revisit the castle ruins of the Knight Templars, see the Kyrenian Mountain Range up close, and journey to the legendary Karpaz region in the northeastern tip of the island. Of course, I'd like to see Lawrence Durrell's house in Bela Pais and have the muddy Turkish coffee in the cafe by the Tree of Idleness, things I missed the last two times I was at the ruins of the legendary Bela Pais Abbey. Author of the Alexandria Quartet, his travelogue The Bitter Lemons of Cyprus is a poignant portrait of the country in the '50s.

I've been reading the Mediterranean writers. I'll probably go through the Greek poets and the Egyptian novelists. I finished Kazantzakis' biographical Report to Greco just a few weeks ago.

I'm leaving for London on the 15th to teach a couple of private students, then fly to Istanbul to visit a Taoist colleague on the 19th. I am supposed to meet the indefatigable and multi-faceted Ed Maranan, who's trying to organize a poetry reading in London. Patrick Rosal, an extraordinarily gifted poet, and I read there last June. I'll be back in the US to teach in Boston and New York in July.

From Cyprus (also called the Lost Continent of Atlantis by some people),

— Rene

P.S., Just got back from the North: At the Green Line the guard said that tourists could stay in the North for up to 3 months without further documentation. I stayed from Wednesday to Friday, mostly up in the Karpaz peninsula in the Northeast territory. The area has wonderful terrain, empty beaches, unpolluted air, the Kyrenian mountain range and clear jade water of the Mediterranean. There's little industry, no radar and mobile phone towers. The cuisine was simple but excellent — olives marinated in olive oil with garlic, lemon and coriander seeds, goat cheese/halloumi, grilled meat (chicken, lamb, and beef), squid, octopus, and fish (chipura, sea bream, is the favorite). I stayed at two hotels, both on the coast. One of them was run for three generations by a Turkish Cypriot family who raise their own sheep and vegetables. It was comforting to see the cook take a stroll to the nearby farm to harvest green beans, steak tomatoes and spring onions for dinner. The other is owned and run by new immigrants from Anatolia, who probably took over the property formerly owned by Greek Cypriots after the country was invaded by Turkey in 1974.

Rene teaching Swimming Dragon in Southern (Greek) Cyprus in 2005.

The Karpaz is still generally unspoiled, although the few developments are an eyesore. A sandy beach on Famagusta Bay was undergoing the hasty construction of several hotels plus a casino: in a year or two, it will look like a miniature Reno. The old couple that owns a ramshackle tienda-cum-bar at the end of the only road will probably not know what hit them when the multi-nationals descend upon this hitherto tranquil retreat. There are infrequent tourist buses; most transport is by rental car, for now. You'll see miles and miles of virgin land along the Mediterranean Sea and every so often you will encounter a herd of wild donkeys. In the summer and fall, there are sea turtles laying eggs on the shore. My guide told me that the Greek South was like this 10 years ago, but has since then gone insanely commercial, with developments rising up most everywhere, especially on the coast, mountains are being gouged to make way for hotels, roads, houses and golf courses.

In the Karpaz, there are abandoned Greek Orthodox churches from the war. The Monastery of San Andreas, probably one of the best Greek Orthodox Churches in Cyprus, is in a sad state of disrepair, looking forlorn and pathetic against a breathtaking landscape. I saw an old church that was actually being used as a mosque, reminiscent of some churches in Toledo and Avila in Spain that carried both Christian and Muslim designs and motifs. In the South there are numerous abandoned mosques. I did not see any still in operation, although I heard that the Al-Kebir Mosque in Larnaca is still in use by Muslims.

Both sides speak of ugly deeds done by the other — massacres and disappearances. I met the owner of a coffee shop in the Karpaz who narrated the story of his own journey as a child from a small village in the South, how he and 30,000 to 40,000 other Muslims had to take refuge in the British compound, airlifted to Turkey and eventually re-settled in the North. Almost similar stories were told by Greek Cypriots who were driven at gunpoint to the South from their homes in the North. After the opening of the borders last year, a Greek Cypriot couple found Turks from Turkey in possession of their farm home, and their wedding photos were still sitting in the bedroom undisturbed. I wrote poems about these stories, but it seems all so futile. How does a writer capture the anguish and the frustration and pain of both sides in this endless war?

In villages on both sides of the Green Line men were rounded up in the night. There are still bodies that are not accounted for 30 years after the war. I walk the country roads and see these abandoned stone houses, doors and shutters falling on their hinges, and wonder if under the floor or in the ancient olive grove nearby there are skeletons. And those old men stooped over their coffee in the village square, what do they know about what happened during those raids that nobody on either side admits?

Called the island of Aphrodite, the goddess of love, Cyprus has probably never experienced real peace at any time perhaps for the last 1000 years or more. You read its long history and from the names you encounter, you see the oscillations of conquest and colonization — Egypt, Assyria, Persia, Cato, Anthony, Cleopatra, Constantine, Alexander, Ottoman, Byzantine, Venetians, Turks, Greeks, UK. Each generation seems to have suffered war, invasion, strife. After 1974, the Green Line was drawn east-west; in many places it is actually a barbed wire fence running the length of this picturesque country of about 800,000 people. In a real, sanguinary way, this little island country mirrors the larger struggle of the world, the religious and political wars, the physical, psychic, and emotional wounds that people all over inflict on each other, the failure to forgive and the limits of human love.

There have been calls for reunification but where do they begin? Last May at a referendum the North voted Yes while the South voted No to the Annan Plan. Indeed, how do these enemies with a common ancestor but separated by religion start all over again?

22.

Dateline: Ubud, Bali, 2012

JANUARY 21, 2012.

We were sitting on the balcony this morning in Sawah Indah (Beautiful Rice Fields) when David Verdesi[1] said that Ian Baker, the writer and explorer, is arriving in Bali. In February 2006, Ian was in Bangkok and was supposed to join us in Java en route to Borobudur to do a documentary for National Geographic. David and I were visiting John Chang, the famous Magus of Java, at the time. I did not know anything about Ian Baker, but David told me stories about him and had an autographed copy of his book, *The Heart of the World: A Journey to the Last Secret Place*. The Preface by the Dalai Lama says it is the search for the lost land, the legendary Beyul Pemako. That's "the hidden land shaped like a lotus," located somewhere in indescribably difficult terrain in no-man's land in the borders of China, Tibet, and India. No doubt it is a fascinating story and from the blurb Ian's exploration sounded better than an Indiana Jones adventure. Hey, the search for Shangri-La is an ancient and continuing human obsession, isn't it? We waited for Ian… and waited and waited. Meantime, in the idle hours in Java, I read the book, arguably one of the best in the genre of travel literature, up there with the works of British writers Colin Thubron, Laurence Durrell, and Simon Winchester. Finally, we got the news that Ian could not come because his mother took sick in Thailand.

When I got back to the US, I bought myself a copy of the book from Strand, my favorite bookstore, south of Union Square in Manhattan. I read the book all over again page after page through the detailed geography, impressive research, and felicitous prose. I learned that there was a National Geographic DVD of the exploration, but I could not find a copy. I bought Ian's other books — *Tibetan Art of Healing* and *The Dalai Lama's Secret Temple: Tantric Wall Paintings from Tibet* — indispensable keys to Ian's oeuvre. The former is an excellent source of information about Tibetan healing, with extraordinary paintings and sketches of different techniques, the model of the body and different organs. The latter particularly is rich in the materials of the esoteric meditation called Dzogchen (the teachings of the Great Perfection) and probably more than any other book shows perhaps for the first time the mysterious and mystical wall paintings that are supposed to guide the Dalai Lama on his road to enlightenment. It is sad to read that His Excellency, the present Fourteenth Dalai Lama, because he had to escape from Tibet, was unable to set foot on the Lukhang (Serpent Deities) Temple in the middle of the lake behind the Potala Palace. Contemplating the murals — in reality, a veritable manual of high Tibetan Buddhist meditation — before the Dalai Lama's retreat appears to have been an obligatory ritual.[2] They were painted by mysterious artists after the Fifth Dalai Lama (1642–1682) had mystical visions apparently due to his encounter with a Lumo (female Naga).

*****

Since I arrived here in Bali on the evening of January 5, 2012, we have tried to avoid the tourist route, focusing on the training and visits to the masters. It was a good idea that David rented a house at the end of a road leading to the rice fields outside the town. We've had the benefit of quiet and privacy and a pleasing landscape, with a view of the coconut groves and the distant volcano.

The ceremonies have really been quite moving. The big initiation attended by the community was itself a magical occasion. I thought of how the community was bound by this faith, united in the charisma and qi of the old master, and in the culture and religion of the islands. It was, I realized, something that was missing in a Westernized culture.

Rene with Nicolai Denisov, a psychic from Russia who was visiting David in Bali.

Sometime when we first visited at his village home and temple, the old priest asked me, through Agung the guide and translator, if my country had the same tradition. I said, No. It was difficult to explain that my country, the Philippines, was colonized, first by Spain (Roman Catholic) and then by the US (Protestant), and took a different historical route, that we have been Westernized, that among other things, we have Christian processions and masses instead of the ritual Hindu dances, that we have/had a Western education …

Last time we — David, Pierre, Ana, Nikolay, and I — went to the village an hour by car from Ubud, the old shaman gave all of us his blessings. As we said goodbye, the old man held both my hands in his and said, "Om, Shantih, Shantih, Shantih." It took me by surprise and touched me deeply. He often took particular attention to hold my hands on the four occasions we visited him and listened to his lectures during the preparation for David's initiation. The old shaman had become a familiar figure after our third visit. I had sat with him as he wrote the mantras and demonstrated mudras of his lineage, heard the explanation for the rituals that he conducted.

Agung, the translator, preparing his ritual chew of betel nut as we waited for the Hindu priest to start the class.

It was different in many ways from my encounter with the Magus of Java John Chang who had this overwhelming power called yin yang gong or the mating of the yin and yang in the dantian that resulted in a strong electrical current. Wehda, his nephew, commented to me that the power was not spiritual. I was of course surprised to hear him say that and I thought about it for a long time, and I concluded that I wanted something else — as I expressed in the concluding paragraphs of my chapter, "Thunder Path in Huangshan" — peace and love and clarity and stillness. It is what I truly believe in. There is a milieu here that is harmonious, soft, and gentle. I found that they have faith in the sacred. I feel that my belief has finally found people who are animated by it.

There are obvious similarities, of course, between Bali and the Philippines — in the language for instance. It is close to Capampangan, the language of my region north of Manila. We share the same or almost similar words — *nasi* (rice), *bulan* (moon), *batu* (stone), *masok* (entrance), *ribu* (thousand), *dua* (two), and so many more. We also are similar in racial and physical characteristics. But at the same time, I notice the big differences in religion and culture. The Philippines is Westernized and Christian. It is a simplistic quotation, I admit, but the remark, "The history of the Philippines is 300 years in a Roman Catholic Convent and 50 years in Hollywood," says a lot. Despite the years of foreign occupation and internecine warfare, Bali's culture seems intact: dances, movements, martial arts, arts and crafts, statuaries. They know their sacred and religious texts. Here, in Bali, I've seen it in the animist Hindu culture.

I've tried to articulate my thoughts and mixed feelings about my country where sadly, there are times when I feel like a misplaced stranger in my own home.

JANUARY 16, 2012.

I have just been through the worst nightmare of a traveler — losing his credit/debit card. I had brought what I thought was sufficient cash for the time I will be in Bali but turned out there were other unexpected expenses when I arrived. So, I decided to ask my son in the US to inform the bank that I am in Bali and will probably use the card. After all the procedures he went through, I could not find the card. I emptied my wallet and my bag. It was nowhere to be found. I drafted an e-mail to my son but did not send it hoping my card would turn up, after all. We were at the performance of the Ramayana, and I tried to focus on the show, but my mind was on the credit card. I recognized some of the characters — Rama, Sita, Hanuman, Garuda ... David, my host, took me home and he and a few other companions proceeded to another shamanic event, a trance dance, in town. On the off chance the card was in my bedroom, I went upstairs and turned the bed sheet over. Lo and behold, it was there staring at me. It was the most beautiful sight in the world at that moment. So, I was there, alone, in the big house listening to Saint Saens' Carnival of the Animals and the cacophony of the frogs and the crickets and nursing a cup of hot espresso coffee.

In 2006, I was invited by David to Java to see the famous Magus. After close to a month, David left for Thailand. Wehda, a nephew of the Magus, invited me to go to Bali with him. He said we were going to meet a strange shaman, a shapeshifter who could change into a monkey right before your eyes. I had heard about something like it from a friend who had seen it in Malaysia. Of course, I was skeptical about it. Anyway, I was supposed to check into a beach hotel, but when we arrived in Bali, Wehda ordered the driver to take us to the home of his relatives in Kuta. His aunt and her husband were in the pool. There was construction going on of a museum for batik, silk, and other arts and crafts I heard later. There were several houses in the compound. The man emerged from the pool, came up to me, and said, "Mr. Navarro, it will be an honor to have you stay with us." I did not know what Wehda said in Bahasa Indonesia, but I was surprised of course and did not know what to say, except give my thanks. I was given the use of a house, a car, and a driver. Wehda was told to sleep in the library. I said he could stay with me.

Lotus and shadow at a Balinese temple.

One of the places I was advised to visit was a Hindu temple where an old Hindu healer was in residence. He was doing a healing when we saw him. There were about 10 foreign guests, apparently students of his, who sat in a semi-circle in front of him as he took them on one by one. He used a small and thin foot-long wand to poke at different parts of the body. I recognized them as acupuncture points. The patient would grimace and/or make a sound as the old man pressed this or that spot. And then it was my turn. I noticed that the probe he used was a wooden stick, shiny from use and in the shape of a snake. He spent about 10 minutes exploring some of the famous acupoints as I moaned and groaned from the pain. When he was done, I went back to my seat. "You have sinus problem," he remarked. "Yes," I said. "Do you want me to treat you?" "Yes," I said. Upon which, he went to his desk. With his back turned to me, I could not see what he was doing. He came up to me and said, "Close your eyes." I closed my eyes. Then, he spit on my face. "Keep them closed for 10 minutes," he ordered. Everybody laughed. As the saliva dripped down my face, I smelled the odor of Sichuan peppercorn, and I felt a clearing in my sinuses. It was, I thought, a different healing modality! Something I or anybody else, no matter what the intention, could not have done in the US.

In retrospect, I realized that it was an approach that was based on a different paradigm. Each healing system has almost invariably its own foundation, its own reality and rationale, its own perception of the body. So, the diagnosis and treatment are different too.

Remember that there is usually a payment required if you are going to see a healer. Inquire ahead of time how much it is. If none is required, it is good practice to make a donation just the same.

Lord Ganesha, the god of beginnings and journeys. You'll find Him in many places, usually at the gate or doorway of every home and temple.

I should not fail to mention another Hindu priest whom three of us saw in Ubud. We called him King since he belonged to a royal family. He had different methods of healing, some of which you might tend to call strange, if not bizarre. One of these methods required the application of a red-hot chisel on the back of your tongue, not once but 9 times in a row. The chisel is then dipped in a glass of rose water which is then used to wash the face and head in a kind of baptism. He did the treatment — "initiation" is the more appropriate name for it — 3 times in one night. As it was explained to me, the purpose was to activate the kundalini, the so-called Serpent Power. From the point of view of eastern medicine, the tongue is an extension of the Heart; hence, the ritual is also intended to cleanse the Heart.

JANUARY 18, 2012.

Yes, I am still enjoying Bali. Most of my time is dedicated to training. No touristing for me here. Whatever extra time we have is spent attending rituals and meeting masters. It is an incredible place, especially if you have connections with the community and if you live outside the city. As mentioned, David rented a house adjacent to the rice fields at the end of the road. When I wake up, I can hear the gecko barking in the dark and the roosters announcing the sunrise. I go to the terrace and see this young woman Man Sri, our help in the house, looking like an ancient priestess, long hair flowing down to the small of her

In Bali with Tynne Clifford and Lee Holden in a moment of levity.

back, carrying a basket of flowers and fruits and palm leaves, her daily gift to the land — coconuts, bananas, rice, the rivers and lakes and mountains — and the gods and ancestors and she goes on bended knees, palms together above her head, and chants quietly facing the spirit house. "There's nothing that is not sacred on this island," David said. When you drive an hour to the hinterlands, past the rice terraces and the farms, the small villages, and the coconut and banana groves, past the quiet temples and deep valleys, and the wood and stone carvers, you'll see a queue of women on certain holy days carrying baskets of fresh flowers on top of their heads, walking to a sacred temple. It was one of the first scenes that astonished me the first time I visited Bali with Wehda in 2006.

I was struck by the natives' familiarity with their culture and religion. Even our taxi-driver, whom I invited to dine with us, knew the religious texts and the gods. He talked about Arjuna and Hanuman. He was like a scholar giving a lecture on his academic specialty. It was quite an experience listening to him. It was like hearing an ordinary man in China talking about Sun Wukong in *Journey to the West* or General Kwan in the *Romance of the Three Kingdoms* or a waiter in Greece telling stories from the *Odyssey* or *Iliad.* I am happy that the big corporations like Walmart haven't gobbled up the island and its arts and crafts — batik and silk industry, singing bowls and bells, statuaries, and woodwork — and dumped mass-produced and consumer goods Made in China. Watching the performance of the Ramayana, I was impressed with two small girls dancing the legong, a long choreographic number, replete with different stylized movements. They must have trained for a long time. I can just see them emerging later as popular folk artists or national treasures.

NB: I did not see any McDonald's in Ubud but I saw one somewhere on one of our excursions to the beach. It had the familiar (and vulgar) arch standing two stories high!

JANUARY 23, 2012.

Ian arrived at the house yesterday. I was in downtown Bali having my camera batteries re-charged at an electronics store. When I got back to the house three hours later, Ian was still there waiting for David. I said hello and he introduced me to his companion and producer Rob. I told him that we were supposed to meet in Java in February 2006. He could not remember. Instantly Ian and I fell into talking about what we were doing: He was researching Tibetan yoga for his new book and was going to interview David. I said I was studying Lei Shan Tao with David and practicing traditional Yang family Tai Chi Chuan. When David came down, we went to a fancy French restaurant (Cozmic?), ordered our dinner, and as we settled down, Ian asked David to answer some questions. We listened to David's mesmerizing talk about Tibetan yoga, lost secrets, nei dan (internal alchemy), and the incredible masters, what had happened to his Chinese connections, the Huangshan hermit Xuan Kong, Wang Liping of the *Opening the Dragon Gate* fame, and the Magus of Java John Chang. Rob talked about *powa*, the Tibetan Buddhist technique of transference of consciousness. Ian mentioned the *wai dan* (external alchemical formulas) of some masters he had studied with on his explorations in remote places in Asia. We swapped information back and forth, bantered, laughed, and guffawed.

Balinese trance dance where the serpentine kris daggers cannot penetrate the body.

The 12-odd tapas-like dishes materialized and disappeared. (I am not familiar with French cuisine. Is there a name for those small servings?) One was flavored with fresh jackfruit, another was raw squid with the lingering taste of an elusive herb, still another was tuna tartare with the piquancy of a tropical spice and yet another was a fish native to Balinese waters. I should have taken notes, but I enjoyed the conversation so much, I forgot to record anything, not even with my still-functioning camera. It was the most engaging, memorable, and informative conversation I've had within memory. Ian said it was like the movie *My Dinner with Andre.* The dinner was also the most expensive I have ever had in my 72 years on the planet. But hey, I had no regrets! It was all worth it. Nobody in the world could have contrived the night in his imagination.

Later, we took Ian and Rob to their hotel. We promised to get together again. But it wasn't meant to be. Nicolay and Marina, the Russian couple famous for their psychic research, had invited me to tour Bali with them. Meanwhile, David had to leave for another island to see a master with incredible powers. And I did not know where Ian and Rob were.

JANUARY 24, 2012.

Just before I left for the airport for the flight back to JFK Airport in NY, David called from an island in Java. He was quite excited by his new discovery and experience. He arrived at his destination in the evening during the celebration of the Festival of Shiva, a huge holy day in Indonesia. He had not eaten anything and was mustered into an overnight sitting meditation that ended at dawn. The master (whom we called the Coconut Man because he discovered his powers after a coconut fell on his head while he was walking on the beach) had given him a powerful initiation, zapped David's dan tian with unbelievable heat, and basically adopted him. It was all he could report at the time, he said. There were certain important details he could not talk about on the phone. And then said he had to go because he was being called back for the continuation of the training. It had been going on for the last two days, non-stop. I wondered if he had eaten yet!

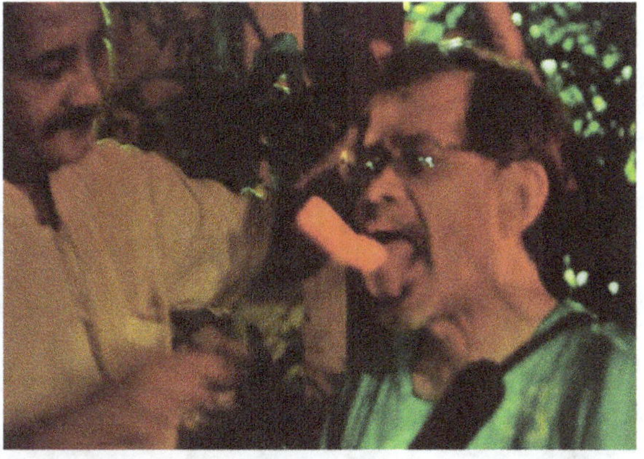

Bali Fire Ritual, hot steel on Rene's tongue

Wayan, the taxi-driver, picked me up early. Nikolay and Martina hitched a ride to town. I dropped them off at a museum. Meeting them was another serendipitous synchronicity in my life. It was a gift that I did not expect. We attended shows and initiations. We participated in the fire rituals.[3] We had breakfasts together. We visited temples and museums. We spent more time together than I had anticipated. In fact, we spent more time with each other than anybody else. Who knew that I would be able to study (and see a psychic phenomenon) with these exceptional Russians when I came to Bali? As arranged by David, Nikolay gave me lessons to give me the power to see with my eyes closed (like Marina) and I gave him treatments over a period of two weeks. When we said good-bye, I knew I would miss them. When I hugged Nikolay, I said: "My friend and teacher." He almost simultaneously said, "My doctor." When Marina and I hugged each other, I felt her gentleness and stillness: she was a disembodied spirit and pure energy. There was nothing else to say.

Cem Sen, a teacher from Istanbul, Turkey, having dinner with Tynne Clifford, Lee Holden, and Rene.

Bali breakfast with David

Bali Ramayana scene

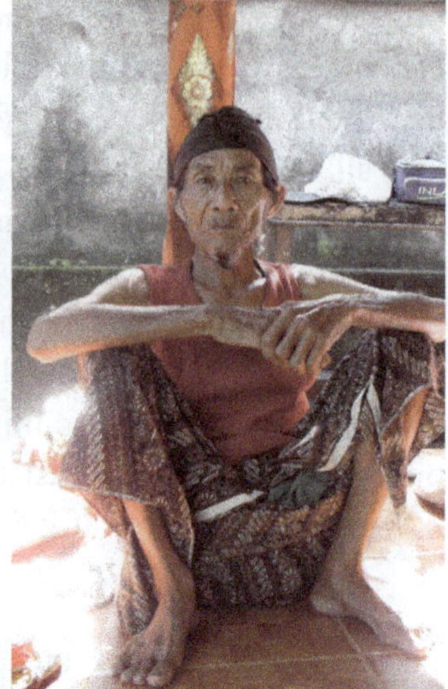
Bali actor at trance and keris show

On the long drive to the airport at Denpasar, I remained quiet, deep in contemplation of my "fortune," what I had gone through and experienced and the wonderful people I had encountered in Bali. Wayan stopped at a batik store. I picked up some sarong and a piece of woven batik material Ava, my granddaughter, asked me to bring. At 11 she designs and sews her clothes.

I treated Wayan to dinner at a restaurant where you could sit barefoot on colorful cushions at low tables and watch the fish in the pond. He ordered fried rice (*nasi goreng*) while I had a deep-fried fish and spicy pickle. We slowly ate and nursed our Indonesian beer. There was nobody else around. He hummed an Indonesian tune. He told me that many people would come to this place with their families on weekends and holidays. They would fish in the pond and grill what they caught. I asked Wayan about his family, how were his kids doing in school. He gave me the usual answers: they were doing well. I thought of the cultural context of his remark. I sensed the stoicism born of his awareness of karma. In some societies, people prefer not to say they are doing very well — or that their daughter is beautiful or son handsome — because it might bring down the anger or jealousy of the gods on them. Sometimes they won't tell the truth about their life because of pride or a sense of privacy. I asked him to write his address in my journal so that we could keep in touch.

When we reached the airport, I asked Wayan how much I owed him for the limousine service. He said in his halting English, "Anything you like." When he picked me up from the airport on my arrival at 3AM, he charged me the equivalent of $30 or $40. It was cheap considering that the airport was very far. He explained that he waited a long time because of the rain and the delayed luggage. He was usually specific about the fee — often between 300,000 and 400,000 Rupiah — when he took us on our expeditions around the island. But for the first time, I got a vague answer. I felt that he and I had crossed a boundary in our relationship.

23.

Jose Rizal: Zen Life, Zen Death

BACKGROUND

Jose P. Rizal was born in 1861 when the Philippines was a colony of Spain. He studied at the Ateneo de Manila and University of Santo Tomas. Due to his desire to further his education and the apprehension of his relatives that he would go to jail if he remained in the Philippines, he left for Europe and studied in Spain at the Universidad Central de Madrid. He spent some time in Germany (Heidelberg and Berlin), England, and France. He wrote two gothic novels — *Noli me Tangere* and *El Filibusterismo* — which were considered subversive by the Spanish authorities. He was also a doctor, a poet, painter, musician, a polyglot (he spoke or understood several languages, including Greek, French, German, Latin, and English), polymath, essayist, and martial artist. Because of his novels, he was banished to Dapitan in Southern Philippines. When the Philippine Revolution exploded in 1896, he was accused of being its instigator, subsequently tried unjustly by a biased tribunal and died a martyr's death by musketry in Bagumbayan (now the Luneta). Before he died, he wrote his immortal valedictory poem which is now a classic in Spanish literature. He is one of the national heroes of the Philippines.

> *"My hands are shaking because I have just had a fencing bout; you know I want to be a swordsman."* — Jose Rizal, age 18, to Enrique Lete, 27 November 1879.

Emerging from the dojo where he had been studying jujitsu, Jose Rizal found the crisp air scented with flowers. It was the Spring of 1888 in Meiji era Japan. The landscape had suddenly been transformed from dead winter to a lively panorama of flowers everywhere. Beyond was Mount Fuji, snow-capped and majestic.

He wandered all over Tokyo, seeing Kabuki and Noh plays, journeying past a Ginza starting to burgeon with emporiums and bazaars, past squat houses with "walls made of paper," to the temples and shrines of Kyoto and Nara and the Daibutsu at Kamakura, hiking through parks and gardens, listening to street bands, visiting museums and libraries, sometimes alone and sometimes with his dear friend, O-Sei-San, and always, his heart was agitated when he saw something new and exotic, and in Springtime, Japan was a tourist's haven, with its rituals out of ancient lore.

The cherry blossoms had burst into white and pink amid the bright colors of Spring. As the storks keened overhead, the blooms touched with raindrops radiated with limpid softness in the sun. Immortalized in painting, music, and poetry, brooded over by samurai and Zen monks, who saw in the flower the symbol of life's fragility, the sakura dominated the Spring festivals.

Jose Rizal, Philippine national hero.

To the mountain village, this spring eve,
I come and listen to the monastery bell,
Watching the cherries in bloom,
And petals softly falling.
–Noin (10th century)

Rizal felt his body stirring as he walked the strange streets.

He had read the haiku and *waka*, in original Japanese, had admired the *sumiye* paintings (those spontaneous, unplanned, and thoroughly intuitive sketches), heard the strains of the *koto* and *samisen* lamenting the fate of the *sakura*, and in the jujitsu academy he had heard of the meaning of the Spring rites. Like the sakura, the warrior's death must be as glorious as his life. The samurai must live every moment intensely because death hovers perpetually over his head. Death and life both must be faced with stoic indifference. Rizal sketched scenery and flowers and common folk in the Zen way of sumiye, which he had started to learn from O-Sei-San.

With his background, Rizal must have reminded O-Sei-San of the ideal of *bunburyudo*, the combination of artistic and martial virtues a samurai aspired to, as exemplified by Miyamoto Musashi, famous swordsman, painter, and poet of feudal Japan, and author of the military classic, *The Book of Five Rings* (*Go Rin No Sho*).

Indeed, Rizal had the characteristics of a true warrior: he had a lifetime commitment to martial arts, an obsession with death, a contemplative mind, an intense involvement with life and nature, a spartan character, and a great sense of loyalty and justice.

ICARUS BY OILLIGHT

Rizal had a difficult birth. His mother vowed to take him on a pilgrimage to the shrine of Our Lady of Peace and Safe Voyage in Antipolo as a gesture of gratitude. It was thought by the family that Rizal would die.

Death was to haunt him all his life. From childhood he had anxious premonitions and dreams of disaster. He recalled the story of the moth:

> *"I looked toward the light and fixed my gaze on the moths which were circling it...The flame rolled its golden tongue to one side and a moth which this movement singed fell into the oil, fluttered for a time, and then became silent... All my attention was fixed on the fate of the insect. I watched it with my whole soul... It had died a martyr to its illusions."*

In Madrid, Spain, he wrote a passage which prefigured his end.

> *"Night. I don't know what vague melancholy, an indefinable loneliness, smothers my soul... Two nights ago, that is 30 December, I had a frightful nightmare when I almost died. I dreamed that, imitating an actor dying on the stage, I felt vividly that my breath was failing, and I was rapidly losing my strength. Then my vision became dim and dense darkness enveloped me — they were pangs of death."*

Separation, celebrations, ruins, even the landscape evoked death. Again, from Madrid:

> *"The trees are shedding their pompous dresses and converted into dry skeletons, completing the sadness of foggy days. A fine rain, an even finer wind, horrible, freezing, comes from the Guaderrama... a thick mist that wraps all objects with its whitish veil giving them a particular aspect and expression are the tones and lines of this penultimate month of the year, the simple notes of its funeral song intoned to the death of nature."*

LIFETIME OF DISCIPLINE

Like Yukio Mishima, Rizal was born a frail, sickly child. To compensate for his small size, he devoted himself to a regimen of exercise and bodybuilding. He had a private pastime he called *higante* (giant), in which he would stand on tiptoe and stretch his body, legs and arms. He studied arnis de mano (stickfighting), dumog (wrestling), suntukan (boxing) and fencing (foil and rapier), which became lifelong disciplines to him.

Even in Europe, he pursued his martial arts interests with almost fanatical zeal, despite illness and near-starvation. In Spain he continued his study of fencing at the famous school of Sala de Armas y Carbonell. He spent afternoons fencing with Nelly Boustead, Juan Luna, and Valentin Ventura.

Rizal fencing with Juan Luna in Paris

Believe it or not, Rizal also pumped iron a la Arnold Schwarzenegger. Dr. Maximo Viola remembered Rizal had boasted to the members of a gym in Berlin, Germany, that he would beat their strongest man within two weeks.

At this time, he had been forced to turn vegetarian due to persistent lack of funds. Said Dr. Viola: "to triumph in his desire he tried lifting great weights under an unaccustomed diet." Although the smallest in the gym, Rizal did succeed in vindicating himself.

A contemporary in Madrid described Rizal: "He was then in his thirty-first year. The first impression one had of him was of wholesome vigor and physical well-being. He was rather slender of build, but all muscle and sinew, compact, for he never remitted in his exercise."

DE CADENA

There is no record of the style of arnis Rizal studied. However, from his uncle he may have learned the prevailing system of stickfighting in the Tagalog region called pananandata or eskrima.

Arnis de mano figured prominently in his college life, when he was called upon to use it against Spaniards who called his countrymen *chonggo* or monkey (Filipinos paid in kind by calling the Spaniards *bangus* or milkfish). Indeed, there were frequent encounters between the two groups. Rizal became something of a street lord of a campus gang, ready to face a whole pack, one at a time.

Unfortunately, at one such encounter, he was deserted by the members of his gang called *Companerisimo* (Comradeship) and was pounced upon by a contingent of about 12 and was left bleeding and nearly unconscious in the street. Taken home, his wounds — and pride — were nursed by his beloved Leonor Rivera. Needless to say, he must have had some mushy entries in his diary that day. The whole scene could have been a page from *West Side Story*, with the Jets on one side and the Sharks on the other, and a radiant Maria nervously waiting to minister to her favorite warrior.

Rizal was, however, not a hot-headed ringleader whose temper exceeded his prowess but a real expert. On one occasion, he and the best eskrimador in Calamba, Laguna, his hometown, had a bout. Rizal was hit on the forehead. Requesting a return match two weeks later, he underwent thorough preparation and won.

To reach that stage where he could defeat the town's master practitioner, Rizal must have had tremendous speed, technique, and calculation. He must have learned to link his techniques fluidly, without interruption, so that they became in the jargon of the art, de cadena, an unbroken concatenation of attacks, parries, feints, and defenses, which left the opponent no breathing space.

MISTER COOL

Rizal became master of the foil, saber, and dueling sword, and acquired a legendary reputation for grace and technique.

He also became an expert marksman. Witnesses from the period say that Rizal could shoot through the mouth of a bottle and put a hole through the bottom without breaking the bottle itself. From 25 yards, "he could pick the circles (*oros*) of a gambling card." Like many of today's martial artists, Rizal could not resist showing off. He mailed a target board full of holes to Valentin Ventura, himself an expert shooter and fencer, who predictably wrote that he was impressed. Writing to Antonio Luna, Rizal said, "I am sending you a target containing ten bullet holes, it was seven and a half meters from me." Then, he added in mock humility it seems to me, "I shoot slowly, but with perseverance I shall become a fair shot." Caveat: Rizal presented no witnesses to these feats.

Ironically, sometime later, the tipsy Luna made some reportedly unsavory remarks about Nelly Boustead. Something like, *baka ang Noli mo maging Nelly* (Your *Noli* might become Nelly). It was a cutting pun and Rizal took umbrage and challenged Luna to a duel. Nothing came of it though because Luna, now sober, apologized. I wonder if he was somehow intimidated by the reputation of Rizal.

Biographer Pedro A. Gagelonia surmised,

> *"Had the duel prospered, Rizal's fate would have been jeopardized. It was a fact that he was probably better at the use of pistols than Luna, but the latter was a better swordsman. In duels, the challenged party had the option of weapons, hence, Luna, logically, would have chosen the sword." This was the consensus of the Filipino exiles in Europe, too, but Rizal had a different view: "Luna is a nervous and impulsive temperament. I am cool and composed. The chances are he would not have hit me, while I could have hit him at will, but certainly would not have killed him."*

Here, Rizal pointed a finger at three *bushido* (samurai) principles. First, know your enemy and exploit his weaknesses (Sun-Tzu). Second, avoid unnecessary killing. And three, strive for serenity. Rizal's suggestion was swordplay demands not just technical proficiency but also psychological balance. He used the words "cool and composed" which in martial arts mean a mind in repose. Like Sekiun and Takuan, Japanese masters of swordsmanship, Rizal emphasized the psychological against the merely technical.

RIZAL: WARRIOR

Rizal's martial qualities have understandably been eclipsed by his other accomplishments. Yet when he died, he had behind him at least 25 years of experience in the native regimen of arnis de mano, suntukan, and dumog; 20 years in fencing and weightlifting; about 15 years in marksmanship.

A layman may find it hard to understand the kind of physical, mental, and emotional peak a martial artist like Rizal achieves. When an eskrima master goes through a pattern, his whole being is behind every movement, every stroke. Totally centered, he focuses all his faculties — power, breath, muscles, body, mind, and spirit — into that single strike. A master marksman reaches the same intensity. He blots out everything, including himself and his ego, and becomes one with the target.

Fighting with a master is a different plateau altogether. How to respond to an attack, which may be real or feigned, demands tremendous coordination of eye and body. When a stick is whipped, it travels a maximum of 150 miles per hour. At close range, this acceleration takes only a split second from inception to impact. A defender has to react instantaneously to avoid, divert or stop the blow. There isn't much time to decide what specific technique the defender must employ — only his instinct, sharpened by training, can help him with a precise and, hopefully, appropriate answer — or else. Within that almost infinitesimal span of time, the martial artist determines different coordinates — the distance, position, direction not only of his body, legs, and arms, but also his opponent's, and moves accordingly. How much more complicated it becomes when one considers that the forces constantly shift. And then again, what does one do in the face of a synchronized multiple attack?

Mark V. Wiley standing at the feet of Jose Rizal, Manila, Philippines, 1994.

The expert acquires a skill so spontaneous it's like second nature. S/He moves without hesitation. Neither fear of death nor injury nor extraneous thought must intrude into his mind. He becomes, after years of discipline, a person who's centered, one who has broken through the dualism of nature and the contradiction of body and mind.

It is not an easy passage to that level of expertise often described as mystical. A student has to endure pain and loneliness until body, mind, and reflexes respond mechanically, until the weapon becomes a mere extension of the hand, until finally the discipline becomes, in the language of Zen, "artless art."

BACK TO BOTHOAN

Rizal lamented the loss of the ancient martial heritage. Said Rizal:

> *"The ancient Filipinos had army and navy with artillery and other implements of warfare. Their prized kris and kampilan (swords) for their magnificent temper are worthy of admiration and some of them are richly damascened. Their coats of mail and helmets, of which there are specimens in various European museums, attest to their great achievement in this industry."*

The ancient barangays had a martial arts culture. With the coming of the Spaniards and Roman Catholicism, it was slowly decimated. When weaponry was banned by the Spaniards, the Filipinos gradually forgot their ancient martial prowess and discipline. They began to adopt the new culture and religion of the foreigners. By the time of Rizal, Filipinos in the colonized areas had been reduced to using sticks instead of the deadly bladed weapons and the schools sometimes called *bothoan*, where the art of war, the techniques of weaponry, herbal medicine, and assorted expertise were taught, had become according to Rizal's Annotations a mere footnote in to Morga's Sucesos.

As if to remedy the situation, Rizal organized martial arts groups for Filipinos. Rizal's public gym in Calamba (circa 1887) combined classes in wrestling, weightlifting, fencing, marksmanship, and arnis de mano. It was probably the first integrated martial arts club in the country. He also proposed the inclusion of martial arts in school curricula.

Of course, it is difficult to visualize Rizal, the intellectual giant, the renaissance man, as the resident sensei of a local dojo or even as an oriental guru but he did teach martial arts to Filipinos of his time, and not for divertissement and sublimation it seems. I suspect he also dreamed of resurrecting an ancient tradition — that of the Filipino as a warrior.

WAR IN MINIATURE

No doubt Rizal's martial arts training taught Rizal the principles of war. As it is understood by martial arts teachers, sparring — with fists or weapons — is actually war in miniature. As on a battlefield, two adversaries size up each other, using spies to study each other's weaknesses, making strategies for victory, considering variables of combat such as speed, strength, size, technique, terrain, distance, and timing. Like it or not, a practitioner who goes through the routine daily, as Rizal must have done, would develop certain reflexes and, as important, an awareness of principles of combat which negate mere size.

The popular belief that a martial artist rushes into battle, without thought or preparation, certainly has no foundation in fact. An eskrima student learns how and when to attack, to ascertain and exploit the vulnerabilities of his opponent, to create a beat (*kumpas*) by which he hypnotizes his foe, to distance himself through footwork and body weaving (*indayog ng katawan),* to create illusions of speed and height, to set traps and ambushes, to wait for his adversary to make a mistake and to initiate the action. He is taught not to be foolhardy or impulsive or temperamental. He must consider all elements, including his own resources and his opponent's strategy, to win.

REQUISITES OF REVOLUTION

Like Sun-Tzu before him, Rizal believed that "prudence and not valor is the first necessary quality of a general."

Preparation, allies, timing, discipline — these were, to him, the prerequisites of a successful revolution. It bothered him no end that the Filipinos had inadequate weapons. He considered how long the logistics would last. Contacting a Japanese minister who offered three merchant ships to ferry arms and ammunitions, Rizal tried to borrow money for the venture but was rejected by a prominent Filipino.

Not the least of his concerns was, who would lead the rebels on the battlefield? He had met but did not know Andres Bonifacio. He dreamed that the noble Elias would lead the Revolution. He settled for Antonio Luna — yes, the hot-headed Luna — to "direct the campaigns in case hostilities broke out." Rizal himself had sketched plans for fortifications in his travels; in fact, he had written notes on military parapets with diagrams.

It is interesting to speculate what would have happened if a man like Rzal, trained in weaponry, a martial artist par excellence, had led the Revolution of 1896. He had rightly perceived the configuration of Asia, with Japan as the ascendant power and America lurking in the wings; had understood the weakened position of Spain in the face of the Cuban revolution and had correctly analyzed the role of the rich and the military in the struggle. Moreover, he appreciated the role of the masses, of materiel and of strategy in revolution, not to mention the need for unity and discipline.

What a tantalizing speculation it is to cast Rizal into the role of a field marshal. However.

STRATEGY OF REVOLUTION

Summarized by historian Teodoro Agoncillo in his classic book, *Revolt of the Masses*, his famous dialogue with Dr. Pio Valenzuela, Andres Bonifacio's personal emissary from the Katipunan, the revolutionary society of the 1890s, Rizal expressed his desire to secure more weapons for the Filipinos before the Spaniards got wind of the revolutionary underground, was willing to lead the revolution and, apparently to augment his military knowledge, was intending to go to Cuba to observe military tactics, "to study war in a practical way, to go through the Cuban soldiery if I find something that would help remedy the bad situation in our country."

Said Rizal, "I will never lead a disorderly revolution and one which has no probability of success because I do not want to burden my conscience with an imprudent and useless spilling of blood; but whoever leads a revolution in the Philippines will have me at his side." In short, Rizal wanted a strategic approach, a revolution by maneuver and tactic, a position that is consistent with his lifetime training as a martial artist.

ZEN DEATH

There are many explanations for why Rizal died cool and composed. It is said he had a clear conscience; he was at peace with God, or he was a patriot who was willing to die for his people.

I agree, but I like to believe also that it was his lifelong practice of the martial arts that gave him that feral nerve. Wielding a sword against an adversary or aiming a pistol at a target, he had to steel himself, empty his mind, achieve egolessness, and surmount the merely physical aspect of survival. He had spent years to attain what the Japanese call *mushin no shin* (*mind of no-mind*), that pinpoint concentration where intuition and reflex both responded instantly, without hesitation, where body and mind and spirit became one in the sword or the gun.

Mark V. Wiley at Rizal's Grave, 1994

While the world tumbled about him, the gentle warrior went about his business of writing notes, saying goodbye, leaving legacies to his heirs, putting his affairs in order. As if nothing affected him. Even his request that he be shot in front or his incredible gesture of twisting around so that he would fall facing the Philippine sky evoked the grandeur or that *idee fixe* which, perhaps, only the warriors and samurai could have mustered.

Rizal wrote his immortal poem just before he died. Perhaps it's no coincidence that before their death, the samurai of Japan wrote poetry, *jisei*, a kind of "parting-with-life-verse" in the words of D.T. Suzuki characterized by what is known as *furyu*, an appreciation of nature amid tragedy and annihilation.

It was perhaps no coincidence either that Rizal died the eternal stoic, pulse normal, eyes alive to the beauty of the dawn, mind lucid and rational. It was a beautiful death, an exit without regrets, a samurai would have been proud of it.

Here was a man. A genius who, at 35, had accomplished bunburyudo, the martial artist's ideal exemplified by Musashi Miyamoto. Now, he faced martyrdom, the unconditional endorsement through death of his beliefs.

As shots rent the morning at Bagumbayan on December 30, 1896, he twisted his body and fell facing the sky.

For the samurai to learn
There's one thing only,
One last thing –
To face death unflinchingly.
– Tsukara Bokudan (1490–1572)

24.

Jose Rizal, Alchemist

...the ultimate subject and object of the alchemical experiment (was) the alchemist himself. —Michael Baigent and Richard Leigh, *The Elixir and the Stone*

...the true end of alchemy is not the manufacture of gold but the purification of the soul and the contemplation of god. —Peter Marshall, *The Philosopher's Stone*

Jose Rizal was a Mason but there's strangely nothing in the record to show what grade he was. Jose Rizal was a Master Mason, probably level 33 in the hierarchy. But as such, what did he do in the organization to reach that grade, apart from observing and following the principles of Masonry in his life? Did he undergo a test or initiation? We can ask other Masons but they'll probably not say anything because the rituals are a secret. Did he discuss Masonry with his colleagues? It is probable but I have not seen any specifics in the record. Did he visit any alchemical laboratory, say, in Prague, a center of alchemical work in Europe where he spent a few days?

One of the traditions and practices associated with Masonry is alchemy, the art of transformation that may have had its origins in Egypt, China, or India. The word itself came from the root *alkemia*, or black lands, the ancient name of Egypt. Alchemy was referred to later as Hermetic knowledge because the Greeks called Thoth, the Egyptian god of wisdom and writing, Hermes. Alchemy was partly based on the Emerald Tablet, the sacred text that was attributed to Thoth. There are different versions, one of them in China. Some of its maxims are:

Dr. Jose P. Rizal

— As above, so below. As below, so above.

— One in all, all in One.

— What's within is without; what's without is within.

— For every positive, there is a negative; for every negative, there is a positive.

These sayings underscore the system of correspondences and parallels between the body and the earth, on one hand, and the external world, on the other. If there's divine in Heaven, there's also divine within. If there's a feminine, there's a masculine and vice versa. The art embraced a paradigm that included certain beliefs and concepts — nature and man as a manifestation of God, the possibility of perfection, of man being capable of reaching godhood. It is a system that established an ancient paradigm of reality and transformation.

We do not know how it developed but in the course of its history, alchemy was supposed to have evolved a method for the transmutation of lead into gold, or the transformation of the raw human being into the perfect sage or magus through the fusion of contrary and opposite ingredients. The process of alchemy was held as a secret, its "formula" was contained in esoteric symbols and images like sulfur and silver, sun (*sol*) and moon (*luna*), masculine and feminine, tiger and dragon, and the different elements like earth, fire, water, wood, and metal in China. In other cultures, like Greece and India, there are four elements: fire, earth, water, ether (air). They are construed not in their ordinary meaning but in their spiritual, energetic roles.

Alchemy itself started as a process of producing gold and immortality through the mixture of four (or five in China) different metaphorical elements: Earth, Air, Fire and Water or their equivalents. This was called external alchemy. In the course of time it became, as in China, a method of prolonging life and achieving perfection (internal alchemy), twin goals of the tradition. By finding the equivalent elements within the body, internal alchemy (also called Philosopher's Stone) made it possible for practitioners to achieve perfection through the transmutation of energies and emotions. There are different paths or ways. In simple terms, the alchemy of fire (li) or yang and water (kan) or yin was able to produce "steam," a higher element in the process. From the raw a new and higher reality or self — or an Immortal Fetus — is born through the secret processes of alchemy.

Since the early 1990s, when I started studying Taoist internal alchemy, I began looking for evidence if Jose Rizal knew and practiced alchemy. His library contained books by Masons like Voltaire (Jean Marie Arouet). He associated with Masons like his friend Blumentritt. No doubt he was exposed to — and was immersed in — the culture of the Enlightenment. There's also evidence that he may have been greatly influenced by Richard Wagner whose operas contained Masonic symbols and images. There is much in the *Noli Me Tangere* and *El Filibusterismo* that is similar to the Wagnerian operas. The characters of Elias and Father Florentino reflect the "pure and spotless" heroes of the Ring Cycle and Parsifal. There are themes that resonate with Masonic motifs.

Rizal, top left, in the Free Masons journal.

But I did not expect Rizal to mention alchemy, much less to talk about it of course because the theory and practice is considered a secret. Studying it without a knowledgeable master is dangerous and we are warned can result in mental derangement or death. It is evident that many of the symbols and images in Rizal's poetry and the arguments in his writings, especially his correspondence with Father Pablo Pastells, were derived from the Enlightenment, the Hermetic transmissions, and Masonry and their vocabulary. There is the suggestion of a transformation from the gross to the subtle, from the earthly to the divine. For instance,

And when in dark night shrouded the graveyard lies
And only, only the dead keep vigil the night through:
Keep holy the peace, keep holy the mystery.
Strains, perhaps, you will hear — of zither, or of psalter:
It is I: O Land I love: it is I who sing to you.

Nothing then matters to place me in oblivion —
Across your air, your space, your valleys shall pass my wraith.
A pure chord, strong and resonant, shall I be in your ears:
Fragrance, light, and color — whisper, lyric, and sigh:
Constantly repeating the essence of my faith.

—Jose Rizal's valedictory poem translated by Nick Joaquin

Jose Rizal made Master Mason.

The Cable Tow

Vol. XIX — Manila, Philippines, June, 1941 — No. 1

OFFICIAL ORGAN OF THE
GRAND LODGE OF FREE AND ACCEPTED MASONS
OF THE PHILIPPINE ISLANDS

PUBLISHED FOR AND IN THE INTEREST OF THE MEMBERS OF THE LODGES OF THIS JURISDICTION

✦ NEVER BEEN A TRAITOR TO ANYBODY ✦

June 19, 1861

Dec. 30, 1896

Dr. Jose Rizal
A Mason to the Core

Rizal on the cover of The Cabletow, Philippine Masonic Newsletter, 1941

The verses suggest the destruction of the physical and its transformation into something subtle, energetic, or spiritual. This is the essence of alchemy — *dissolve et coagula*. The transmutation of lead into gold, the gross human material into divine possibility.

> *"... in the light of the knowledge of the past and present, I weigh things, try to determine their causes and the finality of their activity, and strive to follow the direction they take. I see in everyone an inborn desire to know; I see the world outside full of colors, qualities and incentives that nourish this desire; I see misery as the chastisement of ignorance, well-being as the prize of knowledge. And I come to the conclusion from my humble reasoning that the Creator desires man to perfect himself by growing in knowledge.*
>
> *Regarding the immortality of the soul and life eternal, how can I believe in the death of my consciousness, when everything around me tells me that nothing is lost but things merely change? If the atom cannot be annihilated, is it possible for my consciousness which rules the atom to be annihilated?"*
>
> —The Rizal-Pastells Correspondence by Raul J. Bonoan, SJ

Another poem is even more suggestive of Jose Rizal's interest in and practice of alchemy:

WATER AND FIRE

We're water, you say; you're fire.
As you like it, let it be!
We live in calmness,
And ne'er will fire see us fight;
Rather joined by wise science
In the burning seat of boilers,
Without anger; without rage.
Let's form the steam, the fifth element.
Advancement, life, light, and movement.

—from Pedro Gagelonia's *Rizal's Life, Works and Writings*

It is clear that "the burning seat of boilers" refers to the laboratory that was used by alchemists to produce the Philosopher's Stone. The poem points to the reconciliation and/or the dissolution of opposites — hot and cold, dry and moist — that is followed in all alchemical traditions, whether Egyptian, European, Indian, or Chinese.

A prolific writer, Jose Rizal kept a meticulous and detailed record of his observations, thoughts, and experiences. But sadly, in keeping with the tradition of Masonic secrecy, he did not bequeath us his method of alchemy, the path to human perfection.

25.

Haiyan Recovery Update: Healers on a Mission

The geographic trajectory of my recent journey to Leyte and Samar in Central Philippines is easy to follow: a flight on Sunday February 02 from Manila took us south to Tacloban City, Leyte, one of the most devastated areas in the country. From the Tacloban airport, we took a rental van to Guiuan, a town in Eastern Samar.

It was a three-hour journey through beautiful but desolate landscape, the sea and islands to the right, mountains to the left, and coconut trees that had lost their fruits and leaves dotting the scene. The last hour of the trip at sunset was over cratered roads, a white-knuckle route made scarier by a race-car wannabe for a driver, tricycles (motorbikes with a sidecar, which are called *tuktuk* in Thailand and *cyclo* in Vietnam), and chickens, dogs, and people crossing our path in the darkness.

From what I saw, the destruction — physical, material, psychological, and spiritual — was unimaginable. Photos can suggest but not capture the extent and depth of it or its direction. How do you draw a map of psychic damage and injury?

We were speechless as we passed tent cities, corrugated iron shanties, heaps of garbage and debris, steel and wooden frames bent like match sticks, posts snapped in two, uprooted trees, cars sitting on top of rooftops, an endless assortment of detritus. I haven't seen anything like it in my 73 years on the planet. Estimates could be drawn for the wreckage of buildings and assets, but who can arrive at the cost to the human psyche? How about the damage to the children?

From Guiuan, we rented and crowded into a small pump boat to take us to Victory Island 45 minutes away on a calm blue sea. "We" refers to Annie, Ellen, MariCris, Sonia, and me. Annie, Ellen, and MariCris are INAM Philippines staff and acupuncturists. They did acupuncture. I, an INAM consultant and visiting professor, led qigong and massage exercises. Sonia, a yoga teacher, raw food chef and a volunteer, taught basic yoga to the children. INAM organized the February mission after the first one in January.

When, on a bathroom break between Tacloban and Guiuan, I asked a storekeeper if she had bananas to sell, she said they had all been blown away by the wind. The reconstruction is going to take years. Five years is the minimum period before the coconuts bear fruit again, if at all.

Meantime, where will the people find food to eat? It takes about six months for rice to be harvested. Vegetables take at least a month, pigs and chickens at least two to three months. The land has been salted over by the sea — will that be a problem for agriculture?

At Barangay 88-89, a boy sadly looks at the devastation of his world.

International and local rescue and relief operations are ongoing. The recovery has already started. We saw a group of fishermen building boats at Barangay 89-90 in Tacloban City. But how long will it take just to clear the debris and heal the people of the trauma from the typhoon?

Haiyan — or Yolanda in the Philippines — packed 190-mile winds for several days. Somebody described the experience as like being in a giant washing machine: getting churned this way in the beginning and that way next, and then being squeezed and turned the other way, and then being washed again and again with the repeat cycle on. Well, add the vicious and relentless winds to the mix.

The scene reminded me of the senseless suffering of an innocent child. Why? How do you explain the existence of such existential horror? All it suggested was not only the indifferent universe of Camus (in *The Plague*) but an angry and merciless God or the trial of Job in the Old Testament.

The horror recalled an early childhood time back in the mid-1940s when a typhoon broke. My family (father, mother, and two small children) lived in a 10 feet x 10 feet house standing a foot above the ground in my hometown of Bamban, Tarlac. The wind blew and whistled for hours. Afraid we would drown, an uncle "evacuated" us to his house next door that had a second floor and was definitely more solid than where we lived. The memory has remained with me until now.

We stopped for two nights at Guiuan to teach and share qigong, meditation, and massage techniques. You'll probably not see our next stop, Victory Island, on the map because it's just a dot in the sea. Go now, said an area resident, while it's still there.

The unpredictability of the weather made us anxious: in the region people talked about the *amihan* (northeast monsoon) or the *habagat* (southwest monsoon) winds that descended even during calm days and nights. There was also a tropical depression the day before we departed Manila, strong enough to be called a typhoon; luckily, it left just when we arrived in Tacloban City.

At a session in Guiuan, we listened to the women who arrived in boats from different islands. We heard about their fears and nightmares when there is a strong wind or news of another storm, and what triggers their fright and sense of helplessness.

Rene teaching villagers how to breathe and cope on Victory Island.

Encouraged by her mother, a 16-year-old girl stood up and told the gathering about her vulnerabilities and worries. She was advised by her doctor to see a psychologist. The stories were so horrendous a group of acupuncturists who had come earlier reportedly had to see a psychologist because they were themselves traumatized and were haunted by "ghosts."

One question I have often asked myself, how can you relieve human suffering with an acupuncture needle? I know there are acupoints that are effective for stress, for relaxation, but how do you get people to eventually help themselves and find peace and quiet, and the courage to leave that painful period behind?

My own humble approach is, in addition to acupuncture, to teach qigong, empowerment, tuina (massage), protection and meditation techniques not only to the victims but also to the healers. We named the protocol "INAM TaoRen Terapi," part of the development of a Philippine approach to healing called Integratib Medisin. We combined different acupuncture points—Kiiko's Triple Intestine near the elbow, CV 6, GV 20, LI 4, LV 3, and a few others on the extremities.

The qigong and tuina, involving massage, Six Healing Sounds, and visualization included activating the *jing* (well) points of the hands and certain areas of the body — lung mu, stomach mu, back of the knees, zusanli, the gall bladder line — and covered the sacrum, lumbar, shoulders, and spine. Massage techniques are important because they are an essential link of human connectedness. Touching, a simple gesture, is a way of reaching out. Focused on the spine, the technique can help restore the supportive strength of the Du Mai (Governing Vessel), one of the ancestral channels.

The protocol is not a complete solution; far from it in fact, but it is what we can offer for now. Eventually, the acupuncturists, the teachers, and the healers (there are also psychologists there) will leave and the typhoon survivors will have to fall back on their own resources and face or exorcise their ghosts. Alone, perhaps in the middle of the night, an area resident will need accessible techniques to cope. Or together the victims will have to support each other ultimately with methods of facing up to the traumas — methods of self-cultivation or nurturing the body, mind, and spirit.

So, we advised them to make the practices an integral part of their lives and their culture. We trained them — I hope well enough for the short time we had — to be familiar with the methods so that they can do the practices as well as teach them to friends and relatives in their remote neighborhoods and villages.

Parts of the armamentum are simple methods of breathing, healing sounds and colors, meditation, and movements of *taoyin* (stretching) or qigong and massage, techniques drawn from the Universal Healing Tao, to learn to let go, reestablish human connection, and restore the spirit. Hopefully, the practices will provide some form of relief and strength now and closure later.

26.

Bringing Chi Nei Tsang Organs Massage to Homonhon

We thought we could not leave because there was a typhoon on the horizon, but we took the plane from Manila to Tacloban City anyway. We were picked up at the airport and taken to Guiuan, Samar three hours east. Along the way, I noticed reconstruction work. It was different from the last time we did a mission in February 2014. The tent city along the way was gone. The coconuts had grown leaves and a few fruits, a sign of hope and recovery. We slept over and in the morning we — Melody, Gecil, Emile (all from PMPI national secretariat, the sponsor of the mission), Lotlot, Annie, and I (from INAM PHILIPPINES) — were ferried in a small open lan-tsa, a catamaran pump boat, to Homonhon, Ferdinand Magellan's first landfall in the Philippines before he proceeded to Cebu and Mactan where the explorer was slain in a battle.[1]

It was windy and the sea was rough (*maalon* in Tagalog). We all got soaked during the 3-hour ride. We stayed at the parish house of the Roman Catholic Church in Bgy. Casuguran. That night the storm broke and dropped tons of water on the iron roof as the wind whistled through the night. I woke up and listened. Finally, I fell asleep, and I woke up to dogs barking and roosters crowing. We had great weather the rest of our stay on the island.

The healing mission to Homonhon was part of the closure activity of what was called Early Recovery Phase that included relief and immediate response (after typhoon Haiyan/Yolanda) of Project Pagbangon initiated by the Misereor of Germany and the Philippine Misereor Partnership, Inc. (PMPI). Our group was going to provide massage training to leaders, midwives, and barangay health workers as a continuation of INAM TaoRen Terapi for trauma and wellness that we conducted in Guiuan, Victory Island, and Tacloban City February 2014.

The Integrative Medicine for Alternative Health Care Systems (INAM) Philippines that I belong to as a consultant and trainer is one of the PMPI network members that are responding to the health issues of the island.

Homonhon Closure. Rene and the pump boat that brought the group of healers from Homonhon back to Guiuan, Samar.

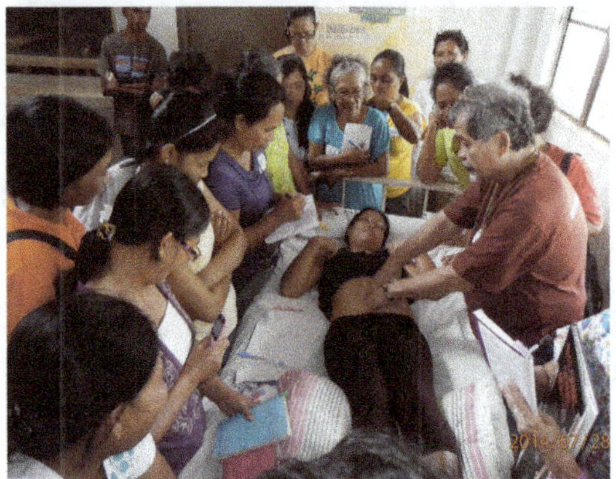

Rene teaching CNT to a group of women from the islands. The photo shows a manipulation of the Small Intestine.

We had a seminar for more than 20 women from different barangays. There were seven or eight men on the first day, but they were all called to a meeting on another initiative relief program of PMPI.

In my introductory remarks, I said that it is important to learn the techniques not only for trauma but also to make them a part of our culture and life, that the healing tradition of the Philippines as represented by the babaylan has to be revived, and that each person in the spirit of self-reliance and autonomy, could be a healer in her own way.

We started the training at the church with CNT (Chi Nei Tsang), the organ massage method developed by the Healing Tao master Mantak Chia in the mid-80s. I was one of the senior instructors who wrote and edited the book that is now a classic in New Age literature. The techniques involve manipulations on the different organs — Liver, Kidneys, Stomach, Colon, Lungs, Heart. In Chinese medicine, these organs hold emotions — anger, fear, worry and anxiety, grief, and sadness — and manifest different illnesses as a result. Especially in cases of severe trauma, these emotions could sit in the organs for a long time and affect the physical and mental balance of a person unless a multi-faceted healing approach is implemented. Unlike ordinary massage on the muscles, CNT goes direct to the source of the problems, the organs themselves.

Since we needed tables, we moved to the local community health center. At first, I wondered how the participants would react to this style of bodywork because the patient has to expose the abdomen in the course of the treatment. I know from years of teaching in different countries that women in certain cultures are averse to or are not allowed to show certain parts of the body like the abdomen or, in a worst-case scenario, even the face. The organ massage was something new to everybody. I demonstrated the first technique, a manipulation of the stomach with Lotlot, my assistant, as the model patient. She was a very funny and cooperative patient, so she was a good example for others to follow.

The participants were surprised to hear that certain shapes of the navel could reflect chronic or lifetime obsessions and emotions, that an experienced practitioner of Chinese and Japanese palpatory diagnosis could actually "read" what it "says."

There was much laughter as we broke into five groups, each one practicing the technique that was demonstrated.

Homonhon Healing Circle

In the course of two-and-a-half days we also covered Six Healing Sounds, an ancient Chinese qigong method from the Universal Healing Tao that deals with emotions and energy; several movements of Xing Shen Zhuang Fa, another qigong tradition that focuses on strengthening the spine; Dragon Well Qigong, my synthesis of several Buddhist and Taoist techniques; and Power Animals (Tiger, Dragon, Crane, Snake). I told the group each animal represents a different virtue and power. I said I'll teach them the monkey next time!

At the end of three days, we had a fire ritual in front of the burning clay kalang.

At the end of three days, we had a fire ritual in front of a burning clay *kalang* (cauldron) for closure. Fire is one of the alchemical elements for transformation in ancient cultures. The other is Water. I gave a Taoist empowerment and protection blessing, to each and every one of the participants.

It was an exhausting procedure for me, partly because of the individual qi work but also because I had almost no sleep for a week. I flew from Newark Airport on Thursday morning, arrived at NAIA on Friday night, and proceeded to Tacloban City that Saturday.

All six of us had a long walk on the beach and watched the sunset beyond the mountains when the training was finished. Emile, the local facilitator and Melody, the Project Officer of PMPI, brought us San Miguel beer and we sat and listened to the night wind and the tides in the dark. We talked about our work and the effects of training that we had just conducted in Homonhon. We wondered how much of what we taught would become a part of the culture of healing and self-cultivation in the local community.

When we left the island to return to Guiuan the next morning, the sea was calm and smooth. To me, it was a sign of good things to come. We were tired but happy we were able to share the different techniques of healing and recovery and bring laughter to the women from the barangays.

27.

Thinking of My Friend, Uncle Rudy

I was leaving for China last August (2006) when I received an e-mail from my college contemporary Isis Sabelino saying that Uncle Rudy had passed away at his house in Sampaloc, Manila.

In my journey through Beijing, Shanghai, Chongqing, Xian, the Three Gorges, I often found myself thinking about him.

Everybody called him Uncle. His full name was Rodolfo C. Vidad. It was sometime in 1968 that Isis introduced me to him. I was in my late 20s, a lawyer working in the Philippine Senate, a student of Shaolin Temple Boxing and Tai Chi Chuan, and married with a child.

Uncle Rudy occupied a room with shelves for records and tapes, a turntable, tape player, and two speakers. His bed sat in the center of it. There was a clear glass window occupying one side facing the other house outside. Another room held more of his records and tapes. It was the largest private collection that I had ever seen, comparable to the one at USIS Jefferson Reading room in the Escolta, where at 17 or 18, a student taking undergraduate studies, I first heard recordings of TS Eliot's *The Wasteland* and Edith Sitwell's *The Canticle of the Rose.*

At the time, I did not know much about Uncle Rudy's life, except that he studied at the Massachusetts Institute of Technology (MIT). He was an engineer with a construction business. He smoked. I did not know if he was Protestant or Catholic. Religion wasn't something we talked about.

I don't have a picture of him, but I can remember how he looked: his pompadour of a hairdo, a smile that was slightly askew, his bright, but sad eyes, the expressive hands. I remember his soft voice, his dry humor, his thoughtfulness. He was tall for a Filipino, slim, with a slight stoop and a gangly walk. He never did wear anything fancy, just a plain shirt and light-colored khaki pants.

I can't exactly remember our first conversation. But I do remember that sometime during my visits I told him that as a child I studied the violin in our hometown, but the teacher stopped coming, and so that was the end of my music studies. I said much of the music I had heard was from the radio. I remember what our church choir, conducted by Josue "Sonny" Villa, sang (Handel, Mozart, and Bach, among others). Sonny became a Philippine ambassador for some time to Thailand and briefly to China. Another Sonny (Fabie) accompanied us on the piano or organ and played Rachmaninoff ("Prelude #2") and Debussy ("Claire de Lune"). What I also listened to but was probably too embarrassed to admit, was what was called "light classical" — Song of India, Barcarolle, Mantovani, Ray Conniff — and a few themes from the popular repertoire. That was my childhood exposure to music.

The next few times that I saw him at his house, Uncle played different types of music, classical and romantic, and sometimes recitations (one of them of Dylan in America by Sir Alec Guinness). It was at his house that I first heard "Britten's Children's Introduction to the Orchestra" and "Peter and the Wolf" narrated by Sean Connery.

He introduced me to Haydn, Mozart, and then to Beethoven. He made me listen to a commentary explaining the similarities and differences between Mozart and the early Beethoven. He gave me materials about the technique of transformation and variations in Beethoven's 5th Symphony and the triad in the 3rd (dedicated to Napoleon). He played the "Eroica" (3rd symphony) and "Wellington's Victory," Beethoven's apologia for Eroica. We listened to Brahms, Schumann (I loved his composition for the piano, "Kinderszenen" ("Scenes from Childhood"), Tchaikovsky, Rachmaninoff, and Ravel and the French impressionists and many composers like Bartok, Mussorgsky, Borodin.

He would play a piece of music, say, Rachmaninoff's Piano Concerto #2 performed by different pianists. Or Tchaikovsky's Violin Concerto also by different performers. Often it was like that. We would also listen to operas and then arias sung by different singers: Callas, Scotto, Sills, among them.

It's not just a matter of recognizing the music, he said, you should be able to recognize the performer. He also said, why buy an expensive stereo equipment if all you are going to play is junk?

I would sometimes drop by his house on Remedios Street after my Tai Chi Chuan or Shaolin lessons in Chinatown or when I was not busy at work. At the time I had grown deeply interested in Chinese kung-fu. My first Shaolin master Johnny Chiuten taught me esoteric Buddhist forms. Later he introduced me to his master Lao Kim, the patriarch of martial arts in Manila's Chinatown. I also had the rare privilege of having a new master in Chan Bun Te, who trained in Yang Tai Chi Chuan style with the Taiwanese master Han Ching Tang.

In the course of time, I was able to listen to many compositions from the classical, romantic, baroque, modern eras. It was a great education. I also got acquainted with the Soviet Army Chorus and Missa Luba.

One time, he told me that he was going to play Rachmaninoff's Piano Concerto #3. It was a composition I had not heard before. It was played by Alexis Weissenberg, of whom I knew nothing before, either. Weissenberg, if I remember from the liner notes, was about eight or nine years old when his teacher played a recording of the concerto for him. It was performed by no less than Rachmaninoff himself. The young boy was enchanted and at that early age committed himself to learning to play it. Years later, when he was in his early 20s or late teens, he became co-winner with the violinist Itzak Perlmann of the Leventritt Competition. Rach 3 was the piece he played at the competition.

Another time Uncle played recordings of Mahler: Symphony #1, the "Titan," and then Symphony #2, "the Resurrection." It was later that I learned — probably from the album cover notes, possibly from one of the books in Uncle Rudy's library — about Mahler's struggle with the superstition about and the "curse" of the 9th symphony and death. It was then that Uncle played Gustav Mahler's "Songs of the Earth," a set of lieders based on the poems of Du-Fu, Li-Po, and others. I had read these two Chinese poets of the Tang dynasty but did not really appreciate them until I heard their words being sung in Mahler. (Perhaps, it had something to do with "colonial mentality," the tendency to dismiss or ignore something from Asia until somebody famous in the west recognized or praised it.)

Uncle talked about the 3 Bs in music. I learned about Hector Berlioz and was awed by his Requiem. Later on, Uncle introduced me to Shostakovich, Takemitsu, and Schoenberg. I fell in love with Tchaikovsky's "Souvenir of Florence."

I learned bits and pieces of the lives of the composers, conductors, and performers. I learned the vocabulary of music. I read Leonard Bernstein explain Beethoven and the concepts of harmony and melody.

Inclined to privacy, Uncle did not say much about himself. He did not really talk a lot. He put on a recording and listened all the while. We would have snatches of conversation here and there. But I learned how he got immersed in this life of music. He was a young postgraduate student at MIT in Cambridge, Massachusetts, when he began attending concerts. When he got to know the doormen and guards at the symphony hall, he was allowed to get in free. If the house was full, he would sit on the stairs in the balcony. It was at this time that he started his giant record collection.

I never heard him sing. He told me that if there was a song he wanted to sing, it was "None but the lonely heart." I did not ask why. He did not explain.

Sometimes, Uncle would tape a recording for me to take home. I had acquired a small second-hand tape recorder at the time and all of a sudden, our small neighborhood apartments in Kamuning were echoing with Tchaikovsky's Violin in D and Dylan Thomas' poetry.

In 1969, Uncle picked up photography probably influenced by his nephew Melvin. He and I started to talk about photography. He opened a dark room. My brother Flor gave me an Asahi Pentax professional camera and I began to take photos, too.

In 1970, Uncle Rudy gave up smoking. He explained to me that he would put a pack of Marlboro in front of him, stare at it and struggled with his addiction, until he succeeded in overcoming it. To me, that was quite a heroic feat.

I gave him my used recording of Shakespeare plays by the Marlowe Reading Society that I got from the Solidaridad Bookstore on Padre Faura.

When I left for the US late in 1970, Uncle gifted me with three tapes. "Rots of Rock," he wrote on the wrapper. One had Wagner, the second stories for children ("Babar, the Elephant" and others) and the third was Jerry Dadap's music from his first concert at PhilamLife Auditorium (including his first symphony and his obra maestra "Alay sa Inang Bayang," a composition for orchestra, chorus and rondalla), and Philippine songs. (I gave Uncle the recording of Dadap's first concert which I got from a DJ at a radio station in Caloocan City somewhere. I was listening to the radio one morning when I heard the music and decided right then to call the DJ to make an appointment to see him.)

In New Jersey, I started my own modest collection of recordings, which included some of what I heard at Uncle's, and readings. I frequented Sam Goody's, Harmony House, and a few other record stores when we lived near Asbury Park. I bought a cheap stereo set.

In Brooklyn, New York City in 1972, I got a Benjamin Miracord II turntable, large Bose speakers, a Japanese tape recorder. Often, my children Norman and Albert, then six and three, and I would sit and listen to "Peter and the Wolf," "Children's Introduction to the Orchestra" (narrated by Sean Connery), Peter Ustinov reading Exupery's "The Little Prince," and others. Albert, at the age of three, had memorized many passages from Exupery, including the famous "mushroom" paragraph that began with, "I know a red-faced gentlemen. He has never smelled the flowers, he has never looked at the stars, he has never loved anyone."

Later, I was also able to acquire bargain recordings of Shakespeare, Greek plays, Dylan Thomas, among them, from closing sales.

Intermittently, I sent Uncle vinyl and CD recordings. A couple of solos by Cleo Laine, a Messiaen, Chinese pipa music, Weissenberg playing Chopin, Maria Farantouri singing Theodorakis, Cleo Laine at Carnegie Hall, Cleo Laine and Ray Charles singing "Porgy and Bess," among others. One time, concerned about a photography book a friend borrowed from him and never returned, I looked around, found a copy, and sent it to Uncle as a replacement.

I saw him when I visited Manila after the fall of Marcos in 1986. By that time, he had become immersed in photography. When I called, he was often out taking pictures. He gave me a copy of his book of photographs which featured many of the famous visiting ballet dancers at the Cultural Center of the Philippines.

Years had passed since I last saw him in the mid-1990s. I had trained in Chinese and Japanese acupuncture and traditional Chinese herbology, left lawyering, became a healer and teacher (of martial arts, massage, meditation, qigong, internal alchemy), wrote poetry and essays (and got published), studied more Taoist arts and Tai Chi Chuan, traveled much, saw my two boys grow up, marry and gift me with five grandchildren, met new teachers who broadened my life and knowledge.

In the middle of it all, music has been very much a part of my life. Over the years I acquired a good collection of vinyl recordings: Tibetan and Buddhist chants, symphonies, Japanese shakuhachi, folk songs from different countries, concertos, solos, new interpretations of the traditional repertoire. Ten years ago, my son Albert asked me if he could have them. I retained a few which are sitting in my library. I have stereo equipment all over the house. Last year, Albert installed a sophisticated stereo set at my house to replace the old one I bought in the early 70s.

Last year, I took a course in Music Theory at a local community college. I have consistently had a stereo — an audio before, now a CD — player in my car and a bunch of recordings.

The grandchildren — Emily, Madalyn, Ava, and Isabel — have just had their first recital. They perform for me when I visit. I've given them CDs of Beethoven's piano sonatas and Peter and the Wolf and Introduction to the Orchestra, along with Pete Seeger's Concert at Town Hall.

I've played "Peter and the Wolf" and Introduction to the Orchestra for Ava and Isabel when they are with me. A few times, we sat in my library and listened to the old vinyl of Peter Ustinov reading "The Little Prince." Both Ava and Isabel have memorized the "mushroom paragraph" and sometimes, moved by the spirit, we three would recite it from memory. They are studying the piano now. Isabel studies the recorder and the trumpet.

Often when I attend a concert — Shostakovich's 13th Symphony ("Babi Yar" with Yevtushenko reading his own poem) at the Met in New York or Yoyo Ma playing Bach's complete suite for the cello at Carnegie Hall — I think about Uncle Rudy and wish he were there with me. When I saw Berlioz's Symphony Fantastique at Royal Albert Hall in London, I sent Uncle a postcard about it.

When I was in China after Uncle's death, I wondered if I had done justice to our friendship. I thought about what he did for me, how he opened experiences I had not imagined, how he enriched my life, how his legacy of music has been passed down to my children and grandchildren. I regretted not seeing Uncle more often when I visited Manila. But I could not do anything about that. Instead, I wrote and mailed a postcard addressed to him saying, "Thank you for everything. I miss you. Love, Rene."

28.

Len Roberts: Poet

It was in the mid-80s, perhaps '84, probably '85, that I first met Len Roberts. Ted Kloss, chair of the English Department at Lafayette College in Easton, PA, was conducting a weekly poetry workshop and I was one of the community residents who attended regularly. One day Ted got sick, and Len took his place.

I had submitted a couple of poems. One was about kite-flying with my children in Prospect Park, Brooklyn; the other was a war poem about a child in the ruins of a town in an island in the Philippines.

Len said that he liked the war poem, that writing political poetry is very difficult. After the workshop, Len told me that I should bring some of my poems to him at his office at the college. That I did. At that time, I was writing a sheaf of poems about Hiroshima. I still have a copy of the notes he had written at the time about 25 years ago. I have kept them like the other letters he has written to me over the years, mostly comments on drafts of poems I had sent him from wherever I was as I traveled the world. Four years ago, as I packed my things to move to another house, I saw these letters again and re-read them.

Poet Len Roberts and Rene in Hellertown, Pennsylvania.

These comments were not only meticulous, they were also generous and gentle. Len would ask for details, suggest another word, or hint that perhaps there is another poem sitting behind what I had written. He would say something truly encouraging and mark certain lines that he liked. There was never a time when he was cruel or nasty. And he was always thoughtful and kind. So, over a period of more than two decades, Len helped me with my poetry.

Rene reading poetry live at the Marble Summer Arts Festival in New York City in 2023. During the pandemic, the festival went online.

I sent him and his wife Nancy postcards from Egypt, UK, Thailand, China, wherever I was. I visited him at his house, sometimes slept over. He would get a pizza or Nancy would cook, I would bring a bottle of red wine, and the three of us would sit in the living room. One time we listened to Yo-Yo Ma, another time I showed a Tai Chi DVD I had done and talked about my Taoist practices. A favorite subject of his was his new project — building a house on an island in Nassau. Always his son Joshua was a concern. Travels with Nancy were a topic that generated much laughter. Sometimes Len and I took a walk in the backyard up the hill where he had planted black walnuts and a grove of pine trees. One night, sitting in front of the fireplace, with a bottle of wine on the table, he read his favorite poems by Thomas Hardy and D.H. Lawrence. For the first time, I saw the other facet of these two fictionists' brilliance.

One summer afternoon, I brought him a new poem I had written in London. Let's think about it, he said and jumped in the pool, did a few laps, and when he came back, he had a few ideas to improve it. Water always seemed to invigorate him: he loved the sea and planned to spend his retirement at the home he was building in the islands.

We often wrote to each other, sometimes long letters, often just short notes. We read together in the Philipsburg Art Center, NJ. Here is our correspondence about a reading the two of us did in Allentown, PA:

At 01:13 PM 3/28/00:

Dear Len,

Thank you for making me a part of that poetry reading at Borders. I truly enjoyed doing it. The tea with you and the others was fun, too. Sometimes I need a break from my otherwise solitary life and the regimen of meditation, qigong, and Tai Chi Chuan.

It's easier now to do these things. I do bits and pieces often. I can go out at any time of the day and do a sword or spear form like it's not really a routine but just the flow of the universe.

Breathe well!

Rene

Dear Rene,

I had a fine time, too, reading with you! One of my students who was there praised and praised your reading presence as well as the poems. Thank you for the kind dedication at the start, also. I am touched whenever I think I have had anything to do with your fine poems.

I admire your practice and wish I could incorporate some of what you do daily into my poetry life. But the world encroaches, snares …

Hopefully this summer will open up new avenues. As well as provide time to see you here!

All best,

Len

Len's poetry often explored and engaged everyday life: none of the big issues of the world but the ordinary happenings in school, at home, in his life. He wrote about the tools of carpentry, the search for the best Christmas tree in the backyard, shopping at the grocery store, doing the laundry, shoveling snow. He talked about the ordinary objects in the house and neighborhood: the gold carp, copper frog, mockingbird mobile, crickets, the periwinkle. Many of the poems are about his childhood at a Catholic school or about alcoholism, recovery, his parents, and his brother. Sometimes he wrote about his early sexual experiences, which were more funny and awkward than erotic.

Even if the poems dealt with the quotidian, they were often metaphors for a bigger, larger universe or symbols of existential conflicts. He wrote about a snapping turtle that wandered in his lawn:

… his departing hiss at me a warning,
I did not take lightly,
having seen those eyes before,
and that thick shell,
that reptile brain,
knowing even as I let him go
that he would be back again.

In a memorable letter-poem, to his friend poet Hayden Carruth, who was sick and dying in a hospital, Len wrote:

… and because I know you're close enough
to death now so you feel its breath,
its stink you've written so often about,
old man who used to sit at our round
oak table those blue-gray dawns

to stare out at the pond, waiting
to catch just one more glimpse
of the great blue heron flapping,
clumsy, its prehistoric wings
as it rose over the telephone wires
and trees, into the mountain
that has no name.

One of my favorite poems, "Talking to the Poison Sumac," recalls his older brother who went mad, was confined to the VA hospital for 24 years, and received electric shocks treatment:

And I didn't know why I was out there
thinking of his soft body I had not held
for more than twenty years, repeating
his story when I knew that nothing
I did or said mattered, that the sky
was powerless, and the sun setting
powerless, that the snow that started
to fall, the beautiful falling
itself, was nothing, the field, the world,
the unlivable, burning stars, the emptiness
of it all contained here in one small human heart.

He did not use any big words. You understood every single word, every single sentence, because they referred to things that we know, things that are familiar; but somehow, there was something else there, something we had to decipher, something we had to translate, something much bigger than the things he seemed to be writing about.

And his long lines are something else again. You read through a whole poem non-stop, possibly in a single breath, as if the poet cannot stop the flow of his narrative, he must take in the whole experience in one gulp. I tried the style — which my father perhaps influenced by Victor Hugo, also used back when I was in high school — and found it very effective.

The body of his work describes a life, from the grades to maturity, the slow transformation, and redemption of a human being through the anguish and pain of growing up in a totally dysfunctional family, through separations and divorces, and nervous breakdowns and drunkenness, and self-inflicted suffering. Somehow, we know that poetry played a great part in that life, poetry shed light on the darkness, cleared the way for him, and fulfilled the destiny that was waiting like a hidden treasure in his heart.

I look at his attainment: selection of "Black Wings" for the National Poetry Series, grants from National Endowment of the Arts and Fulbright and awards from the Guggenheim. There is also an award for his translation of Sandor Csoori's poems. Eight books of poetry and a couple of chapbooks. Decades as a teacher. It is a solid achievement.

When I read his obit in the local newspaper a few days after his death on May 25, 2007, I was dumb struck. I was standing at Wegman's in Nazareth, Pennsylvania, paying for my lunch, and in front of the cashier, I could not hold back the tears. My family consoled me because they knew how much I loved and respected this man. He touched my soul and my life, both, and I've never been the same since the first time I met him at Lafayette College a quarter of a century ago.

LEN ROBERTS' PUBLISHED WORKS:

The Disappearing Trick (posthumous)
The Silent Singer: New and Selected Poems
The Trouble-Making Finch
Counting the Black Angels
Dangerous Angels
Black Wings
Sweet Ones
From the Dark
Cohoes Theatre

Translations from Hungarian:
Waiting and Incurable Wounds (chapbook of Sandor Csoori)
Selected Poems of Sandor Csoori
Call to me in My Mother Tongue (chapbook of Sandor Csoori)

29.

David Cortez Medalla

MEDALLA: IN MEMORIAM (1938–2020)

An announcement in "Art News" in January 2021 hit me this morning. It said:

> *David Medalla, an artist whose open-minded output spanned participatory gestures and sculptures that created themselves, has died at 78. Curator Adam Nankervis, who was Medalla's partner and longtime supporter, said on Facebook that the artist died in Manila on Monday.*
>
> *Medalla was something of a cult figure until recently, with his pioneering sculptures of the 1960s mainly known to European curators and historians, who have featured them in major biennials and surveys over the past decade. But a growing fan base has also come to recognize the artist, who was known for cofounding a key London gallery in the 1960s, his role in a series of influential collectives, his writings, and much more — in addition to a practice that defies easy classification.*

I knew the artist when he was 15 (or perhaps 19, depending on the source). He lived in a shack on A. Mabini close to the Luneta, Manila, Philippines. I was 16 at the time, a college student in 1957.

The shack that he called Le Cave Angely was made of boards. The door was often unlocked (at least the two times I went to visit). As you entered, there was a painting that he called "Crucifixion on the Sea." It showed Jesus on the Cross in a kind of bay. There were fishes in the water at his feet. It was done on plywood with enamel paint and pebbles. Beneath the painting were books. One of them was Walt Whitman's *Leaves of Grass*. In the margins of the book were poems and notes written by hand, presumably by Medalla himself. He marked a famous line: "This is not a book, who touches this touches a man."

He was known as David Cortez Medalla. He used to hold poetry readings on Wednesday nights with some of the beautiful society people like Diana Jean Lopez and Cynthia Sun. I attended one of his poetry readings in Sampaloc, Manila. He read his poem "Young Limbs."

It was about, well, limbs. He compared limbs to Zhu Bei Hong horses and rose petals. He said it took him six months to find a metaphor for limbs. Somebody asked, It took you that long? He read from TS Eliot's *A Game of Chess* (from the Wasteland), Juan Ramon Jimenez's *Fortunate Creature*, and Eugenio Montale's *Dora Marcus* that night. He said the English version of Jimenez that he read was his own translation.

David C. Medalla and Rene, 1957

Looking back, I must acknowledge my debt to him for having introduced me to those great poets. I was a young college student in Manila, a new arrival in the city, and the rare exposure to poetry reading gave me the inspiration to explore the bookstores and libraries. Can you imagine a teenager from the province being exposed to this kind of experience? It was mind-blowing and mind-expanding. The kind of experience that can change you inexorably and totally. I started reading books by Jose Garcia Villa, Nick Joaquin, Rabindranath Tagore, TS Eliot, Nikos Kazantzakis, Albert Camus, Jean Paul Sartre, and Jack Kerouac and listening to the recordings of poetry at the British Reading Room on Recto Avenue and the Jefferson USIS Library in the Escolta. I still have Villa's *Selected Poems and New*, with the rave introduction by Edith Sitwell, published in 1958, that I bought in September of that year for 13 pesos at the National Book Store warehouse on Arlegui Street.

Later in the year, he presented a reading of *The Wasteland* with popular society figures in black at the University of the Philippines.

I read somewhere that he and Jose Garcia Villa walked around the campus of Columbia University with the hand painted iconic Third Eye on their foreheads. Most probably the idea, considered eccentric then, came from one of Villa's Divine Comma Poems where he described "the, true, dark, Hero" as "He, with, the, three-eyed, thunders..." One of Villa's self-portraits shows him with three eyes. I think that was the time when Medalla was taking special classes as a student at the Ivy League university. He must have been 13 or 14 at the time.

The last time I saw Medalla in his shack at Mabini he had just come back from Ethiopia (Abyssinia) on a kind of travel grant associated with Arthur Rimbaud. He said he wrote poems after the Frenchman and that it was going to be published with a photo of him posed like a statue: feet together, knees bent, and arms raised together in front. I do not know if it got published because it was not mentioned in his bios.

But he did publish a magazine in the University of the Philippines where he answered questions about himself: his "terrestrial" and "celestial" addresses, his favorite poets (Dante, Walt Whitman, and Jose Garcia Villa). He published one of his rare poems, "A Psalm," in it:

The Lord is my Gardener.
He shall come to me
A parasite-ridden
Parched tree
Standing in a desert
Of poisonous ponds,
Bull's bones
And granite jewels
Of phosphorescent stones.
He shall come to me
And pluck the worms
From my waterless
Strengthless roots.
And he shall send me
Forth his showers
To drown my thirst
And soothe my sores.
Until once more
I burst into songs
And poems
And flowers.

David Cortez Medalla and Rene in front of Le Cave de Angely in Ermita, Manila in 1957.

I read the poem and that's how I remembered it from memory until now.

I saw him again at an art gallery in Ermita in 1968. Somehow in my memory it was Lyd Arguilla's but I could be wrong. He and his partner had just travelled to Ceylon, and they were wearing batik sarong and white tunic. He was giving a talk about his travel to a small audience. They stopped over in Manila on their way back to London. Sometime around this period, his kinetic sculpture was featured in a British movie: It was a kind of white blob floating in water, constantly changing shape.

His illustration, a line drawing of Sisa changing into a tree, reminiscent of Daphne in Greek mythology, appeared on the cover of Leon Ma Guerrero's translation of the *Noli Me Tangere*.

Every now and then, at the millennium, I would read about his art installations at popular art shows in New York. As described by the *New York Times*, one of his creations involved a piece of cloth hanging from the ceiling and a bowl of needles and thread for anyone to embroider much of anything on the cloth. One time there was a photo of his painting based on the Hindu Goddess Kali with an extraordinarily long red tongue. Except for his poem quoted above and the poem "Laughter in the Slums," published in the mid-1950s in a Philippine magazine, I have not seen any poem under his name. I believe he dedicated himself to kinetic art and stopped writing poetry altogether. But who knows, perhaps he has poems written in journals and on the margins of books, and one day we may find them published posthumously!

30.

The Dragon at 75: Reflections on Growing Older

I heard Ana, a 72-year-old woman of Italian origin, groaning after finishing a routine at a machine at the gym one morning. I said to her, "The things we have to do to keep the body healthy." She replied, "Just to keep it alive."

When I started going to the gym, I thought I was the oldest at 69. It turned out I was one of the youngest in the group that met in the morning. The others on that day were older, some a lot older. A couple were in their late 70s, one or two in their 80s. They were there pumping iron, pushing the pedals of the stationary bike or riding the treadmill. All of them had been doing it for months or years.

When I went to my primary care physician a few years ago, I was surprised to see myself in the waiting room in the company of disabled people, one or two in crutches or quad, usually accompanied by somebody younger. I did not realize then — or in the subsequent visits — that I was already a "senior citizen." I was on Social Security retirement pension, a "retiree" — I did not like the word, I preferred "pensioner." Despite my membership in AARP, I did not think I had actually retired since I was still busy — teaching, studying, writing, traveling, and practicing Taoist arts. I had not gone to pasture yet or started playing shuffleboard or attending senior citizens' gatherings at the local church or community center.

Here are random reflections about different subjects written over a period of three years at this juncture in my life.

CHANGES

One realizes inevitably that the years are creeping up/have crept in and the body isn't the same any longer. There are the pills accumulating on the counter — fiber, fish oils, vitamins A, D, E, Glucosamine and Chondroitin, Cholest-Off, saw palmetto — and the bottles of Cod Liver Oil the doctor recommended one must take two tablespoons twice a day. And of course, the postures and movements in Tai Chi Chuan one did easily before having become a little difficult now. It was one of the reasons I had started going to the gym: I wanted to recover my flexibility and stamina. I do not know if it will happen, but I am slowly regaining strength in my knees, the old pains are diminished, if not gone. I have also been able to do my usual traditional Yang family Tai Chi Chuan practice and some of the Shaolin forms.

What do you do as you get older? When you are in your 40s, 50s, 60s? At a given point in your 40s, perhaps you begin to get bored with what you are doing. Unanticipated when you were in your 20s, the challenge of your job is no longer fascinating or interesting. As a lawyer or even as a financial adviser, the glamour and excitement of the profession is no longer that attractive. And you begin to look into other things that you could do. You have the money and the time: now what do you like to do that would be satisfying and meaningful?

At Dunhuang, an important station on the tour of the Silk Road that started in Xian, passed Flaming Mountain (made famous by Sun Wukong/Monkey King), Gobi Desert and Heaven's Lake and ended in Urumqi.

Change happens all the time, at any age. One usually becomes more aware of it when one retires or at the point of retirement. But I have also seen it happen in people in their 20s.

Perhaps we do not know that we have changed. But even if we did, often we do not acknowledge it. Consequently, we deny it and we continue to do the things that we can no longer do well or even dislike. The body has changed, so has the mind, so has the perspective. The changes one goes through are many and some of them are not even noticeable. If I were to itemize some of them, I would probably neglect or forget to include quite a few. It is said that the body changes every so often, in an inevitable process of metamorphosis: every second, there is a transformation, the body we have now isn't the same as the body we had a few minutes ago. Through a whole lifetime, we must have undergone millions of changes in a gradual intellectual and physical evolution. Where does it lead? We do not notice the profundity of it; we see only the surface: the wrinkles, the scars, the withering, and the osteoporosis as we look at the mirror.

There are deeper changes… the injuries and the wear-and-tear, the effects of gravity and the sun and the years… the psychic and physical damage and trauma… and of course there are the refinements of our consciousness, values, and the mind.

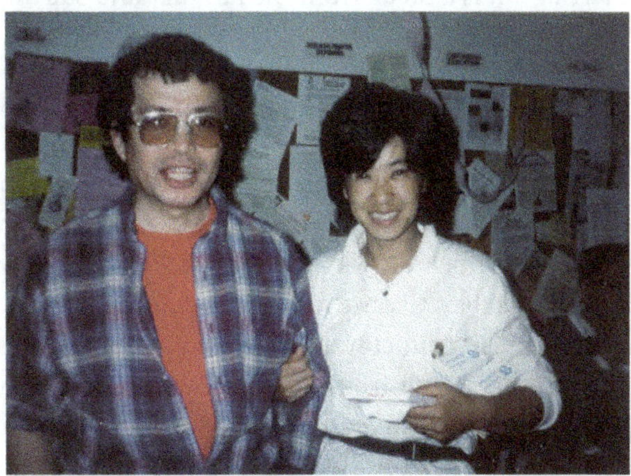

Kiiko Matsumoto, the famous acupuncturist and author of several books like "Hara Diagnosis: Reflections on the Sea." Kiiko sensei was my teacher at the New England School of Acupuncture in the early 1990s. I was her intern in Japanese acupuncture at NESA. I apprenticed with her as a "Moxa boy" — meaning I followed her around the clinic or at her house burning thread- or sesame seed-size moxa on acupuncture points that she indicated for me to do. I've taken several of her weekend seminars since then.

As one learns from life, there are certain ideas and beliefs and practices that become passé, obsolete, absurd. One can no longer hold on to them for one reason or another. Even likes and dislikes change. Desires and priorities get transformed. Sometimes, it is an inspiration — from a teacher, a speaker, a book, a TV show, almost anything — that triggers the change. Who knows?

We undergo indescribable changes in life — physical, material, energetic, vocational, spiritual — that are sometimes intentional, sometimes accidental, sometimes unnoticeable, slow, and gradual, sometimes sudden, and radical. Sometimes they happen early in life, sometimes late. The transformation happens especially among searchers who at one time or another begin to look for something truly enduring and meaningful and fulfilling.

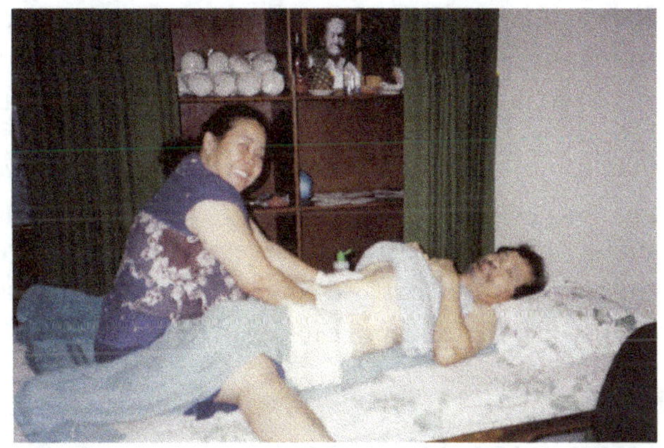

Khun Ni, master of Chi Nei Tsang and Karsai Massage, working on Rene at the millennium at the Tao Garden in Chiangmai. Both methods of therapy involve direct manipulations of the organs and could be uncomfortable, even painful, in the beginning. They are considered "root" treatments as differentiated From "branch" treatments. Rene receives a schedule of several treatments whenever he and Master Khun Ni are in Thailand.

It is not very often that we come upon an epiphany in life, an experience that brings us to a new path, a sudden realization that something is no longer the same, or that we have crossed a bridge we haven't been to before, or we are having a transformation that is life changing. Perhaps the novelty of it was obviously there but we did not see it. If we realize that something has indeed happened, it is possible that we will take a different direction in life. In a real sense, it is similar in many ways to a divorce after decades of marriage. It is a break from the familiar and starting a new life.

I know a student, an engineer, who in her early 30s decided to become a healer, an acupuncturist and herbalist. The shift or jump seems to come quickly but is often the result of years of slow evolution. It has happened to a lot of people, I am sure. In my class at acupuncture school, there was a chemist who was my age. She was making a new beginning in life. There were actually a bunch who switched professions; some were nurses or doctors. There was somebody who had a bachelor's degree, who could not find a meaningful job: she waited on tables to raise funds for acupuncture school. She is now one of the leading lights of Japanese acupuncture. I started acupuncture school at 50. The theme is generally about people who switch from one profession to another, but it is also about people who were floundering and wanted something they could do for the rest of their lives.

I am not saying that people change careers only to make themselves happy and satisfied. Some acquaintances changed jobs not necessarily for psychic rewards but for security and stability. Perhaps they are getting older and want to have a good pension or a nest egg. You cannot entirely blame them; after all, in these uncertain times, you have to prepare for old age.

There are of course people, many of them talented, who do not seem to change. They dwell on the surface, whatever it is they do, and they do not respond to the deeper aspects of life. They may be reading but their books or magazines are really just on the level of the physical and material. They would spend hours watching sports on television. They cannot find a way to go inward. They do not question or examine their values or their occupation.

But change can often be a painful process. It is reinventing oneself. The bigger the change, the more difficult and painful it is. To shift from one path, like a career for instance, to another requires decisions on several levels. It involves not only breaking into another path and training for it, but also confronting family and clan and one's own self-image, ego, and aspirations. There is a price to pay in terms of the psychological, emotional, financial, social, and physical cost.

MY PERSONAL CHOICES

I was a member of the bar for many years in the Philippines and later in NY. My job in Long Island from 1978 to early 1982 was with legal services, an agency that served the disadvantaged and indigent population. When the family moved to New Jersey in the summer of 1982, I became the manager of another legal service office. Towards 1984 or 85, a kind of disillusion set in. I began to ask myself if I was really helping to change society. I saw clients trapped in a cycle of which many of them could not get out. The job was an opportunity to help. But working that way was often like Sisyphean labor: when one got the rock up the hill, it rolled back down, and one had to start all over again. It was frustrating. It was not the way I wanted to help society. I wanted something much more significant than helping somebody fight the bureaucracy and get her on welfare or social security or secure a protective order to get that violent boyfriend who beats her or her children out of the house ... nothing bad about the work, but I wanted something much, much more, a real transformation of people and the culture, a process of healing that would go deep.

In the summer of 1983, I spent a couple of months in China training in contemporary kung-fu, called wu-shu. It was doubtless an exciting time for me, not only because it was my first time in China, but also because I loved the training although it was indescribably painful and difficult. I was with a group of martial artists. From Cheng-Du, Sichuan, where we trained for a month, a few of us traveled to Shanghai and then to Beijing. I realized that wu-shu was not for me. Choreographed under a communist regime, they were fancy and stylized, intended for competition, without much internal substance.

Back in the US, while walking around NY's Chinatown, I chanced upon the work of Healing Tao's Mantak Chia — *Awaken Healing Energy Through the Tao* and *Secrets of Taoist Love and Sex* — in a bookstore and began studying with him until, six years later, I became a senior instructor. It was almost a totally different world, the Taoist one, in which even the vocabulary was built on words like "love," "healing," "gentleness," "kindness," "compassion" and the ultimate achievement seemed to be Stillness. It was right out of the *Tao Te Ching* where water is the predominant symbol and peace and harmony constitute the ideal life. Of course, there was a gap between the theory and the reality but with sincere and serious practice, the possibility of contentment, transformation, healing, and happiness was there. GM Chia showed different methods of attainment, including qigong, Tai Chi Chuan, sexology, massage, and internal alchemy. In retrospect, it was the most profound and various discipline I had ever studied at that point in my life.

In Lake Titicaca, Peru, the highest navigable lake in the world at 12,000 feet above sea level. I broke away from the tour, came down the island of Tanguile and jumped in the cold water. When I told my guide, a shaman, he said it was an ancient ritual of cleansing.

In 1986, at 45 years old, I resigned my job in legal services. I decided that I was not going to do lawyering any longer. I realized that part of my disillusion was due to having followed a cultural script in my country: the eldest son followed the profession or career of the father. I concluded I had done my duty to my ancestors, and it was time to break away and follow my heart. I did not anticipate that it was a decision that would have far-ranging repercussions in the near future. Perhaps coincidentally just at that moment, the Marcos dictatorship was on the verge of collapse. I returned to the Philippines and spent several months there over the next two years giving myself the time to decide what to do for the rest of my life. I traveled the country, met friends from college, got interviewed for newspaper articles, had an essay published, lectured on martial arts, taught Philippine stick-fighting in my alma mater, visited my martial arts teachers. I had kept my Philippine passport and citizenship after 16 years in the US. I wanted to live in the Philippines, but nothing was attractive enough for me to do. I returned to the US.

A CHANGING VIEW OF MARTIAL ARTS

When I started learning martial arts back in the 1960s, I was fascinated by the grace and beauty of the forms. A roommate invited me to watch a demonstration of Chinese martial arts in Manila's Chinatown and I was hooked. Later, martial arts master Johnny Chiuten initiated me into the art in the traditional way: making me stand in the horse stance for almost three hours and basically doing what the masters were supposed to do to novices who were aspiring to join an exclusive priesthood. It was indescribable torture. Every time I saw Johnny, he taught me Shaolin forms, but we spent most hours sparring. He held back, but he was still a deadly machine. He pushed me to my limits.

At the pyramid of Kukulkan in Mexico. At the equinoxes, the Snake descended the pyramid. Back in 1984 and 1985, when I took my family there, there were few pilgrims. After the millennium, you could not find space to stand because so many people (many New Age) came for the celebrations. (I should not really be sitting on the statue!)

The forms were beautiful and challenging. I learned several forms starting with a beginner's set called "Sup Ji Kun," often translated as Cross Pattern. Then it was what Chiuten called "Kata 200" because it had a lot of movements (later I learned that it was actually called "Ching Hua Kun" perhaps translated as "young blossom or flower fist"). The ultimate form in the system was "Dragon-Tiger Combination Fist," a very demanding and long form. I studied more forms with him, more prominently the rare yin form he called "Buddha Fist." Later, after Johnny recommended me to his master Lao Kim, I learned that it was actually named "Red Boy Praying to Kuanyin." The old grandmaster taught me different forms — fist forms like "Kang Li," "Wat Let," "Ut Kit," and others. He taught me the original versions of "Kuanyin," "Cross Fist," "Dragon Fist," and "Tiger Dragon" and weapons forms — broadsword, sword, spear, three staff forms, GuanTao and five sectional chain whip. When Dr. Jopet Laraya joined the training on recommendation of Johnny, Lao Sigong taught us a hoe form. For this purpose, Jopet had a special wooden hoe made. We practiced sometimes at Hua Eng

Athletic Club in old Binondo, sometimes on the roof of a hotel in Ongpin, sometimes in a warehouse in Caloocan City.

For a long while, in the '60s up to '70s, I followed a regimen of toughening the forearms, palms and digits, hitting bags filled with sand and later with beebees and iron filings and washing my hands with dit da jow, a 24-herb liniment bath given to me by GM Lao Kim. (He gave me a 36-herb recipe when I saw him in Hongkong in 1988.) The so-called iron fist was a technique I learned from Johnny Chiuten. It was training the digits, basically to disable an opponent by hitting certain spots on his body. I had reached a decent level of expertise after almost 20 years of serious practice. I'll refrain from describing what I could do, but I felt that I could have done the techniques in an actual fight.

Suddenly, in the mid-80s, it dawned on me: what was I training for? What did it all mean in the long run? I had two young sons whom I might unintentionally hit in a burst of distemper, and it scared me. Or suppose I got into a fight, was I going to the extreme of killing my opponent? There was also a sense that my consciousness was being molded in an uncomfortable matrix — I was spending more and more time with martial arts practitioners and martial arts practice. I realized that although I had met wonderful people in martial arts, the culture of fighting itself as interpreted in contemporary times was often characterized by machismo and egotism and inhabited by practitioners many of whom did not have much interest beyond combat.

At that juncture, there was a convergence of different and varied factors in my life. I had to make important choices under conditions that involved moral, legal, ethical, physical, and spiritual values. I again had to decide what I wanted to do with my life.

I began serious training in energetics — qigong, healing, and internal alchemy. I asked myself, why dedicate my life to learning how to fight and injuring people when I could actually help them get well? Not only get well but also become better people. In July 1986, returning from the Philippines, I accepted Mantak Chia's invitation to undergo training to become a Healing Tao instructor and passed the demanding tests. I began teaching.

In 1988 or thereabout, I decided to study acupuncture and herbology. I won't go into the background of the story and the agonizing decisions I had to make, but I left home and family and moved to Boston and started studying acupuncture and herbology and pursued healing as an important attainment. It was flipping the other side of the coin. I had studied and taught Tai Chi Chuan, but I felt that my knowledge was sorely incomplete. I had observed different styles and masters both in San Francisco and New York. I saw the famous master Cheng Man-Ching in New York in the early '70s and, despite his writings and following, I was not impressed. I studied the Wu family small-frame form with master Leung Shum in New York City but dropped out before the year was over because I thought it was just another version of the Yang family form I had learned in the Philippines. (I learned later that the form was itself drawn from the Yang family curriculum.) When I saw GM Gin Soon Chu in June of 1986, I found the most authentic and complete Tai Chi Chuan system of the

Yang Family. Under the guidance of Master Gin Soon Chu, second disciple of Grandmaster Yang Sau-Chaung, first-born and heir of the legendary Yang Cheng-Fu, I covered the curriculum of fist (108 solo set, Tai Chi Chang Chuan, and sansou sparring) and weapons (knife, staff-spear and sword) forms. Chu shifu was the only teacher I saw who demonstrated the different techniques from the 34 fajing (discharge of jing). It was a martial art of a different order entirely, with its emphasis on "investing in loss," yielding and softness, where your partner was your teacher and not an enemy, and where yin was the most important value and qi was the goal.

That was 32 years ago. I graduated from acupuncture and herbology school, passed the national boards, got licensed, opened a clinic, and taught healing and meditation in different countries.

BUILDING PRIORITIES

As I write these reflections, the narrative seems a bit simplistic and easy and clean. But it was not so in reality. There was plenty of bloody struggle. It was messy sometimes. There were distractions along the way. Sometimes it was difficult to stay focused on my goals. True, acupuncture was not a glamorous profession; it was a new phenomenon in the US. Alternative healing was not yet an accepted modality. It was just making a start in the West. But I had faith that it would make a breakthrough. What was important was that learning it gave me a fulfilling vocation. It was exciting to me, like having a door opened to a new world. As important, I wanted to "complete" my education. I had studied martial arts, massage, meditation, qigong, internal alchemy, nutrition/ dietetics, sexology, feng-shui. Acupuncture and herbs were part of the package of integrated courses and healing modalities that fascinated me to no end.

Rene Navarro's private study, known to students as "the Dragon's Lair."

When acupuncture was introduced to the US back in 1972, after Nixon's ping-pong diplomacy, it was taught almost in isolation, divorced from the other related healing modalities like qigong, meditation, nutrition, and others.

Qigong and Tai Chi Chuan were not a part of its curriculum when I entered the New England School of Acupuncture. I pioneered a qigong course that included Mantak Chia's Microcosmic Orbit Meditation, Six Healing Sounds, Buddha Palm Qigong, and Tai Chi Chi Kung 13 movement form, and my own version of 12 Meridian Meditation. I taught it for several years until I decided to leave Boston in the late 1990s and move to Lake Harmony in the Appalachian Mountains where I owned a house and live a quiet life of semi-rustication. I spent my days in meditation and Tai Chi Chuan practice. I wrote poetry. I did *renga* (linked poems) with my friends the short-story writer Nadine Sarreal who was in Singapore at the time, award-winning poet and Tai Chi Chuan teacher Debra Kang Dean and healer Jaya Ward who was in Switzerland. A few of my students came to take lessons with me. Friends visited occasionally. I was close to nature: mist descended in the valleys and peaks, deer were close by, even bears came down to open the trash bin!

FRIENDSHIPS

I have written about my own experiences with teachers who have taught me many things — healing, poetry, martial arts, qigong and, as important, love, acceptance, and generosity. No, I did not get to learn things by myself. I had the help and support of friends who were there for me when I needed them. To travel the road, I had taken is difficult; it is impossible to do it alone. There are people who have encouraged, inspired, influenced, and taught me. They often stay in the background. In my website, you'll read about these people — Johnny Chiuten, Len Roberts, Uncle Rudy (Vidad), David Verdesi, Mantak Chia, for instance. I would not have reached this place without them.

Johnny was my first Shaolin Kung-Fu master. I trained with him early in the 1960s. He introduced me to the old Grandmaster Lao Kim, the patriarch of martial arts in Manila's Chinatown. Lao accepted me as a private disciple because of Johnny.

Uncle Rudy taught me about music back in the late 1960s. I was introduced to him by Miel Sabelino, a friend from college. He played the classical, romantic, baroque, and modern music repertoire. He played different operas, symphonies, concertos, even plays and songs. I became familiar with composers, performers, and compositions.

Len Roberts mentored me in poetry starting in 1985 at Lafayette College until his death a few years ago. We used to spend time together at his house in Pennsylvania. His wife Nancy would cook dinner in Winter, or we would sit by the pool in Summer and talk poetry. He would critique the poems I would send him. I delivered a eulogy and read one of his poems at his funeral service.

David Verdesi was my student back in 1992 when he was just 15 or 16. He has studied with many masters and over the years he has invited me to join him in his seminars or to meet his masters in Thailand, Indonesia, and China. I studied with him in Chiangmai, Thailand, Bali and Java, Indonesia, Rome, Italy, and Istanbul, Turkey. Mantak Chia was my first Taoist master. I met him sometime in 1984 in New York's Chinatown when I started to study with him. When I became an instructor, I assisted him during the summer retreats in the Catskills, NY. I have also written and/or edited six books for him, four of them on internal alchemy.

There are other masters. It is important to know that friendship — characterized by acceptance, loyalty, generosity, sharing, patience, and love — is an essential ingredient in our search and our life. In a real sense, we are often not alone in our journey.

The Navarro family with Rene, Lolit, Ava, Albert, Laura, and Isabel after a dinner of dim sum at the Joy Luck Garden on Mott Street in New York's Chinatown.

With Ed Maranan, Hall of Fame writer, and F. Sionil Jose, National Artist for Literature, at the Carlos Palanca Literary Awards in the Peninsula Hotel in Makati, Philippines. Both Frankie and Ed have passed on.

While we are pursuing certain goals and dreams, we may be confronted with fears and doubts, the very first obstacles in transformation that we ourselves create. We may also be faced by social pressures and criticisms and cultural taboos: society sending us its message, obvert or subtle, that we cannot or should not do certain things, that we must follow the mainstream route of conformity. How many of these frustrating scripts are there staring at us or playing in our minds! If we seek approval from or listen to others — friends, relatives, authority figures — or if we succumb to our fears, we may even abort our dreams.

In our search, we may be aided by music or literature or even locales and practices. We may have companions in our journey, but basically a quest is done alone; most of our time is spent in solitary study, whether it is a class or a practice. To me, there's music especially from Japan and Tibet and the Yang-Sheng regimens of self-cultivation I have done for 50 years now. Nature has also been a great refuge, companion, and healer to me — the sea and the sky, mountains and lakes, and the stillness and isolation they provide for free.

“COINCIDENCES”

There are a lot of coincidences in my life. Some people would say they are not coincidences but synchronicities because nothing happens by chance. I've heard that special people appear at certain times and open doors to certain opportunities for learning and growth as a part of one's destiny. Johnny Chiuten, I had known for a couple of years while studying in the university for my law degree. He actually invited me to study with him when we bumped into each other in the college cafeteria. It was Johnny who introduced me to the legendary Shaolin master Lao Kim who became my private teacher in Manila's Chinatown until I departed for the US in late 1970. My Chinese godfather told me to study Yang Family Tai Chi Chuan with his cousin Chan Bun Te in 1968 in Hua Eng Athletic Club. (I also learned Pa-Kua Chang there.) Master Chan introduced me to Lao Yun Hsiao, the famous Taiwanese master, who was teaching in Manila at the time. I studied another version of the Yang Family Tai chi Chuan 108 form with him, too. Mantak Chia entered the picture back in 1983 when I was looking for a teacher to guide me. I met David Verdesi in 1993 at Mantak Chia's retreat where I was one of his assistant instructors. David and I developed a close father and son relationship since then, or a period of more than 2 decades. Through David, I met many masters, among them, John Chang, called the Magus of Java, and Xuan Kong, the incredible Breatharian hermit of Huangshan. GM Gin Soon Chu I met in 1986 when I visited Boston and friends Gunther Weill and Rylin Malone from the Healing Tao took me to watch their Tai Chi Chuan practice with him. Chu Sifu's son Vincent, also a master of Traditional Yang Family Tai Chi Chuan, introduced me to my next teacher Master Ou Wen Wei, the founder of Pangu Mystical Qigong.

Lolit and Rene on his 70th birthday in Taiwan with adopted daughter Aishuan Wang, her husband Roger Lai (standing) and her family (mother, sister, and brother). There were 12 dishes, including black chicken, dried fish eggs, steamed fish, long-life noodles, etc, and a birthday cake!

I have often wondered about the strange coincidences in my life. There were many things that happened to me… as if I was made to walk a path although I did not seek it. There were other cases of “coincidences.” Through David Verdesi, I met several Hindu priests and Karma Lhatrul Rinpoche, the Bhutanese Buddhist guru, in Bali in August of 2014. Who knows what or who else is going to materialize in my life of searching?

31.

Encounters with Zhang Sanfeng

Two questions: What are the most important among the many teachings I have studied in the last 65 or so years? What ideas and suggestions can I share with readers and students?

The first is a difficult question to answer because the teachings were all important to me at certain points in my life as I evolved as a human being. As for the second question, please read through the essays carefully, draw your own conclusion from the path I've taken and figure out what you can take away from it, if any. At my age (80 at this writing), I cannot say I have found the answer to any of life's mysteries. I can only say that the experience was mine and that each person has to find his own way in the world to the best of his ability.

My first encounter with East Asian martial arts was in 1962 when I first began studying Wado-ryu karate with my younger brother Florante. I considered it a very valuable style at the time. We did not really do very much, except for a couple of beginner's forms or *pinan*, set exercises that formed the basis for fighting techniques. We also learned a few kicks: front, side, and roundhouse, I guess. We were very excited to have had access to a young man — if I remember right, his name was Robledo Sanchez — from Angeles City who came to town to give private lessons to my brother. We did not know where the style came from or with whom the teacher studied. But we were excited to learn it just the same. Well, I admit, we really did not know very much about martial arts at the time, and we were awe-struck with the knowledge.

Later, at the University of the Philippines, I met Master Johnny F. Chiuten and for the first time encountered a Chinese Shaolin style. I did not know what it was called but I was impressed by it. I told Flor that here was something tremendously better than what we had studied. I started training with Johnny privately in 1964 until he referred me to the legendary Grandmaster Lao Kim, his master in what I learned later was Hong Kuen in 1966. It was an old style based on the five Animals. I trained with Lao Kim until late in 1970 when I migrated to the US. I studied fist and weapons forms. The three signature forms in the system are "Dragon-Tiger," "Plum Blossom," and "Red Boy Prays to Guanyin." They are unusual, if not rare. I studied them with the two masters.

When he heard that I was studying martial arts, my Chinese godfather Chan Tek Lao advised me to study Tai Chi Chuan with his cousin Chan Bun Te, who was with Hua Eng Athletic Club in Binondo, Manila's Chinatown, at the time. I did not know the name of the style, it was the first time I heard about it, but it was an exciting form. The form was taught in the Philippines by a famous Taiwanese master, Han Ching Tang, and was derived from the Yang Family style, with a few variations. It was a long ride from Kamuning to Quiapo, plus a mile walk to the school, but I joined the early morning class, stood at the back and followed what everybody else was doing. There was somebody leading but there was no teacher. After each class, Chan Bun Te made corrections to my form. I also learned Pa Kua at Hua Eng from an old man who was also a Tai Chi Chuan student like me. Later another famous master from Taiwan Liu Yun Hsiao began teaching Tai Chi Chuan in Chinatown. Chan Shifu enrolled me in the class.

When I migrated to the US in 1970, I pursued other training methods. I studied arnis de mano with Mat Marinas in Queens, NY. I studied Wu style Tai Chi with Master Leung Shum in New York City. I travelled to China to study contemporary Wu-Shu, Monkey Fist and Cudgel, Sword, Spear and Hsing-I in the summer of 1983. At about the same time span thereafter I met and studied with Mantak Chia. It was the beginning of a decades-long apprenticeship that covered internal and external methods: Microcosmic Orbit, Six Healing Sounds, Inner Smile, Sexology, the three levels of the Yi Jin Jing, Tai Chi Chi kung, Fusion of the Five Elements, Kan and Li, and Chi Nei Tsang internal organs massage. It was the most complete transmission I had ever encountered: it covered the development of powers and virtue, the physical, energetic, and spiritual, the total transformation of the human being. If properly approached, it offered the possibility of growing the human potential. I became a senior instructor in several areas of his system.

At the Pura Besakih Mother Temple in Bali. We had just arrived from Java where we did a pilgrimage to Burubodor, Mendut, and Prambanan. We were exhausted and kind of templed out: we couldn't do any more climbing. We saw the trance dances and the performance of the Ramayana on a theatre overlooking the sea.

Later in 1989 I lived in the Boston area and studied with Gin Soon Chu, second disciple of Yang Sau Chung in traditional Yang family Tai Chi Chuan. I studied the curriculum of fist and weapons forms for the next decade while I was studying and then teaching at the

New England School of Acupuncture. It was, to me, a milestone because Chu sifu was the greatest Tai Chi Chuan master I had ever seen anywhere and the Tai Chi Chuan curriculum he taught was the most complete I had ever encountered.

During the millennium, I began teaching in different countries — UK, Egypt, Thailand, Philippines, the Netherlands, the US. I was in Amsterdam when I read a book called *The Magus of Java: Teachings of an Authentic Taoist Immortal*. I said to myself, I would like to see this master. Five years later, when I was in Istanbul, I heard David Verdesi talking to somebody he called Sifu. I said, David, who is that? He said, "It is the Magus of Java." I said, I would like to see him. David said, "You will." The next year, he sent me an e-mail inviting me to stay with him in Java for a month. You can read the rest of the story in the essay, "Thunder Path in Huangshan."

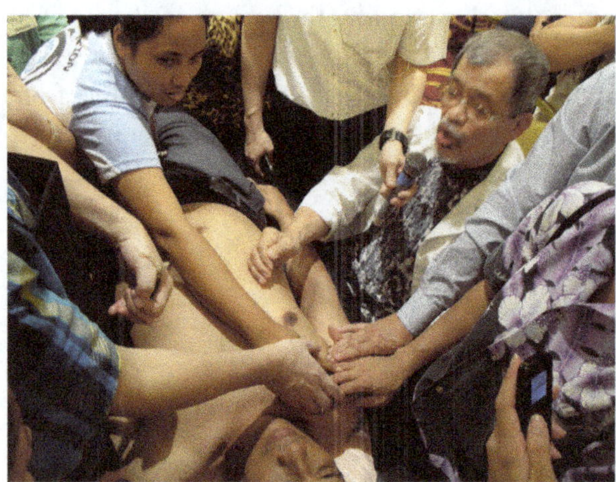

Rene demonstrating CNT internal organ massage at the World Blind Union Asia Pacific Conference in Manila.

Rene speaking at the WBUAP Conference. He was the only speaker who was not blind.

Each of the things I studied had something valuable to me. Wado-ryu karate opened a gate to Asian martial arts. In retrospect what I learned was really quite basic. The experience was like a youthful infatuation, an innocent attraction. With Johnny Chiuten and later Lao Kim, I learned a real discipline and a real martial art, both demanding and deadly. There were techniques in the system that made the forms really sophisticated and effective, but these techniques were not in the forms but supplementary and additional training. I believe that these methods — one was called iron hand training — transformed the movements into lethal combat techniques.

Training is often divided between the martial arts forms on the one hand and the energetic healing and spiritual forms on the other. The martial forms are taught as a separate and complete curriculum. As far as I know, that is how the system operates, whether it is a Wudang/Taoist or a Shaolin/

Buddhist style. That's probably what happened when the martial systems were taken out of the temples (and religion) and opened in a secular background. You can spend decades, even a lifetime, memorizing the forms. There are forms for the fist, there are forms for the weapons. It is basically exercise and fighting. It is possible that the teacher knows both aspects — the martial and the energetic/spiritual — but often to learn the energetic and spiritual curriculum usually you have to study with somebody else.

I realized this was true as well with Tai Chi Chuan, the quintessential Taoist internal martial art. The forms gave you exercises for health and discipline and taught you a vocabulary of movement that became the foundation for fighting but the real internal work was not a part of it. For the supplemental methods, you had to learn something else, but it was not taught usually as part of the curriculum of Tai Chi Chuan forms. I discovered this when I went home to the Philippines and again saw my teacher Chan Bun Te in 1986. He sat me down and told me that he was going to teach me the "secret" of Tai Chi Chuan: he said it wasn't in the 108 movement Tai Chi Chuan form that I had studied, it was the Microcosmic Orbit and sexual practice. It was good but the Tai Chi Chuan form wasn't going to take you very far. So, there was an internal method behind the internal art, after all. I found out later from Mantak Chia, who was teaching and writing about them in public, that these internal methods may also include different Qigong and Yi Jin Jing regimen.

Internal methods are also adopted in external arts or hard martial arts like Shaolin and its different branches and derivatives. Their methods for optimal development are not just the external exercises like toughening the digits or the physical body, they include meditative techniques to discipline and strengthen the mind and body and sexual control to retain the jing (sexual energy). The masters who achieved the peak of development were those who had these internal arts.

Some of these internal methods involved the development and cultivation of what is called the dantian, translated as the elixir field. There are usually three dantian located in ascending vertical order in the body. The lower dantian, the one commonly associated with martial arts, is in the area below the navel. Ideas about the dantian proliferate in the martial arts world. The dantian has acquired an almost mystical status spoken of with admiration and awe. It is to many martial artists the focus of training. The dantian is associated with qi and breathing and mind-training. The student is advised to focus on the area "behind the navel," to concentrate the qi there and he will develop something beyond the merely physical.

While many ideas about the lower dantian are basic and sketchy, I realized in my studies that there are some specific methods that are important in the achievement of internal "gong" and result in powers. One of them is the activation of the meridians that converge around the bowl of the hip and the area of the navel (Shen Que) and the lumbar (Ming Men). These meridians are conduits of qi and set the parameters or the field of the dantian. In certain lineages this field is associated with the "cauldron" or symbolically the "stove" which must be energetically created and filled through breathing and visualization.

But the methods for possibly achieving almost any form of power can often come at a great monetary cost. There are teachers of Tai Chi Chuan who sell a Qigong method or a form at a high price. An acquaintance told me that he had to pay $70,000 to study one technique called "Ultimate Qigong Under Heaven." That is just one technique. (Discipleships are sold at a higher price.) Of course, to recoup his expenses, he must sell his lessons, too. It is a vicious cycle. Looking at these pricey transmissions, I often wonder what they are worth. Why is it so important to hurt somebody or overwhelm an opponent? Why do people spend a lifetime to train in something they'll probably never use unless they deliberately seek an opponent to prove they can do it?

What powers are acquired in the process of developing the lower dantian depends on certain specific methods. David Verdesi, himself a master with exemplary abilities, described to me the way to acquire certain powers and took me to see masters whose area of expertise has nothing much to do with martial arts. But what they did was/is simply amazing and almost beyond comprehension: they are able to move objects from a distance, generate enough intense heat to burn a paper and/or emit electricity (to heal or kill), and drain or rob the energy from a human being, an animal, or a plant. In some cases, masters draw a "golden bell" around their body so that you cannot touch them or hit them. These rare masters do not talk about fighting or martial arts. They do not have a curriculum of expensive fist and weapons forms. They do not need it. They do not show any kind of movement, no punches, attack, or defense. It seems to be all happening within the body. It is a different world altogether. I've met masters like the Magus of Java and the hermits of Huangshan who had psycho-kinetic powers. It was like seeing the miraculous, the impossible feats, the unimaginable. For a period of time — years or decades — these masters who were probably Breatharians trained intensively, away from the world, in a cave or jungle. This was the Lost Horizon of superhumans.

At the ancient temple of Burubodor in Yogjakarta, Java, Indonesia. Lolit stayed at the garden below because at high noon it was too hot to climb the stairs and circumnavigate the temple. She said, "Go. This is your pilgrimage."

This level of achievement is not just being able to push somebody 10-20 feet away, stop somebody cold in his track, manipulate the Qi, or any of the abilities in the list of 28 to 34 fajing methods or killing with a thrust of a digit as in dim mak. It is on the level of extra-extraordinary ability, most of which is achieved with and from the mind. For one reason or another, very few masters are able to develop this gift. I could be wrong, but my suspicion is that many of the secret methods were lost or forgotten and were retained by some lineages like the Mo Pai or the Lei Shan Tao.

Zhang Sanfeng, a Buddhist monk at the Shaolin Monastery in Luoyang and the founder of Tai Chi Chuan in the 12th or 13th Century CE was supposed to have achieved high levels of power himself. If he had it, whatever happened to its transmission? More developed than Push hands, there is available evidence that with the proper mating of yin and yang and the activation of the breath and the meridians in the lower dantian, superhuman powers are a possibility even today.

The upper dantians (usually located in the heart and the brain) involve the development of other abilities and consciousness — compassion, virtue, love, ESP, the soul, spiritual awareness, and knowledge, etc. You need a master to teach you the methods and help you develop this level of transformation over a long period of time.

At the Glastonbury Tor in 2001. The sacred landmark, part of King Arthur's Camelot, has a powerful energy. If you know feng-shui, geomancy, you could find the confluence of the Dragon and Tiger. Jesus' Holy Grail was supposed to have been brought here.

The procedure for the development of these abilities and qualities is often not included in the realm of martial arts. Virtue which encompasses love, compassion, kindness, gentleness is cultivated by those who believe that life is more than ego and fighting, combat and physical endeavor and money and material possessions. It is the path and world of the sages and the saints. Knowledge of the meridians and energy centers, training in meditation and alchemy, a different cosmology and connection to the internal and external world, are required.

My studies in acupuncture school bought me to a different world — the world of needles and meridians and healing. When you spend time learning about the network of channels running up and down the body, yin and yang, five elements, the different cycles, the energetic and spiritual functions of each point, and how to manipulate the points, you begin to have a different understanding of the human being. You are just a step or two away from the physical and material into the world of energetics and spirituality.

I cannot say I remember everything I studied because there was a lot. Perhaps it was just too much to memorize, or more probably, there was not enough time to work on everything. Honestly, at a certain point, as I explored the various Asian disciplines and arts, I believe I began to prioritize the different forms according to my evolving values and goals and the exigencies of daily life. I also started to move away from the physical and external to the more internal healing and spiritual disciplines. Perhaps that was the period in the early

Rene and his younger brother Florante playing in the front yard of their home in Tarlac, a town north of Manila in 1966.

1980s when my search led me to Mantak Chia and his center (now called Universal Healing Tao) in Manhattan's Chinatown and eventually to the New England School of Acupuncture in the Greater Boston area and Gin Soon Chu's Traditional Yang Family Tai Chi Chuan in 1989.

Sometimes I ask myself if I would have preferred to study only certain things and skipped the rest. But we cannot do it that way because we do not have the wisdom or the freedom of choice at certain points, and there are different circumstances that limit us and our life. We can say I can do what I want to do but in reality, our opportunities are really constricted by random factors — money, desire, health, age, circumstances like jobs, family, and whatever obligations we have at the moment. In a real sense, often we do not make radical choices; we evolve, often very slowly. If we decide on something, we've already been prepared for it, intellectually, emotionally, and spiritually. Anything that happens by surprise, we consider as fate or a miracle!

Of course, the world is full of surprises and miracles, but then again how often do they happen to us?

After everything that happened over the course of decades, it all boiled down to, what is it that gives meaning and satisfaction? Partly it is knowledge, the mind opening and receiving facts and information; partly, it is seeing what's out "there" beyond the door and learning something new; partly, it is having something important to do and filling one's life, it is meeting a challenge. You also try to achieve balance in your life: you express yourself through music, painting, or poetry, travel, or relationship. After all, you live in the world, you have a family, you are not a hermit or a renunciate, you crave something deeper for the soul or the heart. Ultimately, of course, what fulfills you too is service — the opportunity to share. As I often tell my granddaughters, your life is your legacy, and your legacy is what you give away. You cannot take it with you, is a truism in life as in death. Which brings us to the questions, Who am I? Why am I here?

Family photo taken in 1956 at the family home in Tarlac.

Now, at the end of this narrative, here is the story of a miracle: When we were in Bali, David Verdesi took me on his motorcycle to a Buddhist couple outside of Ubud. The story I heard is that the wife was a devotee of Guanyin, the Goddess of Mercy. While she was praying, the Goddess came down and touched her big toe. At that very moment, she felt this powerful and mysterious electrical charge in her body. For a year or two she could not channel or control it. But eventually "it" followed her command, and she was able to use it for healing. Her husband was understandably upset that he did not have this power. The two of them beseeched Guanyin to give him the power as well. To make a long story short, it came to him one day and the two of them began healing people together. I experienced their method — a mild current from their hands buzzing on my legs and back — in four healing sessions during two visits to Bali with David.

The story underscores the fact that this couple needed no training. Their power was a gift that was apparently given because of their devotion. It happens that there are people who are blessed; their ability is given to them or perhaps it is in-born and is just lying latent within, waiting to be awakened. There are also people who cannot get what they want, no matter what they do. It is indeed a mystery and forces us to face the question of human destiny or probably karma.

I have some stories about other miraculous and karmic happenings, among them the strange tale of the Indonesian man who developed powers when a coconut fell on his head, but on this note I would like to end this piece because, no matter how much I rack my brain, I cannot find a rational explanation for them myself.

32.

Reflections on the Diaspora, *Burung Babi*, A Favorite Uncle, Malayan Fish Head Curry, and a Trip To The Mountains

I've heard about the Filipinos' nostalgia for Philippine food after a period of stay in a foreign country, that yearning for certain native dishes prepared at home by mother or cousin or an uncle or eaten in a favorite restaurant. I was skeptical of such reports and thought they were exaggerated, although they were common enough. Salivating over Aling Maring's dinuguan or missing Indang Carning's suman sa ibus or a home-made patis from Batangas was something I could not comprehend. It seemed all so silly to me. Earlier in my life in the US, sometime in late 1970, I did not miss Philippine food possibly because it was available and so these tales sounded all the more absurd. Boiled rice (it was Texas long-grain, but okay), linagang baka or manok, adobong baboy or manok, and isdang prito or grilled pork chop (dipped in vinegar with pressed garlic) were often part of our usual diet. There were ingredients missing in some dishes it is true, but we found substitutes.

So, my wife and I regarded this strange craving that we were warned about as more imagined than real, and we began to joke about it. Imagine being told to include in your luggage a bottle of patis and green mangoes to ward off those legendary pangs when you arrived in America. It was as absurd as the suggestion that we should bring tailored clothes from Manila because US ready-made clothes were ill-fitting and *amboy*. How about being gifted with Nora Daza's cookbook at the Manila International Airport? The main drawbacks of migration, to me, were emotional-sociological (loneliness was a big thing, so was anomie, whatever it meant) and political-cultural (losing connection with our country), not gastronomical.

But just a few months after my arrival in New Jersey in late August 1970, I began to crave something like sinigang na bangus with patis spiced with pepper on the side and Pampanga pork sausages dipped in a sauce of vinegar, siling labuyo, sea salt, and lots of garlic. (Salty, spicy and sour seem to be the common flavors a homesick palate seeks.) Not really a major crisis in my life but it was there just the same, something puzzling and unexplainable, and

Four generations of the Navarro clan headed by Paulino Navarro (standing in the back) gathered during the Sunrise Service on the occasion of Easter/Resurrection Sunday in the old hometown in Bamban, Tarlac.

it caught me unawares. Your nose — or imagination — picked up certain scents and you began to fantasize about a certain dish. You tasted something that remotely hinted at a native dish, and you wondered where you could get it. It became a Pavlovian reflex. My wife Lolit valiantly and resourcefully came to my aid and concocted what I wanted with ingredients from Shop Rite across the street. It wasn't the same thing, of course, but when you are in Neptune, New Jersey, you cannot really complain, and you make do with what you have. For sinigang she used lemon instead of crushed sampaloc or camias, for the sausage she used casings — chitlings, I guess — and a mixture of ground pork (a combination of fatty and lean meat) and spices. Instead of bangus, with its clean, pure taste, she used the heavy flavored and oily mackerel (we also used this fish for paksiw). She learned to improvise by using substitute ingredients.

While many things were missing in the local grocery stores, there were compensations though. We lived in Jersey Shore, a few minutes away from the beach. We got fish heads for free at many of the seafood stores in the area. The store owners gave the fish heads away under the impression that they were for Fido. At the Shark River inlet, there were blue claw crabs that we could catch with a raw chicken neck on a string during the "er" months (September, October, November, and December).

The Filipino community in the area used to gather for occasional parties. Somebody would bring calderetta or kari-kari or pansit, an occasional dinuguan. A kind of bayanihan and a mutual support, it was a potlatch feast with cuisine from different Philippine provinces. Sometimes there would be bottles of San Mig. We would share culinary secrets and where to go for that precious sauce or spice. Such parties happened on a more or less regular basis, especially on somebody's birthday or a child's baptism. Invariably, as in the home country, we would all have pabaon of this or that dish.

Mike, a physician in the nearby hospital, would take a few of us for a drive to Philadelphia, where he would buy pig's blood and intestines for dinuguan, or find a bottle of patis, and other Asian dipping sauces (probably from Thailand or Vietnam) in Chinatown. Those trips were an adventure for me. I did not realize that there was a Little China in Pennsylvania right in the heart of the City of Brotherly Love amid the faux classical Greek/Roman architecture, and masonic and revolutionary monuments.

Pete, another doctor, also had the savvy to direct us to the right places in New York City. (He also knew where the museums were — I learned about Guggenheim because of him.) Getting to eat an authentic Philippine dish was just a matter of knowing where to get the right ingredients. At that point, a year or so after my arrival in the US, I had enough information to know where to get most of everything I needed for almost any recipe I needed to cook. I did not miss many of our native dishes because they could be recreated wherever it was we lived.

The Navarro siblings: Sergio, Eduardo, Ricardo, Flora, Odon, Romulo, and Crisencio. Missing: Carmen N. Ocampo.

Besides, there were other cuisines that we explored: Italian, Japanese, Korean and different varieties of Chinese. It was a sporadic education that began in the late 60s in the Philippines and continued when we arrived in the US.

When I lived in Kamuning, Quezon City, there were actually a few affordable foreign restaurants in Manila accessible to us who did not have a good income. I had been to mostly Cantonese but there was a Szechwan restaurant at the Ali Mall in Quezon City in the late 60s which was, in retrospect, not "genoowine." I had been to Atemi, a Japanese restaurant in Ermita my uncle Eduardo and brother Flor took me to. There was also Cucina Italiana in Padre Faura that I tried a couple of times with a girlfriend who would watch me eat spaghetti puttanesca while the waiter in the corner probably wondered why she did not eat (I could not afford another plate on my allowance.) My favorite was a small Chinese noodle shop in Ongpin that served fried bihon in malukong (bowls). After my Shaolin kung-fu lesson with Sigung Lao Kim, the patriarch of Chinatown's kung-fu underground, this street corner grease joint panciteria was where I repaired to for dinner. The Chinoy chef put a layer of crispy fried noodle threads on top. I did not use soy sauce or patis but black vinegar to flavor the dish. There was also another small restaurant up the road where my four-year-old son Norman and I stopped over after my morning Tai Chi Chuan practice that specialized in gawgaw soup, simply a bowl of thick flavorful brown soup with pork bones, and fruit shakes (avocado and papaya).

As a member of Hua Eng Sporting Club in Binondo, I got invited to anniversary banquets sponsored by Kung-Fu associations in Chinatown. They were interminable eating marathons and bouts of lion dancing and martial exhibitions spiked by generous toasts of scotch or gin to the deadly masters.

Father himself would sometimes treat the family and close friends at the patio of our home to the same legendary lauriat, Chinese banquet of 12 to 14 varied dishes covering every imaginable flavor that almost invariably culminated in a plate of fried noodles or rice and soup. He knew something about food. When I was in college in Manila and he had a court hearing in the city, he would take me to a different restaurant every time — San Jacinto and Moderna in Plaza Sta Cruz were frequent destinations — and treat me to something new. Pancit lomi, a bowl of steaming flat noodles with slices of pig liver, shrimp and egg was a favorite among the restaurants on MacArthur Highway in Tarlac. On my 19th or 20th birthday father took me to the San Miguel Hotel outside of the Hacienda Luisita in Tarlac and watched me slowly relish a t-bone steak and a bowl of ice cream and apple pie.

My Chinese godmother in Tarlac used to cook Braised Duck with Lotus Root and Mung Bean Noodles with Bamboo Shoots, among other Cantonese dishes, during the town fiesta in January. (It took me years to discover the secret ingredients but through trial and error, I was able to duplicate them later on when I lived in Long Island.) Many of her relatives from as far as Manila would trek to her kitchen and savor the special recipes she served.

My Shaolin kung-fu master the legendary Johnny Chiuten invited me, sometimes with his family, to many trips to the Chinese gourmet world. Along the way he talked with equal enthusiasm about obscure fighting techniques and rare culinary delicacies, the latter of which were too exotic for my taste.

It was a good introduction to international cuisine. Now, in the Northeast United States, there are so many national and ethnic restaurants, you could get dizzy and bankrupt trying even a tenth of them. They were not exactly mushrooming everywhere in the 70s, but they were slowly inching their inevitable way into the American palate: Korean grilled steak and soybean shops along with grocery stores, Middle Eastern falafel freshly baked, olives in barrels, pastries dripping with honey, and fresh figs.

On the Philippine native dishes front, we could make some dishes like paella/arroz Valenciena or pata tim (one is Hispanic, the other Chinese but are now a part of our eclectic cuisine). Amalia "Mals" Canlas, my mother's help, produced for our delectation dinuguan, kari-kari, sinigang, stuffed bangus and chicken and whatever it was we wanted. She was the most versatile chef in the clan. There was nothing that she could not cook. She did not use any of the prepared sauces that are considered a blessing because they save time and expense. Sauces with their dried ingredients and preservatives have brought New

York closer to Manila, but there's something lacking in the flavors. The packet of powder and desiccated ingredients doesn't really deliver as good and authentic a quality as fresh sampaloc or camias to flavor sinigang. It is convenient to use them, but it is, in my opinion, cheating.

It was not like our family was missing anything.

I did not realize that something was working on expanding my consciousness at the time, however. My wife was the breadwinner employed as an OB-Gyn resident in the hospital next door while I took care of two small kids and kept a double shift working part-time as a recreation director-cum-kung-fu teacher for children in a local church and as a nurses' aide on the graveyard shift in a nursing home. Left to fend for ourselves in Asbury Park, New Jersey, I educated myself in the refinements of the culinary arts, I read cookbooks and collected clippings of recipes, I learned the principles of Chinese dietetics and nutrition (five element and yin/yang guided by, among others, Lin Yutang), and my taste started to become more cosmopolitan and perhaps international. With my exposure to other cuisines, I began trying different ingredients for Philippine dishes — Shanghai bakchoy or pickled Chinese mustard instead of petchay or cabbage for instance — and coming up with more delicious, more subtle flavors, with more balance. I learned to add honey or oyster sauce to adobo, star anise, cloves, and cardamom seeds to paksiw na pata, miso or fermented bean curd to sinigang, lotus root to braised chicken and duck, olives, and capers to Cornish game hen, and it was a better interpretation of the original dishes, as far as I was concerned. I believe the same phenomenon of evolution was occurring among Filipinos in other parts of the US and in the Philippines, too.

Family photo with parents Ricardo and Amelia and children Rene, Flor (standing) and Danilo (sitting) in 1948 in Bamban, Tarlac. Note the Christmas tree in the back.

Our exposure to international dishes and access to different ingredients and spices brought us ideas about how to make our food more complicated and palatable. The ordinary "country" or peasant food — now transformed into haute cuisine — was finding its way to the table of cosmopolitan Filipino restaurants.

But something else was egging on my taste buds. I was actually craving something much, much more, and I was not aware of it. I did not realize it until I saw a frozen steak of venison in a butcher's shop in what was considered the Philippine Town behind the Port Authority Terminal in New York City. As I stared at the label on the package, I began to visualize the tapa of my childhood.

I was born in Bamban, Tarlac, a small town across the northern border of Pampanga. There was a river flowing steadily beside a range of mountains. A tribe of negritos was to be resettled near the highway later on, but from 1945 on, just after the war, we had a run of the place. We kids would cut classes and go for a swim in the Bamban river or in the dam at the family farm. We would wait for the train that passed a few times during the day with a heavy cargo of sugar cane for the mill in town. Some older kids would apply a coat of heavy grease on the rails, the train would skid to a screaming halt and as it trembled helplessly in pain like a huge metal dragon, we would steal from its caboose stalks of sugar cane to chew on. Many times, we would flatten soda lids under the train wheels and make them into sharp buzz saws that we called garlit. Just once in a fit of audacity, I attempted to cross the railroad bridge and made it to the other side before the train came.

In town was an old, smelly warehouse in the Feliciano compound which doubled occasionally as a movie house. Phantom, Flash Gordon, and Tarzan became a big part of the fare in this small-town entertainment. Kids who could not afford to get in would find a sponsor so that they could sneak in for free, which was what I did often successfully. On the rare time that I could not get in, I would peek through a hole in the mildly electrified metal wall for the duration of the movie.

My grandfather, Ingkong Poli to us little kids, was a farmer, patriarch, raconteur. He made me buy old books during the town fiestas — an assortment of corridos and legends that he promised to read to me. As we sat at his feet in the living room of the clan house, he regaled us with stories about Juan Tamad, Matuang Tomas a Bingot (literally, Old Infant Tomas), Siete Infantes de Lara, Bernardo Carpio, and assorted powerful and miraculous beings who could jump from the ground to the roof of a house. I could swear from the distance of 60 years that we actually believed that they existed, not just in our imagination.

With a scout knife, Apung Poli carved slingshots and tops from guava or mango branches that were models of the woodworking craft. He also presided over the circumcision of the adolescents of the clan at the Bamban River after we had undergone a period of initiation. Before the Big Event, we were taught the use of pandakaki sap for freeing the foreskin and assorted other "tricks" for our journey into manhood. Cousins and other distant relatives would gather periodically in odd places to compare notes about each other's progress. The actual ritual was performed with an ordinary razor blade; a piece of guava branch served as a batakan or chopping board; another piece of wood was used to tap the razor and the job was done — unless Ingkong Poli for reasons of aesthetics or practicality thought that more of the prepuce had to be cut. Afterwards, the batakan shaped like a primitive phallus was thrust into the ground repeatedly, presumably as a symbol of coitus, and it was over. No anesthesia was used. None of that sterile hospital stuff for us either. We stuck to spit and guava leaves in the face of infection and swelling. Cousins Dan and Ray and I had survived a rite of passage together in a mystical brotherhood that nothing else in our young lives can compare to.

Ingkong Poli was firm and had an unpredictable melange of rules which resulted in a memorable lesson or two for us children. One time he caught us in different stages of nudity as we exhibited our paraphernalia to each other inside the huge rice basket (*buslo*) under the house and gave our ears a painful twist. (Another punishment he inflicted was hitting you on top of the head with one single knuckle called *sintok*.) He loved to have one of us pulling his gray hair with two rice grain husks as he awaited the customers at the *bigasan* (rice) mill. Imagine how difficult that was for us; it was an undeserved cruel and unusual punishment for little kids. To relieve the tedium, he told me stories about the Philippine American War, the bravery of the ill-equipped Filipino soldiers and the quixotic General Francisco Makabulos, the hero of Tarlac; when he was in good humor, Ingkong talked about his exploits with women. When he began to nod and snore, I would invariably find a way to escape into the woods back of the house or to the market.

Ingkong was also a patient guide. He knew the different plants and herbs. We children picked up some of this knowledge — what leaves, fruits, barks, and roots were good for cuts and wounds, what worked for diarrhea, fever, postpartum depression, bladder problems, what was edible, whatever. He even knew how to train a martin to sing and talk. Apung Poli taught me the method when I was seven — rub the bird's tongue daily with a slice of betel nut — but just as my pet began to say the first word, he was unceremoniously seized from his bamboo cage by a hungry house cat and dragged into the darkness before I could recover from my shock at having witnessed the scene up close and personal.

Sometimes Apung Poli would take me fishing using a net weighted at the outer edges with lead. When he cast it, the net would gradually flare wide from the center and spread out and for a moment one caught a glimpse of a beautiful spider web in midair. He did not catch any big fish, only the swordfish-like balulungi. Often Apung Poli would take one or two of us with him to his farm in Panaisan at the foot of the mountain where he cultivated rice, mangos, and vegetables (prominently eggplants, bitter melon, okras). We learned to look for wild roots — the fibrous singkamas, especially — and set different bamboo traps for birds and fish. We gathered paco, a wild fern, and aya, a Philippine spinach, and suso (snails) and camaru. It was important to have this working knowledge as a tool to survive when you have no food and are stranded in the jungle. Sometimes armed with a bolo, we would climb the mountain and cut lagundi for firewood and bring it down to town.

We pictured the mountains and fields as teeming with creatures and spirits and elementals who came down occasionally to haunt the streams or the trees. There were ghosts and *tikbalangs* and *patyanak* and *duendes*, some of them malevolent, lurking around the *punso* or the giant tree, we believed in *encanto*, and to protect ourselves, we would chant "*bari, bari Apu*." I can on my oath say that once on a hunt for spiders early at dawn I had seen a few of them at the boundary where the town proper ended, and the rice paddies began. Needless to say, I ran as fast as I could the moment they emerged from the mist with their thick fur, monstrous heads and huge claws.

I spent my childhood in that environment of innocence where myth and reality were intertwining threads of a dream life, nature was a habitat for spirits who knew — and rewarded or punished — our every move and Ingkong Poli was a huge presence in our world.

Family photo taken in front of the capitol building in Tarlac with parents Ricardo and Amelia and children Roland, Danilo, Florante, and Rene.

We lived in a compound, with assorted relatives sharing space in a big house. There was a giant caimito tree — it yielded the biggest fruits I have seen of its kind anywhere — in the back, its branches overwhelming the house of Tatang Odon, my father's older brother, and one of Ingkong Poli's children. A patch of wilderness sat dangerously close in the backyard. At times a colorful gekko or a salamander would find its way into the tree, or a poisonous snake would wander nearby. One time while my cousin Ray and I were up a tamarind tree, hundreds of snakes arrived and began working themselves into an agitated sexual frenzy on the ground below.

Not infrequently we would be taken to the local *herbolario* (herbalist) or *hilot* (masseuse) whenever we had a twisted ankle or wrist, and he would apply a magical oil, often on the opposite side of the injury as he mumbled an incomprehensible mantra. (Later on in my life, I learned about the principles of contralateral treatment in Chinese acupuncture). We in the clan reverenced these healers as belonging to a higher species altogether, heirs of an ancient knowledge that was slowly getting lost and forgotten.

There were several colorful uncles in this extended clan. A couple of them had a secret life, which the family only talked about in whispers. Tatang Mulong, the kindest and quietest of them and as far as I know, the only one not cursed or blessed with the Navarro weakness for beautiful women, ran a rice mill (*kiskisan*). It was he who let me in his workshop whenever I needed to load a seashell with splinters of lead, sharpen a scout knife, a buzz saw or an arrow or whatever it was that I fancied to make. Tatang Sergio, who often made you feel you were never good enough whatever you accomplished, was the brilliant child prodigy and renaissance man of the family. At one time or another he became a guerrilla, choir conductor, a Sunday school teacher, a science teacher, a composer, family historian, *dramaturgo*, a singing coach, and a high school principal. He was at home with Handel's The Messiah as he was with Christopher Marlowe's *Faustus*. In another culture, he would have been a national icon, his achievements written up in magazines and textbooks, but he preferred to live in obscurity in our small town all his life. Tatang Crising (we called him Tatang Gara when he wasn't around) was the youngest. A high school teacher, a perennial youth and a Narciso Bernardo, the legendary basketball star, wanna-be, he memorized long lines of inspirational poetry from Tennyson's Ulysses to Wordsworth's Ode to Intimations of Immortality. Tatang Dandong was the politician of the family, determinedly obsessed until his death to become mayor of the town. An Errol Flynn look-alike, he possessed the most beautiful voice among the brothers and with it, he used to serenade the young Japanese waitresses in Ermita with Japanese love songs he picked up during the war. My two aunties, Ymang Flora Catajan and Carmen Ocampo, were benevolent absences who entered our lives with their anonymous but important work in the kitchen.

Tatang Odon was my favorite. He was a schoolteacher and a poet. To me, he appeared to live in an entirely different world and time. A romantic, he was intense, joyous, and sad at the same time. During the war, he owned a set of horses and carretelas. He was a master chef and a butcher. Like my father, he could tell how much a pig weighed to the last ounce just by looking at it. He was also a barber who had the unique ability of cutting his own hair. Setting one mirror in front and another in the back, he would awe us kids with the precision of his scissors. What was remarkable was he also loved a different cuisine from the wilds. We did not know where he got the knowledge (probably from Ingkong Poli), but he knew how to trap birds, snakes, and iguanas, of which there were many in the woods in the back. (This passion earned him the name "Barag," the Pampango word for iguana.) I should not forget to include bats. Come to this, he had installed a net at the end of a long bamboo pole which he used to snare the bats flying out of the church belfry when the bell was rung at angelus. During the postwar, it was a convenient way not only to stave off hunger but to taste an unusual dish (and adventure) as well.

I was not aware if the snakes, bats, and iguanas (*bayawak*) had any nutritional value at the time. But my brother Flor still recalls that they made a good, tasty dish. It was only later on, in my middle age, when I was studying traditional Chinese herbology at the acupuncture school outside of Boston that it occurred to me that Tatang Odon may have been into something nobody in the family suspected, i.e., the wild animals had an effect on the body that was healthy and erotic. After all, of all his siblings, he was the one who had the biggest family.

When Tatang Odon Navarro and his wife Indang Chayong moved to California upon the petition of their son Ray, excellent longaniza, tapa and burong babi found their way occasionally to our table although we lived across the mainland in New Jersey. When he died in his early '90s he left a poetry manuscript. Unfortunately, Tatang Odon's recipes are lost to the clan. They would have been a rare legacy. Ingkong Poli's stories and songs are probably lost, too. But that's often the fate of our heritage: it is not considered important and valuable enough to preserve and to continue, and usually dies with the person who carried it.

The clan children were into kurang-kurangan, patintero, timbang preso, coyut and hide and seek. Spiders as well, which we collected in matchboxes and made to fight on a short baton of thin stick. We made kites from bamboo, string, glue, and manila paper, some of them the giant gurions, and had dogfights in the open field. I was also into gambling with *sigay* (shells) which I adroitly loaded in my favor with lead so that when tossed onto the ground they would always make me win. I was unbeatable in town. I won a lot of colorful rubber bands that way. I could have gotten rich when I was 8 but I did not appreciate the value of money at that age.

Perhaps there wasn't much to eat — after all, it was after the devastation of the war and one or two times early on we had to fall in line outside the US camp for k-ration — but there was in my memory a list of food that we enjoyed. Aside from the supply of tin cans of carne norte, salmon, spam, and pork and beans which my resourceful parents brought from the black market through Clark Air Base and Fort Stotsenberg, we had goat ribs cooked with kalibangang; the pork dish called bulanglang which was flavored with ripe guavas and kangkong or camote tops; bringhi, a derivative of paella, with chicken, prawn and sticky rice; pakbet with slivers of pititsan, crispy pork skin; paco (fern) salad; lelot balatong (toasted mung beans with rice congee); camote tops and calabasa flowers cooked with fermented fish or shrimp; monggo soup with ebi (dried shrimps), slices of ginger, garlic and bitter melon leaves; tender bamboo shoots (available from the surrounding areas) quickly sauteed in a wok with garlic and patis; and last but not least there was frog soup with pepper or malungay leaves and ginger. For desserts we had tibok-tibok, suman bulagta and sa ibus, bobotu, duman, ginataan/sampelut, etc. Frequently, we kids would go to the pineapple orchard of Apung Pitong, who returned home after working in the Hawaiian plantations. When he wasn't around, we treated ourselves freely to his manzanitas, avocados, green mangos (dipped in vinegar and siling labuyo), and cashew nuts.

When I was about seven or eight, I picked up Tatang Odon's fondness for game and learned to use a sling shot to hunt birds. On occasions, I would bring a kingfisher or two back from my solitary escapade in the marsh. I also learned how to dress and cook adobo from bats which I captured from our attic with the use of a pole. (Bats are dressed like snakes; you pressed a knife on the neck and stripped down the skin from top down.) With a bamboo trap I wove myself, I learned to catch birds in their nests. In retrospect, it was a cruel procedure because sometimes the birdlings died along with the mother.

Wild ducks, manok labuyo and hogs and deer were brought down occasionally from the mountain. It may have been this exposure to an exotic, rare cuisine, that began to come to the surface when I saw that frozen piece of expensive deer meat at this butcher's shop in Manhattan.

No, I did not progress to catching reptiles because by the time I was 11 my father decided to move the family to the capital for his law practice. The world of my childhood was lost to me afterwards because it was no longer there in our new home.

Only on two occasions did I again experience returning to that environment. Both trips were taken with my father to the remote mountains somewhere between Tarlac and Batangas. He was seeing a tribe of *negritos* who had retained him to represent them in their fight to take title to their ancestral land. We had travelled for a day across rivers and mountains, into forests, on precipitous terrain. As night fell, we arrived at a clearing between a mountain and a river past what I imagined were crocodile-infested lakes. There were huts lighted by *paritan*. A deer had just been shot and it was being dressed over a campfire. A piece of the liver was grilled and its blood still dripping, the chief gave it for me to eat. That night my dad and I slept on a bed of hay on the flatbed of the 6x6 under a clear cold night sky and the stars.

Rene with Ed Maranan and Dr. Temy Rivera, two famous activists and writers in the Philippines during their reunion dinner at Café Via Mare.

I returned to Bamban a couple of times and visited Panaisan, Ingkong Poli's farm, but the enchantment was gone. The mountain that had loomed large in my memory was reduced in size, the dam where we learned to swim was now but a small stream. The mango trees had been cut down. The old house where I spent my early childhood was gone, too. Even the concrete stairs that sheltered us from the bombing during the war was razed. Nothing was left of the landscape I remembered so well. The spell of the past was lost.

It is puzzling how events happen that way. Sometimes we cherish a memory, and we keep it alive for a long time; and then somehow for no discernible reason it evaporates like mist. Suddenly our world changes. A familiar place is different now. We wake up in the morning and things are not the same. But I wonder if we realize that we must have changed, too. Perhaps we have grown up and matured and now see with different eyes. Or perhaps we have become skeptical of other dimensions, or earlier beliefs and values. Who knows what we have gone through, what we have become, what the world has done to us? Who knows where the spirits of the earth we communicated with have disappeared to?

In the late 70s, with the family settled in a small neighborhood in Malverne, Long Island, NY, I began experimenting with tapa, burung babi, burung asan and patis. Fresh fish was cheap at the harbor in Bay Shore just 30 minutes away. $10 was all it cost to buy a basin of fish. There were also dilis (I never learned what kind of fish they were, but they may have been sardines) at Oyster Bay that I caught with a net and stocked in a clay jar with salt. They made a good fish sauce, probably better than Rufina's, the most popular brand at the time. Burung asan (fermented fish with rice) was the most delicate procedure of all because it required a thoroughly sterile environment — clean hands and utensils, fresh fish and cold rice were mandatory, else you ended up with a pot of rotten, inedible fish and rice. It's believed that you also need a clean heart, hence making the sauce was considered a test of character. Burung babi I was able to make with the help of the salitre I got from my brother Danny and his wife Edna. Somehow like illicit drugs, certain rare preservatives and spices were passed from hand to hand among relatives and friends.

Nowadays, I am sure I don't feel any nostalgia for Philippine food because there are many places one can get it. There are many Filipino restaurants in New York city especially in Elmhurst, Queens. In Jersey City there are a few catering to a large clientele of Filipinos. You can get most of anything there, including prepared food in the turo-turo, which is what my wife and I do when we find time to stopover on our way to or from Manhattan. Need instant sauces, cooked kari-kari, crispy pata, lumpiang ubod, maja blanca, inihaw na tilapia, leche flan, turrones de casoy or Magnolia's ube or macapuno ice cream? Name it, they have it. Just say the word.

Life changes are signposted by one's lifestyle, wardrobe, age, marital status, children, interests, commitments, and other factors. I should add, the choice of what and how one cooks and eats. For many years now, since I reached middle age, I've avoided greasy, salty, and sweet, the most common characteristics that plague much of Filipino food and possibly the Filipinos (think heart attack, obesity, hypertension, and diabetes, some of our health problems). I believe that because of my familiarity with different national and ethnic cuisines through the different restaurants especially in the Northeast United States and through my travels in different continents, I have right now a stronger craving for gastronomical adventure than for the familiar home recipes. Even my granddaughters Isabel, eight, and Ava, five, born in the US, are picking up the spirit of exploration. Not only are they into chicken adobo and pansit guisado but also sushi and sashimi and the soupy Xiao Long Bao (Little Dragon Treasure) on Pell Street. My children Albert and Norman who grew up on Philippine food can whip up a Philippine dish or two when called upon, but they prefer Shanghai Joe's or Caballo's Italian when there is a family celebration.

Something else has obviously changed in my life. My formal training in Chinese medicine, acupuncture, herbology, nutrition and dietetics, with their principles of balance, yin and yang, Five Elements, cycles and correspondences (color, flavor, season, organs), and astrological, natal charts has had a strong influence on my approach to cooking. When I look at the person I am cooking for, I often think of what they need. I've frequently been using Chinese herbs and produce. I make bottles of tonics for certain deficiencies (there is a great demand nowadays for sexual energy formulas) — with deer horn and tendon, sea horse, He Shou Wu (dark-haired Mr. Wu) and such like steeped in vodka or brandy — in lieu of viagra). I go to EWA, a Chinese pharmacy on Mulberry Street in Chinatown, to buy herbs. Often, I make a soup of black chicken with ginseng, dangui, and wolfberries. I regularly make tea with chrysanthemum flowers, gu ci zi, and bodhi fruit. These are just a few of the innovations in my kitchen. The Chinese herbal pharmacopeia offers many an alternative approach to cooking.

The way I cook certain items has changed too. Poultry (especially Cornish Game Hen) is a favorite but often I cook it not as adobo but with soy sauce, pineapple juice, cinnamon bark, ginger, raisins, and fresh figs. (My apologies to those who keep exact measurements: I hardly follow recipes, I ignore proportions, I am often guided by experience and intuition, so each dish is never the same.) It's probably my several sojourns in the Mediterranean that inspired this eclectic dish. Our travels have exposed us to a variety of cuisines. We Filipinos have also found a rich source of information in books, the internet, TV, and cooking classes; we have ventured into wine and are ready to experiment. Perhaps eventually we'll stamp Filipino names on these mestizo dishes that are coming out of our travels and the diaspora and our creative imagination. Chicken Banyaga, perhaps, sounds good.

Ulo ng salmon is of course still one of my favorites, but again, I would rather cook the fish head in a different way now: Malayan Fish Head Curry with coconut milk and okra. I read the recipe in the New York Times in the mid-70s and have duplicated it many times. On a visit to our country in 1987, I saw it in the menu of a restaurant near the Quezon Memorial Circle. It was the first time I had eaten it in the Philippines. Perhaps, the chef and I both copied the recipe from the NYTimes.

We eat for a variety of reasons. There is the need to fill our belly and it does not matter much what it is we eat as long as it fulfills certain predictable criteria or habit. There is the need for nutrition: there are times when we are seeking something for our health (vegetarianism and the other popular vogue diets are part of this development), a vitamin perhaps for a specific deficiency or a particular dish (like liver) that has the reputation of building stamina or helping cure an illness (like bitter melon for diabetes). There is the yearning for something, sweet, spicy, salty, or sour: the nostalgia for certain dishes and comfort food probably falls under this category. There is also a kind of indulgence where we don't think of fortifying the body or filling the belly or searching a flavor, we just want to enjoy, to be with friends, to try something together, perhaps with wine or beer, in a camaraderie of taste. There is a rare time, too, when we feel a deep possibly subconscious longing for a connection to a life that we miss, that recalls a more basic rhythm, something in the past.

To me, it is game that most satisfies my taste buds and something in my psyche and spirit. Venison especially, that lean, red muscle from the flank or thigh. Pheasant, too, is satisfying. So are quails and an assortment of birds. They have a flavor that is enhanced when cooked with laurel leaves, olives, hot sausages (especially made from ground wild boar meat), butter, cloves, and capers. But, whether sliced thin for tapa or cubed for stew, venison has always fortified me in ways that no other meat has.

I don't think I can pick up a rifle to shoot that squirrel scampering up the sycamore in the backyard or that Canadian goose waddling down to the pond. I must confess I could have done it earlier in my life but not now. Hunting to me is for survival, not recreation. There are also certain food items I can't eat any more like batute (frog stuffed with ground pork, chopped onions and garlic, ground pepper, and sometimes raisins) or camaru (an insect harvested from the fresh-harrowed field during the planting season), even if my life depended on it.

I am sure it is not love of the hunt and much more than the flavor of game or nutrition that is involved here. It is I suggest rooted partly in the myth and mystique of our people who have emerged in different stages from a long tableau of history, from island to island, from shore to mountain, from mountain to plains, spanning centuries. We may have wandered far from our homes, we may have left those legacies of our ancestry, we may have broken that chain of connectedness to our past, the traditions, and values of our people, but still sitting in our blood and our DNA is the ancient love of nature and the environment and a taste for the untamed, a link that is past understanding.

I feel a strange pulse whenever I see a white-tailed deer or a black bear in the distance as I am taking a walk through the woods in Phoenicia, Catskill, New York, or catch a quick glimpse of a ring-necked pheasant in its frantic flight on my descent into the valley in Lake Harmony, Pennsylvania. Something clicks, the senses open a gate, and I am transported somewhere almost familiar, but unknown, a spot in a distant forest, and a man in a loin cloth is drawing a line of choreography in the dust beside a bonfire.

Afterword

I met Rene in 1995, my first year at the New England School of Acupuncture in Watertown, MA. Like him, I had left a conventional career in search of something more meaningful. Something that touched the mysteries of life and healing on a deeper level.

Rene was teaching a required first year course that he was instrumental in developing. The focus was on personal cultivation through Tai Chi Chuan and Taoist meditation techniques. It was my first foray into any disciplined study of cultivating my own energy.

I already knew, beyond doubt, that the body boundary does not end at the skin. On several occasions, I had felt energy from the world, and from encounters with others, hit me like a powerful force. These experiences were among the things that drew me to the Eastern healing arts in the first place.

In Rene, I found a person who not only confirmed what I had experienced but had the knowledge and ability to teach how to work with it, control it, and use it for good. He taught how to cultivate it, gather it, and project it through the body for self-healing, and to others to assist in their healing.

Rene enjoying lunch with Karen Borla and Manny Maramara

Now that was interesting! It meant that your intentions mattered. It meant that while the acupuncture needle is an important tool, the practitioner, herself, would also influence outcome, based on intention and the quality of personal cultivation. It also meant that being an acupuncturist wasn't just about healing the patient but could also be an avenue for self-healing.

Rene taught Sifu Mantak Chia's 13 movement Tai Chi Chuan form, which is an abbreviated form perfect for beginners. While I was athletic, my training had been limited to body building, power lifting, and running. I had never studied dance or any other discipline that required sequenced movement. I was clumsy, clunky, and awkward, but nevertheless, I could feel the qi (intrinsic energy). I wanted more, and Rene took me on as a private student.

Upon arriving at his house in Weston, MA, I was instructed to light three joss sticks and stand in the horse stance until they burned down completely. It took about 45 minutes, during which time Rene would press on my shoulders and lean against my shins, encouraging a lower stance and firm grounding. It was excruciating. When the time was up, we would begin working on the basic stances and movement patterns of the system Sifu Lao Kim taught him in the Philippines.

After six months, I had learned the first form of Lao Kim's system, known as "Red Boy Prays to Guanyin," and went on to learn several other empty fist forms, a broad sword form, and the staff form. In the first two years we trained three or four days a week for several hours a day, at his house in Weston, MA. He was always cooking something while we trained, and afterwards we would sit to eat his wonderful creations filled with Chinese Herbs and exotic ingredients, like lotus root, deer tendon, and pig kidney. Sometimes we would watch Jackie Chan movies, or the videos of Lao Kim doing the forms.

Karen Borla assumes the Kwanyin Twist posture.

It was never just about marital arts. Rene's philosophy was that the forms were as much for healing and personal transformation as they were for fighting. Each martial move also had an application in healing. If you knew the points you could either disable an opponent or apply healing techniques to the muscles and tendons.

He also stressed the importance of practicing the Taoist meditation techniques of the "Six Healing Sounds," the "Inner Smile," and the "Microcosmic Orbit." Mastering these, while also mastering the forms, would transform the forms into a shamanistic healing ritual for self-cultivation. Having this background during my years studying acupuncture and Chinese Herbal medicine was invaluable to my development as a practitioner.

What struck me most about Rene was that he himself never stopped learning and cultivating. He was always working on one aspect of his development or another, whether it was developing his poetic voice with the help of his mentor, Len Roberts, or traveling the world to meet different masters with his friend David Verdesi. He studied calligraphy, traveled, taught all over the world, meditated, cultivated, and shared his gifts wherever he could.

Through the years since we both left Boston, I have continued to study with Rene. We have trained in various places; Walden Pond, Central Park, the terminal at Newark Airport (before 9/11), in the Poconos, at various tennis courts in West Hartford, CT and Watertown, MA, on a pool deck in Thailand, in Columbus Park, NY, and in a parking lot near his residence in Easton, PA.

The nature of the material and the distance between us requires that I spend the bulk of the time practicing on my own, but each time we get together, Rene offers pearls (he calls them corrections). It may be a simple movement, or a demonstration of application, but so much more is communicated in these small offerings than can ever be described. The man's own 60 plus years of developing his art is transmitted in these meetings.

The essays in this book reveal the depth and breadth of this generous, fun-loving, adventurous soul. May you, dear Reader, receive the pearls of his offerings, too.

Karen Borla, L.Ac
Quan Yin Healing Arts
West Hartford, Connecticut

End Notes

FRONT MATTER

1) Sifu Tak Wah Eng has been involved with martial art traditions since the age of four. Growing up in Hong Kong and later moving to the United States, Sifu Eng has had the opportunity of studying with the world's top martial arts masters. Today, after four decades of training, he is recognized as one of the most accomplished Masters, earning him respect and distinction. He has won many prestigious awards for forms competition, full contact fighting, and has served as a judge in numerous tournaments and demonstrations. Sifu Eng has also served as a fight choreographer and technical advisor for many feature films and has appeared on a variety of national television series. Not only is Sifu Eng a revered Shaolin martial arts master, but also a skilled painter and calligrapher who has exhibited his work in New York, San Francisco, Los Angeles, and the Far East. His conception of balance incorporates his passion for painting. His work is dynamic and unusual in its use of vibrant colors and ancient brushstrokes, melding the modern with centuries past. It is in this balance of Yin and Yang, the spiritual and the physical, that Tak Wah Eng exists.

AUTHOR'S PREFACE

1) Here in a nutshell is part of what I found during my studies of Asian healing modalities: The different aspects of the human being or the Human Body — Physical, Intellectual (Mental), Three Souls (Shen), Seven Spirits (Ling), Consciousness (Mind), Heart-Mind (Xin), Jing, Qi, Chakras, Three Dantian (Elixir Fields), Meridians, Yin-Yang, Five Element/ Phases, Correspondences (in Hermetic terms: What's outside is inside, what's inside is outside; what's above is below; what's below is above), Interface with the World (what the Vietnamese Buddhist monk Thich Nhat Hanh calls inter-being in his commentary on the Heart Sutra). — Therefore, we should be holistic in our view of the human being.

In healing and in life, there are different approaches and modalities and choices:

Meditation (Silence/Stillness), Qigong (Self-Cultivation), Martial arts (movement, empowerment, strategy, survival), Diet and Nutrition (Food), Massage (Tuina, Die Da, Chi Nei Tsang), Internal Alchemy (Neidan; Fire and Water, Yin and Yang, Five Elements), Sexology (Jing, Qi, and Shen), Feng-shui (Earth), Astrology (Earth, Heaven, Stars, and Planets), Crystals, Minerals and Stones (Essence of the Earth), Essential oils and Flower Essences (Aromatherapy, Essence of Plants), Herbs (Essence of Nature), Acupuncture (Qi).

These healing practices and modalities address the different aspects of the human being. They are indeed a way of living, a culture that we could follow. It is important to know what constitutes the human being. Look at the Western paradigm and compare it with the Eastern. That is a good start for the process of decolonization. As you can see from the list of what the human is composed of, there is so much more we have, more than just the Cartesian body-mind or the New Age body, mind, and spirit. And the methods of healing and living are so much more varied than just working, eating, and the pursuit of happiness (which we often seek in the wrong places).

Which modality or regimen is appropriate for a problem or the time of your life? These practices address the different aspects of the human being. They show a road to a life that is much richer and satisfying and authentic.

Martial art is not just fighting. There's empowerment for one, and wellness and self-discovery and the experience of Stillness and going to the Source. It brings us to the classics of warfare like Sun Tzu and Mao and how different they are from the shock and awe methods we've read about and seen in the west.

I learned the precepts of Sun Tzu, among them that the highest type of victory is not in winning a war but winning without fighting. The study of acupuncture gives us a picture of the human being as a grid of energy that runs through the body. Qigong offers a connection to us and to the earth and a regimen that can transform the Human Body and its different aspects in pursuit of longevity. Alchemy takes us on a search for transformation and guided by the *I-Ching*, the *Tao Te Ching*, the *Chuang Tzu*, and a master, we reconcile and dissolve the polarities and dualisms in being human in the world and give birth to a new spirit that could span the length of the universe.

CHAPTER 1 – SELF-CULTIVATION: INTRODUCTION TO CHINESE CULTURE

1) *The Yellow Emperor's Classic of Medicine* (*Huang Di Neijing Suwen)*, translated by Maoshing Ni, PhD

2) Lung and Kidney are not supposed to be pluralized because they stand not only for the physical organs but also for their functions.

3) Dan tian literally means the field of pills or elixir field. Dan is a medicine or elixir; tian refers to a field. It therefore refers to an area that is often the focus of self-cultivation. I have written about this in an essay titled, "The Source and Taoist Root Energetics."

4) Apologies if I am repetitious. The different disciplines and arts of self-cultivation are related, if not in the execution, at least in principles. I am also making general statements here qualified by "usually" because there are exceptions. External techniques may likewise use soft techniques in combination with harder techniques. Internal techniques may use hard techniques in combination with more soft techniques. External techniques work on the level of the physical body and to some extent the qi/energy; internal techniques work more on the level of the energetic and spiritual. In alchemy, external refers to the consumption of minerals and herbs (wai dan or external alchemy) while internal refers to the use of meditation/qiqong and/or sexual practices (nei dan or internal alchemy). There are practitioners

and schools that combine both internal and external techniques, depending on what they are trying to achieve. To have a better understanding of these different concepts, you must study the classics and find a qualified teacher.

CHAPTER 2 – THE INTERFACE OF CHINESE HEALING MODALITIES

1) The paper was delivered in February 2002 at the conference before there was a law to certify practitioners of acupuncture in the Philippines. I was involved in having a law passed. Since then, Congress passed a law regulating the certification of healers and the practice of healing outside of mainstream Western medicine. PITAHC (Philippine Institute of Traditional and Alternative Health Care) is the government agency that is now in-charge. I am certified to practice acupuncture and Traditional Chinese Medicine in the Philippines.

CHAPTER 4 – LAO KIM: MYSTERIOUS MASTER OF KUNG-FU

1) The essay has undergone a number of changes as I discovered a few things about Grandmaster Lao Kim (aka Goon Tiong) and his system of martial arts over the years. On the authority of my teacher Johnny Chiuten (Wong Fiak San) I called the style Hong Cha: that was how I heard him say it back in the mid-1960s. I understand that it also could be spelled Hung Kuen depending on the dialect and descended from the 5 Animal System of fighting. Since then, I discovered that there are several styles or offshoots of the art that were developed by families in the regions of Guangdong and Fujian and Lao Kim's was just one of them. At the same time, what I also heard from Johnny Chiuten and Jose Santiago Laraya is that Lao Kim studied in a Buddhist Temple in Fujian (Fukien). But I could not establish which one. There was a Shaolin Temple in Fujian, the brother temple of the one in Songshan, Loyang Province, Hunan, but it was reportedly burned sometime in the early 1900. There is really no way of verifying the facts now. Mark V. Wiley, Manny Maramara, Karen Borla, and I have attempted to secure more information. Based on our research, and adhering to the available information, we decided to call the Lao Kim system "Dragon Tiger Fujian Temple Kungfu." Lao Kim passed when he was 114 years old at the millennium in Hongkong.

2) Johnny called the style "Hong Cha" or "Angka." We did research into the Hung Gar/Angka/Hong cha system and could not find credible documentary or oral evidence of the alleged original founder Jee Sin Sim See or his student Hung Hei-gun. There is also no evidence of what he studied and taught or the curriculum that was passed down to the later generations.

3) In the course of the work on the book, Mark Wiley did research into the different martial arts of Fujian Province where Lao Kim's system came from. He discovered that there are martial arts schools with the names: Dragon Tiger, Plum Blossom, and Red Boy Praying to Kuanyin. Lao Kim's teaching include these forms. We have been calling the last form "Fairy Child Praying to the Goddess of Mercy" but, as we found out, it is really "Red Boy," after the demonic character, son of Princess Iron Fan and Bull Demon King, in the picaresque epic *Journey to the West* who was the antagonist of Sun Wukong and Kuanyin. When I studied

the form from Lao Kim, in the 1960s, I heard the name "Tong zi" but later I realized what I heard was really "Hong zi" or Red Boy. In *Journey to the West* the posture towards the end of the epic is called Kuanyin Twist: the hands, palms together, are held in front of the heart in a praying mudra and the legs are in a scissor or woman's stance. Red Boy was put under control and whenever he misbehaved Kuanyin recited the magic words that made the bracelets constrict on his head, ankles, and wrists. It was so painful, Red Boy put his hands together and begged for mercy. Chapters 42-43, *Journey to the West* (translated by Anthony C. Yu).

CHAPTER 5 – JOHNNY F. CHIUTEN: FIGHTER AND SAGE

1) I met Johnny's father in the Manila Doctor's Hospital. He looked like Johnny: the same build and looks. The old man got off his bed and asked me to attack him. I did and his move surprised me: it was the exact replica of what Johnny would have done!

2) In 1966, on a Wednesday noon, it was during Holy Week, if I remember, we had a memorable match. During a furious exchange, he stabbed my left leg and I fell. A bubble of blood formed immediately. It was one of those moments when life passes in front of your eyes. Johnny showed me how to massage the leg and put the blood back into the vein. Later, the bubble appeared again and grew to the size of a baseball. I went to see Johnny at his house on the campus. He slapped the "baseball" and spread the blood all over my leg. He made me drink two cups of dit da jow liniment made of 36 herbs. The recipe came from Lao Kim. (In 1988, the Grandmaster gave me a copy of the recipe in Hongkong.) My leg was black and blue for a few weeks. It was one of the scariest times of my life. Asked about it years later, he replied, "You were going to kill me. I had to defend myself." Dr. Guillermo Lengson, vice president of the Karate Federation of the Philippines under Johnny in the 60s, said of his sparring sessions with Johnny: "Sinagasa ako," referring to the technique of non-stop attack that Johnny had honed to perfection. Johnny showed me different dim mak methods over the years, the last two during my visit to Bantayan Island in February 2002.

CHAPTER 8 – GILAS ARNIS: AMANTE MARINAS

1) Antonio Pigafetta, First Voyage Around the World. An eyewitness account.

2) This obsession with death is, perhaps, what distinguishes the martial arts from other arts. The martial artist recognizes that he may have to use the daily routine to kill, if necessary, in self-preservation. Says Paul Leonard Turse, Jr., Ph.D., in his article "What is art?" in the April 1972 issue of the Black Belt magazine, "the rhythm of karate and its bodily movement in relation to the environment is an imitation of the original life-and-death struggle which gave impetus to the behavior pattern. Thus, the impulse is retained (along with the need to face death.) But the end — kill or be killed in the life-and-death struggle — is transcended through the symbolic nature of karate practice. In this way, the karate artist learns to overcome his fear of death... It is important to stress (again) that in karate one does not practice killing. Rather one practices how to kill. Art is, therefore, evolved because according to

behavioral psychology, anytime the perfection of form takes precedence over completion of an end, art is created."

CHAPTER 10 – LOOKING FOR YANG CHENG FU

1) I turned 83 before the publication of this book.

2) Gin Soon has since passed away. The school is now 54 years old and run by Chu Sifu's son, Vincent Fong Chu.

CHAPTER 11 – THE CURRICULUM OF YANG FAMILY TAI CHI CHUAN

1) from *Tai Chi Touchstones: Yang Family Transmissions*, p. 7, by Douglas Wile

2) I studied Tai Chi Chuan with Sifu Chan Bun Te from 1968-1970 in Binondo, Philippines. When I saw him again in 1986, Chan Sifu taught me the Microcosmic Orbit and Huan Jing Bu Nao (sex and qigong).

CHAPTER 12 – THE MYSTERIOUS TRADITIONAL YANG FAMILY CHANG CHUAN FORM

1) I am not sure either if he verified his information about the Yang Family, but he said that Yang Cheng Fu "had four sons. They are teaching Tai chi in either Hong Kong or Hawaii." (p. 47). He must have had in mind the descendants of Tung Ying Chieh who lived in Hongkong and Hawaii. The children of Yang Cheng Fu lived in China and Hongkong. Only Yang Sau-Chung lived in Hongkong. The rest of the children lived in China. The Tung family re-settled in Hawaii. The most famous was Tung Ying-Jieh's son, Tung Hu-ling, who died many years ago in Hawaii. I interviewed his son Tung (now spelled Dong) Sheng Chen and grandson Alex Dong and observed their classes doing Fist and Knife and Sword forms at the Chinese school in Oahu's Chinatown. One of the senior students, a disciple of Tung Hu Ling, privately demonstrated some of the forms to me, one of them the so-called Fast Tai chi.

2) Master Gin Soon Chu prefers to describe the lineage system he teaches as Traditional Yang Family Tai Chi Chuan as distinguished from other derivatives of the style (like Cheng Man-Ching's and Wu-Shu competition forms).

3) This was probably the last interview just before Master Ip Tai Tak died in April of 2004. It was published in *Tai Chi Magazine*. Robert Boyd is the second disciple of Master Ip. (The first disciple is John Ding of England. Both Boyd and Ding also studied with Gin Soon Chu or Chu's student.)

4) I was surprised to read that Master Ip did not include the 2-Person Fighting Set (San-sou) in the list of forms to learn for martial application. Without disrespecting Master Ip, I believe this form is the traditional way of learning the martial application of Tai Chi Chuan.

Perhaps he did not study it? It is common in martial arts that some students, no matter how advanced they are, do not learn all the forms. The famous disciple of Yang Cheng-Fu, Tung Ying Jieh, for instance, probably studied the Yang Family Solo form, Spear form, one Broadsword form, one Sword form and Push hands. Cheng Man Ching claims to have studied "everything" that the Yang Chengfu had to teach, but like Ip and Tung, he probably did not learn the whole curriculum. From what I have seen and read, he did only 2 forms — the solo fist form with 47 movements and the first sword form - but it is difficult to say who taught them to him. What the Tung Family told me is that he studied with Yang Cheng Fu for at most 2 years. As I said earlier, this is not to disrespect or to undermine the talents and training of these masters; to me, one of the realities in martial arts is that the master does not always teach everything to the student.

CHAPTER 13 – THE SWORD OF THE IMMORTAL LU DONGBIN

1) From *On Seeing a Pupil of Lady Kung-Sun Dance with the Sword*, by Du-Fu (712-770) translated by Mark Salzman

2) Al Huang in his book *Embrace Tiger Carry to the Mountain*, explains the calligraphy.

CHAPTER 16 – THE MYSTERY OF CHENG MAN CHING

1) Robert W. Smith. *Chinese Boxing: Masters and Methods*, p. 38

2) Robert Smith, *Chinese Boxing Masters and Methods*, p. 35.

3) Wolf Lowenthal (1993). *There Are No Secrets: Professor Cheng Man Ch'ing and His T'ai Chi Chuan*. North Atlantic Books

4) Cheng, MC and Smith RW. (1967). *T'ai-Chi: The Supreme Ultimate Exercise for Health, Sport, and Self-Defense.* Tuttle. P. 4.

5) *Cheng Tzu's Thirteen Treatises on T'ai Chi Ch'uan* (1947) by Cheng Man-ch'ing (Author), Benjamin Pang Jeng Lo (Translator). R. Smith in *Journal of Asian Martial Arts*, Vol. 6, Number 1, p. 51

6) Here is Vincent F. Chu's letter to me:

> *Hi Rene, Are you still into Cheng Man Ching's story? I came across an article written by an over 80 years old man Jin Yen Lin of Shanghai recently. He said Cheng Man Ching started studied with Yang Cheng Fu in 1932. However, before this time, he already studied tai chi chuan from his teacher 6 to 7 years. His teacher was Ye Da Mi (1888-1973), a middle frame Yang Style student of Tian Zhalin, studied Wu Dan Sword from Li Jing Lin (1884-1931) and a good friend of Sun Lu Tang's second son. Some of his students and grand students in Shanghai called his tai chi chuan the Ye Style Tai Chi Chuan. You know Yang Cheng Fu died in 1936. He moved from Beijing to Nanking sometime in 1928. The first time he was in Shanghai and stayed with Ye Da Mi was in 1929. Between 1929 to 1936, he traveled to Wuhan, Hangzhou, and Guangzhou. Fong*

UNANSWERED QUESTIONS REQUIRING FURTHER RESEARCH:

Q1) What forms did Cheng actually study with Yang or any of his assistants?

Said Yang Cheng-Fu: "The Tai Chi Chuan curriculum consists of hand forms first (i.e., empty hand), such as Tai Chi Chuan and Tai Chi Long Boxing. Next comes One Hand Push-Hands, Fixed Position Push-Hands, Push-Hands with Active Steps, Ta Lu, and Free Sparring. Last comes weapons, such as Tai Chi Doubled-Edged Sword, Tai Chi Broadsword, Tai Chi Spear (Thirteen Spear). And so forth." (Wile, *Tai Chi Touchstones: Yang Family Transmissions*, p. 7)

So much is known about Cheng, yet nobody has written about what he actually studied. Did anybody ever ask him about it? If so, what was his answer? I have asked a couple of Cheng's followers about it, but nobody has an answer. One authority on Cheng's life told me that Cheng studied "everything" with Yang Cheng-Fu. Robert Smith unequivocally states, "Cheng absorbed the lessons like a sponge." (*Journal of Asian Martial Arts*, p.51). What these lessons were, nobody has explained.

It is an interesting conundrum for researchers. What did the famous Cheng, considered by his students as the greatest Tai Chi Chuan master of the century, actually study with Yang Cheng-Fu? The question can be raised about a number of Yang Cheng-Fu's students – Chen Weiming, Fu Xiaowen and Tung Yingchieh, among others. As far as I can make out, Chen and Tung studied the Solo Form, Push Hands, and Sword forms. Tung also studied the Broadsword/Knife (I saw his grandson's class doing the form in Hawaii). The Tung family also have their own version of the Tai Chi Fast Form, which they themselves choreographed. During his last years, Yang Cheng-Fu practically stopped teaching. He had apparently gained weight and was not active at all. The photographs of him show a man who had a big girth. There were a few of his famous students in the photographs – Chen Weiming, Tung Yingchieh, Sun Lutang, and Yang Sau-chung.

Q2) In the book, *Martial Musings: A Portrayal of Martial Arts in the 20th Century*, published in 1999, Robert Smith said: "In Masters and Methods (p. 38), I wrote of this and implied that these were the only two times Zheng pushed hands with Yang. I was wrong. They pushed often. Rather, these were the only two times that Master Yang displayed his sansou (free-fighting) ability." p. 200. Sadly, Mr. Smith passed away a few years ago. He did not cite any authority for his change of mind.

Q3) I showed the original version of the essay to Vincent F. Chu, lineage instructor of Traditional Yang Family Tai chi Chuan and one of the most knowledgeable scholars of Tai Chi Chuan I know, based in Boston, Massachusetts. He corrected a few sentences. I have incorporated his comments. Still, I would like to quote his letter to me for the richness of information. Among other things, he said:

> *"1. On page five, you quoted me as saying, 'Cheng's father said that Yang could assign somebody to teach Cheng.' It should be the mayor, not Cheng's father. Cheng Man Ching*

was raised by his mother, his father died when he was very young. 2. On page eight, you wrote Sun Lutang was one of Yang Cheng Fu's students. This is not correct. Yang Cheng Fu and Sun Lutang were good friends. 3. On page eight, you wrote Ye Da Mi (1888-1973) was Yang Cheng Fu's student. Although Ye studied from Yang Cheng Fu and Yang Shaohou when they moved to Nanking City in 1928, Ye was known as Tian Zhaolin's (1891-1960) student. Ye studied from Tian in 1917 and blood brother with Sun Lutang's second son in 1919 so he studied from Sun Lutang as well. Ye opened the "Wu Dang Tai Chi Chuan Club" in Shanghai in November 1926 and Chen Wei Ming opened his Tai Chi Chuan school in Shanghai in May 1925. Ye's students and students' students in Shanghai called it the Ye Style Tai Chi Chuan today. You mentioned the name "Po (Pu) Qiucheng on page three. Po was the mayor of Shanghai in the Qing Dynasty. Po's daughter Po Bing Ru (1907-1997) and Cheng Man Ching studied painting together at Shanghai Fine Art College. After graduation, Cheng Man Ching remained at the college to teach. Po Bing Ru studied Tai Chi Chuan from Ye Da Mi in 1924. Po was one of four of Ye's best students. The three other best students studied from Ye in 1953. Among them, one of them is called Jian Yin Lin who said that Cheng Man Ching studied from Ye in 1928. 4. The 37-movement form of Master Cheng Man-Ch'ing is not a part of the Traditional Yang Family Tai Chi Chuan Curriculum in the Yang Cheng-Fu lineage."

CHAPTER 17 – MANTAK CHIA: MODERN TAOIST MASTER AND ALCHEMIST

1) When referring to Mantak Chia's specific courses, we will use the Wades-Giles spelling instead of the Pinyin as is being used otherwise. Example: Chi Kung vs. QiGong.

CHAPTER 19 – DISCOVERING INTERNAL ALCHEMY: OF FIRE AND WATER

1) Chapter 7, section 7, *Inner Chapters, Wandering on the Way, Early Taoist Tales, and Parables of Chuan-Tzu*, Translated by Victor H. Mair.

2) Balance' is a useful word but not the keyword in internal alchemy: it is in Chinese medicine and Taoist healing. The keywords in internal alchemy are "dissolution"' and "transformation." That is, usually. The practitioner does not aim to balance the polarities but to dissolve them and eventually transform them into something else. Thus, Fire and Water mated and gave birth to "steam."

CHAPTER 20 – THUNDER PATH IN HUANGSHAN

1) Yin Yang Gong, the mating of Yin and Yang in the dantian, is considered 4th level achievement in the Mo-Pai tradition. Some people believe that this is the real Tai chi, the marriage of yin and yang in the dantian. Generating "electricity" can also happen in other cases but Yin Yang Gong — one of many gongs in Lei Shan Tao — is the more potent type. Strangely, the "type" of power is missing from the list of 28-35 fajing, discharge of fajing techniques in Tai Chu Chuan. Was it concealed in one of them or has it been lost or forgotten?

The question for me is, "What is the nature of this Qi that makes it possible, when manipulated in a certain way, to produce electricity and fire?" I understand that the Magus could withstand attacks with a knife: the master could not be cut, the weapon just bounces off as if there is a shield that covers his body. When scientists were solving the problem of "reality" or certain objects and phenomena, they used different words: singularity, particle, waves, string, big bang, annihilation, sizigy, quarks. They borrowed words from the Greeks, even James Joyce, and names of scientists. So, what is this phenomenon that manifests itself as "power" when certain things — breath, muscular contraction, focus, energy, visualization — are aligned? How can a human being produce something that only a machine could produce? Scientists should investigate this "singularity." At least, there should be a name for it.

2) The first time I saw what has been called "Holy Water" technique, it was done by Lao Cang Wen at the Tao Garden. Others have copied the technique since then. Lao Sifu was a Buddhist and Taoist master who had been teaching different methods, including "Chi Knife," using a knife to project Qi onto a patient. The water did not acquire any flavor (I drank it for an allergy, but it did not have any obvious effect), I don't think, only healing properties and probably a rearrangement of the molecules. Jiang sifu's water was transformed in different ways. Laboratory tests, I heard, confirmed that there was an unknown element in it which wasn't present in ordinary water. Other students who attended the seminar in Shangrila witnessed other demos — setting a bush on fire with nothing but qi, draining the lifeforce out of a rabbit, etc.

3) The documentarian, Lawrence Blair, returned to Java sometime and filmed another — longer — demonstration which is shown on youtube.com. While you are on youtube.com you can type in the name of Lao Kim, my teacher in Shaolin in the 60s, to see his Fujian Temple form. He was in his 70s at the time. You can also look at Vincent F. Chu, the son of Gin Soon Chu, my sifu in Traditional Yang Family Tai Chi Chuan in Boston and second disciple of GM Yang Sau-Chaung.

4) The ancient master took his position similar to Brush Knee and Push in Tai Chi Chuan, aimed the right palm at the bull 20 feet away and in a few seconds, the bull bellowed and groaned and collapsed in indescribable agony. I heard that the master could have killed the bull right then and there, but it is against the principles of his religion (he is a Buddhist). It would die in a week to a month, we were told. Fourteen bulls were sacrificed that afternoon. There is a considerable debate about the ethics of this procedure similar to the slaughter of animals for food. I understand that the transfer of qi from the bulls is necessary for people who have depleted qi, or who need to make quick progress in the work. It is also a sacred ritual from an ancient tradition of animal sacrifice to honor the ancestors and seek the intercession of heaven.

When I verified some of the information, I learned (1) that the grandmaster was just in his 90s. The Chinese have a tendency to exaggerate their age; and (2) the Magus was not born in the year of the Dragon but 5 years earlier.

CHAPTER 21 – LETTER FROM CYPRUS

1) Nadine R. Sarreal, writer and friend who was living in Singapore at the time.

CHAPTER 22 – DATELINE: UBUD, BALI, 2012

1) For more information about David, go to www.davidverdesi.com

2) Caveat: In his introduction to the book, HH the Fourteenth Dali Lama Tenzin Gyatso says: "Originally, the Tantric practices illustrated by these murals were revealed only after years of study and meditation under a qualified teacher. Without understanding the context of compassion, the awakening mind, and the emptiness of inherent existence within which they function, the methods of Dzogchen and the Highest Yoga Tantra could easily be misunderstood. Nevertheless, I believe that these paintings can be a source of profound inspiration even for those who have had no previous exposure to Tibetan Buddhism."

3) The Hindu priest and shaman held the red-hot chisel as I waited. Marina was waiting too. He asked me to open my mouth and stick out my tongue. I knew what he was going to do because I was warned about it, but I was nervous anyway. He touched the back of my tongue with the chisel 9 times in a row and then dipped it in a glass of water with rose petals. There was a hissing sound as the burning chisel turned cold. I was told to wash my head with the water. The priest did the ritual 3 times that night. We returned the next night and endured the process all over again. What was it for? From my point of view as a healer, the tongue is the extension and opening of the heart and fire is one of the elements for cleansing and exorcism, like water. I was told something else, but I cannot share it here because it is supposed to be a secret. When I was in Lake Titicaca, the highest navigable lake in the world at 12,000 feet, I took off my clothes and jumped in the water. My guide, a native shaman, told me that it was a cleansing and healing ritual in Peru.

CHAPTER 23 – JOSE RIZAL: ZEN LIFE, ZEN DEATH

To avoid the clutter of excessive footnotes, I have worked certain explanations into the article itself. After all, this was written for a popular audience, not for academics and scholars.

*However, grateful acknowledgment is due the following which provided useful insights and data: D.T. Suzuki's *Zen and Japanese Culture*; Yukio Mishima's *Sun and Steel* and *Hagakure* (Hidden Leaves); Sun-Tzu's *The Art of War*; Yambao and Mirafuente's *Mga Karunungan sa Larong Arnis*, (the first book on arnis de mano); Teodoro Agoncillo's *Revolt of the Masses*; Pedro Gagelonia's *Rizal's Life, Works and Writings*; other materials published by the Jose Rizal Centennial Commission. These were the main authorities I consulted when I researched the article in late 1970s in the United States. Many materials have come out since then. Among them: Mark V. Wiley's *Filipino Martial Culture* and William Henry Scott's work on the ancient barangays/pre-Hispanic Filipino.

*His physical training also made his death more poignant and beautiful since he developed a strong and muscular body. It is a traditional belief among warriors that if they are going to die for a cause, they should be young and strong. As Yukio Mishima said, "A powerful, tragic frame and sculpturesque muscles (were) indispensable in a romantically noble death. Any confrontation between weak, flabby flesh and death seemed to me absurdly inappropriate." The cult of the romantic death — dying for a noble cause at the height of one's powers — has many followers among the samurai and warriors. It is enshrined as one of the cardinal rules of Bushido or the warrior's code. There is perhaps in certain cases the inarticulate death-wish.

Dr. Rizal was also obsessed with Elias, the Noble Hero, who was to be the leader of the revolution. I suspect that this obsession had its origin in the Siegfried legend, in Wagner's Ring of the Nibelung. In fact, a close reading of the Noli and Fili would reveal many German influences - the necklace of Maria Clara, the treasures of Simoun, the opening chapters of both novels, and of course the ethics of the Revolution. There's more but this requires another essay.

*This essay was first published by the "Philippine News" in San Francisco some 20 years ago. When Dr. Alejandro Roces read it at LaMama ETC, NY in 1980, he thought it should be published in the Philippines. (He was giving lectures on Philippine culture, and I was teaching arnis and appearing in Cecille Guidote Alvarez's PETAL productions.) I was told it was published in *Malaya Magazine* but reportedly copies of the magazine that carried it did not reach the readers because the publication's office was raided and closed by the Marcos government for alleged subversive activities. When the author went home for the celebrations of the February Revolution in 1986, Dr. Alejandro Roces read the article again and decided to publish it in the "Manila Times" Sunday magazine on the anniversary of Jose Rizal's death. This essay was also published in the Rapid Journal edited by Daniel Go of Manila and in the book *Arnis: Reflections on the History and Development of Philippine Martial Arts* edited by Mark V. Wiley (Tuttle, 2001).

Acknowledgements

I cannot list all the people who have helped me with this book, from the teachers who are the subjects to the friends and relatives who have encouraged me one way or another. These essays were written in different places — Cyprus, Long Island, NY, Lake Harmony, PA, London, England, Cyprus, Egypt, Thailand, Indonesia (Java and Bali) — as I stayed with friends in my travels.

Special mention must be made of Danny Go, editor and publisher, who featured many of these essays in his magazine *Rapid Journal* in the Philippines. Sadly, he passed some years ago and *Rapid* consequently ceased publication.

Special thanks to GM Mantak Chia for permission to use illustrations from his work.

"Reflections on the diaspora, Burung Babi, a Favorite Uncle, Malayan Fish Head Curry, and a Trip to the Mountains" was first published in "A Taste of Home".

"Opening the Body to Nature" was first published in *Yang-Sheng Magazine.*

"Gilas Arnis: Amante Marinas" was first published in *Ningas-Cogon Magazine.*

"Haiyan Recovery Update: Healers on a Mission" was first published in *Positively Filipino.*

"A Man of Parts, Master of Chinese Arts" by Ed Maranan (and featured here with his permission) was first published in *Philippine Star.*

"Letter from Cyprus" was first published in *Our Own Voice.*

"Jose Rizal: Zen Life, Zen Death" was first published in "Philippine News."

Deep gratitude should also go to:

My family and relatives — Lolit, Norm, Jen, Al, Laura, Isabel and Ava, Roland and Vicky Navarro, Dan and Edna Navarro, Sarah, Emily, Madalyn, Aryn and Riley, Jonathan and Ruth Navarro, Andre and Cathy Persaud, Dely and June ArranzaMendez, Cely Fernandez, Claire and Joe Billingham, Luisito and April Fernandez, Aishuan Wang, and Roger Lai.

My brothers Florante, Danny, and Roland, cousins Ray Navarro, Letty Espinelli, Nick Navarro, Alice Camaya, and Dan Catajan. My students Annie Sollestre, Janet Paredes, Ric Caminade, Isabel "Chingbee" Templo, Buenie de Guzman, Jackson Tan, Florentina Urag, Isidro Sia, Claudine Najera, and Vivien Tan (at INAM Philippines), Jutta and Walter Kellenberger, Annette Derksen, Muriel Kirton, Peter Wayne, and Barry Spendlove (at Universal Healing Tao), Dale Dugas, Mike Arsenault, Henry McCann, Lynn Swirda, Karen Borla, and Lynda

Danzig (at the New England School of Acupuncture), and Manny Maramara, Karen Borla, and Mark Wiley (in Dragon Tiger Fujian Temple Kung-fu).

My friends and colleagues Lee Holden, James McConnell, Randi Brochman, Renu Li, Juan Li, Mikael Hoij (Tao Garden Herbalist), Karin Sorvik, John Loupos, Barry Spendlove, Sharon Smith, Ron Diana, Rylin Malone, Gunther Weil, Michael Winn, Andrew and Fiona Jan, Sharon Smith, William U. Wei, Walter Kellenberger, David Twicken, Karin Sorvik, Gilles Marin, and Reinoud Eleveld in the Healing Tao (now Universal Healing Tao); poets and writers Ed Maranan, Alfred "Krip" Yuson, Leny M. Strobel, Nelson Navarro, Belinda Aquino, Eileen Tabios, Bino Realuyo, Luis Francia, Debra Kang Dean, Nadine R. Sarreal, Jenny, and Frankie Llaguno and Carol Purington; martial artists Alex Co, Edgar Sulite, Topher Rickett, Mark Nowak, Kenton Venzant, Christopher Viggiano, Waikeung Lau, Keith Cini, David Miller, Robin Shou, and Cyndi Rothrock; Banana Club stalwarts Vic Ramos, Agustin Que, Jimmy Yambao, Chibu Lagman, Jose Rebano, Vic de Jesus, Lito Imperio, Temy Rivera, and Salvador Carlota; Ben Muego, Ed Labitag, Leo Quisumbing, Alenn Nidea, Herson and theatre director Cecille Guidote Alvarez, Miel Sabelino, Ululani Young, Loida Nicolas and Reggie Lewis, master photographer Carlos and Arlene Esguerra, Master chefs Romy Dorotan and Amy Besa (of Purple Yam), DR Teodoro, Christian Bautista, Reynan Dale Esquillo, Art Talbo, Dante Raul Teodoro, Badong Tuy, Rommel Manuel; Lingling and Archie King, Guru and Suh Bose, Dianne and Bill Craft, Malula Longo and Janet Lehman, Mike Arsenault and Chi Sun, Michael and Lois Posner, Jeanne Christianson, Muriel Kirton, Henry McCann, Sarah Pirtle, Ilene Bellerue, Amirah Snaith, Andrew Snaith, Aiten Snaith, Janice MacKenzie, Alma Quema, Cathy Wessels, Nora Favelukes, Francesca Stefani, Jenny Madamba, Kellie Bach, Nick Lekas, Ilene Aleshire, Mario Sprouse, Karla Hendrick, Peter and Ziva Wengert, Lynda Danzig, Lisa Bersanini, Erin Owen, Evelyn Cameron, John Rogers, Eric Baculinao, Chito Sta.Romana, Jimi FlorCruz, Tynne Clifford, Peter Wayne, Jane Ward, Ana Vladimirova, Obin Kommara, Gonca Denizmen, Jessica Sommar, Carmen Graganza, Cesar Graganza, Romy Liwanag, Josue "Sonny" and Carol Villa, Letty Nacpil, Grace Magdamo Teoxon, Fely Santos, Ollie Jumao-as, Lingling Maranan Claver, Luchie Maranan, Ellen Maranan, Corbelita Jose Palima, Cathy Sanders, Melina Salerno, Denise Veres, Ilina Abadjieva, Maryann Horvath, Kurt Kraus, Nancy Roberts, Isidro Sia, and Vivien Tan whose support and encouragement have always been there.

My classmates in Boston's Chinatown H. Kim Won, Mary Beth Soares, Gordon Chu, Gary Woolf, Seal Freed, Jean Young, Tony Chu, Art Soohoo, and Linda Sugiyama (in Traditional Yang Family Tai Chi Chuan); Dr. Jose Santiago "Dr Joe" Laraya, Florante Navarro and Ching/Chang See San (in Dragon Tiger Fujian Temple Kungfu); and David Twicken, Cathy Umphress, Marie Favorito, John Zielinski, John Loupos, Sharon Smith, and Mackenzie Jampa Stewart (in Healing Tao, now Universal Healing Tao).

The masters who shared their expertise with me, among them: David Verdesi , John Chang, Xuan Kong, and Jiang Feng (Thunder Path), Mantak Chia (Universal Healing Tao), Lao Cang Wan (Qigong), Vincent F. Chu and Gin Soon Chu (Traditional Yang Family Tai

Chi Chuan) , Leung Shum (Wu Family Tai Chi Chuan), Johnny F. Chiuten and Lao Kim (Dragon Tiger Fujian Temple Kungfu), Mat Marinas, Filemon Caburnay, Ondo Caburnay, Johnny F. Chiuten, and Guiling Tinga (arnis de mano), Xiao Yingpeng (Monkey Hand and Staff), Ye Tao Qin (Hsing-I Chuan), John Loupos (Wah Lum Praying Mantis Green Dragon GuanTao), Len Roberts (poetry), Rodolfo C. Vidad (music), Jeffrey Yuen (Chinese medicine and the classics), Ping Chan (die da/traumatology and its herbal recipes), Khun Ni (Chi Nei Tsang/internal organs manipulation and Karsai Nei Tsang/genital massage), Chan Bun Te and Lao Yun Hsiao (Yang Tai Chi Chuan), Master Chan (Pa-Kua Chuan), Kiiko Matsumoto Sensei (Japanese acupuncture), Yao Zhang, Patrick Cunningham and Lu Weidong (Chinese medicine) and my other teachers at the New England School of Acupuncture, the Russian psychics Nicolai and Marina Denisov (Inner Eye method), David Twicken, and Li Po (Feng Shui/Geomancy) and countless others. There were other masters whose names I have not been able to keep: the coaches who taught me the Northern Sword and Spear in the Sichuan Sports College in Chengdu in 1983 and the anonymous classmates who taught me the spear form of Han Ching Tang at the Hua Eng Athletic Club in Manila's Chinatown in 1970.

Special mention for their work on the book and warm companionship: the multi-faceted Mark V. Wiley, the publisher of Tambuli Media, a friend and associate in the Society of Black Belts of America (SOBBA), whose idea it was to get my writings published in book form. Until he urged me to gather this collection, I did not have any interest in putting them together. But he insisted that I have something important to share. Most of these essays were published in an obscure magazine in the Philippines and perhaps reprinting them will give them a new lease on life. It was also Mark who did singularly research the martial arts of Fujian and uncovered different family styles that might have been related Lao Kim's temple Kungfu system. To Manny Maramara who formatted the earlier version of the book, edited the interview with Vincent F. Chu, and collated the photos for the essays. And last but not least Karen Borla who shared her private and invaluable notes from her personal training with the extraordinary master Johnny F. Chiuten in the remote island of Bantayan.

Photo Credits

Alex Co: 71, 74 (left), 77 (bottom), 87-89

Alex Dong: 5, 8

Gin Soon Tai Chi Club: 92-94, 96, 97, 99, 100, 116, 123-126, 128, 133, 140

Johnny Chiuten: 46 (bottom), 47 (top and middle), 48 (bottom)

Jopet Santiago Laraya: 40 (bottom), 41 (top), 57, 62, 63 (top), 64, 67, 90

Karen Borla: 52, 279

Lao Kim: 39, 40 (top), 41 (bottom), 42 (top)

Laura Billingham: 16, 20, 72 (all photos except top left), 73, 103 (top), 104, 108, 109, 111 (top right), 118

Mark V. Wiley: VII, 75-76 (courtesy of), 77 (top), 83, 95 (R, courtesy of), 145 (courtesy of), 216, 219

Rene J. Navarro: ix, xvi, 11, 12, 15, 19, 20, 21, 22, 23, 26, 27, 28, 29, 30, 31 (2 bottom), 32, 33, 35, 36, 37, 38, 42 (bottom), 43, 44 (top), 46 (top photo), 47 (top), 48 (top photo), 49, 50, 51, 55, 58, 60, 61, 70, 71 (top), 72 (top), 74 (top right), 80, 87 (top), 88 (top and bottom right), 89, 95 (left), 102, 103 (bottom), 105, 106, 111 (top right), 117, 119, 120, 123 (bottom), 126, 128, 133, 140, 152, 153, 154, 158, 159, 160, 167, 168, 170, 172, 175, 176, 177, 178, 182, 183, 184, 185, 186, 187, 189, 190, 191, 193, 194, 196, 199, 200, 201, 202, 203, 204, 205, 206, 222, 223, 226, 227, 233, 234, 239, 240, 242, 243, 245, 246,248, 250, 251, 253, 254, 256, 257, 258, 259, 261, 262, 264, 267, 270, 275

Tak Wah Eng: Cover Image and calligraphy on page 3.

Universal Healing Tao: 150, 151, 161, 162, 167, 168, 172-175

TAMBULI
MEDIA

中華柔術大全
CHINESE GENTLE ART COMPLETE:
THE BIBLE OF
NGO CHO KUN
BY
YU CHIOK SAM
TRANSLATED BY
ALEXANDER LIM CO

THE WAY OF
NGO CHO KUN
KUNG FU
TRANSLATED & EDITED BY
ALEXANDER CO
UNDER SUPERVISION OF
MASTER TAN KA HONG
福建五祖拳法

MARK V. WILEY
FILIPINO
FIGHTING
ARTS
THEORY AND PRACTICE
VOLUME I

MASTERING
ESKRIMA
DISARMS
MARK V. WILEY

www.ingramcontent.com/pod-product-compliance
Lightning Source LLC
Chambersburg PA
CBHW081327090726
47907CB00010B/2396

* 9 7 8 1 9 4 3 1 5 5 4 0 8 *